A Drama of Souls

EGIL TÖRNQVIST

A Drama of Souls

Studies in
O'Neill's Super-naturalistic
Technique

YALE UNIVERSITY PRESS

NEW HAVEN AND LONDON, 1969

For permission to study and quote from Eugene O'Neill's unpublished manuscripts, typescripts, and letters, I am indebted to Mrs. Carlotta Monterey O'Neill and to the authorities of Cornell University Library, Dartmouth College Library, Harvard College Library, Princeton University Library, and Yale University Library. I am also indebted to Mrs. O'Neill and to the Princeton and Yale University Libraries for permission to reproduce some of O'Neill's sketches for the settings of his plays as well as sections from the original longhand drafts of *The Web* and *The Emperor Jones* (both in Princeton University Library), and from the scenario for *Long Day's Journey Into Night* (in Yale University Library). Of the sketches, the one representing the house in *Desire Under the Elms*, appearing on page sixty, belongs to Princeton University Library; the rest are in the Eugene O'Neill Collection in Yale University Library. This material may not be reproduced without written permission from Mrs. O'Neill and the libraries concerned.

Grateful acknowledgment is extended to the Estate of Eugene O'Neill, Random House, Inc., and Jonathan Cape Ltd. for permission to quote from *The Plays of Eugene O'Neill*, 3 vols., from *Ten "Lost" Plays by Eugene O'Neill* and from *A Moon for the Misbegotten*. Thanks are also due the Yale University Press for permission to quote from *Long Day's Journey Into Night*, *A Touch of the Poet*, and *Hughie*, and for valuable editorial assistance.

A number of persons, too many to list here, have given their help and cooperation in the preparation of this book. For valuable criticism and encouragement I wish to thank especially teachers and students at the Uppsala Institute of Literature. For helpful services in various matters pertaining to my work I am grateful to many kind librarians at Uppsala University and at the universities mentioned above. I especially wish to thank Dr. Donald C. Gallup, Curator of the Collection of American Literature at the Yale University Library.

A fellowship from the American Council of Learned Societies enabled me to spend a precious year in and around American libraries. I have also received grants from Uppsala University and from the Foundation of Karl and Betty Warburg.

Also published in Sweden as
Acta Universitatis Upsaliensis,
Historia litterarum, 3

Standard book number: 300-01152-0

Printed in Sweden by

Almqvist & Wiksells Boktryckeri AB, Uppsala 1968

To Rita

CONTENTS

EXPLANATORY NOTE

In the ensuing pages, references to O'Neill's plays are always made through page numbers within parenthesis following quotations or references. All other sources are referred to through page numbers preceded by 'p.' or 'pp.' Thus, (10) indicates that the reference is to an O'Neill play, (p. 10) that it is to another source. The indication (= 10) means that a mentioned word or passage in a draft version appears in a place corresponding to page 10 in the published play.

In the source references, dates of publication are given only when it is necessary to distinguish between different works by the same author. The indication (O'Neill, 1926/Clark, p. 105) means that a statement by O'Neill, originally published in 1926, is reprinted in the work by Clark found in the bibliography; the page number refers to the reprint in Clark's book; for details about the original source, the reader is asked to look for the year 1926 under the published, non-dramatic works by O'Neill as listed in the bibliography. Information about reprints is given in the bibliography only when the page references in the text concern reprinted material. Only with regard to O'Neill's writings has the reprinted source been indicated in the text as well as in the bibliography.

Unless otherwise indicated, a play manuscript (including notes) cited or referred to is found in the library holding the longhand draft, as listed in the bibliography. For the location of unpublished letters cited or referred to, see the name of the addressee in the bibliography.

For quotations from the dramas I have followed the typography of the Random House edition of O'Neill's plays. In some respects I have, however, departed from the typography in this edition. Thus, for song texts and quotations from poetry, which may properly be considered parts of the dialogue, I have used roman letters throughout; the Random House edition usually has italics in these cases. For all passages which are not part of the dialogue I use italics. In accordance with O'Neill's practice in the typewritten versions of the plays, stage directions in the drafts have been italicized throughout.

American dating practice is adhered to; thus, 2.1 stands for February 1. I use single quotes (') not only for quotations within quotations but also for setting off a word or a phrase, usually to indicate that it is not used in its common or literal sense.

O'Neill always wrote the original drafts of his plays, as well as the notes and scenarios preceding them, in longhand. At the top a section of the original draft of *The Web*, showing the relatively large handwriting that is characteristic of the author's earliest manuscripts. In the middle the opening section of the original draft of *The Emperor Jones*, indicating how minute O'Neill's handwriting had become already by 1920; the whole play, which comprises 32 pages in the Random House edition, is written on three pieces of typewriting paper. Below a section of the scenario for *Long Day's Journey Into Night*, showing O'Neill's almost illegible handwriting in the late manuscripts.

I. INTRODUCTION

O'Neill's Tragic Vision

In a remark to the critic Joseph Wood Krutch, presumably made in the early thirties, O'Neill pointed out the fundamental difference between himself and the majority of modern dramatists: "Most modern plays are concerned with the relation between man and man, but that does not interest me at all. I am interested only in the relation between man and God" (Krutch, 1932, p. xvii).[1] O'Neill, in other words, thought of himself as primarily a religious playwright; not, of course, in the strict sense with which such a designation can be bestowed on Eliot or Claudel—O'Neill never demonstrates the salvation of any one creed—but in the wide sense, that what chiefly concerns him are ultimate, transcendental phenomena (cf. Trilling, 1936, p. 299).

Although this concern was perhaps mainly constitutional, it may well have been accentuated by the religious upbringing O'Neill received as a child and the conflict he was eventually to experience between the faith he was taught to believe in and the realities that surrounded him. Like most Irish-Americans, O'Neill's parents were devout Catholics (Clark, p. 11; Bowen, 1959, p. 10; Gelb, pp. 45 f.).[2] As a girl his mother had dreamed of becoming a nun (Gelb, p. 14); his famous actor-father, who was frequently taken for a Catholic priest, played the part of Christ in a play called *The Passion* with such intensity that people fell on their knees in prayer (Gelb, p. 46). From his seventh to his thirteenth year O'Neill received abundant religious instruction at the Catholic boarding schools he then attended. At the age of twelve, when he received his first Holy Communion, O'Neill's Catholic faith seems to have been at its peak. He then believed that he had achieved union with God. But the shattering discoveries that his father had an illegitimate child, that his brother was turning into an alcoholic and, worst of all, that his mother had been a drug addict for years, undoubtedly contributed to work

---

[1] For reference principles, se the Explanatory Note, p. 9.

[2] A general remark on the biographical evidence is appropriate. Naturally, I rely to a great extent on the information given in the existing O'Neill biographies, especially on the information provided in the very comprehensive one by Arthur and Barbara Gelb. Unfortunately none of them quite fulfills scholarly demands as to exact dating, critical evaluation of sources, clear references, etc. For this reason the possibility that my external evidence at one point or another is fallacious cannot be wholly excluded.

a spiritual change in him. In 1902, the year that according to O'Neill himself marked the turning point in his life, he entered a nonsectarian boarding school. A year later he stopped attending church. At the age of thirteen he had become a renegade (Gelb, pp. 71 ff.).

Although O'Neill was never to return to his childhood faith (Bowen, 1959, p. 233), there is ample evidence that he always felt an urgent desire to return to a belief in a benevolent God. In 1918, recently married to Agnes Boulton by a Methodist minister, he told a friend: "I caught myself wishing I could believe in the same gentle God he seemed so sure of" (Gelb, p. 372). In 1932 he told Philip Moeller, the director of *Days*,[3] that the hero's return to his Catholic childhood faith was a wish fulfillment on his, O'Neill's, part (Gelb, p. 779). And in 1946, when the question whether he had returned to Catholicism was posed, he replied: "Unfortunately, no" (Bowen, 1959, p. 316). Throughout his mature life O'Neill remained "an agnostic ... in search of redemption" (Sergeant, p. 83), a renegade "haunted by the God whom he had discarded" (Boulton, p. 280; cf. Skinner, p. 115).

Five years after he had given up Catholicism, O'Neill became acquainted with Nietzsche's writings,[4] and Doris Alexander (1962, p. 103) is doubtless right in assuming that it was above all as a (comparatively) meaningful substitute for his shattered faith that Nietzsche's philosophy appealed to him. What teaching could be more attractive to a young man who shunned the creed of the Church, yet who declared himself primarily concerned with ultimates!

O'Neill's view of life and of tragedy bears an unmistakable kinship with Nietzsche's. Undoubtedly he was to some extent influenced by Nietzsche's thinking, but it is more meaningful to see the similarity in their ideas as a manifestation of a basic spiritual affinity. To Nietzsche, who in this respect of course adheres to a long and well established tradition, Greek tragedy meant the unsurpassed example of art. As we shall see, O'Neill shared this view. Enacted in theatres that were also temples, the Attic tragedies had a religious spirit which the dramatist found completely lacking in modern life.[5]

---

[3] For abbreviations of O'Neill's play titles, see the key on p. 275.

[4] It was in the spring of 1907 that O'Neill came across *Thus Spake Zarathustra* (Gelb, p. 119), a book which, he said, "has influenced me more than any other book I've ever read" (letter to Benjamin De Casseres 6.22.1927). By 1917 he had read several works by the philosopher (Boulton, p. 61). It is likely that he was acquainted at this time with *The Birth of Tragedy,* a work of particular interest to a burgeoning tragedian; it was brought out by Oscar Levy in 1909.—For an examination of Nietzsche's importance for O'Neill, see Olson and Törnqvist (Aug. 1968).

[5] One of the notes for *Lazarus* reads: "What did the Greeks have that we haven't got? First, faith in their own lives as symbols of life! Hence, faith in their own courage [.] Hence, faith in their own nobility. Hence, faith in the nobility of Fate. Hence, in a word—True Faith!"

12

"If in three or four years I'm able to read Greek tragedy in the original and enjoy it," he once told a friend, "I'll have made a grand refuge for my soul to dive deeply and coolly into at moments when modern life—and drama—become too damn humid and shallow to be borne" (O'Neill to Manuel Komroff in 1926/Gelb, p. 699). O'Neill rarely felt that he fully belonged to life and he probably never felt himself as part of *modern* life. The evolution he believed in was of the crayfish variety: a regressive decline from the glory that was Greece to the empty values of contemporary life. To recreate the Greek spirit in modern life was the goal he set for himself both as a playwright and as a man.[6] The mystical, Dionysian experience of being, not an individual, but part of the Life Force, which Nietzsche found communicated in the plays of Aeschylus and Sophocles, O'Neill hoped to impart, through his plays, to a modern audience. "What has influenced my plays the most," he stated in 1929, "is my knowledge of the drama of all time—particularly Greek tragedy" (Nethercot, p. 248).[7]

Like most modern dramatists—Ibsen, Strindberg, Synge, Chekhov, to mention the ones who can lay the greatest claim to having written modern tragedies and who have at the same time influenced O'Neill—he never evolved any elaborate theory of tragedy. Yet in interviews and letters, especially in the early twenties, he occasionally expressed his tragic vision—rather than his view of tragedy. Thus, in a letter to the *New York Tribune* (2.13.1921) he declared that to him "the tragic alone" had "that significant beauty which is truth. It is the meaning of life—and the hope" (Cargill et al., p. 104). The most complete formulation of his tragic vision he gave in an interview a year later:

People talk of the "tragedy" in them [my plays], and call it "sordid," "depressing," "pessimistic"—the words usually applied to anything of a tragic nature. But tragedy, I think, has the meaning the Greeks gave it. To them it brought exaltation, an urge toward life and ever more life. It roused them to deeper spiritual understandings and released them from the petty greeds of everyday existence. When they saw a tragedy on the stage they felt their own hopeless hopes ennobled in art.

... any victory we *may* win is never the one we dreamed of winning. The point is that life in itself is nothing. It is the *dream* that keeps us fighting, willing—living! Achievement in the narrow sense of possession, is a stale finale.

[6] There is no unanimity as to his success in realizing this dream. Among many statements on the matter, see Engel's polemics (1953, pp. 257 ff.) against Krutch's view that *Electra* is a play true to the Greek spirit.

[7] It was, it seems, in his first playwriting year, 1913, that O'Neill for the first time thoroughly acquainted himself with Greek tragedy (Clark, p. 25). In George Cram Cook, the leader of the Provincetown Players, and the writer John Reed, also connected with this theatre group, he soon found other ardent admirers of Greek tragedy, men who like himself longed to recreate the Greek spirit in modern America (Gelb, pp. 303, 308).

The dreams that can be completely realized are not worth dreaming. The higher the dream, the more impossible it is to realize it fully. But you would not say, since this is true, that we should dream only of easily attained ideals. A man wills his own defeat when he pursues the unattainable. But his *struggle* is his success! He is an example of the spiritual significance which life attains when it aims high enough, when the individual fights all the hostile forces within and without himself to achieve a future of nobler values.

Such a figure is necessarily tragic. But to me he is not depressing; he is exhilarating! He may be a failure in our materialistic sense. His treasures are in other kingdoms. Yet isn't he the most inspiring of all successes? (Mullett, pp. 118, 120).

In another interview the same year he repeated the opinion that true tragedy expresses a "higher optimism," again equating his own view with the Greek one (Mollan/Clark, pp. 96 f.). And in an often quoted letter to Arthur Hobson Quinn, probably written in 1925, he declared it his ambition

to see the transfiguring nobility of tragedy, in as near the Greek sense as one can grasp it, in seemingly the most ignoble, debased lives. And just here is where I am a most confirmed mystic, too, for I'm always, always trying to interpret Life in terms of lives, never just lives in terms of character. I'm always acutely conscious of the Force behind—Fate, God, our biological past creating our present, whatever one calls it—Mystery certainly—and of the one eternal tragedy of Man in his glorious, self-destructive struggle to make the Force express him instead of being, as an animal is, an infinitesimal incident in its expression. And my profound conviction is that this is the only subject worth writing about and that it is possible—or can be—to develop a tragic expression in terms of transfigured modern values and symbols in the theatre which may to some degree bring home to members of a modern audience their ennobling identity with the tragic figures on the stage. Of course, this is very much of a dream, but where the theatre is concerned, one must have a dream, and the Greek dream in tragedy is the noblest ever! (Quinn, 2, p. 199).

That O'Neill applied the "glorious, self-destructive struggle" to himself appears from a letter, in which he describes himself—he is commenting on the playwright rather than the man—as an unbent Prometheus, plucked by the vultures of self-criticism:

My vultures are still flapping around, thank God, hungry and undismayed; and I am very proud of them for they are my test and my self-justification. I would feel a success and a total loss if they should ever desert me to gorge themselves fat and comforted on what the newspaper boys naively call fame. But luckily they are birds that fly from the great dark behind and inside and not from the bright lights without. Each visit they wax stranger and more pitiless—which is, naturally, a matter of boast between them and me!—and I look forward to some last visit when their wings will blot out the sky and they'll wrench the last of my liver out; and then I predict they'll turn out to be angels of some God or other who have given me in exchange the germ of a soul (letter to Benjamin De Casseres 8.11.[1927]).

Although these statements all stem from a limited period, their consistency indicates a certain permanence in the author's views, a deeply rooted tragic vision which, as far as we can judge, the writer adhered to throughout his life.

Its essence is found in the postulate that the goal of life is to acquire spiritual nobility. Few men attain this goal, and therefore life on the whole is both sad and repulsive. The tragic hero, by contrast, possesses such spiritual nobility or comes at least to possess it at the time of his undoing. He is therefore only seemingly defeated; spiritually he is triumphant. His development is a high example set before us, and tragedy, by revealing man's power to change himself for the better, is in a deep sense highly optimistic, exulting rather than depressing. Since precisely those heroes who harbor the highest dreams and therefore have to struggle the hardest to make them come true are the most exulting, we arrive at the paradoxical conclusion that the most "optimistic" tragedies are the ones in which fate seems most inexorable.

This brings us to the important question of what place fate holds in O'Neill's conception of life. It is not difficult to find fatalistic statements in the plays; for example:

It ain't your fault, and it ain't mine, and it ain't his neither. We're all poor nuts, and things happen, and we yust get mixed in wrong, that's all (*Christie,* 65).

We're never free—except to do what we have to do (*Chillun,* 315).

None of us can help the things life has done to us. They're done before you realize it, and once they're done they make you do other things until at last everything comes between you and what you'd like to be, and you've lost your true self forever (*Journey,* 61).

We can, of course, object to an equation of O'Neill's views with those of his characters. But this objection is of little consequence, since we find the author expressing himself in much the same vein outside the plays. Thus, in a letter to Agnes Boulton, probably written in 1928, he voices the same view as Anna Christie and Mary Tyrone (*Journey*) in the preceding quotations:

I am not blaming you. I have been [to blame] as much as you, perhaps more so. Or rather, neither of us is to blame. It is life which made us what we are. ... it is perhaps not in the nature of living life itself that fine beautiful things may exist for any great length of time, that human beings are fated to destroy just that in each other which constitutes their mutual happiness. Fits of cosmic Irish melancholia, I guess!

Eugene O'Neill, Jr., who shared his father's enthusiasm for Greek drama and was an outstanding classicist, has declared that "the Greek tragedies, the concept of fate in the Greek sense, had a tremendous influence" on his father

(Bowen, 1959, p. 299).[1] And in the 1946 *Iceman* interview O'Neill publicly voiced his fatalism: "It's struck me as time goes on, how something funny, even farcical, can suddenly without any apparent reason, break up into something gloomy and tragic.... A sort of unfair *non sequitur,* as though events, as though life, were being manipulated just to confuse us" (Gelb, p. 871). These remarks reveal that O'Neill could experience life itself as hostile to man, as a malign fate thwarting his hopes and desires. The majority of men, he indicated, adjust to life as it is, satisfied with what is little more than a vegetative existence. The noble spirit, however, can never do this. He must fight it at every turn and suffer greatly in the process in the hope that by this struggle a better kind of life, "a future of nobler values," may dawn.

O'Neill's deeply rooted skepticism of all outward success and, conversely, enthusiastic acceptance of resistance should be seen in relation to the fate of his father. James O'Neill was an outstanding Shakespearean actor when, allured by the easy success of melodramatic pieces, he gave up serious acting and devoted himself especially to one part—that of Edmond Dantes in the Fechter version of *The Count of Monte Cristo*—which he played season after season and which turned him into a wealthy though embittered man. To his son he came to incarnate the biblical word about the futility of gaining the world while losing one's soul—so much so, that this was to be one of the dominant themes in O'Neill's plays. "My father's last words," the dramatist wrote to Tyler in 1920, "are written indelibly-seared on my brain—a warning from the Beyond to be true to the best that is in me though the heavens fall" (McAneny, p. 87).

A counterpart of the father's development he could see in that of his country. Starting out under better auspices than any other country America had become, not the most successful country in the world, but "the greatest failure"; it too had traded its soul for shallow possessions. Therefore, O'Neill was convinced, "there's bound to be a retribution" (1946 interview; Bowen, 1959, p. 313).

The idea of retribution presupposes that man has a free will; if this were not so the dictum "whatsoever a man soweth, that shall he also reap" would be meaningless as a moral principle. O'Neill's fatalism did not prevent him from believing in a free will. In a letter to Mary Clark (8.5.1923) he points out that in his struggle with fate, "the brave individual always wins," for "fate can never conquer his—or her—spirit." In the letter to Agnes Boulton

---

[1] The Gelbs indicate (p. 352) that O'Neill considered Greek tragedy wholly fatalistic. But the statement on this matter they ascribe to the dramatist is an utterance recalled by one of his friends forty years after it was made. In view of this it can be given very little credit. That the concept of free will was not foreign to Greek tragedy is now generally recognized (see especially Greene, pp. 90–219, *passim,* notably p. 91).

just quoted we have seen how he hesitates between blaming life and blaming his wife and himself. Neither O'Neill nor such fatalistic characters as Anna Christie and Mary Tyrone refrain from blaming both themselves and others, although their fatalism, were it absolute, should really invalidate such an attitude; obviously they also—or at times—take a free will into account. The strong sense of guilt characteristic both of O'Neill and of his protagonists further implies a feeling of *personal* responsibility. A remark by the dramatist in 1946, although it is a slight overstatement, seems to clinch the matter: "In all my plays sin is punished and redemption takes place" (Bowen, 1946, p. 82).

Thus, while O'Neill's fatalism is certainly more conspicuous than his insistence on man's free will, it did not hold absolute sway over him; his ambivalence has been well described by Agnes Boulton: "firmly convinced that he could not alter that heavy hand of Fate, he must believe that it *was* possible—even if it were never to be possible. *The hopeless hope*—'Life's a Tragedy, hurrah!'" (Boulton, p. 280). On one hand the strong sense of man's utter helplessness (fatalism); on the other the high dream that by giving his utmost man may conquer his fate (free will).[2]

It is characteristic that O'Neill himself, when referring to his concept of fate never talked about it in the terms of a rational determinist but rather in those of a mystic; he would use expressions like "inscrutable forces behind life" (letter presumably written in 1919; Clark, p. 59), "the Force behind," "Mystery," etc., and when specifying his meaning he would group together old and new ideas and talk about "Fate, God, our biological past creating our present" (Quinn, 2, p. 199). This indicates that O'Neill's concept of fate did not spring merely, or even primarily, from modern scientific thinking, as Winther holds (pp. 149–62, *passim*), but is rather a blend of modern psychological determinism and ancient popular fatalism, Greek or Irish.[3]

O'Neill's continuous struggle against life as it usually is—i.e., death-in-life —was fought with a lusty joy when he felt himself strong enough to wage the battle. At other times, when the weight of existence seemed too overpowering, life would be rejected and death greeted as a welcome release. Spells of death longing were not alien to O'Neill. Early in his life—in 1912— he tried to commit suicide, and towards the end of it, shattered by the world war and suffering from an incurable sickness which gradually incapacitated

[2] A full discussion of the relationship between fate and free will is found in Krämer's unpubl. diss. In his conclusion Krämer assesses (p. 114) that the determinism in O'Neill's plays in no way excludes a sense of freedom on the part of the characters and that the tragic tension of the plays is intimately connected with the tension between freedom and necessity.

[3] Cf. Asselineau's observation (p. 147) that the psychological fate in *Electra* does not "entirely supersede the traditional belief in an external fate."

him for work, he joined the Euthanasia Society of America and often contemplated suicide. The doctor who attended his death bed has stated that "there seemed to be no will to live" (Gelb, pp. 900, 938 f.).

These are but the most conspicuous manifestations of a death impulse that always seems to have been latent with O'Neill[4] and which he himself recognized, when he made his alter ego in *Journey,* Edmund Tyrone, admit that he had always felt like a stranger on earth, never belonging, always "a little in love with death" (154 f.). Belonging and peace are invariably the attributes of death in O'Neill's plays; life is characterized by the opposite qualities: loneliness and struggle. This is partly the reason why the death of an O'Neill protagonist is never felt to be so much a punishment as a reward, "the right of release," as Robert Mayo puts it (*Horizon,* 168). And it is significant that in the late plays—O'Neill's darkest—there are hardly any deaths; the characters are doomed to go on living; the release of death is denied them.

Naturally, there was also a death fear in O'Neill (cf. Gelb, p. 361), which kept him fettered to life despite his sickness with it. But besides this negative reason for adhering to life, there was, as we have seen, a more positive one. To make life in all its stupidity and cruelty at all meaningful, O'Neill came to see it as a test, which man must pass to become worthy of what comes after death. Thus considered, the pain of existence could be explained and even welcomed, since pain, suffering and inner struggle would be the cost one had to pay to insure a blissful journey beyond the night of death. This hope or dream, which gives meaning to life and beauty to death, is ultimately what keeps O'Neill's tragic protagonists struggling through existence, much as their creator did. When O'Neill talks about "a future of nobler values" and "treasures ... in other kingdoms" he is expressing a utopian idea of a certain vagueness which reflects his uncertainty as to whether these kingdoms will ever be found on earth, as he hoped with Nietzsche, or whether they will be found in another existence, beyond death, as he hoped with Christ.

The Physical Theatre and the Dream Theatre

The whole period from O'Neill's birth in 1888 to his debut in 1914 was marked by the commercialization of the American theatre. In 1896 the first Theatrical Syndicate was formed, and despite the opposition from a number of producers and actors, James O'Neill being one of them, it had within ten

---

[4] Cf. Dorothy Day's remark, based on her acquaintance with O'Neill in 1918: "He was absorbed by death and darkness" (Gelb, p. 362). Dr. Gilbert V. Hamilton, from whom O'Neill received therapeutic treatment in 1926, told Macgowan: "There's a death wish in O'Neill" (Gelb, p. 597).

years gained control over most theatres in the country (Hughes, pp. 317 f.; Hewitt, p. 257). The repertoire was dominated by light entertainment, sentimental and sensational pieces (Hughes, p. 354). Playwriting meant adjustment to what the masses desired. The playwright's main task was to learn the tricks of the trade by which he could allure his audience (Krutch, 1957, p. 15; cf. Gelb, pp. 28, 34). There was no native tradition to boast of, and even the best American dramatists of the time—men like Moody, Herne and Fitch —seemed rather mediocre when compared to their European contemporaries: Ibsen, Strindberg, Maeterlinck, Hauptmann, Wedekind, Schnitzler, Chekhov, Shaw and Synge. Not only did Europe have much more to offer in the way of serious drama, but ever since the foundation of the Théâtre Libre in 1887 it also had a number of experimental theatres where this drama could be staged.

There was obviously little in the American theatre that could appeal to the young O'Neill. "My early experience with the theatre through my father," he once said, "really made me revolt against it." And he added: "As a boy I saw so much of the old, ranting, artificial romantic stuff that I always had a sort of contempt for the theatre" (Gelb, p. 64). It is difficult to ascertain to what extent O'Neill's revolt was a revolt against the conventional theatre and to what extent it was a rebellion against the father who was associated with it. The dramatist himself once pointed out that he found it "perfectly natural that having been brought up around the old conventional theatre, and having identified it with my father, I should rebel and go in a new direction" (Gelb, p. 451). In a letter to the *New York Times,* composed at the death of Professor George Pierce Baker and published on January 13, 1935, O'Neill summed up his impressions of the American theatre at the time of his debut as follows:

Only those of us who had the privilege in the drama class of George Pierce Baker back in the dark age when the American theatre was still, for playwrights, the closed shop, star system, amusement racket, can know what a profound influence Professor Baker ... exerted toward the encouragement and birth of modern American drama.

It is difficult in these days, when the native playwright can function in comparative freedom, to realize that in that benighted period a play of any imagination, originality or integrity by an American was almost automatically barred from a hearing in our theatre. To write plays of life as one saw and felt it, instead of concocting the conventional theatrical drivel of the time, seemed utterly hopeless (Gelb, p. 793).

Whatever O'Neill learned from this artificial and traditional type of theatre was a negative knowledge; "it helped me," he once said, "because I knew what I wanted to *avoid* doing" (Mullett, p. 116).

A more varied view he held with regard to the American theatre of the

twenties and thirties. Occasionally he would take a rather favorable attitude
to it (Gelb, pp. 584, 611; O'Neill, 1936/Frenz, p. 41). At other times he
would be as negative about it as about the Broadway of his youth. Thus in
1925 he contemptuously characterized the contemporary (American) theatre
as "a realtor's medium" and pessimistically viewed an artistic theatre as "an
unrealizable dream" (O'Neill 11.6.1925/Deutsch-Hanau, p. 198). In 1929,
after the failure of *Dynamo,* he wrote Eleanor Fitzgerald, manager of the
Provincetown Playhouse:

My faith in theatres, Provincetown or otherwise, has bogged down a bit. I'm
miscast among the True Believers. The future appears to me completely sterilized
against the conception of miracles. ... My motto just now is "Write 'em and
leave 'em!" and my morose intuition is that it is better not to do things at all—
especially the most beautiful things (*First Editions,* p. 44).

In 1946, on a copy of *Iceman* dedicated to Lawrence Langner, the dramatist
wrote (1963, p. 37): "To Lawrence—what can I write after all these years in
which we have tried to create a theatre? I can't write the truth that it's ten
times more rotten than when we started—in so many ways."

It was apparently the acquaintance with modern European drama that
opened O'Neill's eyes to his own possibilities. In 1907 the nineteen-year-old
boy saw Alla Nazimova's troupe in *Hedda Gabler* "for ten successive nights":
"That experience discovered an entire new world of the drama for me. It gave
me my first conception of a modern theatre where truth might live" (O'Neill,
6.2.1938). Four years later he saw the Irish players doing Yeats, Synge and
Lady Gregory: "It was seeing the Irish players for the first time that gave
me a glimpse of my opportunity. The first year that they came over here I
went to see everything they did" (O'Neill to Charles Merrill/Alexander, 1962,
p. 154). Two years after this event he discovered Strindberg:

It was reading his plays when I first started to write back in the winter of 1913–
14 that, above all else, first gave me the vision of what modern drama could be,
and first inspired me with the urge to write for the theatre myself. If there is
anything of lasting worth in my work, it is due to that original impulse from
him, which has continued as my inspiration down all the years since then—to
the ambition I received then to follow in the footsteps of his genius as worthily
as my talent might permit, and with the same integrity of purpose (O'Neill,
1936/Frenz, pp. 41 f.).[5]

Feeling the need "to study the technique of play-writing" (Mullett, p. 116),
O'Neill in 1914–15 attended George Pierce Baker's famous 47 Workshop, a
course in playwriting and play production. As his tribute to Baker indicates,

[5] Strindberg's importance for O'Neill has been examined especially by Hartman
(1960).

O'Neill respected the man more than the teacher.[6] Most of what Baker had to tell his students about the theatre as a physical medium was "old stuff" to O'Neill.[7] What he learned from the course was mainly a practical work method (Alexander, 1962, p. 197).[8] "Without the shortcut of your advice," he wrote Baker in 1919, "I would have learned (if I have learned!) by a laborious process of elimination" (Kinne, p. 207). Aside from this, Baker's importance, as O'Neill made plain in his letter to the *Times,* consisted chiefly in the encouragement he gave his students that a new era would dawn in which the serious playwright would get a hearing in the theatre.

Of greater importance was O'Neill's connection with the Provincetown Players. This group, which consisted of some radical intellectuals and artists —novelists, journalists, sculptors, teachers, architects—who spent their summers in Provincetown, Massachusetts, began its activities very modestly at about the time when O'Neill left Baker's course. When he arrived in the little fishing village in the summer of 1916, apparently in the hope of getting one of his sixteen plays produced, he was immediately recognized as a dramatist of stature; and, ironically, he won his recognition almost solely on the basis of the play Professor Baker had thought no play at all (Clark, pp. 27 f.). "So Gene took 'Bound East for Cardiff' from his trunk," Susan Glaspell has recalled, "and Freddie Burt read it to us. ... Then we knew what we were for" (Deutsch-Hanau, p. 15). The play was produced the same summer in what was by this time called "The Wharf Theater," a deserted old shed for fishing gear and boat repair. The production marked not only the first staging of an O'Neill play but also the beginning of a new era in the American theatre (Krutch, 1957, p. 3), an era characterized by greater sincerity and integrity.

It is likely that the Provincetown Players would have continued their activities even without O'Neill. And O'Neill, for his part, has stated that he would have gone on writing plays even without the Players (Clark, p. 31). Yet it is obvious—and acknowledged by both parties—that each benefited enormously

[6] One of his classmates has recalled that O'Neill often accused Baker of teaching commercial drama (Gelb, p. 279).

[7] Skinner tends to doubt that Baker's teaching had any influence at all on O'Neill. "In content and feeling and technique," he points out (p. 38), "there is little noticeable difference between the first and the last three of the Glencairn series," i.e. between work done before and after Baker. Koischwitz (pp. 83 ff.) goes even further and depicts Baker as a rigid academician against whom O'Neill had to rebel. Since Koischwitz gives a simplified caricature of Baker's ideas, his opinion is of very limited value. Cargill (p. 333) claims that O'Neill's interest in writing plays with Negro protagonists was derived from Baker, but he provides no supporting evidence for this view.

[8] For a discussion of O'Neill's work method, see Törnqvist (1968).

from the other. George Cram Cook, the leader of the group, O'Neill found to be

the big man, the dominating and inspiring genius of the Players. Always enthusiastic, vital, impatient with everything that smacked of falsity or compromise, he represented the spirit of revolt against the old worn-out traditions, the commercial theatre, the tawdry artificialities of the stage. I owe a tremendous lot to the Players—they encouraged me to write, and produced all my early and many of my later plays (Clark, p. 31).[9]

Precisely because the members of the group were not professionally engaged in the theatre, they had no prejudices about plays or play production (Deutsch-Hanau, p. 6). In the manifesto, drawn up on September 5, 1916, it was stated that the primary object of the Provincetown Players was

to encourage the writing of American plays of artistic, literary and dramatic—as opposed to Broadway—merit.

That such plays be considered without reference to their commercial value, since this theatre is not to be run for pecuniary profit. . . .

That the president shall cooperate with the author in producing the play under the author's direction. The resources of the theatre ... shall be placed at the disposal of the author. . . . The author shall produce the play without hindrance, according to his own ideas (Gelb, p. 315).

Thinking perhaps of Strindberg's Intimate Theatre (Gelb, p. 316), O'Neill suggested that the group name their theatre on Macdougal Street in New York "The Playwright's Theatre" (Deutsch-Hanau, p. 16). Nevertheless, he seems from the very first to have been relatively disinterested in the production of his own plays. Although, as we have seen, the Players granted the playwright the right to supervise the staging of his plays, O'Neill would leave most of this work to George Cram Cook, despite the fact that "he was not always in agreement with 'Jig's' ideas" (Clark, p. 40). The Gelbs report that O'Neill would "reluctantly" agree to supervise the staging of Cardiff in New York (Gelb, p. 318). Since this is a play which O'Neill valued highly (cf. Skinner, p. viii), and since it meant the first production of an O'Neill play in New York, this reluctance is surprising.

Again, Agnes Boulton recalls (p. 251) that O'Neill would become moody when he was expected to attend rehearsals of Caribbees: "He really wanted to settle down to work on his plays. At times he even tried to persuade himself and me that it would be just as well if he attended only the last rehearsal or so and left the rest of it up to Jig Cook." Finally, because Caribbees was his favorite play (Clark, p. 58) and because Cook had no time for it, O'Neill resigned himself to attending rehearsals, but apparently without any enthu-

[9] The statement is somewhat inaccurate; the Provincetown Players did not produce all the early plays by O'Neill; cf. the chronology, p. 265.

siasm; less than a month after the play opened he complained about the production and could not even remember the name of the director (letter to Nina Moise 1.17.1919). O'Neill once told Nina Moise, who directed *Rope*: "When I finish writing a play, I'm through with it." And Moise, in line with this, has observed that "Gene was concerned with plays, not theatre" (Gelb, p. 325).

While attending rehearsals of *Horizon* O'Neill wrote his wife Agnes: "I'd never go near a rehearsal if I didn't have to—and I'll certainly never see a performance" (letter 1.23.1920). In 1929 he told Eleanor Fitzgerald: "I'm a bit weary and disillusioned with scenery and actors.... I sigh for the old P'town days, the old crowd and zest.... I think I will wind up writing plays to be published with 'No Productions Allowed' in red letters on the first page" (letter 5.13.1929/*First Editions*, p. 44). The twelve-year absence of a new O'Neill play from Broadway (1934–46) his wife Carlotta has partly explained as due to the dramatist's dislike of attending rehearsals: "The only thing he cared about was his writing. He used to say, 'Oh, God, if only some Good Fairy would give me some money, so I'd never have to produce a play, and I could just write, write, write and never go near a theatre!'" (Gelb, p. 787). O'Neill's disinterest in play production is also indicated by his rare visits—except during his boyhood (Gelb, pp. 79, 128; Alexander, 1962, p. 66)—to the theatre. In 1924 he told an interviewer:

I hardly ever go to the theatre, although I read all the plays I can get. I don't go to the theatre because I can always do a better production in my mind than the one on the stage. ... Nor do I ever go to see one of my own plays—have seen only three of them since they started coming out. My real reason for this is that I was practically brought up in the theatre—in the wings—and I know all the technique of acting. I know everything that everyone is doing from the electrician to the stage hands. So I see the machinery going around all the time unless the play is wonderfully acted and produced. Then, too, in my own plays all the time I watch them I am acting all the parts and living them so intensely that by the time the performance is over I am exhausted—as if I had gone through a clothes wringer (Anon./Cargill et al., p. 111 f.).

He might have added that seeing a play of his own was a painful experience for him also because of the discrepancy between the production he had done in his mind as he wrote the play and the one executed on the stage. O'Neill frequently drew attention to this aspect. While attending rehearsals of *Horizon* he complained: "Those people will never—can never—be my Robert, Ruth, and Andy—and what would be the use of my watching another lot of actors perform—after all these years of watching them?" (letter to Agnes Boulton 1.23.1920). By 1929 he had seen no performance which fully realized his intentions: "I've had many plays in which the acting was excellent. I've never had one I recognized on the stage as being deeply my play. That's why I never see them."[1] By 1946 he had seen only one actor—Charles Gilpin as Brutus Jones—who in all respects incarnated the character he felt he had written into his script:

I am not saying that some of the actors and actresses who interpreted my plays did not add something to them. But, after all, even an owl thinks her owlets are the most beautiful babies in the world and that's the way an author feels about his stage children. It is for this reason that I always attend the rehearsals of my plays. While I do not want to change the personalities of the artists acting in them, I want to make it clear to them what was in my mind when I wrote the play (Woolf, p. 62).

O'Neill's disappointment with most actors is partly due to the high standard of acting he demanded. But more important is the fact that he felt unusually close to his characters: "I've always tried to *write* my characters out. That's why I've sometimes been disappointed in the actors who played them—the characters were too real and alive in my imagination" (O'Neill/Bowen, 1959, p. 329). As is now well known, many of the characters are intimately auto-biographical; presumably O'Neill found it especially hard to accept the actors' interpretations of parts into which he had written a good deal of himself, his parents, his brother or his wives (cf. Gelb, p. 882).

To O'Neill the staged version of a great play could never equal the written one. Even a perfect and imaginative production would have the limiting boundaries inherent in a physical production as compared to a purely ima-gined one. It would also lack the unity found in the written play, being the product of but one mind: "After all, is not the written play a thing? Is not *Hamlet,* seen in the dream theatre of the imagination as one reads, a greater play than *Hamlet* interpreted even by a perfect production?" (Sayler, p. 24). O'Neill, the avid play reader who never went to the theatre and who attended rehearsals of his own plays mainly to prevent his work from being misinter-preted, obviously thought so. In 1929 he wrote De Casseres: "A play's fate after I have written it—I mean outside of my creation, the play in the book —is just roulette to me with a fat percentage in favor of the author losing *his* play either artistically or financially or both" (letter 3.12.[1929]). In 1931 he repeated:

To me it is axiomatic that any play that reads as a good play *is* a good play, and the whole history of drama bears me out. Production may help to bring the values of a play out or it may blur them into meaninglessness but the play as written remains a thing in itself which no good or bad acting or directing can touch (letter to De Casseres, 11.12.1931).

[1] Undated letter to De Casseres, written at Cap D'Ail, France, where O'Neill stayed in the winter and early spring of 1929.

Considering the author's high evaluation of the written play, it is not surprising that the epic or novelistic trend should be rather marked in his work. When outlining *Horizon,* O'Neill revealed in a letter to the *New York Times* (4.11.1920), he "dreamed of wedding the theme for a novel to the play form in a way that would still leave the play master of the house." He characterized *Chris* as an attempt "to compress the theme for a novel into play form without losing the flavor of the novel" (letter to George Tyler 3.26. 1920). In *Interlude* with its long time span and its constant thought asides the novelistic tendency is very evident. About the plays in the projected series *By Way of Obit,* of which only *Hughie* was completed, O'Neill told Nathan that they were written "more to be read than staged, although they could be played" (letter 6.19.1942). The ample, descriptive stage directions, to which the dramatist appears to have devoted as much attention as to the dialogue,[2] give an epic touch to all O'Neill's plays, as does the unusual length of some of them. From one point of view this tendency may be regarded as an attempt to overcome the limitations inherent in the dramatic form. From another, relevant in this context, it may be said to constitute an attempt to give artistic confirmation of O'Neill's view that the written play is the thing.

Yet it would clearly be absurd to argue that O'Neill wrote solely for the reader.[3] Despite his skeptical attitude to the theatre of his day, O'Neill never wrote a closet drama and he was clearly interested in having his plays produced; in 1926 he even nourished plans for an O'Neill repertory theatre (Gelb, p. 619). Many of the effects in the plays are also of a strongly theatrical nature.

Moreover, there are statements by the author which support the view that O'Neill wrote also, perhaps preeminently, for the physical theatre—if not for the one of his time. In the wake of Nietzsche he dreamt of an ennobled theatre, filled with artists of a higher order than the ones he saw crowding the New York stages; in 1921 he told an interviewer:

Yes, I can almost hear the birth cry of the Higher Man in the theatre. There is a goal, blessedly difficult of attainment. And what will he be? ... Well, the Higher Man of the theatre will be a playwright, say. He will have his own theatre for his own plays, as Strindberg had his Intimate Theatre in Stockholm. He will have grouped around him as fellow workers in that theatre the most imaginative of all the artists in the different crafts. In no sense will he be their master, except his imagination of his work will be the director of their imagina-

[2] This may be inferred from the many changes undertaken in the stage directions of the various play versions. Agnes Boulton also observes (p. 113) that O'Neill wrote the scene descriptions for *Horizon* "with as much creative absorption as when he wrote the dialogue."

[3] Several critics have pointed out that O'Neill wrote both for the reader and for the spectator. See, for example, Shipley (1928, p. 15), Lamm (p. 325) and Biese (p. 22).

tions. He will tell them the inner meaning and spiritual significance of his play as revealed to him. He will explain the truth—the unity—underlying his conception. And then all will work together to express that unity. The playwright will not interfere except where he sees the harmony of his imaginative whole is threatened. Rather, he will learn from his associates, help them to set their imaginations free as they help to find in the actual theatre a medium ever-broadening in which even his seventh last solitude may hope to speak and be interpreted. And soon all of these would be Higher Men of the theatre (Sayler, p. 24).

It was for such a theatre, it might be held, that most of O'Neill's plays were written, a theatre which he hoped would be "the theatre of tomorrow."[4] And it was presumably this kind of theatre he had in mind when he subtitled *Lazarus* "*A Play for an Imaginative Theatre.*" In his letter to the Kamerny Theatre, whose production of *Chillun* impressed him, O'Neill stated: "A theatre of creative imagination has always been my ideal! To see my plays given by such a theatre has always been my dream!" (O'Neill, 6.19.1932/ Cargill et al., p. 123).

Along with George Cram Cook (Alexander, 1962, p. 224) and Kenneth Macgowan (Engel, 1964, p. 107) O'Neill, the renegade Catholic, dreamt of the theatre as a "Living Church," the one 'church' left to modern man after "the death of the old God and the failure of science and materialism to give any satisfying new one" (O'Neill/Nathan, 1929, p. 119).[5] In an unpublished "Author's foreword" to *Brown* he states: "The theatre should stand as apart from existence as the church did in the days when it was the church. It should give us what the church no longer gives us—a meaning. In brief, it should return to the spirit of the Greek grandeur." The idea returns in "A Dramatist's Notebook," where the author pleads for

a theatre returned to its highest and sole significant function as a Temple where the religion of a poetical interpretation and symbolical celebration of life is communicated to human beings, starved in spirit by their soul-stifling daily struggle to exist as masks among the masks of living (O'Neill, 1933/Cargill et al., pp. 121 ff.).

Lazarus is a concrete example of O'Neill's attempt to create "a legitimate descendant of the first theatre that sprang, by virtue of man's imaginative interpretation of life, out of his worship of Dionysus" (ibid., p. 121). To the playwright Paul Green he confided in late 1926 his desire to write plays in which the audience could participate in much the same way as a congregation does in a church service:

[4] This is the title of the book by Kenneth Macgowan published in 1921.
[5] When staging *The Miracle*, brought to New York in 1924, Max Reinhardt actually transformed the playhouse into a church (Gassner, 1965, p. 55). O'Neill undoubtedly heard of this famous production from Nathan, who was greatly impressed by it (Engel, 1953, p. 86).

As it is now there is a too cold and cut division between the stage and the auditorium. The whole environment of the piece—stage and auditorium, actors and spectators—should be emotionally charged. This can only happen when the audience actively participates in what is being said, seen and done. ... What I would like to see in the production of *Lazarus* is for the audience to be caught up enough to join in the responses—the laughter and chorus statements even, much as Negroes do in one of their revival meetings (Gelb, pp. 602 f.).

Convinced that "reason has no business in the theatre ..., any more than it has in a church" (letter 5.7.1923 to Nathan/Caputi, p. 449), O'Neill always aimed at stirring the emotions rather than the intellect of his audience. Frequently, he found, audiences would applaud ideas to which they were actually opposed, "because they had been appealed to through their emotions" (Mullett, p. 34).

It would appear, then, that O'Neill, hostile towards the physical theatre of his day, wrote both for what he himself termed "the dream theatre," i.e. the theatre of the mind, and for an "emotionally charged" imaginative theatre of the future, hence for two audiences: a reading and a viewing audience. Since he never published any of the original acting versions,[6] we must assume that he meant the published plays to function not merely as reading matter but also as texts for future productions. And even of the passages that seem directed primarily to the general reader we cannot feel sure that they are not meant as much for the actor and director.[7] Thus, when O'Neill has Murray in *Straw* clench his fists *"in impotent rage at himself and at Fate"* (392) or assures us that *"for the first time Death confronts him* [Murray] *face to face as a menacing reality"* (412), when he has the Cabot brothers in *Desire "smell of earth"* (204), or when he has Margaret in *Brown* kiss *"with a timeless kiss"* (325) and Cybel in the same play chew gum *"like a sacred cow forgetting time with an eternal end"* (278), he is, I believe, doing two things at the same time. He is explaining the significance of the characters' actions to the *reader* to help him do a better production in his mind. And he is providing "road signs for the intelligent actor" (Gelb, p. 325) to help him do a better production for the *spectator*. To what extent we consider stage directions such as these primarily meant for the general reader or for the actor and thus, indirectly, for the spectator, depends on to what extent we consider them realizable in the theatre.

[6] For the difference between these and the published versions, see Arbenz.

[7] O'Neill's note on the title page of the first typewritten version of *Interlude* does not contradict this statement; there it says: "The published book of this play is *not* identical with the staged version. I kept material in the book which I felt was necessary when the play was *read* but which was not needed when one *heard* and *saw* the play acted. This was done in the case of many of my other plays, too."

O'Neill's Super-naturalism

When O'Neill began writing plays in 1913,[8] naturalism and symbolism had already had their heyday, but both were still vital forces in the theatre. The first expressionist plays had recently been staged, but expressionism was as yet little known outside Germany and the term, though coined already in 1901 (Sokel, pp. 1 f.), had barely been applied to the new literary movement, whose major pioneer, Strindberg, died the year before O'Neill started out as a playwright.

Rather than enroll himself in any of the current movements O'Neill very early appears to have been searching for a style of his own. When the producer George Tyler suggested, in 1920, that he use the *Monte Cristo* plot for a drama, O'Neill wrote back:

I can only imagine one way in which the project could call forth any genuine creative interest on my part. If I could say to myself: "Throw everything overboard—all precedent, all existing dogmas of what is practicable, and what is not, in the theatre of today, all well-regulated ideas of what a play is or isn't, etc. Create your own form just as you did in the *Emperor Jones*" (McAneny, p. 87).

Two years later he stated in an interview:

I intend to use whatever I can make my own, to write about anything under the sun in any manner that fits or can be invented to fit the subject. And I shall never be influenced by any consideration but one: Is it the truth as I know it—or, better still, feel it? If so, shoot, and let the splinters fly wherever they may. If not, not (Clark, p. 163).

In 1925 he complained to Quinn (2, p. 199):

To be called a "sordid realist" one day, a "grim pessimistic Naturalist" the next, a "lying Moral Romanticist" the next, etc. is quite perplexing—not to add the *Times* editorial that settled *Desire* once and for all by calling it a "Neo-Primitive," a Matisse of the drama, as it were! So I'm really longing to explain and try and convince some sympathetic ear that I've tried to make myself a melting pot for all these methods, seeing some virtues for my ends in each of them, and thereby, if there is enough real fire in me, boil down to my own technique.

Again, in 1933, he declared: "I do not plan to confine myself to any one type of technique. Rather, I plan to use the method, whether it be naturalism

---

[8] A statement by Frederick P. Latimer (Clark, p. 19) suggests that O'Neill had written "play-manuscripts" already in 1912. In agreement with this, the Gelbs maintain (pp. 195, 216) that O'Neill wrote snatches of dialogue and made sketches of characters and notations for settings in the fall of 1912. In a letter to the present writer, Louis Sheaffer, who is working on a two-volume O'Neill biography, claims, however, that O'Neill's decision to turn playwright "came at the TB san in 1913, not in 1912, as the Gelbs maintain." This agrees with O'Neill's own dating (cf. Clark, p. 21).

or symbolism, that happens to fit in with the sort of drama I am writing" (Gelb, p. 770). O'Neill's proneness to experiment with dramatic form— especially during his formative years he often refers to his plays as "experiments" (Clark, pp. 69, 72; Cargill et al., p. 102)—follows logically from the assumption that just as every play has its own subject matter, so it must also have its own form. This demand for artistic freedom within the theatre, which was inaugurated practically in *Sturm und Drang* drama and theoretically in Victor Hugo's preface to *Cromwell,* and which has proved highly seminal in modern drama, was hardly a generally accepted view in the American theatre of the early twenties. In the United States O'Neill was, as Dickinson points out (p. 122), "the first playwright to be a free agent in the theatre."

Not only O'Neill himself but also his critics have drawn attention to the syncretistic nature of his work. Thus Lamm remarks about *Cardiff* (p. 320): "This little play is usually included with O'Neill's early naturalistic plays. But it might just as properly be called symbolistic." Gassner (1951, p. 326), similarly, finds that O'Neill "fused naturalistic detail with symbolist mood, suggestiveness and symbol." And Goldberg (1922, p. 457), commenting on the expressionistic aspects of *Jones* and *Ape,* from a somewhat different point of view notes that "even when his [O'Neill's] contact with external reality seems least firm, he yet maintains his grip upon the roots of things."

From naturalism O'Neill overtook the modern, 'scientific' view of heredity and environment as the powers determining man's fate. With Darwin and Zola he revealed the beast in man, seeing him as a victim of his own biological past, of his own animal instincts or of a corrupt society. As Gassner notes (1951, p. 326), O'Neill was "virtually the first serious American dramatist of any standing to bring characters from all walks of life on to the stage," and the number of characters in his work belonging to the lower strata of society—farmers, stokers, Negroes, prostitutes, gangsters—is noteworthy. The 'vulgar' tongue of these characters, which frequently brought O'Neill into trouble with censorship, associated him in the popular mind with naturalism.

Yet the naturalists' positivism was foreign to O'Neill's anti-rationalistic, mystical mind.[9] Fundamentally he had more in common with their opponents,

[9] Krutch notes (1932, p. xv) that even in his earliest plays O'Neill was "reaching out for something more" than realism, and Koischwitz similarly points out (p. 45) that "schon in den nach Form und Inhalt naturalistischen Frühdramen O'Neills verrät sich die mystische (durchaus antipositivistische) Haltung des Dichters." Cf. Trilling, 1937, pp. ix ff.

It is significant that politically committed or socially concerned critics usually have taken a negative attitude to O'Neill's plays. See, for example, Flexner, Gorelik, Lawson, and Bentley (1946).

the symbolists and especially the expressionists.[1] Once, probably in the early thirties, he told Langner (p. 288) that "he had sometimes been referred to as a 'naturalistic' or 'realistic' writer whereas he had never actually written along these lines except on rare occasions."

O'Neill's concern with what underlies the fleeting phenomena of life[2] rather than with these phenomena themselves can be traced to his very beginning as a playwright. It is significant that he began as a poet and always stressed the poetical nature of his work.[3] In the fall of 1912 he worked as a cub reporter on the *New London Telegraph,* to which he regularly contributed poems, some of which anticipate his later concern with the eternal mysteries of existence: love, death, God (cf. Sanborn–Clark, pp. 111–61). Malcolm Mollan, City Editor of the *Telegraph,* has recalled that as a reporter O'Neill left something to be desired, because facts, standing by themselves, did not interest him: "It was what they signified, what led to them and what they in turn led to, their proportionate values in the great canvas of life, that intrigued his rapt attention" (Gelb, p. 197). Mollan found O'Neill deep-probing and "sensitive as a seismograph" (Clark, p. 20; cf. Latimer's statement, ibid., pp. 18 ff.).

It was in the winter and spring of 1913, which O'Neill spent at Gaylord sanatorium, that the urge to write first made itself strongly felt (Clark, p. 21). The discovery of Strindberg around this time further inspired him to write for the theatre. The reason why Strindberg had a greater impact on him than Ibsen[4] and Synge, with whose work he was earlier acquainted, seems indicated in a statement by the playwright from around 1925, in which he claimed that if it had not been for Dostoevsky's *The Idiot* and Strindberg's *Dance of Death,* he might never have begun writing. These two works had "the feeling and sensation" O'Neill wished to communicate to an audience. They were tangible evidence that "a powerful emotional ecstasy, approaching a kind of

[1] O'Neill denied, however, that he had been influenced by German expressionism in such plays as *Jones* and *Ape* (Clark, p. 83). For convincing evidence of O'Neill's indebtedness especially to Kaiser, see Blackburn and Valgemae.

[2] This concern, noted by many critics, has been especially stressed by Koischwitz (see, in particular, p. 40).

[3] Cf. Clark, pp. 24, 43; Alexander, 1962, p. 63; Quinn, 2, p. 199; O'Neill, Jan. 1933/Cargill et al., p. 121; and Goldberg, 1926, pp. 158 f.

[4] This is not saying, of course, that Ibsen's work has been of little consequence to O'Neill. The influence of the Norwegian is, in fact, more readily detectable in O'Neill's early and late plays than is that of Strindberg. In a public letter (6.2.1938) the dramatist stated: "Not long ago I read all of Ibsen's plays again. The same living truth is there. Only to fools with a superficial eye cocked to detect the incidental can they have anything dated or outworn about them. As dramas revealing the souls of men and women they are as great to-day as they will be a hundred years from now." But whereas O'Neill always expressed his admiration of Strindberg, his attitude to Ibsen was ambivalent (cf. Törnqvist, 1965, pp. 214 f.).

frenzy" could be communicated by a writer (O'Neill/Gelb, p. 233). It seems obvious, that what appealed to O'Neill in Strindberg's work was, among other things, what he was later to term its "super-naturalism." In 1919 he wrote Clark that he wanted to explain to the critic his "feeling for the impelling, inscrutable forces behind life which it is my ambition to at least faintly shadow at their work in my plays" (Clark, p. 59). Five years later he would refer to some of Strindberg's plays as "behind-life" dramas.

In a letter to Nathan (5.7.1923), he wrote in reference to *Welded*:

Damn that word, "realism"! When I first spoke to you of the play as a "last word in realism," I meant something "really real," in the sense of being spiritually true, not meticulously life-like—an interpretation of actuality by a distillation, an elimination of most realistic trappings, an intensification of human lives into clear symbols of truth (Caputi, p. 449).

The description fits not only what O'Neill was trying to do in *Welded* but also what he found Strindberg had done in some of his plays. When finishing the drama he stated that he wanted to write "a truly realistic play" which dealt with "what might be called the soul of the character" and mentioned *The Dance of Death* as an example of this true kind of realism (Gelb, p. 520).

It is interesting to note that O'Neill in the spring of 1923 called the two plays realistic rather than expressionistic. He had used the latter term in a letter a year earlier when stating that he was working out a scheme for filming *Ape* "along Expressionistic lines" (letter to Harry Weinberger 1.26. 1922). His knowledge of expressionism at this time was based mainly on Isaac Goldberg's discussion of it in *The Drama of Transition*.[5] Obviously, O'Neill did not feel that the term expressionism fitted *Welded*. The reason for his unwillingness to adopt this term appears in his statement on the movement a year later:

... expressionism denies the value of characterization. As I understand it, expressionism tries to minimize everything on the stage that stands between the author and the audience. It strives to get the author talking directly to the audience. ...

I personally do not believe that an idea can be readily put over to an audience except through characters. When it sees "A Man" and "A Woman"—just abstractions, it loses the human contact by which it identifies itself with the protagonist of the play. ... The real contribution of the expressionist has been in the dynamic qualities of his plays. They express something in modern life better than did the old plays (Anon./Cargill et al., p. 111).

If O'Neill discarded the expressionist faith in purely abstract characters, he even more violently opposed the shallow meticulousness of the naturalists, which turned characters into mere individuals. When depicting characters he

---

[5] This appears from a letter to Goldberg 9.22.1925.

always tried to find a balance, a synthesis, between these warring tendencies. Emma in *Diff'rent,* he indicated, is both "the eternal, romantic idealist who is in all of us" and "a whaling captain's daughter in a small New England seacoast town" (O'Neill, 2.13.1921/Cargill et al., pp. 104 f.). Cape in *Welded* is both "a man" and "Man" (Caputi, p. 449). Yank in *Ape* is both an American stoker and "a symbol of man" (Anon./Cargill et al., p. 110). *Brown* deals both with "recognizable human beings" and with "conflicting tides in the soul of Man" (O'Neill, 1926/Clark, pp. 105 f.). The characters in the Cycle plays are, he said, in part "extraordinary examples and symbols in the drama of American possessiveness and materialism" (Langner, p. 286).

Also the plays are attempts at synthesis. *Ape,* he once wrote, "isn't Expressionism. It isn't Naturalism. It is a blend—and, as far as my knowledge goes, a uniquely successful one" (letter to Robert Sisk 3.15.1935). *Dynamo,* he said, is "a symbolical and factual biography of what is happening in a large section of the American (and not only American) soul right now (Nathan, 1929, p. 119). *Electra,* he found, is "realistic and not realistic at the same time" (letter to Sisk 8.28.1930).

Misunderstood by Nathan in his use of the term "realism" and aware of the difference between his own work and that of the expressionists, O'Neill coined the term "super-naturalism," which, he felt, adequately described Strindberg's position, both historically and stylistically, his ability of transcending naturalism without losing touch with recognizable reality. The term appeared in what might be called O'Neill's first artistic manifesto, his program note for *The Spook Sonata,* produced on January 3, 1924. The note is worth quoting at length:

Strindberg still remains among the most modern of moderns, the greatest interpreter in the theater of the characteristic spiritual conflicts which constitute the drama—the blood—of our lives today. He carried Naturalism to a logical attainment of such poignant intensity that, if the work of any other playwright is to be called "naturalism", we must classify a play like "The Dance of Death" as "super-naturalism", and place it in a class by itself, exclusively Strindberg's since no one before or after him has had the genius to qualify.

Yet it is only by means of some form of "super-naturalism" that we may express in the theater what we comprehend intuitively of that self-defeating self-obsession which is the discount we moderns have to pay for the loan of life. The old "naturalism"—or "realism" if you prefer (would to God some genius were gigantic enough to define clearly the separateness of these terms once and for all!) no longer applies. It represents our Fathers' daring aspirations toward self-recognition by holding the family kodak up to ill-nature. But to us their old audacity is blague; we have taken too many snap-shots of each other in every graceless position; we have endured too much from the banality of surfaces. We are ashamed of having peeked through so many keyholes, squinting always at heavy, uninspired bodies—the fat facts—with not a nude spirit among them;

we have been sick with appearances and are convalescing; we "wipe out and pass on" to some as yet unrealized region where our souls, maddened by loneliness and the ignoble inarticulateness of flesh, are slowly evolving their new language of kinship.

Strindberg knew and suffered with our struggle years before many of us were born. He expressed it by intensifying the method of his time and by foreshadowing both in content and form the methods to come. All that is enduring in what we loosely call "Expressionism"—all that is artistically valid and sound theater—can be clearly traced back through Wedekind to Strindberg's "The Dream Play", "There Are Crimes and Crimes", "The Spook Sonata", etc.

Hence, "The Spook Sonata" at our Playhouse. One of the most difficult of Strindberg's "behind-life" (if I may coin the term) plays to interpret with insight and distinction—but the difficult is properly our special task, or we have no good reason for existing. Truth, in the theater as in life, is eternally difficult, just as the easy is the everlasting lie (O'Neill, 1924/Deutsch-Hanau, pp. 191 ff.).

If we compare this characterization of Strindberg's work with O'Neill's description, quoted earlier, of the style employed in *Welded,* it will appear, that there is virtually no difference; that O'Neill, as he strongly suggests in the Strindberg note, considered himself a (humble) pursuer of Strindberg's super-naturalism.[6]

The second coinage—"behind-life" plays—can also be related to O'Neill's own work. Already in 1919, as we have noted, he had declared it his ambition as a playwright to suggest "the impelling, inscrutable forces behind life." Cape in *Welded,* he wrote Nathan in 1923, is "Man dimly aware of recurring experience, groping for the truth behind the realistic appearances of himself, and of love and life. For the moment his agony gives him vision of the truth behind the real" (Caputi, p. 449). In 1925 he wrote Quinn that he was always "acutely conscious of the Force behind" (Quinn, 2, p. 199). In *Brown,* he explained a year later, there is a "mystical pattern" manifesting itself as an overtone "dimly behind and beyond the words and actions of the characters" (Clark, p. 104). *Electra,* he noted in 1929, was to be "primarily drama of hidden life forces" (O'Neill, 1931/Frenz, p. 4).

The fact that O'Neill uses the term "super-naturalism" about *The Dance of Death* and reserves the term "behind-life" for *The Dream Play, There Are Crimes and Crimes* and *The Spook Sonata* may suggest to some readers that he considered the mysticism, the departure from naturalism in these later plays greater than in *The Dance of Death.* Such a reasoning presupposes that O'Neill uses both terms as descriptive of the *form* of the plays and was

---

[6] Only a few critics have used the term super-naturalism with regard to O'Neill's work (see Clark, p. 52; Stuart, p. 649; and Dietrich, p. 206). Dietrich understands the term in a narrower sense than I do; to her it means "innere Realität mit äusserlich unrealistischen Mitteln, teils symbolisch, teils abstrakt, teils grotesk dargestellt." Thus understood, the term, it seems to me, comes to mean much the same as 'expressionism.'

anxious to point out the difference in technique between them. Actually, there is nothing in the note that supports such a view. It is plain that O'Neill does not evaluate one type of play against another, although this would have been natural had he considered them notably different in style. It is therefore much more likely that O'Neill considered the terms complementary; that he found a super-naturalistic technique the fitting form for a behind-life drama, just as a naturalistic technique would suit a play that limited itself to the description of surface reality.

The term "behind-life" relates directly to O'Neill's concept of fate. It suggests the existence of an external, supernatural force ruling man's life, what Strindberg termed "the Powers" and O'Neill simply called "Fate" or "God." It also indicates the existence of an internal, psychological fate. In Strindberg's chamber plays the veil of the material world is often momentarily torn apart and beyond its floating shreds we divine both a supernatural world, a product of Strindberg's religious concern, and a subterranean one, a creation of the author's keen psychological insight.

These two worlds are also to be found in O'Neill's plays. We have already discussed the dramatist's concern with the supernatural one. His preoccupation with the subterranean one has been noted by many critics, anxious to point out the Freudian, Jungian or Adlerian ideas they have found embodied in the plays.[7] O'Neill's relationship to psychoanalysis is of interest, since it indirectly informs us of the playwright's concern with depth-psychological issues. I shall therefore discuss it at some length.

When *Desire*, the O'Neill play in which the Oedipal conflict makes its first obvious appearance, was produced in 1924, some theatregoers remarked on the Freudian influence. O'Neill, who regarded himself as an "intuitively keen analytical psychologist" (Gelb, p. 577), protested to a friend: "The Freudian brethren and sistern seem quite set up about *Desire* and, after reading quite astonishing complexes between the lines of my simplicities, claim it for their own. Well, so some of them did with *Emperor Jones*. They are hard to shake!" To an acquaintance he said: "I respect Freud's work tremendously—but I'm not an addict!" And he added: "Whatever of Freudianism is in *Desire* must have walked right in 'through my unconscious'" (ibid.).

In reply to a friend, who had commented on the "complexes" of the characters in *Interlude*, O'Neill stated: "... I feel that, although [*Interlude*] is full of psychoanalytical ideas, still these same ideas are age-old to the artist and that any artist who was a good psychologist ... could have written 'S.I.' without ever having heard of Freud, Jung, Adler & Co ..." (Gelb, p. 631). A more complete statement of his acquaintance with psychoanalysis O'Neill

[7] See especially Engel (1953) and (1964), Alexander (Dec. 1953), Sievers, and Falk. Nethercot provides a useful survey.

gave in a reply to Martha Carolyn Sparrow, who was preparing a thesis on the use of modern psychology, especially of psychoanalysis, in O'Neill's plays. The letter (10.13.1929) reads in part:

There is no conscious use of psychoanalytical material in any of my plays. All of them could easily be written by a dramatist who had never heard of the Freudian theory and was simply guided by an intuitive psychological insight into human beings and their life-impulsions that is as old as Greek drama. It is true that I am enough of a student of modern psychology to be fairly familiar with the Freudian implications inherent in the actions of some of my characters while I was portraying them; but this was always an afterthought and never consciously was I for a moment influenced to shape my material along the lines of any psychological theory. It was my dramatic instinct and my own personal experience with human life that alone guided me.

I most certainly *did not* get my idea of Nina's compulsion from a dream mentioned by Freud in "A General Introduction to Psychoanalysis." I have only read two books of Freud's, "Totem and Taboo" and "Beyond the Pleasure Principle." The book that interested me the most of all those of the Freudian school is Jung's "Psychology of the Unconscious" which I read many years ago. If I have been influenced unconsciously it must have been by this book more than any other psychological work. But the "unconscious" influence stuff strikes me as always extremely suspicious! It is so darned easy to prove! I would say that what has influenced my plays the most is my knowledge of the drama of all time— particularly Greek tragedy—and not any books on psychology (Nethercot, p. 248).

About two years later, rejecting Barrett Clark's criticism that *Electra* was patterned a little too precisely after Freud and Jung, O'Neill repeated his earlier view:

I don't agree with your Freudian objection. Taken from my author's angle, I find fault with critics on exactly the same point—that they read too damn much Freud into stuff that could very well have been written exactly as is before psychoanalysis was ever heard of. ... I think I know enough about men and women to have written *Mourning Becomes Electra* almost exactly as it is if I had never heard of Freud or Jung or the others. Authors were psychologists, you know, and profound ones, before psychology was invented. And I am no deep student of psychoanalysis. As far as I can remember, of all the books written by Freud, Jung, etc., I have read only four, and Jung is the only one of the lot who interests me. Some of his suggestions I find extraordinarily illuminating in the light of my own experience with hidden human motives (Clark, p. 136).

These are the direct comments we have by O'Neill concerning his relations to psychoanalysis. In all of them he claims his independence of the new psychological school. Yet, as Hoffman has shown (pp. 58–84, *passim*), interest in the "new psychology" was strong among the radical intellectuals of Greenwich Village, to whom it became a weapon against bourgeois and puritan values.

O'Neill, who spent most of his time between 1915 and 1917 in Greenwich Village and who joined the Provincetown Players in 1916, can hardly have avoided noticing the general interest in psychoanalysis. "We all had a rationale about sex," a friend of John Reed and his wife Louise Bryant has said, referring to the Provincetown group; "we had discovered Freud—and we considered being libidinous a kind of sacred duty" (Gelb, p. 324). O'Neill, who in late 1916 found himself in a love relationship with Louise Bryant, was probably no exception to this rule.

By 1925 O'Neill possessed not only Freud's *Beyond the Pleasure Principle* but also *Group Psychology and the Analysis of the Ego*.[8] And while working on *Lazarus* he discussed Freud's *Wit and Its Relation to the Unconscious* with Manuel Komroff (Gelb, p. 600). It is of course possible—but unlikely—that O'Neill never read *Group Psychology* and *Wit*, that he discussed the latter merely on the basis of what Komroff told him about it. O'Neill also possessed Krafft-Ebing's *Psychopathia Sexualis* (copy now at C. W. Post College, L.I.), published in 1922 and, apparently, Stekel's treatise on sexual aberrations, *Disguises of Love*, which he showed Malcolm Cowley in November 1923. He told Cowley that there were enough case histories in the book "to furnish plots to all the playwrights who ever lived," and gave as an example the record of a mother who seduced her only son and drove him insane (Cowley, 1957, pp. 45 f.). It was at about this time O'Neill got the first idea for *Desire*, where he employed the incest theme in Oedipal fashion, as he was later to do in a number of plays.

O'Neill also had personal contacts with at least three psychoanalysts. Between 1923 and 1925 he sporadically saw Dr. Smith Ely Jelliffe, a well-known New York psychiatrist. He was not psychoanalyzed by Dr. Jelliffe but received therapeutic help for various problems (Gelb, p. 565).[9] In 1925 he frequently saw his neighbor Dr. Louis Bisch, with whom he discussed psychoanalysis in general, its curative effects, etc. (Gelb, pp. 573, 595). In the spring of 1926 O'Neill actually underwent 'psychoanalysis'—the analyst himself referred to it as that!—for a period of six weeks. When the six weeks were over O'Neill said he had no trouble understanding that he both loved and hated his father (dead since 1920), and that he was suffering from

[8] Both copies, which are now in Yale University Library, are signed "Eugene O'Neill, Bermuda '25." Freud's *The Problem of Anxiety* also belonged to the O'Neill library. This copy, now at C. W. Post College, L.I., is, however, signed "Carlotta Monterey O'Neill."

O'Neill's knowledge of foreign languages was apparently very limited. In a letter to Goldberg (9.22.1925) he speaks of his "very dim knowledge of German." It can therefore be taken for granted that he read all psychological works in English translation.

[9] It is interesting to note that Jelliffe, together with Louise Brink, already in 1922 had brought out a volume entitled *Psychoanalysis and the Drama* (mentioned in Goldberg, 1922, p. 50).

an unresolved Oedipus complex (Gelb, p. 596). He had come in contact with the analyst, Dr. Gilbert V. Hamilton, through his friend Kenneth Macgowan. Hamilton was undertaking a research program, the purpose of which was to investigate the problems of sexual adjustment in marital relationships. Two hundred married men and women were selected, four of whom were the Macgowans and the O'Neills.

Like many other intellectual Americans Macgowan was interested in the new trends in psychology. If his views had a special relevance to O'Neill, it was because Macgowan saw the opportunity for a rebirth of tragedy in the new psychology. The play of tomorrow, he wrote, thinking perhaps of *Jones,*

will attempt to transfer to dramatic art the illumination of those deep and vigorous and eternal processes of the human soul which the psychology of Freud and Jung has given us through study of the unconscious, striking to the heart of emotion and linking our commonest life today with the emanations of the primitive racial mind (Macgowan, 1923, p. 248).

What Macgowan, from a dramatic point of view, found valuable in the new psychology was its probings into the deeper levels of the human soul (the unconscious) and, as a consequence of these probings, its demonstration of civilized man's basic similitarity to primitive man and partnership in the "mysterious processes of nature." By working along the same lines as the psychoanalysts, Macgowan felt, the future dramatists would give a deeper and more universal picture of man than the realistic or naturalistic playwrights had been able to do.[1]

In O'Neill's plays there are some direct references to psychoanalysis or employment of psychoanalytic terminology. Already in *Now I Ask You* O'Neill briefly refers to the new rage when Mrs. Ashleigh wonders whether her daughter Lucy has "gone in for psycho-analysis again" (8). Since Lucy's ideas in other respects faithfully reflect the young O'Neill's—she worships Nietzsche and Strindberg, is obsessed with *Hedda Gabler,* has anarchistic leanings, etc.—it seems reasonable to assume that also her concern with psychoanalysis reflects at least a vague interest in the new psychology on the part of the author.

Less convincing as proofs of O'Neill's familiarity with psychoanalysis are the passages in the original, 1920, edition of *Horizon* quoted by Nethercot

---

[1] Robert Edmond Jones, O'Neill's other collaborator in the 'triumvirate' formed in 1923, expresses similar ideas. *The Dramatic Imagination,* "the fruit of twenty-five years of ... work in the American theatre" (p. 13), opens with the following sentence (p. 15): "In the last quarter century we have begun to be interested in the exploration of man's inner life, in the unexpressed and hitherto inexpressible depths of the self." And Jones further observes (pp. 16 f.): "Our playwrights ... are attempting to express directly to the audience the unspoken thoughts of their characters, to show us not only the patterns of their conscious behavior but the pattern of their subconscious lives."

(p. 249). Yet the fact that these passages were omitted in the second edition, published in January 1925, is of interest. A few months earlier *Desire* had been produced and to O'Neill's great irritation it had, as we have noted, caused some people to remark on his indebtedness to Freud. It seems likely, in view of this, that the omissions were undertaken largely to counteract any linking of *Horizon* with psychoanalysis.

Other examples mentioned by Nethercot are more relevant. Thus Dion Anthony in *Brown* talks about "fixation on old Mamma Christianity" (269), and Dr. Edmund Darrell in *Interlude,* who as a neurologist is naturally fully entitled to use psychoanalytic terminology, states that Nina "needs normal love objects for the emotional life Gordon's death blocked up in her" (37). To Marsden, the novelist with a sexual trauma, Darrell is the type for a Freudian psychoanalyst:

... what is his specialty? ... neurologist, I think ... I hope not psychoanalyst ... a lot to account for, Herr Freud! ... punishment to fit his crimes, be forced to listen eternally during breakfast while innumerable plain ones tell him dreams about snakes ... pah, what an easy cure-all! ... sex the philosopher's stone ... "O Oedipus, O my king! The world is adopting you!" ... (34; O'Neill's dots).

O'Neill has admitted that he discussed the "psychological aspect" of *Interlude* with Dr. Hamilton while writing the play (Lewis, p. 16). It is hard to reconcile this fact with the dramatist's view that the play could have been written by someone who had never heard of "Freud, Jung, Adler & Co." Bowen assumes (1959, p. 169)—as did Miss Sparrow—that O'Neill had read Freud's *General Introduction to Psychoanalysis.* It would certainly seem natural if he had partaken of this survey of the depth psychology before tackling the play which, by his own admission, was full of psychoanalytical material, or if he had glanced at Freud's main work, *The Interpretation of Dreams,* before having Marsden refer to phallic dream symbolism and Oedipal conflicts.

In the "Working Notes" for *Electra* O'Neill gave a reason for Christine's hatred of her husband, which would have seemed quite unsatisfactory before Freud (and still does to some critics): "sexual frustration by his puritan sense of guilt turning love to lust." He talked about the "hidden psychic identity" between the women in the play and observed that the characters' desire to leave for their South Sea island expresses a "longing for the primitive" and for the mother, a "yearning for prenatal non-competitive freedom from fear." He talked about "'Island' death fear and death wish" (O'Neill, 1931/Frenz, pp. 5, 8 f., 12), and after the play was completed, he spoke about "the life and death impulses that drive the characters on to their fates" (O'Neill, Dec. 1932/Cargill et al., p. 120). In the notes for *Days* he would similarly speak of "mother worship, repressed and turned morbid," turning into "Death-love and longing," and of the wife of the protagonist as a "mother substitute" (Falk, p. 150).

While these examples are of interest as proofs of O'Neill's acquaintance with and interest in the new psychology, they do not indicate any deeper indebtedness on his part and do not disprove his claim that he was himself a keen psychologist, that his indebtedness concerned earlier men of letters rather than contemporary psychologists, and that he could have written the plays almost the way he had without any knowledge of modern depth psychology. This view can only be rejected if we can convincingly reveal that O'Neill has made use of decidedly Freudian, Jungian or Adlerian ideas in a more fundamental way in his work.

To present more of a man's inner consciousness than a man would ordinarily reveal had, as Macgowan notes (1929, pp. 449 ff.), always been a central concern with O'Neill. By a variety of means, ranging from realistic states of mind such as death fever, madness or drunkenness to theatrical devices such as the employment of masks[2] and thought asides, O'Neill sought to depict the deeper workings of the human mind.

When, in 1926, he declared that he had attempted, in *Brown,* to describe the "pattern of conflicting tides in the soul of Man," he was drawing attention to a central aim throughout his work. The pattern, he further explained, would be suggested by the use of "mysterious words, symbols, actions they [the characters] do not themselves comprehend" (Clark, pp. 105 f.). O'Neill apparently attempted to depict man's "fundamental impulses," to quote Macgowan, his "unity with the dumb, mysterious processes of nature," in a word: his unconscious desires.

That O'Neill's interest in the mask—an interest he shared with his associates in the Experimental Theater, Inc., Kenneth Macgowan and Robert Edmond Jones[3]—was directly related to this concern with the underlying spiritual reality, O'Neill made clear in his "Memoranda on Masks." In this article he advocated masks to

express those profound hidden conflicts of the mind which the probings of psychology continue to disclose to us. He [the modern dramatist] must find some method to present this inner drama in his work, or confess himself incapable of portraying one of the most characteristic preoccupations and uniquely significant, spiritual impulses of his time.

[2] Proper masks were first used in the production of *Ape,* but the mask technique, as Falk notes (p. 18), is implied already in *Servitude.*

[3] In 1921 Jones, influenced by Craig, designed masks for the witches in *Macbeth.* In 1923 Macgowan, in collaboration with the designer Herman Rosse, published his *Masks and Demons.*—For a brief survey of the interest in the theatrical mask in the first decades of the 20th century, see Engel (1953, pp. 89 ff.).

The mask, O'Neill believed, was the most satisfying solution to the

new form of drama projected from a fresh insight into the inner forces motivating the actions and reactions of men and women (a new and truer characterization, in other words), a drama of souls, and the adventures of "Free wills," with the masks that govern them and constitute their fates.

For what, at bottom, is the new psychological insight into human cause and effect but a study in masks, an exercise in unmasking? (O'Neill, Nov. 1932/ Cargill et al., p. 116).

O'Neill applied the idea of the unconscious not only to his characters but also to his audience. Our emotions, he once declared with a reasoning that sounds very Jungian,

are a better guide than our thoughts. Our emotions are instinctive. They are the result not only of our individual experiences but of the experiences of the whole human race, back through all the ages. They are the deep undercurrent, whereas our thoughts are often only the small individual surface reactions. Truth usually goes deep. So it reaches you through your emotions.

Thus, although the audience might not intellectually understand the visual symbolism in *Horizon,* it would, O'Neill was convinced, "unconsciously" get the effect he had intended (Mullett, pp. 34, 118). "The big, universal meaning in back of" *Ape,* he believed, "is sensed, emotionally felt, by a great many people ... even if their intelligences fail to grasp it" (letter to Marjorie Griesser 5.5.1922). *Brown,* he declared, describes "the mystery any one man or woman can feel but not understand as the meaning of any event—or accident —in any life on earth. And it is this mystery I want to realize in the theater" (Clark, p. 106). About *Electra* he remarked: "audiences will unconsciously grasp at once, it is primarily drama of hidden life forces" (O'Neill, 1931/ Frenz, p. 4).

O'Neill's concern with "hidden life forces" testifies, of course, to his probing mind. But it is also related to a dramaturgical need. A problem of central importance to him as a playwright was how to find a modern equivalent for the Greek sense of fate. His first note for *Electra* might have been a note for almost any one of his plays: "Is it possible to get modern psychological approximation of Greek sense of fate ..., which an intelligent audience of today, possessed of no belief in gods or supernatural retribution, could accept and be moved by?" (O'Neill, 1931/Frenz, p. 3). In 1925, a year before this question was asked, O'Neill had implied an answer to it. In the unpublished "Author's foreword" to *Brown* he wrote: "if we have no gods, [*sic*] or heroes to portray we have the subconscious the mother of all Gods and heroes." By postulating the unconscious O'Neill could eliminate the contrast between the ancient, religious tragedian and the modern, secular one. What is more, with the help of it he could construct an internal fate as powerful and mysterious as a hidden god. In short, the idea of the unconscious made the writing of tragedy possible in a godless age.

Since the unconscious impulses are to a great extent universal, as especially Jung's concept of the collective unconscious indicates, an emphasis on these would necessarily tend not only to deepen but also to widen the scope of the drama. And this in two respects: the same impulses would be recognizable in different characters; they would also be shared by the audience. Thus a deep emotional rapport could be established between characters and audience. And drama could be restored to its ancient function of religious ritual.

The statement in the foreword to *Brown* indicates that O'Neill considered the awareness of the unconscious a substitute for traditional religion, which modern man could no longer believe in, and that he was attracted to the mystical aspect of psychoanalysis rather than to the scientific one. (It is characteristic that he was particularly interested in Jung who takes a more positive attitude to religion than Freud and Adler.) In an early note for *Days* he wrote:

Make Loving a doctor who has gone in for psycho-a- (?) brilliant doctor before but not satisfied—p-a caused by religious promptings and desire to understand self (unconsciously) although consciously rationalized as imperative to cure $^1/_2$ of patients.

While literary scholars, who are concerned with the plays rather than the author, usually tend to oppose O'Neill's claim that he was "no deep student of psychoanalysis,"[4] biographers and psychoanalysts, whose interests are in the author rather than in the plays, indirectly tend to confirm the playwright's view. Thus, Weissman asserts (p. 135) that O'Neill's dramas "embody an amazing amount of psychoanalytic insight, often related to his own specific conflicts." To Weissman it is clear that O'Neill's frequent use of the Oedipus complex should be seen, not as a Freudian influence, but as a manifestation of the fact that O'Neill, as he himself came to realize, suffered from reminiscences of this complex (cf. Alexander, 1962, p. 84). Weissman convincingly reads *Desire,* not in the light of any psychoanalytic work, but in a psychoanalytic manner, as an unconscious autobiography. More casually the Gelbs have done the same with regard to other plays.

[4] Engel (1953) implies an influence from Adler's individual psychology on *Chillun* (pp. 119 ff.) and finds *Desire* indebted to Freud's ideas in *Totem and Taboo* (p. 133). Falk assumes an influence from Jung's concept of the collective unconscious on *Christie* and *Jones* (pp. 51 f.). Cargill (p. 699) takes for granted that the typified crowds in *Lazarus* owe something to Jung's "*Psychological Types* volume." The only convincing evidence of O'Neill's indebtedness to a psychoanalytic work that I have come across is Alexander's demonstration (Dec. 1953) of the striking resemblances between the ideas in *Electra* and in Hamilton–Macgowan's Freudian book *What is Wrong with Marriage.*

There are thus several ways to account for the playwright's concern with depth-psychological issues. There is the view that O'Neill, like the pre-Freudian writers who were "great psychologists," intuitively arrived at results similar to those reached clinically by the psychoanalysts; this is the view held by O'Neill himself as well as (on the whole) by Falk and Weissman. There is the view that he was directly and deeply influenced by Freud; Sievers, Nethercot and, in a measure, Engel subscribe to this opinion.[5] There is, finally, the view that the similarities between O'Neill's work and the writings of Freud, Jung and Adler are due largely to parallel influences from Schopenhauer, Nietzsche, Ibsen, Strindberg and others. This possibility, which in view of O'Neill's ready admission of his indebtedness to Nietzsche and Strindberg and denial of any noteworthy influence from the psychoanalysts might prove rewarding, has hitherto been largely ignored.[6]

Precisely the fact that O'Neill himself was a "keen psychologist" makes it exceedingly hard, if at all possible, to prove that any of his more fundamental psychological ideas are derived from psychoanalysis. The notes for the plays give ample evidence of his psychoanalytic way of reasoning. Yet very little use is made of psychoanalytic terminology. The impression one gets is that of an independent mind, attuned to modern psychological thinking. His references to earlier writers who were "great psychologists" further complicate the matter. Nietzsche, Ibsen and Strindberg belong to those writers who influenced O'Neill the most. They are also writers who expressed many of the ideas later embraced by modern depth psychology. Freud himself observed (1948, p. 86) that Nietzsche's "Ahnungen und Einsichten sich oft in der erstaunlichsten Weise mit den mühsamen Ergebnissen der Psychoanalyse decken," and he might have said the same about the two Scandinavian dramatists.[7]

For these reasons it will probably always remain hard to prove that O'Neill was "a deep student of psychoanalysis," profoundly indebted to its findings. He may have been a little more indebted to Freud and Jung than he liked to admit. Yet it seems more reasonable to view his interest in the new psychology not as an indication of indebtedness but simply as a sign of his concern with depth-psychological issues. When Doris Falk shows how O'Neill has

[5] Engel, however, also assumes (1953, pp. 214 f.) that O'Neill disliked the more scientific aspects of psychoanalysis.

[6] Alexander does a little in this line in her "*Strange Interlude* and Schopenhauer" (May 1953). Her conclusion that the play "expresses not Freud's psychology, but Schopenhauer's philosophy" (p. 213) is, however, much too categorical.

[7] While Freud's influence on modern literature has been commented on at length by many scholars, little attention has been paid to the other side of the picture: Freud's indebtedness to the literature of his time. For an illuminating study of this latter aspect, see Brandell (1967).

anticipated Horney and Fromm, she actually applies O'Neill's own view that authors may be profound and independent psychologists to the playwright himself. There is reason to believe that this evaluation of O'Neill as a psychologist will essentially remain valid.

Aims of the Examination

For a dramatist who is primarily concerned, not with the relationship between man and man, but with the relationship between man and God, between man and his own soul, between his conscious and unconscious needs and desires, realism and naturalism are clearly insufficient. To describe these 'irrational' inner phenomena, "some form of 'super-naturalism'," an intensification and distillation of the naturalistic technique, is necessary. But the super-naturalism, as O'Neill indicates, can assume different shades. It can be fairly moderate as in Strindberg's so-called naturalistic plays (cf. Dahlström, pp. 91–117); or it can be rather extreme as in the Swede's so-called expressionistic dramas.

Also with regard to O'Neill it is clear that the super-naturalism assumes different forms. Thus, it is evident that most of the plays written between 1920 and 1932 (from *Jones* through *Days*) employ super-naturalistic devices in a more conspicuous way than do, with few exceptions,[8] the early and late plays. It is not my aim to demonstrate this obvious phenomenon. On the contrary I hope to show that the explicit, super-naturalistic devices found in the middle period can be found implicitly also in the early and late periods, that the undeniable differences in technique are differences on a comparatively superficial level, and that beneath the seeming protean variety in O'Neill's work there is an organic unity. As for the formal variety of the individual plays, I would suggest that it is there not for its own sake but because O'Neill needed a wide range of dramatic and theatrical devices to say what he wanted to say, a multitude of effects which, juxtaposed, could suggest the overtones without which the plays would veer dangerously towards the melodramatic.[9]

The present examination, then, is concerned with both the implicit and with the explicit type of O'Neill's super-naturalism, both with that disguised by a surface layer of realism and that frankly breaking with illusionism. In agreement with O'Neill's own usage of the term as I understand it, 'super-naturalism' will thus be employed in a wide sense. Any play element or

---

[8] Such as the mystical crying in *Fog* and the ghost scene in *Cross*.

[9] O'Neill's remark to Nathan (Cargill et al., p. 56) that he had tried hard, in *Electra*, "to prevent the surface melodrama of the plot from overwhelming the real drama," has general application.

dramatic device—characterization, stage business, scenery, lighting, sound effects, dialogue, nomenclature, use of parallelisms—will be considered super-naturalistic if it is dealt with in such a way by the dramatist, that it transcends (deepens, intensifies, stylizes or openly breaks with) realism in the attempt to project what O'Neill terms "behind-life" values to the reader or spectator. To separate psychological issues from metaphysical ones in the plays would be artificial and indeed impossible. Unlike most other modern dramatists O'Neill was deeply concerned with both. His protagonists are nearly always divided souls in search of a faith, which can integrate them and give them peace. As William Brown tersely puts it: "Man is born broken. He lives by mending. The grace of God is glue!" (*Brown,* 318).

A super-naturalistic technique involves a frequent use of symbols. A general comment on dramatic symbolism may therefore be appropriate. When speaking of symbolism in drama we tend to think of the use of obvious symbols, play ingredients whose meaning may well be—perhaps must be—obscure but whose symbolic significance most commentators would agree about. Ibsen's wild duck and white horses, O'Neill's gorilla and dynamo are symbols of this kind.

But, besides these overt symbols, both Ibsen and O'Neill resort to a multitude of more or less concealed symbols, dramatic or theatrical elements whose symbolic significance does not appear when they are considered in isolation but which becomes manifest or highly credible, as the case may be, when they are seen in relation to other elements or brought together into thematic patterns. Since the meaning of a symbol usually depends on the context in which it appears, it follows that it often varies from play to play, from character to character. This is especially true of those elements which symbolize concepts of great abstraction or complexity such as life and death. Nevertheless, as the ensuing analyses will demonstrate, there is a high degree of consistency in O'Neill's employment of symbols.

When we experience a play for the first time, we are naturally not very sensitive to the symbolic significance of those play elements which can be accounted for in perfectly realistic terms. For fundamental dramaturgical reasons—especially the need of presenting a story before one deals with its significance—the symbolic meaning is usually least apparent in the opening part of a play. However, as the play develops many elements which initially seemed quite simple—even trivial and irrelevant—take on a deeper significance. When the play ends this deeper meaning may completely have superseded the initial, everyday meaning. In the course of the play, assisted by the dramatist's use of gradual revelation, we have journeyed from a judging of appearances to a more profound, more essential perspective. And if we now, familiar with the play, experience it again, we are likely to see a symbolic significance also in those parts which we earlier experienced merely on the realistic level. The whole play has gained in depth and unity.

To do full justice to O'Neill's plays we must, however, not only be aware of this cumulative technique; we must also attempt to share O'Neill's own viewpoint, which might be described as that of the ideal reader, the reader who is sensitive both to the more subtle intellectual aspects of the plays and to their theatrical—visual and aural—values. The analytical approach should thus be neither merely 'literary' nor merely theatrical but a fusion of the two.

In the attempt to practice this approach I have been especially influenced by some of the works which deal with related problems concerning other playwrights. Thus my discussions of visual suggestion (Chapters II and III) and illustrative parallels (Chapter VI) owe much to John Northam's penetrating and concise study of these matters in Ibsen's prose plays. My discussion of O'Neill's dialogue technique (Chapter V) owes something to Una Ellis-Fermor's interesting investigations of the various ways in which dramatists have attempted to transcend the limitations inherent in the dramatic form. The excellent studies in Shakespeare's imagery by Wolfgang Clemen and Robert Heilman have also served as sources of inspiration. Generally speaking, I have found the very extensive literature about O'Neill somewhat less rewarding for my particular purposes. Statements and interpretations that have seemed significant and relevant to my subject have been duly referred to and, at times, commented on.

In order to give a fairly complete picture of O'Neill's super-naturalistic technique I have taken my examples from practically all the plays. The space apportioned to the various dramas has been determined primarily by how rewarding they have seemed to me for my particular purposes. Whenever illustrative examples have been found in O'Neill's major dramatic works, I have, however, tended to resort to these works. On the other hand, more attention has been paid to some of the earliest plays than is usually the case, since it has seemed important to me to demonstrate how O'Neill's super-naturalistic technique can be traced back to his debut as a playwright.

Although some familiarity with the plays is almost necessary for an understanding of the ensuing analyses, I have deliberately abstained from space-consuming plot outlines, since such outlines can readily be found in a number of books.[1]

In the attempt to give a clear picture of the aspect of O'Neill's dramatic technique that concerns me, I have made formal rather than thematic criteria

---

[1] Apart from such handbooks as those by Shipley (1956), Sprinchorn, and Hart, many of the books on O'Neill naturally give plot outlines of varying completeness. Engel's study (1953) is particularly helpful in this respect.

the basis of my composition. For the same reason I have tried to isolate the various formal elements in the different plays rather than discuss them in relation to one another. Formal criteria have also been decisive for the arrangement within the chapters, although, whenever possible, I have dealt with the plays in the order they were written (cf. the chronology). Naturally, it has often been necessary to see the various formal elements in *some* relation to one another; strict isolation would have invalidated any deeper analysis.

Since I deal with the plays from a special, if central, point of view and am not concerned with strictly dramaturgical problems, it has been outside my scope to evaluate O'Neill's dramatic technique in general. Even with regard to the aspect of it considered here, I have tried to suspend judgement in the conviction that the analyses themselves will be a better guide to the merits or demerits of O'Neill's technique than any direct esthetic evaluation of it.

II. THE HUMAN SETTING

Shortly after finishing *Lazarus* O'Neill told Clark: "I've worked out every detail of the setting and action, even the lighting. Incidentally, I've done the same thing with all my plays, only ... I didn't get credit for it" (Clark, p. 117). An examination of the attention paid to scenery and lighting in the plays bears the author out. In the stage directions of almost every act and scene throughout O'Neill's entire *oeuvre,* the reader will find ample descriptions of the setting and lighting, written in a poetically narrative style which is very different from the laconic, technical one most modern dramatists employ in their stage directions. In addition he will find the characters frequently commenting on matters that directly pertain to the scenery and the lighting: the environment, the light, the time of day, the temperature, and other elements.

Scenery

A stage setting, as Robert Edmond Jones reminds us (p. 70), has no independent life. Separated from the characters it virtually ceases to exist. O'Neill early revealed an interest in making his stage settings not merely true to the characters in a superficial sense but actually expressive of their thoughts and emotions. The seamen's forecastle in *Cardiff* looks in every respect the way we would expect it to. It is filled with sleeping bunks, wooden benches, a lamp in a bracket, a pail with a dipper, sea-chest, sea-boots, oilskins. Even the narrowness of the room is what we would expect in a ship (cf. Gelb, p. 159):

An irregular-shaped compartment, the sides of which almost meet at the far end to form a triangle. ...
The far side ... is so narrow that it contains only one series of bunks (477).

Yet the shape of the forecastle was hardly chosen by the dramatist out of any Zolaesque anxiety for exactness. Rather, it was selected because this shape enabled O'Neill to suggest scenically Yank's anguished feeling of loneliness and imprisonment in life, which reaches a climax in his death struggle. By placing Yank at the apex of the triangle, in the narrowest part of the room, isolated from his mates, O'Neill could modestly indicate both his loneliness and his anguish.

After employing the idea of cramped space within a realistic framework also in *Ile* and *Christie,* O'Neill was ready to use it in a bolder, more expressionistic manner. The first description of the forecastle in *Ape* sounds realistic; we are reminded of the forecastle in *Cardiff: "Tiers of narrow, steel bunks, three deep, on all sides. An entrance in rear. Benches on the floor before the bunks"* (207). But this is followed by an expressionistic declaration:

> *The treatment of this scene, or of any other scene in the play, should by no means be naturalistic. The effect sought after is a cramped space in the bowels of a ship, imprisoned by white steel. The lines of bunks, the uprights supporting them, cross each other like the steel framework of a cage. The ceiling crushes down upon the men's heads. They cannot stand upright* (207).

The difference in technique is based on a difference in theme. In *Cardiff* Yank's precarious state is both physical and spiritual. And he fully realizes his situation. The setting at once enhances and objectifies his feelings of anguish and isolation. In *Ape* his namesake's precarious situation—that of being enslaved by modern, mechanized society and being out of touch with the harmony of nature—is primarily spiritual. Moreover, Yank is not aware of his situation when the play opens. On the contrary, he boasts of being a ruling power in the modern world, wholly content with his lot. Because it contradicts rather than supports Yank's view, the forecastle scenery in *Ape* is much more conspicuous and emphatic than its equivalent in *Cardiff.* And O'Neill makes it even more striking by having Yank give vent to his hubris in a room, where he cannot stand upright like a man but is forced to a *"stooping posture,"* that *"Neanderthal"* (207) position between beast and man. Although the room is still recognizable as a forecastle, it is an intensified, distilled version of a real-life forecastle. The realistic properties are gone; there is no indication of a light source. Sea-boots and oilskins would merely detract our attention from the all-important impression that must be conveyed at once, that what we are faced with is not so much stokers in a forecastle as beasts in a cage.

The cage image pervades the play. Appearing in all the scenes in one form or another[1] except in the second—the only one in which Yank does not take part—it is, in O'Neill's words, essentially an expression of Yank's "struggle with his own fate" (Anon./Cargill et al., p. 111), for Yank, as Dickinson points out (p. 113), is his own cage (cf. Gump, p. 183).[2] From the initial

---

[1] In the Fifth Avenue scene, as Blackburn points out (p. 117), the procession of marionettes constitutes "a cage against the bars of which he [Yank] beats in vain."

[2] In this respect Yank is a representative O'Neill character, reminiscent of such autobiographical figures as Eben Cabot in *Desire,* for whom *"each day is a cage in which he finds himself trapped but inwardly unsubdued"* (203), and Dion Anthony in *Brown,* who asks himself: "Why must I live in a cage like a criminal ..." (264). In *Lazarus* the feeling of imprisonment is considered archetypal: "Life is for each man a solitary cell whose walls are mirrors" (309).

forecastle approximating a cage, Yank moves to the human cage of the prison and from there to the animal cage in the Zoo. In the first scene the cage is merely implied, for Yank is here unaware of, or at most only vaguely senses, his predicament. Later, as this becomes more clear to him, the cage in which he lives also becomes more obvious to us. That Yank's feelings of imprisonment have universal validity is indicated in the opening scene by the fact that *"all the civilized white races"* are to be found in the forecastle (207). In the prison and Zoo scenes a similar effect is gained by having the cages multiply *"into infinity"* (239). In the I.W.W. scene the cage walls are formed by the black buildings surrounding the narrow street in which Yank, gorilla fashion, comes to the insight that the world owns him rather than vice versa.

The play is subtitled "A Comedy of Ancient and Modern Life in Eight Scenes," and the steamer, in which the action in the first half of the play takes place, apparently symbolizes modern life, while the beautiful windjammer, evoked in Paddy's romantic reverie, epitomizes the ancient life. The contrast had appeared earlier in the conflict between old Chris, a sailor of the sailing ship era, and Mat Burke, a stoker of the steamship period (*Christie,* 49). The tangible signs of a mechanized, industrialized age are found in the modern steamer: steel, smoke, coal, engines (i.e. machines) and speed.[3] Appropriately this ship, unlike the 'real' ones in the earlier sea plays, is unnamed. And fittingly it is manned by an international, hard-working crew below and peopled by capitalist passengers up above, lazily reclining in their deck chairs.

It would be rash to conclude that *Ape* is a 'protest' drama directed against a particular social class. O'Neill's maintenance that Yank is less a worker than a symbol of man, "who has lost his old harmony with nature, the harmony which he used to have as an animal and has not yet acquired in a spiritual way" (Anon./Cargill et al., p. 110), opposes such a view and assigns instead, by implication, a symbolic role also to Yank's antagonists, the superrace people, whose marionettish sauntering (236), resembling the stokers' mechanized work (223), reveals that they too—and in fact to an even greater extent—are removed from nature.

That the evil is ascribed to the modern spirit rather than to any particular social class appears not only from the fact that the superrace, too, is victimized; it appears also from the descriptions of the ship, the symbol of this spirit. Its forecastle is likened to *"bowels"* (207), its bell to a *"heart"* (217), the *"throbbing"* (223) of the engines suggests the pulsation of the blood, and the open furnaces appear now as greedy mouths with sharp teeth (223),

[3] Cf. Dickinson, p. 109: "The liner is a microcosm of our industrial civilization."

now as fiery eyes (224); the latter is an old retribution symbol with O'Neill (cf. *Thirst*, 3). By this kind of animism O'Neill tries to indicate the fact that modern life constitutes a monstrous Fate which man futilely struggles against. The symbolism recalls the one employed in *Christie*; but here it is the ship, a man-made product, which is the devil, whereas the old sea represents *"the beautiful, vivid life"* (218) of nature.

In *Ape* the locale is changed in practically every scene, but in the second act of *Chillun* all three scenes are set in the same locale: the parlor of the Harris apartment in a New York Negro district. In the first scene we see the parlor 'objectively,' in normal proportions. It is still inhabited by Jim's sister and mother, both Negro women. They are a natural part of the environment. When Jim and Ella, the black-and-white couple, have spent six months in it, *"the walls of the room appear shrunken in, the ceiling lowered, so that the furniture, the portrait, the mask look unnaturally large and domineering"* (331). The room now expresses the white woman's sense of imprisonment in the Negro environment, her feeling that she is fighting an uneven struggle against a blackness (epitomized in the Congo mask) which is crowding in on her. Another six months pass: *"The walls appear shrunken in still more, the ceiling now seems barely to clear the people's heads, the furniture and the characters appear enormously magnified"* (338). Ella's sense of being pent up has reached a culmination. The scene witnesses how she goes insane. Moreover Jim, after repeated failures to justify himself in his own eyes and in the eyes of the world, is bordering on insanity. The room has become an intolerable prison cell.[4]

In *Horizon,* settings of cramped space alternate with spacious sets, giving a distinct visual rhythm to the play. O'Neill explained the device as follows:

In "Beyond the Horizon," there are three acts of two scenes each. One scene is out of doors, showing the horizon, suggesting the man's desire and dream. The other is indoors, the horizon gone, suggesting what has come between him and his dream. In that way I tried to get rhythm, the alternation of longing and of loss (Mullett, p. 118).

O'Neill characteristically interprets the scenery from the protagonist Robert Mayo's point of view. Also taking his brother Andrew into account, the contrast between exterior and interior settings may be seen as illustrative of the conflicting desires of the two brothers as they are outlined in the opening scene. The winding road and distant view in the outdoor settings give a

---

[4] Raleigh (p. 189) sees the change from outdoors (Act I) to indoors (Act II), from larger to smaller space, as an expression of man's growing away from nature until he, as a modern city dweller, finds himself "locked in his cell." With this interpretation Jim's and Ella's 'imprisonment' begins already in Act II.1.

suggestion of movement, which complements Robert's beyond dream. The indoor scenes, by contrast, are all laid in the same small room and therefore appear static,[5] imprisoning; in Robert's words: "It seemed as if all my life —I'd been cooped in a room" (167).[6]

The unity of interior setting also enables O'Neill to show, by changes in *"little significant details"* (112), the development from prospering family concord through disintegration and hatred to resigned apathy. Thus the *"orderly comfort"* and cleanliness of the Mayo sitting-room (93 f.) is transformed into slovenliness after Robert has taken over the farm from his father. That the change must in part be ascribed to Robert is indicated in the set: *"a hoe stands in a corner; a man's coat is flung on the couch in the rear; the desk is cluttered up with odds and ends; a number of books are piled carelessly on the sideboard"* (112). But Ruth's indifference is also apparent: *"the table cover is spotted and askew; holes show in the curtains; a child's doll, with one arm gone, lies under the table"* (112). In the final act the decay is complete. There is now no cover on the table, which is *"stained with the imprints of hot dishes and spilt food"* (144), signs of a solely vegetative existence. The curtains are torn and dirty, the wallpaper blotched, the stove rusty, the desk covered with dust. No mention is made of any books, an indication, it would seem, that Robert's dreams have been quenched by the drabness of farm life, of life on earth.

The outdoor settings are more complex, since they express the conflicting desires embraced by Robert and Andrew. The description for Act I.1 reads:

A section of country highway. The road runs diagonally from the left, forward, to the right, rear, and can be seen in the distance winding toward the horizon like a pale ribbon between the low rolling hills with their freshly plowed fields clearly divided from each other, checkerboard fashion, by the lines of stone walls and rough snake fences.

The forward triangle cut off by the road is a section of a field from the dark earth of which myriad bright-green blades of fall-sown rye are sprouting. A straggling line of piled rocks, too low to be called a wall, separates this field from the road.

To the rear of the road is a ditch with a sloping, grassy bank on the far side. From the center of this an old, gnarled apple tree, just budding into leaf, strains its twisted branches heavenwards, black against the pallor of distance. A snake-fence sidles from left to right along the top of the bank, passing beneath the apple tree (81).

[5] Shortly after the opening of the play, O'Neill pointed out that Clark was the only critic who had sensed the meaning of the alternating scenes (Clark, p. 67). Alexander Woolcott, for one, writing for the *New York Times,* did not see their value (Cargill et al., p. 137).

[6] Robert's feeling of encagement is not limited to the house or even to the farm; it concerns this earth; in the longhand draft he remarks: "Even the hills are powerless to shut me in now" (= 167).

To Andrew, who as yet remains faithful to the earth, belongs the part on this side and below the horizon. As Robert tells his brother: "You're wedded to the soil. You're as much a product of it as an ear of corn is, or a tree" (84). The harmonious growth of nature expresses Andrew's inherent creative faculties, the faculties he betrays, when he starts to gamble "with the thing [he] used to love to create" (161 f.). His gambling characteristically concerns not rye but wheat (161), a socially superior, 'decadent' grain.

Already Robert's initial action links him with the upper part of the set: he *"turns his head toward the horizon"* (82). The apple tree, although rooted in the earth like Andrew, is in part also Robert's attribute. Like the day-dreaming young man with *"a touch of the poet about him,"* it *"strains its twisted branches heavenwards"* (81).[7] The connection is most clearly seen in the final scene, where *"the apple tree is leafless and seems dead"* (166), and where the dying Robert, *"straining his eyes"* (167), *"raises himself with his last remaining strength and points to the horizon"* (168).

The tree thus indicates the symbiotic nature of the fraternal relationship, the brothers' love for each other despite their contrasting natures; as their father puts it: "you wouldn't believe how them boys o' mine sticks together. They ain't like most brothers. They've been thick as thieves all their lives ..." (97 f.). The same attachment despite conflicting desires characterizes, in fact, the whole Mayo family, and the tree may well be taken as a symbol of the family fate: fruitful and budding in the opening scene, dead and leafless—everything suggests the extinction of the family—at the end.

In Act II.2, set on top of a hill on the farm, overlooking the sea, the grass is *"bleached"* and *"sun-scorched"* (129). The inclusion of both sea and farm in the stage picture dramatizes Andrew's curse of the former, Robert's of the latter. The *"big boulder"* and the *"large oak tree"* give an impression of strength and earthiness, which in a measure still apply to Andrew, now an *"authoritative"* ship's captain (130), but which are totally lacking in Robert, whose initial weakness has become more accentuated. Having experienced what it means to live with a poetical soul like Robert, Ruth is strongly attracted by Andrew's simple strength,[8] which he has inherited from his father.

The final scene brings us back to the country highway:

[7] The longhand draft adds: *"with despairing gestures."*

[8] Andrew is not unlike John in *Welded* who, in the longhand draft, is described as a kindly, steadfast man, *"a cool rock for the fevered,"* and, in a crossed-out passage, as being *"as healthy & wholesome as a farmer's boy"* (= 450). Peter Niles in *Electra* is a similar type; in the second galley proofs Lavinia tells him: "I love you because you're simple and clean and strong—like a great oak tree!" (= 167). Cf. the oak table in the Mayo sitting room (93 f.) with which especially the healthy and sturdy Captain Scott is connected.

The field in the foreground has a wild uncultivated appearance as if it had been allowed to remain fallow the preceding summer. Parts of the snake-fence in the rear have been broken down. The apple tree is leafless and seems dead (166).

The vernal birth of the opening scene has given way to the autumnal death of nature, brought about by the characters' common failure to make things grow. We connect the fallow state of the field not only with the death of Robert's and Ruth's child eight months earlier and with Robert's consecutive illness, but also with Andrew's gambling in the last year, which has left him almost "dead broke" (157). Its *"wild uncultivated appearance"* goes with Robert's *"long and unkempt"* hair (145). On the other hand the initial 'dying' —the sunset—has been replaced by an awakening, a sunrise. And the broken-down snake-fence is perhaps not merely a sign of earthly decay; it may equally well be seen, with Robert, as a sign that the wall barring him from the true life, from eternity, is annihilated.

The scenery in *Horizon* has, I believe, been designed not only to bring out the nature of the characters but also to suggest that their fate is archetypal. The story of Robert and Ruth, I would suggest, is akin to the story of the Fall. In Act I they still dwell in a terrestrial paradise. Around them the well-kept and frugal Mayo farm bathes in beautiful May twilight. In the center of the stage the *"old, gnarled apple tree"* is budding into leaf and beneath it, on a grassy bank, the snake-fence *"sidles"*[9] from left to right. It is when sitting on the snake-fence that Ruth beguiles Robert to give up his 'beyond' dream and make his Eden come true on the farm in a marriage with her. In the second act we find Robert tilling the unrewarding ground of the "cursed farm" (122) in the sweat of his face. When he appears for his joyless meal, *"streaks of sweat have smudged the layer of dust on his cheeks"* (119). Ruth's situation is no better. To a man she does not love (127) she has born a child in sorrow, whose shrieking is loudly heard in the background. Coming from the kitchen, where she has been preparing food in the oven, she complains: "Land sakes, if this isn't a scorcher! That kitchen's like a furnace. Phew!" (116). We are reminded of the biblical "furnace of fire" (Mat. 13: 42; cf. *Ape,* 222); Ruth is punished to live in a hell on earth; and she wears the stain of the fallen Eve: *"a soiled apron"* (116). Moreover, "the good fairies who performed beautiful miracles" beyond the horizon (90) and for whom Robert has always been longing seem to correspond to the Cherubims God placed at the east of Eden.

They sang their little songs to me, songs that told of all the wonderful things they had in their home on the other side of the hills; and they promised to show me all of them, if I'd only come, come! (90).

---

[9] The longhand draft adds: *"grotesquely."*

In the *"line of flame"* on the horizon at the beginning (81) and end (166) of the play we can see a counterpart of the flaming sword. When the play opens, this flame is *"faint"* and it soon fades away, just as Robert substitutes a dream of earthly love and happiness for his 'beyond' longing. When it closes, the flame is *"quivering"* (166) and increases its light until, finally, the sun itself rises beyond the dead tree in token of the fact that Robert has discovered that "only through sacrifice" (168)—only "where the cross is made" (*Cross,* 573)[1]—can man discover his true treasures, which are found, not "upon earth" but "in heaven" (Mat. 6: 19 f.).

Already in some of his earliest plays O'Neill resorts to an obvious use of color symbolism. In *Thirst* the note of sin and imminent death is struck by the prominent use of blackness. In the first scene of *Warnings,* set in James Knapp's flat in the Bronx, there is a predominance of green in the interior setting, foreshadowing Knapp's death and burial "in the cold green water" (*Thirst,* 17). The color scheme in these plays is relatively simple. It underlines the idea that the characters cannot escape their fate, but has little psychological significance.

A more complex employment of color symbolism is found in *Jones.* The first scene shows the Emperor's audience chamber; it is

a spacious, high-ceilinged room with bare, whitewashed walls. The floor is of white tiles. In the rear, to the left of center a wide archway giving out on a portico with white pillars. ... The room is bare of furniture with the exception of one huge chair made of uncut wood which stands at center, its back to rear. This is very apparently the Emperor's throne. It is painted a dazzling, eye-smiting scarlet. There is a brilliant orange cushion on the seat and another smaller one is placed on the floor to serve as a footstool. Strips of matting, dyed scarlet, lead from the foot of the throne to the two entrances (173).

By selecting the audience chamber rather than any other room in the palace and by furnishing it only with the throne, O'Neill stresses that the room is the Emperor's and his alone; whatever characteristics it has should be ascribed to him. The most striking thing about it is perhaps the predominance of whiteness. Since the protagonist is a black man, the whiteness has not only a moral but also a racial meaning, and Jones' tragedy consists, in fact, in his inability to distinguish between the two. Jones has made his way from a humble origin to his present high position by imitating the clever recklessness of white business people, American and European (Smithers).

But when the "nigger" part, which wants to throw off the "white debil" (195) within him, proves the stronger, he returns to the black forest of his

[1] The Christian implication of the cross mark in *Cross* has been noted by Winther (pp. 272 f.) and Day (1958, p. 8).

childhood to atone for his sins. He is gradually stripped of his 'white,' imperial veneer and emerges visibly as an increasingly black man; by recognizing his guilt, he returns to his original innocence (nakedness). Thus the whiteness of the audience chamber which at first seemed factual, revealing Jones as an innocent man, has proved to be substitutive, revealing only his longing for purity, i.e. his factual lack of it.

One more aspect of the whiteness must be added; to Smithers it is that of the "tomb" (174). The association not only forebodes Jones' physical death and the purity that goes with it; it also implies that Jones' 'white,' imperial existence is a death-in-life; we shall later meet these aspects of the tomb symbol with regard to the house in *Electra,* which also bears other similarities to Jones' palace: like the Mannon home, Jones' residence is *"situated on high ground,"* is *"spacious, high-ceilinged"* and without intimacy—characteristics of Jones' 'white' hubris, coldness of heart and—grandeur.

Scarlet, the other dominating color in the play, is also used in an ironically deceptive way. To Jones it is an imperial color; he mistakes it for purple. Its true connotations are sinfulness, wordliness and blood.[2] Smithers stresses the last meaning by his constant use of the British swearwords "bloody" and "bleeding," which occur twenty times in this scene. He refers, for example, to Jones as "the bleedin' nigger" (187), an accurate description, as we have seen, of Jones' status when he suffers his bloody death; and he calls the forest, where Jones meets his end, "a bleedin' queer place" (185). It is of course only natural that Jones, as an American Negro, does not use these words; but it seems significant in a deeper sense too.

It should be noticed that Jones proceeds on a bloody trail. Bloodstained, he has entered the palace two years earlier; his Emperorship has presumably been marked by bloodshed; soon he will atone for his brutalities with his own blood. All this is suggested visually in the opening scene. Jones enters from right, seats himself on the throne and remains there until he makes his exit through the rear doorway; he thus sticks to the scarlet throughout the scene and literally "leaves de way he comes" (186). Boasting of his imperial superiority while standing on the scarlet matting he adds, much like Agamemnon treading his purple path, the sin of hubris to that of manslaughter, thereby pronouncing his own death sentence.

Jones places himself on the *"huge"* throne in order to emphasize his superiority to Smithers. Similarly, in the slave market scene he places himself on *"a big dead stump worn by time into a curious resemblance to an auction block"* (195) in order *"to get as far away from"* the white planters as possible

---

[2] Cf. the Scarlet Woman in the *Book of Revelation,* Chapter 17, whom O'Neill refers to in *Desire* (210). For the author's interest in this biblical book, see the adaptation listed in the chronology as no. 46.

(197); his fear has here become explicit. In either case Jones ironically seeks refuge in the very place that symbolizes his destruction, in the former case death, in the latter slavery. The throne, we can now see, is nothing but a dead tree stump; by uprooting himself from his native soil in the black forest, symbolizing the black race,[3] Jones has stunted himself, has become a dead tree.

In the second scene Jones has descended from his height and is on a level with his former subjects. He is now seen at

the end of the plain where the Great Forest begins. ... Only when the eye becomes accustomed to the gloom can the outlines of separate trunks of the nearest trees be made out, enormous pillars of deeper blackness (187).

It is evident that his white 'mask' is shrinking: the white stone pillars have become little white stones or have transformed themselves into living, black trees; and, crawling on the ground, Jones is now identified, through the *"stunted bushes,"* with the low-flung "bush niggers" he has earlier (182 f.) held in contempt.

Once inside the forest Jones is confronted with his own sinful past, a monster waylaying him with its underbrush, momentarily stepping aside only to display some horrifying memory, then again closing in on him. The clearings are of different shapes and sizes: *"small triangular"* (Sc. 3), *"wide dirt road"* (Sc. 4), *"large circular"* (Sc. 5), like the *"hold of some ancient vessel"* (Sc. 6), an open space with only one tree (Sc. 7). On the whole we move from narrower to larger clearings. Susan Glaspell (p. 24) has quoted O'Neill as describing the development as follows: "... it begins ... thick forest at first ... steadily thinning out ... scene after scene ... to pure space ..." (Glaspell's dots). The arrangement seems to be a spatial illustration of Jones' increasing awareness, his gradual conquering of the forest by his acceptance of it; by living with his black furies he finds, much like Lavinia Mannon, expiation.

The final vision—the Congo scene—is devised with regard to the opening setting; the values Jones liked and disliked as an Emperor are now found to have reversed their meaning for him. Thus the stones and the scarlet, which he used to admire, are now linked with the altar, where Jones is to be sacrificed, whereas the primitive, dead tree stump—the throne—which he formerly hid beneath a cover of bright red paint, seems to have grown into a *"gigantic tree"* (199), signifying that Jones has now taken his place in the living forest. By the irony of fate he is destroyed by what he cherished and saved by what he despised.

[3] The forest may, of course, also be seen as a symbol of the unconscious, which Jones has tried to repress and to which he (therefore) falls a victim. Cf. Zeller, pp. 104 ff.

Recognizing that a realistic setting is not particularly called for in a play dealing with Man and Woman in their eternal conflict, O'Neill designed a very simple decor for *Welded*—as he was later to do for the thematically related *Brown* and *Days*. An examination of the three sets of the play reveals a basic similarity: all have a door in the rear and a chaise longue, couch and bed respectively as the focal property. *"A balcony with a stairway"* (443) is at the back of the Cape studio apartment, and a stairway is found also at the rear of John's library and the Woman's hotel room (479).[4]

The pervasive stairway is the major symbol of the play. It has both a sexual and a religious significance, just as love, the central concept for the "welded" ones, has both a physical and a spiritual aspect. The matrimonial stairway of the framing acts (Acts I and III) is contrasted with the two adulterous ones of the middle act (Act II.1–2) in much the same way as in *Wilderness,* where Richard, pondering the dismal night he has spent with a prostitute in a disreputable hotel, thinks aloud: "Muriel and I will go upstairs ... when we're married ... but that will be beautiful ..." (276). Michael and Eleanor, although they are married, share Richard's view that what takes place upstairs, in the nuptial bedroom, should be "beautiful"; but they fall short of realizing their ideal. Whether or not O'Neill has been aware of the fact that in Freudian dream psychology the act of mounting stairs, the breath-taking movement up to a climactic point, is a symbol of sexual intercourse, the Capes' words and actions (448 f.) suggest the sexual nature of their stair-climbing. The two doors—one upstairs leading inward, another downstairs leading out—represent two directions, two attitudes—and two levels. On one hand "the common[5] loves of the world" (446), on the other the "true sacrament" (448) Michael wants their marriage to be; in his words: *"Our life is to bear together our burden which is our goal—on and up! Above the world, beyond its vision—our meaning!"* (488).[6] The stairway and the two doors thus present a visual image of the conflict within the Cape marriage between the flesh and the spirit, the allurement and the hostility of the out-side world, the need to remain free and independent and the longing to transcend and annihilate the self. From the point of imagery the central action of the play is actually the Capes' failure to climb the matrimonial stairway

[4] In the first two editions, where the set descriptions are more profuse than in later editions, the similarity between the Cape studio and John's library is further indicated by the fact that both rooms are spacious, tastefully and comfortably furnished, lined with books, etc. As a result these two rooms are set off from the prostitute's ugly and sparsely furnished bedroom. It is likely that O'Neill shortened the set descriptions out of a wish to stress the basic similarity between the three locales.

[5] The longhand draft has "earthy."

[6] Cf. the longhand draft where Eleanor, in a crossed-out sentence, refers even more obviously to the two levels of the setting: "Through you I knew myself merged into something beyond me, living on some higher plane!" (= 447).

(Act I); their escape to other, adulterous stairways (Act II); and their final return to and successful ascension of the nuptial stairway (Act III).

The stairway scenes in Act II.1 are designed as pendants of those in the other acts. Again Eleanor fails to climb the stairs—this time leading to John's bedroom. Her inability to ascend is the outward dramatization of an inner revelation: that her love for Michael is stronger than she had thought; conversely, that her love for John is weaker than she wills it. The discovery that there is a force inside her—love itself—which she cannot master, comes as a startling insight to her, for it makes her at once free and dependent with regard to Michael. Once she obeys the "angel" in her breast, once she decides to return home, she has no difficulties in climbing the stairs (470). Michael, although he does climb the stairs leading to the prostitute's bedroom, makes the same discovery as Eleanor: that he cannot kill his love.

The stairway scene which ends the play (488 f.) echoes the one in Act I, but Michael's mystical yearning for oneness, which was earlier expressed with physical abandon, has now, after his suffering, become purged into a largely spiritual, sacrificial love. It is characteristic that in their final lines Eleanor limits herself to the two words "I love," whereas Michael adds the "you." After their respective revelations the initial imbalance has been transformed into equipoise. The possessive playwright has discovered that he is a dependent "child"; the suppressed actress that she is a needed 'mother'; as such she has an integrity that cannot be destroyed. Realizing this, it is now *she* who takes the lead up the stairs, guiding her husband with her *"tender gesture"* to a love, "deeper and more beautiful" (489) than the one experienced in Act I, because it is *"passionate"* in a religious as well as in a physical sense. It is O'Neill's "das ewig Weibliche zieht uns hinan" scene.

The final gesture—*for a moment as their hands touch they form together one cross* (489)—expresses visually the couple's new-gained conviction that only through sacrifice, only by discarding their selfishness, can their marriage become a "true sacrament" (448). Their love for one another must be conceived in imitation of Christ; their marriage must henceforth be a realization of the Christian love gospel; and the suffering that stems from the struggle upwards to a nobler plane must be greeted with joy. "The great cross—love for mankind," to quote Michael's final words in the original, longhand version, is the key to all true love, the symbol that defeats the *"auras of egoism"* (443) that have separated Michael and Eleanor, the sign by which they finally become "welded."[7] To Michael, the golden rule is the key to all human

---

[7] Earlier in the longhand draft, Michael is even more explicit about the Christian foundation of his love concept as he prays that a transfiguring truth be born in the hearts of men: "One truth of Christ, say—'love one another'—simple, direct—truth!" (= Act III).

relations. The inference of the play is therefore: if husband and wife can live up to this "Grand Ideal," then there is hope also for humanity at large. Thus *Welded* is a play about love, not solely about married love.

"The great cross" has, in fact, been present in the Cape home all along. When Eleanor and Michael unite in the final cross gesture, we discover in a flash that the combined stairway-balcony arrangement actually forms a big tau cross. Presumably having designed his setting with this effect in mind, O'Neill thus adds to the revelation of the Capes a visual revelation on the part of the audience.

"Ghosts of some sort," Nina Leeds in *Interlude* finds, "are the only normal life a house has—like our minds" (49). The statement applies to many of O'Neill's settings. Captain Bartlett (*Cross* and *Gold*) struggles with ghosts in his 'cabin.' Ella Harris (*Chillun*) fights the spirit of the black race in her Bronx apartment. The Evans homestead, which Nina is commenting on, is haunted by a family curse: hereditary insanity. But the most obvious examples of haunted houses are to be found in *Desire* and *Electra*.

In *Desire* the entire action is performed in the shade of the enormous elm trees and inside the stone wall, symbols of the maternal and paternal forces respectively:

The south end of the house faces front to a stone wall with a wooden gate at center opening on a country road. The house is in good condition but in need of paint. Its walls are sickly grayish, the green of the shutters faded. Two enormous elms are on each side of the house. They bend their trailing branches down over the roof. They appear to protect and at the same time subdue. There is a sinister maternity in their aspect, a crushing, jealous absorption. They have developed from their intimate contact with the life of man in the house an appalling humaneness. They brood oppressively over the house. They are like exhausted women resting their sagging breasts and hands and hair on its roof, and when it rains their tears trickle down monotonously and rot on the shingles (202).

The set provides striking similarities with the exterior set for *Electra*; the Cabot farmhouse is a puritan equivalent of the Mannon residence. Here too the *"sickly grayish"* stone color of the house stands for somber, hard puritanism, and the green of the elms for the vegetative, life-affirming forces, denied in the Cabot house since the death of Eben's mother: the green of the shutters is faded! The stage directions for Act I.1 emphasize the contrast between the 'living' elms and the 'dead' house: *"The sky above the roof is suffused with deep colors, the green of the elms glows, but the house is in shadow, seeming pale and washed out by contrast"* (203). The most direct human counterpart of the elms we find in Ephraim's two former wives, who must indeed have been *"exhausted women"* with *"sagging breasts,"* weeping

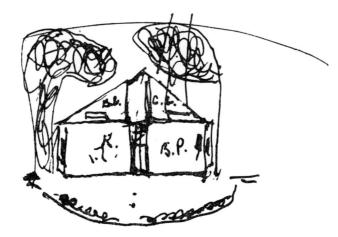

O'Neill's sketch of the house and elms in *Desire*. To the left are the "Br[others']
b[edroom]." and the "K[itchen].", to the right "C[abot's]. b[edroom]." and the
"B[est]. P[arlor]." A comparison with the printed stage directions (202) reveals
that left and right are the audience's. This is always the case with O'Neill.

tears which would *"trickle down monotonously"* from their sad eyes. This is
true especially of the second wife, Eben's mother (cf. Falk, pp. 95, 98), whom
Ephraim worked to death, and whose eyes used to be "weepin' an' bloody
with smoke an' cinders" (209). It is Eben who tells us this. We know that he
hates his father. Can we trust his statement? The author's description of the
elms appears to verify its truth. In the trees we find the mother's monotonous
slavery on the farm visualized.

The elms, then, seem to signify both the dead woman herself—her original,
healthy lust for life—and the wrong done to her, both nature and the
thwarting of nature, both her unselfish love and the Cabots' lovelessness towards her. Above all, the *"enormous"* trees seem to represent their guilt,
which has been growing ever since she died, sucking the blood, as it were,
from the *"pale"* house below; thus the puritan concern with past sins leaves
the Cabots less than living.

"Nature'll beat ye, Eben" (229), Abbie says, and this is precisely what
happens. It is not so much that Eben succumbs to Abbie's or his own sexual
desire, for it is made quite clear that he does not accept her until she has
become identified in his mind with the mother. Once he sees Abbie, not as a
rival of the mother, but as her tool of vengeance on Ephraim, can he give
free rein to his desire (243 f.). Yet, since the mother, as we have seen,
represents nature-gradually-thwarted-by-life-denying-puritanism, Abbie's seduc-
tion of Eben, indicating how nature triumphs over puritanism, is clearly a

retributive act. It is in this sense that nature beats him. When Abbie compares their sexual desire to the growth of the elm trees—it is as natural and power-ful—she draws attention to the trees as symbols of nature, the nature that is suppressed by the Cabots (as the dead woman was suppressed) and therefore has grown *"enormous"* and revengeful and soon will "bust" (211), to use Eben's expressive word (cf. Falk, p. 98).

To summarize: the elms represent, above all, nature, and, obliquely, nature thwarted by intimate contact with puritanism (the house). All the women in the play—note Jenn's long hair (204) as compared to the hair-like trailing branches and Min's resemblance to a fruitful Earth Mother (211)—and especially the dead woman and Abbie are basically in harmony with nature and therefore resemble the elms.[8] Although nature has been suppressed, it cannot remain so for long; finally it takes its revenge on its oppressors; hence the elms come to represent a brooding and ultimately triumphant fate, which operates from without through one of the allies of nature—Abbie—and from within through an accumulating guilt demanding atonement.

Inside the house Eben's mother is associated with the stove in the kitchen, where she was toiling away her life. Eben, we learn, never tried to prevent Ephraim from slaving her to her grave and

It was on'y arter she died I come to think o' it. Me cookin'—doin' her work— that made me know her, suffer her sufferin'—she'd come back t' help—come back t' bile potatoes—come back t' fry bacon—come back t' bake biscuits—come back all cramped up t' shake the fire, an' carry ashes, her eyes weepin' an' bloody with smoke an' cinders same's they used t' be. She still comes back—stands by the stove thar in the evenin'—she can't find it nateral sleepin' an' restin' in peace. She can't git used t' bein' free—even in her grave (209).

Ephraim finds Eben "soft—like his Maw" (231 f., 246). It must have seemed only natural to him that the fifteen-year-old boy—Eben's age at his mother's death—should take over her chores but Eben, by suffering her suffering, came to identify himself with the mother.

The stove is, however, connected with the mother in yet another sense. Under it Ephraim has hidden the money he had hoarded from the farm that by rights belonged to Eben's mother; the mother had discovered the hiding-place and told Eben about it. Eben's feeling that the mother is unable to find peace in the grave and "stands by the stove" every evening is un-doubtedly related to the treasure hidden underneath it. Psychologically, we may interpret these hallucinatory experiences as self-reproaches: Eben is

[8] Engel (1953, p. 129) links the "fecundity and maternity" of the elms with Abbie. Hartman (1961, pp. 364 ff.) connects their *"sinister maternity"* with Eben's three loves: the mother, Min and Abbie. Winther (p. 273), paying (too much) attention to the other aspect of the trees, takes the elms to signify "the New England Puritan."

painfully aware that both the hidden money and the farm are still Ephraim's, that he has still not revenged the mother.

The first opportunity comes when the brothers express their wish to go to California. By providing them with the hidden money Eben performs several desirable things in one stroke: (1) he steals back the money from Ephraim, (2) he deprives the old man of two valuable laborers, and (3) he makes himself sole heir to the farm. The transaction settled, Eben *"sits down at the table, faces the stove and pulls out the paper. He looks from it to the stove. His face, lighted up by the shaft of sunlight from the window, has an expression of trance. His lips move"* (220). Eben is apparently communicating with his mother; the first step in his attempt to justify the dead women has been taken. Once the money is gone and Abbie has replaced Eben by the stove and his mother in his mind, the stove loses its importance: in Act III.1 we learn that *"the stove has been taken down to give more room to the dancers"* (247).

Desire ends with the Sheriff's envious remark: "It's a jim-dandy farm, no denyin'. Wished I owned it!" (269). The line is starkly ironical. The curse of the land, of material possessions, has just been forcefully brought home to us. Then comes the ignorant outsider and declares that he wishes to possess that which has brought only misery to its possessors. The Sheriff and his companions are comparable to the town choruses in *Electra*,[9] which also see without seeing and lack the moral stature of the main characters. His words could have been ours, had we not witnessed the Cabot tragedy. They express precisely what we feel at the beginning of *Electra,* when we take in the *"special curtain"* (2), showing the extensive Mannon estate. This curtain may in a sense be regarded as a fragmentary counterpart of the widely known myth the Greek tragedians could rely on. For it offers the audience a background story of sorts and introduces it to the major conflict in the trilogy, that between green 'paganism' and gray puritanism. What we see is the Mannon house surrounded by rich vegetation.

"As seen from the street" (2), i.e. from the perspective of the town-dwellers (the world outside including the audience), the estate with its *"extensive grounds"* is most impressive. Significantly there is nothing in O'Neill's description of the house as depicted on the curtain that makes us think otherwise. From a distance it appears "purty" (7) to us as it does to the town chorus. We too are under the illusion that what we see is, to use the Sheriff's words in *Desire,* "a jim-dandy farm." Thus, even before the play has begun, we are grouped with the chorus, "the world outside which always sees without really seeing or understanding" (O'Neill, 1931/Frenz, p. 12).

---

[9] Racey (p. 46) actually regards the Sheriff "as a kind of ironic chorus."

Once inside the estate we can better see what the house is like; the stage directions for Act I read in part:

At front is the driveway which leads up to the house from the two entrances on the street. Behind the driveway the white Grecian temple portico with its six tall columns extends across the stage. A big pine tree is on the lawn at the edge of the drive before the right corner of the house. Its trunk is a black column in striking contrast to the white columns of the portico. ...

It is shortly before sunset and the soft light of the declining sun shines directly on the front of the house, shimmering in a luminous mist on the white portico and the gray stone wall behind, intensifying the whiteness of the columns, the somber grayness of the wall, the green of the open shutters, the green of the lawn and shrubbery, the black and green of the pine tree. The white columns cast black bars of shadow on the gray wall behind them. The windows of the lower floor reflect the sun's rays in a resentful glare. The temple portico is like an incongruous white mask fixed on the house to hide its somber gray ugliness (5).

Surrounded by "the green beauty of their land," the Mannons—so the curtain told us—"live in as near the Garden of Paradise ... as you'll find on this earth" (24), to quote Brant's description of the South Sea islands. Or so they would if it was not for the house. After generations of nature-trimming puritanism Abe Mannon, out of revenge on the love he was incapable of himself and which was therefore denied him by Marie Brantôme,[1] tore down the old mansion and built his monstrous "temple of Hate and Death" (171). Yet the vegetation that still surrounds the Mannon estate indicates that nature and the spirit of love, if repressed, are not extinguished. The white portico, like the puritan version of the story, which is the one offered to the world, is a false façade hiding the grim truth visualized in the house itself, the truth, which says that hatred rather than righteousness and revenge rather than justice, motivated Abe's destruction of the old house[2] and erection of the present one. Visualizing modern man's dilemma, the Mannon house is fittingly a "grotesque perversion of everything Greek temple expressed of meaning of life" (O'Neill, 1931/Frenz, p. 4). In its imitation of pagan love of life, beauty, and purity, the portico is incongruously a part of the

[1] In the play we can reconstruct this from Seth's remark that everybody liked Marie and from the violence of Abe's hatred for her, which presupposes an intense desire, which has become thwarted, as it does in Ezra's parallel reaction to Marie and Lavinia's to Brant. In the first typewritten version O'Neill was explicit: Abe had seduced Marie, who gave way to him solely because she was afraid of losing her position; later she fell in love with David (= 17).

[2] A "nice old house," Christine calls the destroyed one in the first typewritten version (= 17). Christine's hatred of the Mannon house may be compared to Mary's dislike of the Tyrone summer home in *Journey*: "I never wanted to live here in the first place, but your father liked it and insisted on building this house, and I've had to come here every summer ..." (44). The connection is made clear by a line in the scenario for *Electra*: "Clementina [Christine] has always loathed the town of N[ew]. L[ondon]. ..."

puritan house built in hatred of life and love; it is itself a perversion of the pagan spirit, for its whiteness is biblical and sepulchral rather than Greek (17).

The inescapability of the fate is underlined by the static setting: the house —exterior or interior—is nearly always before our eyes. Only once—in the ship scene close to the middle of the trilogy (Part II.IV)—do the Mannons get away from it. Here, for a brief moment, the sea promises "escape and release" (O'Neill, 1931/Frenz, p. 8), but the escape is illusory and the main effect of this futile attempt at breakthrough is, in fact, a strengthening of the feeling that the characters are chained to the house, doomed to spend their lives in it. Fittingly, Ezra, Christine, Orin, and eventually, we must assume, Lavinia all die in the house which symbolizes the Mannon way of life, in the house which has worked their destruction: Ezra in the matrimonial bed which he had abused by his inability to love his wife naturally; Christine in the room where she succumbed to the evil Mannon spirit the moment she decided to murder her husband; Orin in the room where his mother committed suicide, partly due to his Mannon harshness.

The house is like a monster swallowing its own breed. Its windows are *"revengeful eyes"* (169), rejecting rather than accepting the warm sunlight, and the shutters are like eyelids. The play begins with open windows and shutters, but when Ezra returns the windows and shutters are closed; the house front becomes a death mask (43), expressive both of Ezra's life-denying puritanism and Christine's evil spirit. When Ezra tells her about the Mannon death worship, she keeps her eyes closed (53 f.), her face resembling a death mask,[3] indicating that she is a victim of the very tradition he is commenting on and which is expressed in the house front. He asks her to open her eyes, but almost immediately entreats her to close them again—an illustration, it seems, of Ezra's willingness but utter inability to free Christine of her death mask. The shutters remain closed also after Ezra's death, for with his corpse in it, the house is literally a tomb (74), and besides it is now Lavinia who rules the house.

In the third part Lavinia's attitude has changed. It is now Orin who locks himself up behind closed blinds in the study, hiding from the world with his guilt (150). Lavinia, on the other hand, is firmly determined to drive the ghosts away. She has strength enough to open the shutters in the study (151), claiming that the air in it is "suffocating" for Orin—as indeed it will shortly prove to be: soon he is to kill himself in the study. It is also due to her that

---

[3] O'Neill rather frequently has his characters close their eyes as an illustration of their deathly state of mind. In Act III of *Straw* Eileen keeps her eyes closed most of the time until Murray declares his love for her (410). In *Iceman* Hugo's words to Larry are explicit: "Why you keep eyes shut? You look dead" (724).

the shutters are fastened back and that the windows are open in the final act. With Orin dead and escape from the Mannons imminent, Lavinia repeats her mother's worship of light and air. Then, in a crushing *anagnorisis,* she discovers that she can rid herself of the evil Mannon spirit only by living with it. She closes her eyes, that is, she 'dies.' And, *"without opening her eyes,"* she says, *"strangely, as if to herself"*: "Why can't the dead die!" (174). She is not merely thinking of the Mannon ghosts; she is also addressing herself, wishing her own death. 'Dead' herself now, it only remains for her, the last Mannon, to prepare her own tomb. She orders the shutters nailed tight and buries herself in the darkened house.[4]

Of the rich vegetation revealed in the special curtain, the stage picture shows only the blooming lilac shrubbery on the left and one of the pine trees on the right. Christine is linked with the shrubbery; she appears close to it twice on her way to and back from the flower garden (8, 15), the second time carrying a bunch of flowers. The pine tree is visually linked with the house, the dark green of its needles matching the *"dark green"* (2) shutters,[5] its column-like trunk in form resembling the house columns and in color the *"black bars"* (5) they cast on the house, turning it, as it were, into a prison. As an evergreen never visibly in bloom (and in this respect contrasting with the rest of the surrounding vegetation) and mournful in color, it adequately expresses the Mannon sterility and hatefulness.[6]

When O'Neill at one point makes Ezra appear close to and turned towards the pine tree (53), he may wish to underline the fact that the man's feelings of hatred and jealousy do not merely concern the present situation but also a traumatic experience in the past. Christine's rejection of him (in favor of Brant) reminds him of Marie Brantôme who similarly 'rejected' him and his father Abe, in favor of David.[7]

More obviously, Lavinia is connected with the pine tree, her black costume in color resembling the trunk of the tree. We are reminded of that especially towards the very end when Lavinia, like *"an ebony pillar"* (43)—O'Neill's description of the pine tree—*"woodenly"* (179) passes between the white columns of the house on her way into its gloomy darkness. Six unnatural deaths—those of David, Marie, Ezra, Adam, Christine and Orin—have oc-

---

[4] Cf. Mrs. Bartlett in *Gold* who, as a living corpse, is carried into her home with its *"tightly closed"* shutters barring all light (658, 674).

[5] In the original longhand draft O'Neill states explicitly in the scene description for Part I.I that the green of the pine trees—in this version the whole grove is apparently included in the stage picture—matches the green of the shutters.

[6] It is significant that the table in the cabin of the "Flying Trades," the Mannon ship, is of pine wood (109).

[7] In the second typewritten version it is made quite clear that this is what is on Ezra's mind as he moves from Christine to the pine tree.

curred in the family since Abe Mannon built his "temple of Hate and Death"; there are six puritan columns in front of the tomblike house.[8] Differing from the other Mannons—except Abe—both by her excessive guilt and by her decision to punish herself to death-in-life, Lavinia is like a seventh black column matching the tree, symbol of the Mannons', especially Abe's, life hatred. As hateful as the grandfather, she has no Mannon to punish—but herself.

Unlike the pine trees, the rest of the vegetation is light green—it is either spring or summer—and subordinated to the seasonal and lifelike rhythm of budding, blooming, decay, death. As we have noted, it links the estate with the islands. This is especially true of the flowers, worn by the natives in Dionysian fashion, "stuck over their ears" (145), symbols of youthful innocence, happiness and love.[9] Thus Christine's brightening up of the Mannon "tomb" with flowers (17) is not merely a sign of her joyous acceptance of Brant, her lover, or even of her attempt to transform the deadly house into a temple of love. As an unhappy, ageing and guilt-ridden woman—she is already planning to murder her husband—Christine longs for all the values represented by the flowers. Her act is one of exorcism.

This is even more true of Lavinia in the final act. Repeating her mother's flower-picking, she is much more desperate. Filling every room in the house with flowers (169 f.), she frankly tells Peter: "Take me in this house of the dead and love me! Our love will drive the dead away!" (176). But her black costume, unlike her mother's green, harmonizes, not with the flowers, but with the dark pine tree. At last she realizes and accepts her Mannon nature. Her final words are: "... tell Hannah to throw out all the flowers" (179). Innocence, happiness and love are incompatible with the Mannon house and do not become Lavinia. It adds considerably to her tragic stature that, despite the intense love for flowers she has just demonstrated, she has the strength to condemn herself to a life without them.

If the Mannon house exemplifies ugliness hidden behind a false face of virtue, the Hogan shanty in *Misbegotten* represents the very opposite: boastful depravity. The house is an ugly, splotched, lemon-and-gray-colored, *"clap-boarded affair," "moved to its present site,"* sedate New England, whose pride and image are prim, white, colonial houses, forming *"a harmonious part of the landscape, rooted in the earth"* (2). The house thus symbolizes a piece of American history: the difficulties of the Catholic, shanty Irish to establish

[8] Cf. Christine's observation about the house in the first typewritten version: "[It is] waiting for something it knows must happen to fulfill some secret purpose for which it was built! It is like an empty tomb which waits for the living to die and give it meaning!" (= 17).

[9] In the first typewritten version Lavinia remarks: "Flowers are gay and innocent and happy, like little children! Life loves them. I never was a child" (= 170).

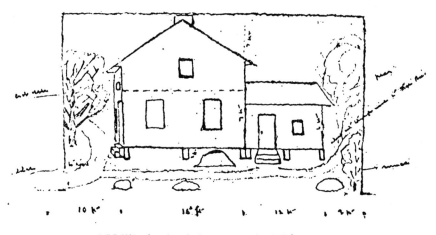

O'Neill's sketch of the scenery in *Misbegotten*.

themselves in Protestant, puritan New England. Like its inhabitants the Hogan home with its *"repulsive"* color, visualizing, in particular, Josie's reputation as a local prostitute,[1] is an outrage and a blasphemy not only to Harder but to the proper Yankee environment in general.

There is perhaps also a point to the fact that Josie sleeps in a one-room addition tacked on to the main building. By sleeping away from the father she can go on pretending to him that she receives male visitors every night; the bedroom part is, in this sense, a monument to her pipe dream.

Even more illuminating is the setting provided another pipe dreamer: Cornelius Melody in *Poet*. Gentleman by upbringing and peasant by birth, Melody is the owner of a tavern in *"a village a few miles from Boston"* (7). Untouched nature is found within his estate; close by is the center of learning and puritanism (Harvard). In the marriage between Sara Melody and Simon Harford, between the Irish strain and the New England puritan stock, nature and culture are brought together in a fateful way. The tavern itself *"had once been prosperous, a breakfast stop for the stagecoach, but the stage line had been discontinued and for some years now the tavern has fallen upon neglected days"* (7). This is as much a description of the tavern-keeper as of the tavern.

---

[1] Cf. the yellow color of the house with Mike's remark to Josie: "You've always been brazen as brass and proud of your disgrace" (9), and with the saffron-colored hotel interior in *Wilderness* (236). That O'Neill meant the high, malproportioned, boxlike house to correspond to Josie's oversize figure is suggested in the stage directions for Act I in the first typewritten version, where it says: *"In the sunlight the Hogan home is pitilessly revealed in all its ugliness, without the shadow of a cloud, or the shade of a tree to clothe its misbegotten nudity"* (= 3).

O'Neill's sketch of the dining room in *Poet*. Note the crossed-out section of the upper story, representing "Simon's bedroom." Originally the action of the play was meant to alternate between the dining room and the bedroom.

Melody himself points out the parallel, when he observes that "this inn, like myself, has fallen upon unlucky days" (69). Similarly, Melody's present estate —"a bit of farm land no one would work any more, and the rest all wilderness" (30)—may, as Falk notes (p. 166), be seen as a travesty of the enormous estate, Melody Castle, he once inherited in Ireland (48 f.). The decline and Melody's attempts to cover it up seem indicated in the description of the dining room:

The dining room and barroom were once a single spacious room, low-ceilinged, with heavy oak beams and paneled walls—the taproom of the tavern in its prosperous days, now divided into two rooms by a flimsy partition, the barroom being off left. The partition is painted to imitate the old paneled walls but this only makes it more of an eyesore (7).

The owner of the place, Melody, in other words, suffers from serious inner division. The painted partition is the visual sign of his attempts to be counted a true gentleman, although his blood—and of late also his reputation—deny him this right and make his overdone, polished behavior *"more of an eyesore."*

The left (partition) wall is especially connected with Melody, since it contains, apart from the door leading to the bar, the mirror in which he finds consolation for his aristocratic dreams and the door leading to his bedroom up above, not surprisingly "the best room in the house" (44). This latter door is used almost exclusively by Melody, a fact which makes the two steps leading up to it suggestive of his imagined superior station and obsessive pride.

The full value of an O'Neill setting often does not emerge until we see it in relation to settings that precede and/or follow it. The hotel scene (Act III.1) and the beach scene (Act IV.2) in *Wilderness,* for example, obviously are counterparts: the hotel witnesses Richard's confrontation with prostituted love (Belle), the beach his confrontation with higher, virginal love (Muriel). The scenes have certain similarities—visual, aural, nominal—which link them with one another, but these general resemblances inevitably point to the differences that are contained in each of them. The lighting in the hotel, a hangout for barflies, is provided by *"two fly-specked globes in a fly-specked gilt chandelier"* (236)—a visualization of Belle's remark that "even the little flies" copulate (243)[2]—whereas in the beach scene *"the crescent of the new moon casts a soft, mysterious, caressing light over everything"* (275). Similarly, the mechanical, noisy and sex-stirring player-piano music in the hotel—"Bedelia, I'd like to feel yer" (237)—is followed by live, faint music from *"the orchestra of a summer hotel"* (275) in the beach scene. And the *"small, dingy room"* in the *"small hotel"*—the implication of pettiness and confinement is obvious —is opposed to the beauty and magnitude of the beach: by having it run *"half-diagonally back"* across the stage O'Neill creates a sense of extension into eternity, which is the proper visualization of Richard's pantheistic sense of belonging: "I love the sand, and the trees, and the grass, and the water and the sky, and the moon ... it's all in me and I'm in it ... God, it's so beautiful!" (277; O'Neill's dots).

In terms of color the hotel setting is dominated by a false and sickly yellow: *"a fly-specked gilt chandelier," "hideous saffron-colored wall-paper"* which is *"blotched and spotted"* and Belle's *"peroxide blonde"* hair (236). In the beach scene the colors are pure and natural: the green of the grass and the willows, the white of the moon, the sand and the rowboat, the dark blue of the sky and the sea.

[2] Cf. Mrs. Miller's worry early in Act I that the house "will be alive with flies" due to the fact that Tommy has left the screendoor open (187 f.); the implication is that the Miller home, unlike the hotel, is kept free from sordidness thanks to the care and responsibility of the parents.

Early in Act I Richard recites his favorite verse from *The Rubaiyat of Omar Khayyam*:

> A Book of Verses underneath the Bough,
> A Jug of Wine, A Loaf of Bread—and Thou
> Beside me singing in the Wilderness— (199).[3]

He also quotes Carlyle: "The days grow hot, O Babylon! 'Tis cool beneath thy willow trees!" (195). In the beach scene we see him and his beloved in the cool moonlight underneath *"the trailing boughs of willow trees"* (275). Richard, after his interlude of seething, passionate desire (indicated by the first part of the Carlyle quotation) has found his way back to soothing, romantic love.

It is thus clear that the beach scene represents the fulfillment of Richard's dreamt Paradise. The wilderness of the verse and of the play title actually appears to have a threefold meaning: in the life of man—and Richard's experience typifies a universal human experience—it stands for the brief, beautiful, unsullied time of youth; in the life of a nation—the action takes place on July 4 and 5—it signifies the (relatively) virginal and unspoiled America of 1776 with its lofty idealism; in the life of mankind it represents the biblical or Rousseauan paradise lost. And the implication seems to be that through the wilderness of youth—by being true to its spiritual innocence and naturalness—man can find a way back to the genuine, life-giving sources from which modern life has cut him off.

Dynamo provides another interesting example of O'Neill's attempt to convey suggestive overtones through unifying factors in seemingly contrasting settings. The play can be read primarily as a psychological drama or as a metaphysical parable continuing the tradition begun with *Ape* (cf. Broussard, pp. 23 ff.). O'Neill apparently meant it to be both. The trilogy of which *Dynamo* was intended to form the first part was to have for its theme, he said, "the failure of science and materialism" to satisfy modern man's religious cravings (O'Neill/Nathan, 1929, p. 119). In *Dynamo* science and materialism are symbolically represented by the utilization of electricity. In many respects electricity satisfies the demands one might have on a new divinity. As a human 'invention' it coincides in time roughly with the Darwinian attacks on the old God. It is world-wide, largely 'benevolent' and allowing itself to be dominated by man. At the same time it has a cosmic aspect. Above all: it is mystical. No one knows exactly what electricity is, only how it manifests itself. It is like a hidden, yet ever-present god.

---

[3] The galley proofs still retained the last line of the verse: "Oh, Wilderness were Paradise enow!" The reason why O'Neill cut this line may have been that it too obviously alludes to the play title. For the change from "Oh" to "Ah," see Gelb, p. 85.

To make the religious issue of *Dynamo* clear, O'Neill pits a representative of the old religion against one adhering to the new. Hutchins Light, a Fundamentalist minister, lives next door to his archenemy Ramsay Fife, an atheistic superintendent of a hydroelectric plant. The action of the play shows the son of the minister, Reuben, rebelling against his father's tyrannical religion and seeking a satisfactory substitute for it in a mystical faith in Electricity and its image, the dynamo. But the boy cannot rest content with Fife's atheism and belief in meaningless chance. He must at all costs find himself a new object of worship, something to belong to. Ironically, he identifies himself with what finally destroys him: having electrocuted the old God, Reuben is himself electrocuted by the new idol, killed by the high currency of the dynamo.

That the dynamo takes the place of the old God is suggested in the sets showing the hydroelectric plant:

The building is red brick. The section on the left, the dynamo room, is much wider than the right section but is a story less in height. An immense window and a big sliding door are in the lower part of the dynamo-room wall, and there is a similar window in the upper part of the section on right. Through the window and the open door of the dynamo room, which is brilliantly lighted by a row of powerful bulbs in white globes set in brackets along both walls, there is a clear view of a dynamo, huge and black, with something of a massive female idol about it, the exciter set on the main structure like a head with blank, oblong eyes above a gross rounded torso (473).

A comparison with O'Neill's drawing of the exterior of the power plant in the notes (cf. p. 72) clarifies that the hydroelectric plant is visualized as a church with its tower, basilica and high windows. The lights in brackets along the walls recall the wall candelabra of a church. And the dynamo fulfills the dual function of divine image[4] and religious instrument; the "singing" of the dynamo, Reuben finds, "beats all organs in church" (474).[5] He also points out that the power houses are "the new churches" (477); and inside the building he tells Fife's daughter Ada that she must realize that they are in dynamo's "temple" (484).

Just as important as the religious significance of the dynamo is the psychological one. The reason why it is conceived of as a *female* idol, Reuben himself indicates; its body, he notes, is "round like a woman's ... as if it had breasts ... but not like a girl ... not like Ada ... no, like a woman ... like her mother ... or mine ... a great, dark mother! .. that's what the dynamo is! ... that's what life is! ..." (474; O'Neill's dots). If we compare this descrip-

---

[4] In the notes O'Neill indicates that the dynamo to Reuben represents "the new idol given to man for God so that in it they may meet again."

[5] In the typewritten version the steel platform on the dynamo with its railing is furthermore compared to a pulpit.

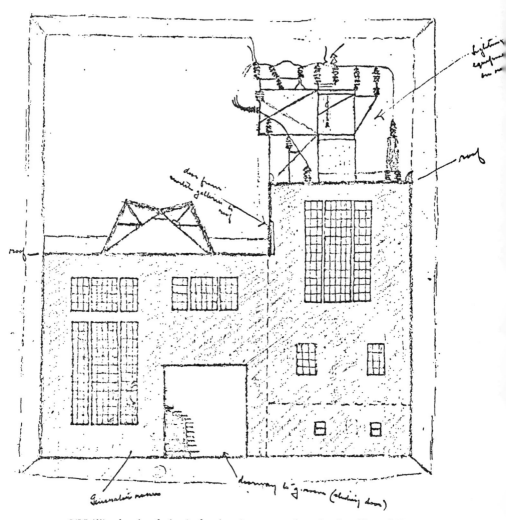

O'Neill's sketch of the hydroelectric power plant in Act II.3 of *Dynamo*.

tion with those of Mrs. Light and Mrs. Fife, the resemblance is obvious. Mrs. Light has a *"stout figure,"* which *"is still firm and active, with large breasts and broad, round hips."* She has a *"dark-complected face"* and *"wavy black hair."* Fifteen years the junior of her husband (who is sixty) she *"appears even younger"* (422).[6] Mrs. Fife, similarly, in contrast to her petite husband, is

[6] The idea of linking Mrs. Light with the stout, dark, 'young' dynamo had apparently not yet occurred to O'Neill, when he was making notes for the play. In the notes Mrs. Light is described as "small" and "old-looking."

*tall and stout, weighing well over two hundred. ... Her figure is not formless nor
flabby. It suggests, rather, an inert strength. A mass of heavy copper-colored hair
is piled without apparent design around her face. ... Her eyes are round and dark
blue. Their expression is blank and dreamy* (428).

By linking the dynamo with the two mother figures—Reuben's own
mother and the one who, to some extent, becomes a substitute for her—
O'Neill could account psychologically for Reuben's development. In a letter
to Nathan (3.19.1929) the author interestingly outlined this as follows:

... what is "Dynamo" primarily but the story of a minister's son and the psychological mess into which hatred and fear of his bullying Fundamentalist father
and an over-emphasis on love for the mother who betrays his trust, lead him
when his life suddenly becomes complicated by love for an atheist's daughter.
When this is further complicated by his devouring popular science manuals—in
final rebellion against his father and his father's god—and weaving a new
besotted dogma out of them, never really getting away from his mother (witness
the postcards) and then finding she has died wanting him, longing for him—
why then in his unbalanced state of mind he makes his mother into an atheistic
deity out of the popular science books,—a dynamo, since dynamos fascinate him—
and, when he is unfaithful to her with the girl she hated, kills the girl as an
expiatory sacrifice and then runs back into his mother—death in her, one with
her, possessing her again—as his final effort in flight from life to security.

In a letter to De Casseres written a week earlier, O'Neill commented on the
symbolic role of the dynamo:

Is not the boy's whole fight to repudiate his father's God humanly a fight to
conquer his father? Isn't this plain in the second act scene between them? Isn't
his feeling about his dead mother plain—the drag her influence from the grave
immediately has on him so that a moment later he tries to kiss the girl and
can't. That the dynamo is his mother that he has elevated by devious ways hidden
from himself into God the Mother so that he can possess and be possessed by
her, his electrocution of the Father God in her name, etc., seems to me to stand
out in the play like red paint.

The obese dynamo, we can now see, serves O'Neill's symbolic purposes in
its suggestion of generative, maternal power—when Reuben remarks that the
song of the dynamo is "the hymn of eternal generation, the song of eternal
life" (482), he is using the word "generation" both in its electrical and its
propagative sense. It also visualizes his idea of the dynamo as a "Great
Mother" (477), a mother of cosmic proportions, the loving deity Reuben
would naturally seek, having fled from the punishing paternal God.

The settings for the first two acts are designed to bring out the religious
conflict in the play. The Fife and Light houses, on the left and right respectively, stand side by side, separated only by a narrow strip of lawn. The Light
house reflects the puritan mind of its owner. It is an old, white New England

cottage with shutters to hide behind or to close out the light with (419). Inside, too, it is old-fashioned, *"spotlessly clean and in order"* (421). The strong sense of guilt and concomitant need for purification seem modestly indicated by the *"washstand with bowl and pitcher"* (421) in Reuben's bedroom upstairs; even after he has converted to his religion of electricity he sees, as of old, mainly the purificatory meaning of water; thus the water in the dam of the power plant seems to him to wash "all dirt and sin away" (476).

The Fife home, similarly, expresses the modern, atheistic mind of *its* owner. It is of an earth-colored bungalow type, *"recently built"* (419). Inside, it is *"of a glaring newness"* (428). The three windows on either story indicate an open, unafraid attitude and worship of light in sharp contrast to the secretiveness of the Light cottage. The contrast is even more apparent in the interior lighting: while the Fife house is *"bright with all their electric lights on"* (428), the Light home is inefficiently lit by a single *"cheap oil reading lamp"* in the sitting room and a kerosene lamp in Reuben's bedroom (421). But like their owners, both houses are small, imprisoning, unsatisfactory as dwellings for Reuben, who seeks to come to meaningful terms with life, and for the voluminous Mother Earth figures who inhabit them—it is characteristic that Mrs. Light complains about having to live in "this awful little house" (425) and that Mrs. Fife is constantly found by the windows, staring at the sky.

Although O'Neill makes it quite plain that Reuben suffers from an unresolved Oedipus complex, it may not be altogether clear to what extent his various actions are determined by this circumstance. His ravishment of Ada at the end of Act III.2 is a case in point. On the most obvious level, this act is an illustration of the confused boy's inability to rid himself of the temptations of the flesh, his failure to pass the test he sets himself. By resisting Ada he would resist not only the physical allurement which the puritan in him—still vital, although Reuben does not think so—condemns as the devil's invention; he would also resist the girl his mother hated. But Reuben is passionately attracted to Ada; unable to restrain himself, he rapes her. Afterwards, filled with remorse on account of this betrayal against the mother and feeling that their sin demands expiation, he kills first Ada then himself.

Yet from another point of view which seems inferred in the play, the ravishment may be considered an expression of Reuben's desperate attempt to seek the dead mother in the living Ada, to possess the one by possessing the other. That the two women are fused in his mind is indicated by the manner in which he wants Ada to pray to the Dynamo-Mother: "I want you to pray to her ... with your arms like her arms, stretching out for me" (484). In the galley proofs O'Neill makes the Oedipal nature of Reuben's desire for Ada

74

rather clear.[7] In the play version he is more restrictive. Here the Oedipal connotations seem conveyed mostly through O'Neill's manipulation of the settings.

Because of their position, height—the term *"bungalow"* (419) suggests that the Fife house is lower than the Light *"cottage"*—and interior lighting, we tend to associate the Fife home containing a Victrola playing modern, mechanical music with the well-lit dynamo room and the Light one with the dimly lit switch galleries, the lilac hedge between the two houses corresponding to the wall between the two parts of the power house. The upper gallery would then correspond to Reuben's bedroom, and the raised platform, where the ravishment takes place, would be the counterpart of Reuben's bed, the bed on which his mother used to sing him to sleep (476) and on which he had cuddled up to her after he had first kissed Ada, scared of his sin and of the lightning, embraced by her tender, maternal arms (445 f.). To make love to Ada on the raised platform under the dangerous electrical equipment in the dimly lit gallery would be to recreate the situation when Reuben last saw his mother, the last time she embraced him and protected him from life. When Reuben rapes Ada he is thus, by implication, revealing his Oedipal desire to "possess and be possessed" by the mother. The opening of Act III.3, playing immediately after the rape, characteristically shows Reuben and Ada in positions which recall those of Reuben and Mrs. Light in Act I.4 (446):

REUBEN *is on his knees, his back bowed, his face covered by his hands.* ADA *is standing before him, directly beneath the switches as before. She is bending over him in a tender attitude, one hand reaching down, touching his hair* (486).

Having failed to turn Ada into a mother substitute and (therefore) seeing their sexual union as a sacrilege against the maternal love he desires, Reuben desperately seeks reconciliation with the mother by killing her rival, Ada, before he hurries to the protective maternal bosom, much as he had done in Act I.4:

REUBEN. (*pleading to the dynamo like a little boy*) ... I only want you to hide me, Mother! Never let me go from you again! Please, Mother! (*He throws his arms out over the exciter, his hands grasp the carbon brushes. There is a flash of bluish light about him and all the lights in the plant dim down until they are almost out and the noise of the dynamo dies until it is the faintest purring hum. Simultaneously* REUBEN'S *voice rises in a moan that is a mingling of pain and loving consummation, and this cry dies into a sound that is like the crooning of a baby and merges and is lost in the dynamo's hum* (488).

[7] There it is stated that Reuben's voice, as the scene opens, is *"strangely like the voice of the young boy reproaching his mother in Part One,"* while Ada speaks *"in a complacent, motherly tone as if she were soothing an unreasonable child"* (= 487).

In other words: Reuben finds belonging in death. The loving embrace and the deathly hug are equated; both protect from the suffering that makes up life. Dying Reuben reenters the mother's womb.

By linking sets and actions in this manner O'Neill demonstrates how Reuben's conversion touches only the surface and how, underneath this surface, there is one governing principle, which determines his actions from beginning to end: his attachment to the mother.

In the dramas which display only one setting it is obviously not possible to resort to such visual echoes as the ones just dealt with. Here the author must find other means to make the scenery expressive.

O'Neill's description for the setting of *Journey* reads in part:

Living room of James Tyrone's summer home on a morning in August, 1912.
At rear are two double doorways with portieres. The one at right leads into a front parlor with the formally arranged, set appearance of a room rarely occupied. The other opens on a dark, windowless back parlor, never used except as a passage from living room to dining room (11).[8]

During the long day we witness a struggle not only between the four Tyrones. We also witness a battle within them between the past and the present, between, on one hand, the desire to forget one's own guilt and misery in the past and remember only the innocent and happy part of it, and, on the other, the need to remember the past guilt of others. Thus all four vacillate between a desire to live in the present and to live in the past, to forget and to remember. It is this complex psychological situation, I would suggest, that O'Neill has attempted to illustrate spatially in his setting.

The three rooms may be said to correspond to three basic experiences of life. There is the living room in front, where all the visible action takes place, representing the living present. And there are the two parlors at the back of it corresponding to the past. The dark back parlor may be taken to represent the guilt and misery of the past; no one wants to dwell in it; yet all must occasionally pass through it. And the bright, well-lit, neatly furnished and well-ordered, yet rarely used front parlor with its musical instrument may be taken to signify those rare moments of deep harmony with life, when we have a feeling that a benevolent, divine light is shining on an orderly uni-

[8] Cf. the description in *Wilderness* (185), where, again, the back parlor is *"dark, windowless."* In O'Neill's drawing of the New London house (see the next page), found among the notes for *Journey,* the back parlor is, however, provided with one window and it is furnished with table, sofa and chairs, a sign that it was used by the family. When I visited the house in the summer of 1966, its present owner confirmed that when the O'Neills owned it, there was a fairly small window in the back parlor.

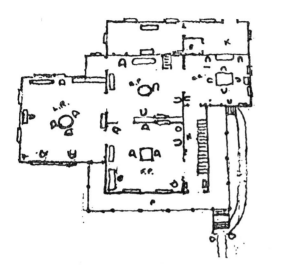

O'Neill's plan of his parents' summer house in New London, Connecticut, which has provided the scenery for *Journey*. To the left is the "L[iving]. R[oom]."; in the middle the "F[ront]. P[arlor]." and the "B[ack]. P[arlor]"; to the right (not visible in the play) are the "H[all]," the "D[ining]. R[oom]." and the "K[itchen]."

verse; Edmund and Mary have both had such moments; Mary, be it noted, is the only one who occupies the front parlor, and she does it precisely when she has rid herself of her past guilt and reverted to her innocent, happy youth and is reliving her pianist dream.[9]

Lighting

Already in his earliest plays O'Neill employs lighting not merely to evoke a mood but to suggest an inner state of mind as well as a relationship between man and some external fate. Thus, in *Thirst* the author makes it clear that the sun that scorches the three human wrecks on the life raft represents a punishing divinity: "*The sun glares down from straight overhead like a great angry eye of God. The heat is terrific. Writhing, fantastic heat waves rise from the*

---

[9] Falk (p. 181) interprets the symbolism somewhat differently: "The family 'lives' in that mid-region between the bright formality of the exterior front parlor—the mask—and the little-known dark of the rear room."

white deck of the raft" (3). The destructive effect of the sun is evident in all three. The Gentleman's bald head is *"burnt crimson"* and his face is *"blistered with sunburn"*; his eyes are "like two balls of fire" and he feels a little out of his head (4 ff.). The Dancer, similarly, notes that her brain is "scorched with sun-fire and dream-fire" (17) and that she is going mad. The Sailor has a *"swollen tongue"* (20).[1]

Having revealed themselves to be essentially beasts of prey, the three are retributively swallowed by sharks, while the Dancer's necklace—symbol of their selfishness—as the sole 'survivor' *"lies glittering in the blazing sunshine"* on the empty raft (32). Whereas their bodies disappear in the hellish depths and leave only a black stain behind, their souls move in the opposite direction:

The heat waves rising from the raft near the woman's body seem like her soul departing into the great unknown (30).

The eerie heat waves float upward in the still air like the souls of the drowned (32).

Whether there is any reconciliation in this upward movement O'Neill does not tell us.[2]

Earlier the sky appears red, as if "raining drops of blood" (5), to the Dancer and the Gentleman; though it is, of course, the heat that works this effect on their eyes, the Gentleman has another explanation: "Perhaps it is the blood of all those who were drowned that night rising to the surface" (5). This fantastic thought may occur to him because he feels guilty, having done nothing to diminish the number of casualties, or because he is thirsty and secretly nourishes the same desire to drink blood as the Sailor, or simply because O'Neill wants to prepare for the bloody ending of the play. The dramatist may well have wished to suggest all these alternatives.

---

[1] The whole play, including the references to the sun, seems inspired by Coleridge's *Rime of the Ancient Mariner,* which O'Neill was to dramatize ten years later. Cf. the following lines in Coleridge's poem:

> ... like God's own head,
> The glorious sun uprist. ...

> "All in a hot and copper sky,
> The bloody Sun, at noon,
> Right up above the mast did stand,
> No bigger than the Moon."

Quoted from O'Neill's dramatization of the poem (68).

[2] The play in this respect ends with the question implicit in the following lines in *The Ancient Mariner,* which undoubtedly served as an inspiration for O'Neill's idea of the heat waves; says the Mariner about the dying sailors:

> "Their souls did from their bodies fly,—
> They fled to bliss or woe ..." (*Mariner,* 73).

The lighting in the first act of *Gold* bears an obvious resemblance to the one in *Thirst*. Again we are introduced to the thirst-maddened survivors of a shipwreck in the tropic seas. The scene represents a small, barren coral island:

The coral sand, blazing white under the full glare of the sun, lifts in the right foreground to a long hummock a few feet above sea-level. ... The far horizon to seaward is marked by a broad band of purplish haze which separates the bright blue of the water from the metallic gray-blue of the sky. The island bakes. The intensity of the sun's rays is flung back skyward in a quivering mist of heat-waves which distorts the outlines of things, giving the visible world an intangible eerie quality, as if it were floating submerged in some colorless molten fluid (623).

Here the blood is seen not only by the characters themselves but also by the audience. By subjecting us to the hallucinatory vision of men maddened by thirst and scorched by the sun, O'Neill equates the sailors and the audience and blots out the demarcation line between the normal and the abnormal mind. The purplish haze and the *"quivering mist of heat-waves,"* which distorts *"the outlines of things"* enable us to empathize with the Captain's state of mind and in a measure understand how he can become a murderer.

The *"angry eye of God"* glares down on Bartlett too. All his life, he admits, he has been dreaming of ambergris and gold, riches which would enable him to give up whaling and make it possible for him and his family to live in comfort together. He longs to "rest to home" (629). But the angry God wants none of this. Punishment awaits those who seek peace and comfort for themselves. Unable or unwilling to see that his materialistic dream is unworthy of the nobler part of him, Bartlett is insensitive to the retributive nature of the scorching sun. To him it is, on the contrary, the sun which is to blame for the island events; it is a malignant fate from which the Captain hides himself in shady obscurity (639).

His religious wife is, not surprisingly, an intense sun worshipper: "I'm sick o' the house. I need sun and fresh air, and today's so nice I couldn't stay indoors. ... I'd best get out quick while it's still sunny and warm" (644). While the Captain seeks cure away from the sun in the damp and shady boatshed, his wife seeks it out-of-doors in sun and fresh air. Their attitudes to God are clearly antithetical.

O'Neill also utilizes each of the positions of the sun for his symbolic purposes. The noon sun, we have already noted, is experienced as a plagueing curse. The sunset usually carries the traditional meaning of death. The sunrise, as we shall see, represents spiritual birth or rebirth.

All three positions are found in *Horizon,* which proceeds from sunset (Act I.1), through night (Act I.2), noon (Act II), dawn (Act III.1), to sunrise

(Act III.2). In Act I.1 *"the horizon hills are still rimmed by a faint line of flame, and the sky above them glows with the crimson flush of the sunset. This fades gradually as the action of the scene progresses"* (81). Robert's connection with the sun is indicated by two illustrative actions: *"He is reading a book by the fading sunset light. He ... turns his head toward the horizon ..."* (82). Recapturing memories of his childhood, Robert further elucidates the nature of this connection. We learn that he was a sick child, who spent much time by the west window learning "all the different kinds of sunsets by heart. And all those sunsets took place over there ... beyond the horizon" (90). The sickness is a sickness with life, the concern with the sunset a longing for death. But Robert does not as yet realize this. As a child he would believe in good fairies—as he still does—and would "dance with them down the road in the dusk in a game of hide-and-seek to find out where the sun was hiding himself" (90). The sun, then, is masculine—like God; and the good fairies we have already linked with the biblical Cherubims. Robert's metaphysical concern thus seems essentially Christian. That he has not given up his dreams of old is indicated by his present decision to go "beyond the horizon" on an old sailing vessel named the "Sunda" (83).

The following interior scene plays shortly afterwards, at 9:00 P.M. Visually, this is suggested by the after-sunset coloring of the walls in the sitting-room: the papering is of *"a dark red"* (93). The cover on the table center has the same color. On it stands *"a large oil reading lamp,"* the single source of light in the room, the sun of this little world. That O'Neill meant the lamp to symbolize the sun is indicated, apart from the coloring of the wall paper, by the fact that he specifically calls it a reading lamp, for that, as we have seen, is exactly the function the sun has for Robert in Act I.1.

As Andrew blows out the lamp at the end of Act I.2, the room lies in darkness. O'Neill insistently points to the symbolic significance of this blackout: Andrew states that he feels "dead"; Robert *"does not move"* and sits "mourning" (111). But the darkness does not signify death. If Robert looks and acts like a corpse, he does so because of his intense guilt feelings vis-à-vis the beloved brother. If Andrew feels "dead," it is because he is sorry to leave the farm. We have already come to identify the light—the sun—with the life beyond, the true life. The darkness belongs to this side of the horizon, to life, signifying not only its prosaic grimness but also its unintelligibility, its seeming futility—a view of life that rules supreme with both brothers at this point in the play. Visually, it is expressed by their *"groping their way"* (111) through the darkness at the close of the scene.

Act II.1 occurs *"about half past twelve in the afternoon of a hot, sun-baked day in midsummer, three years later. All the windows are open, but no breeze stirs.... The noon enervation of the sultry, scorching day seems to have pene-*

trated indoors ..." (112). The scorching noon sun recalls *Thirst* and Act I of *Gold.* Here, too, it seems to represent "*the angry eye of God.*" O'Neill early in the act makes Mrs. Atkins talk about "God's punishment" (114). Her words refer to Mayo, dead for two years, but apply also to Robert, whose "*eyes are dull and lifeless*" and whose face is "*burned by the sun*" (119). Robert's first words significantly are: "Phew! The sun's hot today!" (119). Robert's settling down on the farm, laying up treasures on earth, meant a treason against his true life task such as he saw it already as a child: to seek the sun, the kingdom of God, beyond the horizon. That is why he is retributively burned by the sun.

Ruth, too, as we have seen, suffers from the heat. And Andrew's situation is no better; in a letter he reports: "We're in Singapore now. It's a dirty hole of a place and hotter than hell. Two of the crew are down with fever and we're short-handed on the work.... tacking back and forth in these blistering seas is a rotten job ..." (126). This is just as much a description of the Mayo marriage and farm. Robert and Ruth are feverish; one of the hands has just quit; and Robert's "sweating in the sun like a slave"—the phrase is Andrew's in Act I.2 (107)—is a "blistering" and "rotten" job, as his outward looks make plain.

The difficulty to breathe, the lack of fresh air—these are characteristics of the hell of marriage the Mayo farm has come to accommodate. On the psychological level the noon heat corresponds to the heated relations between Robert and Ruth, the suffocating atmosphere of their married life.[3] When Mrs. Mayo states that little Mary cries because "the heat upsets her" (116), her remark may thus be seen as an implicit comment on the child's suffering from its mismated parents; when they attack each other at the end of the scene, the child's crying significantly rises to its loudest pitch.

The characters seek escape in the shade of the large oak tree on top of the hill. "I come up here now," Robert says, "because it is the coolest place on the farm" (131), and Ruth echoes him: "It's so fine and cool up here after the house" (136). Yet even here Robert finds that Ruth cries, because "the sun hurts her eyes" (142).

Five years later the heat is gone: Ruth is "*sitting by the stove with hands outstretched to the warmth as if the air in the room were damp and cold. ... Her mother is asleep in her wheel chair beside the stove ..., wrapped up in a blanket*" (144 f.). It is just before dawn "*toward the end of October*"; "*the darkness outside the windows gradually fades to gray.*" The sun still keeps hiding itself. Also inside, the lighting is dismal, darkened: "*the shadeless oil lamp*" has "*a smoky chimney*"; and the sun cover on the table is gone

---

[3] Cf. the "*sultry night*" in *Servitude* (227) as an expression of "the stifling environment of married life" (238), and Marsden's view of the "scorching zenith sun" as symbolizing "passion and possession" (*Interlude,* 187).

(144). Robert's dreams of "the dawn of a new life together" (150) in the city, removed from the cursed farm, gets no encouragement from the gray daylight outside or the inefficient light inside. He is deluding himself about the harmless nature of his illness. And yet he is right, in a deeper sense, when he refers to it as a "bad cold" (147). The illness set in when little Mary died (Mrs. Mayo has died still earlier), that is, when love disappeared from his life. But Robert does not *feel* cold; on the contrary he is "burning up" (145) with fever. Ruth's apathy has only increased his beyond longing; the sun has come to possess him. During the scene between them Ruth avoids looking at Robert. She stares dully at the stove instead. Her closeness to it indicates both her need and her lack of warmth, of love; her frozen emotions.

Midway in the scene, just before Doctor Fawcett and Andrew arrive, there is a change of lighting. Ruth places another, clean lamp beside the smoky one, and this clean lamp is later carried in to Robert's bed, when the doctor examines him. With the doctor comes certainty of Robert's imminent death. The darkness of life begins to disperse before the light of death, the greater light Robert faces in the final sunrise scene, which is clearly written as a pendant to the initial sunset scene and in counterpoint to the night scene at the end of Act I.2. The contrast between earth and sky is more distinct than in the opening scene:

The sky to the east is already alight with bright color and a thin, quivering line of flame is spreading slowly along the horizon rim of the dark hills. The road-side, however, is still steeped in the grayness of the dawn, shadowy and vague (166).[4]

In the same way the contrast between Robert, on one hand, and Ruth and Andrew, on the other, is much greater than in the initial scene. The final setting includes, as it were, both the heavenly light of Act I.1 and the blinding earthly darkness of Act I.2. In the latter scene the guilt-laden Robert suffers more than his victimized brother, who strikes an optimistic note. In the final sunrise scene we find Ruth sobbing and repeating Robert's gesture of remorse in the darkness scene, while Robert, now the victim, rejoices in death. Andrew's optimism stemmed from the fact that he did not really love Ruth and so could leave the farm—at "sun-up" (111)—without feeling too tragic about it. In the same way Robert's death joy stems from the fact that he never really loved this world and so could greet a departure from it as a release. Life to him is a purgatory preparing us for the paradise beyond the horizon, and the horizon itself is the black rim of death that we must pass on our way from this gray shadow world into the radiant one beyond.

[4] From a realistic point of view, it is of course impossible to imagine that the sun could set and rise in practically the same place. O'Neill was obviously not interested in subjecting his lighting to the laws of verisimilitude.

Robert is recompensed with a sunrise death: *"the sun's disc is rising from the rim of the hills"* (168) the moment he gives up his ghost. With death comes enlightenment: sacrifice, Robert finds in his dying moment, is the secret of life, the prize we must pay for the voyage beyond the horizon, the crucifixion that must precede the resurrection of which the sunrise, the "augury of good fortune" (150), gives promise. This realization is the "real accretion from his ... dreaming, a thing intangible but real and precious beyond compare, which he [has] successfully made his own."[5] The tragic touch and the 'death' remain with Andrew and Ruth, who are left with *"the grayness of the dawn"* (166)—much as the two brothers were left in the dark unintelligibility of life in the earlier scene.[6]

The twilight in *Chillun* has a somewhat special significance. As Jim and Ella declare that he is her "feller" and she is his "girl," the sun sets and gives place to twilight (304). Their togetherness, recently ridiculed by the other children, is thus accompanied by a light that is neither white nor black but both: twilight; their union, though dismissed by mankind, has, we might say, a divine sanction. The following scenes witness them growing up in the cold and cruel light of the arc-lamp at the street corner,[7] between the black and the white world, fighting in vain against a deepening darkness (306, 312; cf. Raleigh, p. 27). In the wedding scene we see them stepping out from the darkness within the church, which so readily dismisses the mixed couple, into the sunlight (319). By turning their eyes upward they barely manage to pass through the hostile racial lines of society and assure themselves of the rightness of what they have done:

JIM. ... See the sun! Feel his warm eye lookin' down! Feel how kind he looks! Feel his blessing deep in your heart, your bones! ... We're all the same —equally just—under the sky—under the sun—under God— (320).

This is the Christian gospel the church and mankind tend to forget; the "warm eye" of God contrasts with the *"brutal eyes"* (318)—the windows—of the tenements. And Jim and Ella cannot for long isolate themselves from the world. In Act II.3 the arc-lamp spills its cruel, pale light into their apartment, throwing Jim's face into relief (331); it is a visualization of Ella's white skin—she is now fully a victim of white racial prejudices—next to

---

[5] O'Neill to Olin Downes about his early ideas for the Robert character. Quoted from Bowen, 1959, p. 124.

[6] This interpretation agrees with Quinn's (2, p. 172) and Skinner's (pp. 60, 75); it runs counter to the views of Winther (p. 21) and Falk (p. 41).

[7] The *"pale"* (306) and cruel (312) glare of the arc-lamp may also be related to Ella's indifference to Jim in these scenes. She is significantly described as *"repelling"* (309), *"pale"* and *"cold"* (312).

Jim's black one. But in the final scene, where Ella's insane regression returns them to their childhood world and makes them "beaux" (342) again, black and white once more blend into twilight (338).

To consider Jim's revelation at the end delusory because it is made in a state of mind bordering on insanity (Falk, p. 90), is to reduce the stature both of him and of the play. On the contrary, the implication is that in a 'sane' world of warped values only insanity can give Jim and Ella back their true vision. As in the initial scene, their black-and-white union—an exemplar of the brotherhood of man—receives divine sanction in the twilight, as it were. When Jim realizes the religious significance of their struggle, when he sees that theirs has been a suffering in imitation of Christ, he can accept it and bless it, convinced now that as God's true chillun they will soon reach "the gates of Heaven" (342).

In *Ape* lighting plays a part in underlining the contrast between the modes of life of the two classes in modern society, the superrace and the subrace. While the superrace scenes (Sc. 2, 5) bathe in heavenly sunlight, the subrace scenes are set in darkness; while the stokers' life is "six days in hell" (209) —the creative working week—that of the capitalists is one long Sunday (217, 233). This contrast is, however, not an end in itself; it is there to strike home an illuminating parallel: that modern man (Yank, Mildred), unless he is spiritually dead, cannot find harmony in either mode of life.

The "warm sun on the clean decks" (214), the old harmony with the universe, which Paddy exultantly recalls, is visualized in the second scene— but not to the superrace members who are too removed from nature to be able to enjoy it; Mildred can "get *in* it" (252) no more than Yank can. In the Fifth Avenue scene the *"intermittent electric lights"* (233) winking out their commercial messages in broad Sunday light reveal the substitution of man-made, artificial light for the natural light of God.

The same substitute appears in two of the subrace scenes, where the per-vasive darkness—in itself suggestive of the death of God—is dispelled only by the sparse light from *"one ... electric bulb"* hanging *"high overhead"* (222) or *"from the ... ceiling"* (239). The correspondences between celestial and artificial lights are indicated by the scene sequence; the sun of the deck scene (Sc. 2) is transformed into the electric bulb of the stokehole scene (Sc. 3), which again appears in the prison scene (Sc. 6). In the I.W.W. scene (Sc. 7) Yank, encaged by *"buildings massed in black shadow"* (245), for the first time turns to the universe—to the moon—in recognition of his spiritual needs: "I can't see—it's all dark, get me? It's all wrong!" (250). These words draw attention to the basic light contrast in the play, that between the spiritual light of the past and the spiritual darkness of the present; Yank is modern man in search of God. As his inability to return to the past is made manifest in his confrontation with the gorilla, the light fades into darkness. The final *mot d'auteur*—"*and, perhaps, the Hairy Ape at last belongs*" (254)—implies a blessing-beyond-death for Yank as for his namesake in *Cardiff*. It is the gorilla who shuffles off into "*the darkness*" of life (254).

The symbolic significance of the lighting in *Brown* is indicated in several places in the dialogue. Thus, in the Prologue, Dion notes that "the days are dimmer than they used to be" (262), and later, referring to himself, he tells Brown: "When Pan was forbidden the light and warmth of the sun he grew sensitive and self-conscious and proud and revengeful—and became Prince of Darkness" (297). Locked like his mother in the "dark closet" of life "without any explanation" (282), Dion is a Lucifer unjustly barred from a blissful heaven. The defiant, Mephistophelean mask serves as protection against the horrors of the darkness. As Brown, holding Dion's mask in his hands, is later to find: "I need the devil when I'm in the dark!" (308). When he dies, Brown tells Cybel: "It was dark and I couldn't see where I was going ..." (322). Life is a blinding darkness. But Cybel consolingly tells Billy that once he is dead, the sun of love and grace will be rising again (322).

In view of these statements it is not surprising that no scene in the play is set in clear sunlight and that most of them are set in darkness (evening or night).[8] The "*dim, street-lighted view of black houses*" (290) behind Brown's office in Act II.2 visually confirms Dion's remark in the Prologue. In Act III.2 Brown "*can be heard feeling his way in through the dark*" of his library (306)—an illustration of his groping through life. The moonlight of the Prologue and Epilogue, we can now see, does not merely set a romantic mood. As modern man has been forbidden the warm sunlight, so he has been excluded from the warm moonlight. The nights are not only dimmer but also colder than they used to be, Mrs. Brown (259), Mrs. Anthony (261), Dion (262) and Margaret (324) agree. And while Dion's "old-fashioned" grandmother could still believe that "the full of the moon was the time to sow," his father finds the moonlight merely "bringing on [his] rheumatism" (261). Instead of being experienced as a fertile promoter of life, the moon is felt to promote sickness. The intimate oneness with nature has become lost.

As we have just seen, moonlight has its special connotations in O'Neill's plays. It appears with great frequency from *Caribbees* onwards, sometimes setting a romantic mood for the action—Marco and Donata (*Marco*), Dion and Margaret (*Brown*), Reuben and Ada (*Dynamo*), Richard and Muriel

---

[8] Raleigh points out (p. 18) that each act is "a journey into night."

(*Wilderness*) all exchange tokens of love in a beautiful moonlight—, sometimes striking a note of hauntedness and death[9] as in *Cross, Gold, Jones* and *Ape,* sometimes mingling the two as in *Caribbees* and *Misbegotten.*

Of paramount importance is the lighting in *Cross.* When the curtain rises Captain Bartlett's 'cabin' is empty, unlit—except for the moonlight and the faint light from the binnacle up above on the 'bridge' (555); it sets a mood of unreality. The dialogue soon helps to clarify the relationship between the lighting and the owner of the room. The Captain has been 'moonstruck' for three years (556)—since the death of his wife and the report that the ship he had fitted out (by mortgaging his house) to bring back a hidden treasure from an island in the Indian Ocean had been wrecked. It was then he erected the 'cabin' "*as a lookout post at the top of his house*" (555). And every night since, he keeps watch on the bridge up above for the lost ship, the *Mary Allen,* named after his dead wife. For, as his son Nat puts it, "the things he wants to see can't be made out in daylight—dreams and such" (557). The Captain is not, however, the victim of a complete falsification of reality. He has his moments of clear-sightedness. Nat gives us the key to his psyche, when he says: "he *knows*—but he won't *believe.* He can't—and keep living" (558). Belief and knowledge, dreams and facts, gold and brass, obscurity and light —these are the thematic antitheses in the play.

The moonlight harmonizes with the Captain's need for a world set apart from the everyday one, a world in which his dreams can come true, in which his dear departed Mary Allen—the treasure ship *and* the wife—can be brought back to relieve him of his guilt and to fulfill his longing. The Doctor finds the moonlight "a trifle spooky" (557); even the rational scientist has "the root of belief" (560) in him. But just as Bartlett wants none of facts, so the Doctor suppresses his inclination to dream. Nat, as we shall see, fights out the struggle between the two attitudes, moving from the Doctor's factual view to his father's dreamy one.

This is illustrated very well by Nat's preoccupation with the lantern in the cabin. As soon as he and the Doctor have entered the room, Nat suggests that the Doctor fetch the lantern from the sideboard. He then explains the symbolic significance of this act: "Understand that I want you to get all the facts—just that, facts!—and for that light is necessary. Without that—they become dreams up here—dreams, Doctor" (557). After which Nat proceeds to light the lantern. The dreamy moonlight gone, Nat can enlighten the Doctor about the facts concerning his father's insanity.

But Nat's alliance with the forces of light and reason is too demonstrative

[9] That moonlight had connotations of death to O'Neill appears from the fact that he at several times talked about ending his life by "swimming out into the wake of the moon" (Gelb, pp. 212, 642).

86

to ring true. When the Doctor leaves and Nat is alone, he *"goes over to the table, turning the lantern very low, and sits down, resting his elbow, his chin on his hand, staring somberly before him"* (562). The Doctor gone, Nat's rationality is dwindling. Action and position—doubly significant because of his solitude on the stage—proclaim him at heart a supporter of the father's dreamy obscurity. Nat's concern with the lantern thus reveals his divided nature, his conscious fight against the part in himself that is linked with the father and his dreams.

This fight culminates in a striking illustrative action, which again draws attention to the lantern. Sue, Nat's sister, appears. Like the Doctor she allies herself with reason, sanity, facts. But she combines this attitude with a genuine love both for her father and brother. Nat has shown the Doctor a map of the treasure island, which the father has given him as "heir to the secret" (560). The treasure may be a mad dream, he has told the Doctor, but the map is a fact; it exists. Now, as he confesses to Sue that the father has stolen his brain and made him heir to the mad dream, the map becomes the symbol of the obsession Nat wants to free himself of:

He opens the lantern and sets fire to the map in his hand. When he shuts the lantern again it flickers and goes out. ...) See how I free myself and become sane. ... It must all be destroyed—this poisonous madness (567).

The lighting tells us that Nat's attempt to set himself free has been in vain: when the map has burned to ashes, the dreamy moonlight again rules supreme in the cabin.

The light is now set for the appearance of the Captain, whose influence over the son immediately makes itself felt. Soon both men see the lost ship "clear in the moonlight" (569). To underline the intensity of their dream and to demonstrate that the root of belief is in all of us, O'Neill at this point visualizes the hypertrophied wish-thinking of father and son rather than Sue's matter-of-fact view (retained in the last act of *Gold* which corresponds to *Cross*). Hence we witness how *"a dense green glow floods slowly in rhythmic waves like a liquid into the room—as of great depths of the sea faintly penetrated by light"* (570). Nat's reaction clarifies the meaning of the green light:

(catching at his sister's hand—chokingly) See how the light changes! Green and gold! *(He shivers)* Deep under the sea! I've been drowned for years! *(Hysterically)* Save me! Save me! (570).

Marinely obscure, the green glow seems to signify Captain Bartlett's *idée fixe*. Nat has earlier revealed the close connection in his mind between the father and the sea: the father forced him to go to sea as a boy and the sea made him the cripple he now is, deprived of his right arm; "another one of *his* wrecks" (564), Nat bitterly comments, referring not only to the wrecked ship but also to the 'wrecked' mother. The green light thus visualizes the two forces that have crippled Nat: the sea and the Captain's obsession. The light is effective because the room in which it appears—so we must suppose—is a faithful copy of the cabin in the wrecked *Mary Allen*. When the drowned sailors come swaying into the 'cabin' as if swept by "*long swells of the deep sea*" (571), we have at once a picture of the fate they have met with and a parallel to Bartlett's and Nat's 'drowned' existence.

While Bartlett disappears on the 'bridge' with the three ghosts, the Doctor reappears and dispels the green light with his searching analytical light of reason:

HIGGINS. I can't see—where's my flash. Ah. (*He flashes it ... quickly around the room. The green glow disappears. ... Clear moonlight floods through the portholes.*) (572).

It is now Sue who lights the lantern. Bartlett is carried down dead. With brutal possessiveness Nat forces a crumpled ball of paper out of the dead man's hand. It is another map of the island, handed to Bartlett by one of the ghost sailors. Nat "*bends down and spreads it out in the light of the lantern ... There's still a chance—my chance!*" (573). Nat does not heed the light of reason and sanity any more. For Sue the map does not exist. Like the ghosts and the green light it is a product of a diseased mind. Nat is now truly "heir to the secret." The father has "stolen [his] brain" (567).

The most important aspect of the ghost scene is O'Neill's "experiment in treating the audience as insane" (O'Neill/Cargill et al., p. 102). Before this scene we trust the judgement of the rational characters (Dr. Higgins, Sue); the light change forces us to a sudden shift of ground and we now ally ourselves with those characters we have so far considered insane or at least mentally disturbed—or we cannot give credence to the testimony of our own eyes. The conflict between our knowledge that Sue sees things as they are and our awareness that we see things differently from her illustrates, in a most violent way, the clash between two visions of reality. The result is a radical blotting out of the border line between the normal and the abnormal.

Cross marks O'Neill's first attempt to work forcefully on the nerves of the audience, to include it as co-actor and thereby upset its conventional evaluation and gain a sense of universality for his theme. Yet the demonstration of how the root of belief, of dreams, of madness is in all of us fails, since Sue is inconsistently left out of this universal, hence 'normal,' abnormality. The different treatment of the corresponding scene in *Gold* suggests that O'Neill was aware of this flaw.

In *Misbegotten* we only gradually discover the meaning of the moonlight. At first it seems merely attractive, creating a beautiful and poetical setting for Jim's and Josie's odd romance. Then its connotations of death and guilt become clear. Finally, its connection with the dead mother is revealed when Josie says: "I feel her in the moonlight, her soul wrapped in it like a silver mantle, and I know she understands and forgives me, too, and her blessing lies on me" (152 f.). Josie's words relate directly to the play title; it is because the moon is related to the mother that it belongs in the play, shedding its blessed light on the two misbegotten ones. And it is for the same reason that Jim feels both attracted to and haunted by the moonlight. As a Christian emblem the moon represents the Virgin Mary, and the Catholic Josie seems to allude to this when she mentions the silver mantle. At the same time the full September moon has connotations of harvest, fertility, motherhood. It is because of this virgin-mother combination that the moon can be related both to Jim's mother, who was "pure of heart" (151)—hence spiritually a virgin —and to Josie, "who bears a dead child in the night" and yet remains "a virgin" (160). And it is this combination of maternity and purity that is the only form of love acceptable to the self-loathing Jim Tyrone.

The beautiful sunrise that ends the play is also the first sunrise in a life filled with gray dawns. It is clear that this dawn is different from all others not only because Jim has received absolution during the night preceding it and feels clean inside, but also because it signals the "promise of God's peace" (153), the final release from the gray turmoil of life.[1]

More unusual as a scenic device and apparently more disturbing to the playwright than any of the weather conditions dealt with so far, is the fog.[2]

In *Fog* the gradual dissolving of the fog is obviously O'Neill's device to bring the play to a conclusion—the rescue ship discovers the lifeboat when the fog has lifted—but the playwright has treated the weather condition as something more than a plot device. Two different aspects may be distinguished. First, the characters only gradually appear to the audience. In the beginning we see merely some shadowy figures. O'Neill indicates this by referring to the speaking characters as the "FIRST VOICE" and the "SECOND VOICE" (86 ff.). A little later we can make out their faces and are introduced to the "DARK MAN" and the "OTHER MAN" (91 f.). Finally, the dialogue helps to establish them as the "POET" and the "BUSINESSMAN" (92 ff.). This technique forewarns us that the play is not primarily about two individuals but about two outlooks: pessimistic altruism (Poet) versus optimistic egoism (Businessman).

---

[1] Cf. Jim's words about his dead mother: "Free at last. Free from worry. From pain" (147).

[2] Louis Kalonyme has related that fog made O'Neill uneasy (Gelb, p. 474).

The gradual disclosure of the men's contrasting appearances corresponds to our gradual understanding of their inner natures. The second aspect is related to the fog as a symbol: the play opens in gray dawn with a *"still"* sea, a *"dense"* fog and *"a menacing silence, like the genius of the fog"* (85); it ends in sunrise, the white iceberg now appearing *"vivid"* and beginning to melt (102), and a *"fresh morning breeze"* rippling the water (107).

This movement from something deathlike to something lifelike fits the situation of the two men, who dwell in the shadow of death next to the iceberg, but who are finally saved and brought back to life. To the Businessman, who is not inclined to see beyond physical surface reality, this is the only meaning the fog has; he curses it solely as a threat to his life. The Poet dislikes it for quite another reason. He fears not death but life. The fog signifies for him both the meaninglessness of human existence and the attitude largely responsible for this meaninglessness, an attitude here represented by the Businessman; says the Poet:

... supposing we—the self-satisfied, successful members of society—are responsible for the injustice visited upon the head of our less fortunate "brothers-in-Christ" because of our shameful indifference to it. We see misery all around us and we do not care. We do nothing to prevent it. Are we not then, in part at least, responsible for it? (90).

The Poet is not talking in the abstract; he is commenting on the life possibilities of their fellow-passenger, the dead Child.

The Businessman in *Fog* is a cruel egotist, indifferent to his family but keenly interested in his business, which he characteristically refers to as his "child" (91). It is this indifference, this disregard for the golden rule of Christianity, which, visualized in the cold, menacing fog,[3] really kills the woman and her child.[4] It is because he sees it as signifying human selfishness that the Poet shows little hope that the fog will lift—until life is over. His remark on man's difficulty to "see the sun on account of the fog" (87) has a moral and religious implication.

[3] This is presumably what Winther means by his somewhat vague remark (p. 119) that the Businessman "has a mental outlook enveloped in a deeper fog than that which surrounds the drifting life-boat." Falk's view (p. 19) that the fog represents "ignorance and fear" seems less apt.

[4] *Fog* seems transparently autobiographical. The Connecticut Businessman may be seen as a portrait of O'Neill's father, who was not merely an actor but also a land speculator. The Poet is obviously a self-portrait. The poor woman crying over her dead child is, I take it, O'Neill's mother bemoaning her son Edmund, who died when he was "not yet a year and a half" (Gelb, p. 53). It was in connection with Eugene's birth that his mother became acquainted with morphine. It seems highly credible that O'Neill already in *Fog,* as later in *Journey,* has been thinking of the fog in terms of his mother's morphinism and the family tragedy this led to and for which the father was, perhaps, most responsible.

When the fog finally does lift, it is not because the Businessman's attitude has changed. Rather, it is the Child who, in acknowledgement of the Poet's genuine concern for him, saves the men. Although both men assert that the Child has been dead for twenty-four hours, the rescuing crew claim that it is the crying of the Child that has guided them to the lifeboat. The Poet reveals that he is prepared to believe in the miracle, whereas the Businessman considers it "almost unbelievable" (107).

The association of this with that other, familiar miracle—Christ's resurrection—is apt. The poor peasant woman and her dead Child, which, *"wrapped in a white shawl"* (96), she clutches to her, form a kind of pietà grouping, and this was no ordinary death; says the Poet: "It was the most horrible thing I have ever seen or even heard of. I never dreamed anything could be so full of tragedy" (87). But the Child's "weird" crying (105) transcends death and saves the 'murderer' (the Businessman). The final sunrise is that of resurrection; it is also that of Love and Grace.

The indifference of the Businessman and the concern of the Poet have their counterparts in *Cardiff,* where the robust unconcern of the seamates with regard to the dying Yank is set off against Driscoll's anxiety. The tramp steamer is midway between New York and Cardiff; it is *"a foggy night"* (477), the steamer's whistle tells us, and the outer fog is visible also in the forecastle: *"Four of the men are pulling on pipes and the air is heavy with rancid tobacco smoke"* (477).[5] The fog presents a very real danger to the sailors, since it increases the risk of shipwreck. Driscoll, in fact, relates how he and Yank have earlier suffered a shipwreck on "such a night as this" (481). This sets the men on edge and they curse the fog. For Yank the fog has its special significance. Since it retards the crossing to Cardiff (481), where he can get proper medical treatment, it is partly to blame if he dies and has to be buried at sea.

The fog is slowly closing in on Yank, shutting out hope both for survival and burial on dry land. Cocky reports from the alleyway that "the fog's thick as soup" (482) and a little later Yank asks: "How'd all the fog git in here?" (487). It is, of course, the tobacco smoke which he mistakes for the fog; the smoke thus comes to illustrate the direct bearing of the fog on Yank's fate; his death struggle may be said to begin with a hallucinatory awareness of the fog. At the same time it suggests that the mates are 'producing' the fog, that their indifference to Yank's fate—they joke and laugh and snore in his presence—intensifies his life sickness, breaks down his resistance against death and thus, in a sense, kills him. It seems in this context significant that

[5] The longhand draft has *"black"* instead of *"heavy."* Both adjectives fit the nightly fog outside.

four of the five men sitting in the forecastle are smoking; the nonsmoker, we may guess, is Driscoll, Yank's close friend.

Representing an attitude of lovelessness found in most men the fog is an essential feature of life; that Yank's life has been fog-bound in this sense he himself makes plain. But the fog also represents the death struggle, when the eyesight grows faint and we fear the unknown.[6] Cocky's announcement the minute after Yank has given up the ghost verifies that Yank's death coincides with the dissolving of the fog. Yank's last words, his vision of "a pretty lady dressed in black" (489),[7] imply, in fact, the same, for with the lifting of the fog, the starlit night has again become visible, "pretty" and "black" like the lady. This means a fulfillment of Yank's wish that the stars and the moon were out to "make it easier to go" (489) and an answer to Driscoll's "*half-remembered prayer*" (490) for the soul of the man who once saved his life. In Yank's death there is the suggestion of release and resurrection (cf. Skinner, p. 42; Koischwitz, p. 106; Falk, p. 22).

The fog appears also in another *Glencairn* play: *Voyage*. In a low London dive, "*dimly lighted*" and smoky (493), Ivan drinks himself into a coma— he is referred to as "a blarsted corpse" (503)—and Olson, the protagonist, is drugged into unconsciousness. Both are, in other words, reduced to a state of befoggedness.

It is when Ivan is carried away and Olson opens the door that we discover the nightly fog outside; says Freda: "Fur Gawd's sake, shet that door! I'm fair freezin' to death wiv the fog" (504). The fog obviously carries connotations of death. When Olson has just emptied the drug, he unwittingly pronounces his own death sentence: "... I pity poor fallers make dat trip round Cape Stiff dis time year. I bet you some of dem never see port once again" (507). The implication is apparently that the *Amindra*, the "damn ship" (507) Olson is carried to after he has been shanghaied, is in for a fog-bound trip ending in shipwreck and death. The play title and Olson's final words—"I go home" (508)—are both ironical and prophetic; the long voyage has for its goal the ultimate home: death.

Old Chris Christopherson in *Christie* could have been one of the sailors on board the *S. S. Glencairn* had he not given up deepwater sailing. Back in New

---

[6] In a letter to his wife Agnes (7.29.[1920]) describing his father's death struggle, O'Neill talks about the father's soul as suspended "in that veiled borderland between Life and Death." Cf. also the following lines in *Fountain:* "Death is a mist / Veiling sunrise" (441).

[7] The longhand draft has it: "A pretty lady all in black." In the forementioned letter O'Neill speaks of "the soft beauty of Death." Cf. also Juan's words to the Figure of Death in *Fountain:* "Delightful Lady, you are enigmatic" (438).

York from one of his coastal trips he complains: "Ve make slow voyage—dirty vedder—yust fog, fog, fog, all bloody time!" (7). Chris thus appears, as it were, out of the fog. His dark suit, his faded gray cap and his befogged state of mind—he has just emptied half a bottle of whiskey—make him part of the outer gloom.

In Act II, set on Chris' barge, the fog is made visible:

It is ten o'clock at night. Dense fog shrouds the barge on all sides, and she floats motionless in a calm. ...

As the curtain rises, ANNA *is discovered. ... She is staring out into the fog astern with an expression of awed wonder* (25).

The darkness, the sickly lights on board the barge, the stillness, broken only by the *"doleful tolling of bells"* (25)—everything speaks of death. Scenery and lighting set the right mood for Chris' keening to Anna about the men in the family who have died at sea—a fate that has befallen all except one (27)—and for Mat's report of the many who were drowned in the shipwreck he has survived (36). Yet to Anna the fog and the sea have only positive connotations:

... why d'you s'pose I feel so—so—like I'd found something I'd missed and been looking for—'s if this was the right place for me to fit in? And I seem to have forgot—everything that's happened—like it didn't matter no more. And I feel clean, somehow—like you feel yust after you've took a bath (28).

Anna, in other words, suffers a sea change; the fog purifies her of her former prostituted life ashore[8] and mystically reunites her with her seafaring ancestors. For the first time Anna affirms the sea that is in her blood; it brings her a sense of belonging. She is exultant when she declares her love for the fog, which, "funny and still," takes her "out of things altogether" (25).[9] Her experience of the fog—a rapturous feeling of annihilation of the self—comes exceedingly close to such joyous deaths as Robert Mayo's and Juan Ponce de Leon's (*Fountain*).

After the sunny interlude of Act III the nightly fog returns in the final act, displaying Chris' cabin. The room must be fairly dark, for it is lit only by a small lamp. Chris' first words—"It's foggy" (63)—draw attention to the weather outside as well as to his own befogged state of mind. They set the

---

[8] In the longhand draft Anna is even more explicit. She tells Chris not to bring up the past, which she wants to forget: "That's why this fog gets me. It seems to wipe it all out, somehow, I feel as if—I'd always been out here—and nothing had ever happened" (= 26).

[9] The longhand draft has it: "out of the world altogether." O'Neill may have had his own ecstatic experiences at sea in mind when he wrote this line; or he may have been thinking of his mother's morphinism or attempt to drown herself (*Journey*, 118).

tone for the act, which also ends with Chris' ominous reference to the fog, the closing lines of the play:

(*looking out into the night—lost in his somber preoccupation—shakes his head and mutters*) Fog, fog, fog, all bloody time. You can't see vhere you vas going, no. Only dat ole davil, sea—she knows! (*The two stare at him. From the harbor comes the muffled, mournful wail of steamers' whistles.*) (78).

Chris' words may be taken in a general sense as a warning to Anna and Mat that their happiness is merely momentary, that life is full of miseries and that there is sure to be one waiting around the corner. However, since the basis for Chris' pessimism is his awareness of the family fate, it seems clear that his and Anna's renewed bond with the sea—his decision to sign on a ship again and her decision to marry a sailor—means an acceptance of the family fate: death at sea and widowhood.

O'Neill evidently did not want Anna's and Mat's happiness to speak louder than Chris' gloom. Rather, he wished Chris to take on the stature—if not the dignity—of an ominous sooth-sayer, expressing a truth which concerns them all.[1] As he himself pointed out (O'Neill 12.18.1921, 6, p. 1), he had Mat for the first time agree with Chris' somber notions; Anna, too, as her forced optimism reveals, is affected. Yet we cannot speak of a conversion on Anna's part to Chris' view. Her positive attitude to the fog and the sea remain essentially the same. As a result, we are left at the end with the question whether the sea means good or not. And our divided attitude to the fog is never resolved. The fog remains—and O'Neill probably meant it so—mysterious.[2]

The close connection between homecoming, death, water and fog that we have noted especially with regard to Olson and Anna, is found in *Jones* too. Brutus Jones echoes Anna, when he returns to the spot where he had entered the forest: "seems like I been heah befo'" (200). In front of him is the calm

---

[1] Winther's interpretation of the fog as representing the "fog of ignorance" clouding Chris' vision (p. 271) comes close to reducing Chris to a mental case and is insufficient as an explanation of the significance of the play ending.

[2] The end did not come easily to O'Neill. Two versions precede the final one. The first is discussed by Bogard (pp. 69 f.). It shows Mat opposing Chris' fatalism with his own belief that "the sea means good." And Anna, agreeing, ends the play laughing. In the second version O'Neill strengthens the tragic note. Mat now agrees with Chris. Anna alone tries to remain optimistic, but her optimism is forced.

In the play the closing lines are given to Chris. Instead of having Anna refer verbally to a funeral (as she does in the second version), O'Neill creates a funereal mood by visual and aural means. Chris opens the door, so that we can see the dark fog outside and hear all the louder the *"mournful wail"* of the steamers' whistles. It gives impact to his closing lines.

surface of a river, presumably symbolizing life,[3] *"blotted out and merged into a veil of bluish mist in the distance"* (199). This is the place where Jones is fated to die.

Again, in Act VIII of *Interlude,* a *"soft golden haze"* glowing over a river (158) announces the impending death of Sam Evans. And Orin's killing of the Rebels (*Electra*) characteristically occurred in "a thick mist" which was "so still you could hear the fog seeping into the ground" (95). The weather condition expresses the state of mind of the victims, whose eyes "dimmed and went out" (95). But since Orin's killing is in the nature of a spiritual suicide, the deathly fog has a direct bearing upon his own state of mind.

The fog, it appears, is a comprehensive and complex symbol with O'Neill. In all the plays we have considered, it can be seen as a symbol of the "veiled borderland between Life and Death," for in all of them the fog is connected either with violent deaths or with forebodings of such deaths. In some of them it can, in addition, be taken to represent the (seeming) meaninglessness and cruelty of life, our helpless groping through existence. In all these cases the fog is viewed either impartially or negatively. Only Anna Christie takes a positive attitude to the fog. In part this is so because to her the fog, as we have seen, holds a somewhat special meaning: it at once wipes out her dreary past and reunites her with her ancestors. But in addition to this there is the suggestion that Anna loves the fog because it blots out the world altogether, that, sick of life, she welcomes the separation from it that fog allows her to experience.

Anna's attitude is very like Mary Tyrone's in *Journey,* where the fog becomes a dominant leitmotif. The weather progression is one from morning sunshine (Act I) to *"faint haziness"* (Act II.1) around lunch time; the haze becomes increasingly dense in the early afternoon (Act II.2) and thickens into fog later in the day (98); in the early evening the fog resembles *"a white curtain drawn outside the windows"* (Act III); and around midnight *"the wall of fog appears denser than ever"* (Act IV).

The gradual thickening of the fog outside has an obvious counterpart in the gradually befogged state of mind of the Tyrone household. It is presumably after Mary has taken a morphine injection and while the men start their drinking that the sky begins to turn hazy (Act II.1). During the following scene Mary has another injection. In the opening of the third act the servants drink whiskey, and Cathleen, affected by it, begins to think *"hazily"* (101). Meanwhile the men are drinking in town, and Tyrone and Edmund continue to do so after they get home. Between Acts III and IV Edmund visits the inn

---

[3] Cf. *Marco,* where Kublai speaks of "the river of man's life so deep and silent" (385).

twice and procures more drinks, while Tyrone, left alone in the living room, goes on drinking as the *"three-quarters empty"* whiskey bottle and Tyrone's *"misted"* look at the opening of Act IV (125) bear witness. In this act Jamie returns home intoxicated and joins Edmund and Tyrone, who are by now nearly as drunk as he is, in a continued orgy. Shortly before the final curtain we see three drunken men with filled glasses before them in frozen stillness listening to a woman who, dulled by morphine, dreams aloud, hidden in "a bank of fog" (139) as impenetrable as the outer *"wall of fog"* (125).

All this seems clear enough. But what are we to make of the night preceding the long day? We learn that it was a foggy one, and that Mary spent it in the spare room, where she always takes her injections. Jamie obviously suspects that she has relapsed into her earlier morphinism during the previous night (38).

Although O'Neill does not make the matter completely clear, Mary's negative reaction to the fog of the preceding night, which contrasts with her love of it during the night following the long day, indicates that she has kept away from the drug. Only if we assume this does the morning sunshine harmonize with Mary's state of mind. From a psychological and dramaturgical point of view it is also more satisfactory to imagine that Mary does not take her first injection until lunch time (between Acts I and II.1). For then it would be the unjustified suspicions of the men, especially of Edmund, that drive her to a relapse; their responsibility is increased, and Mary's addiction truly comes to constitute a family fate not only in its effect but also in its cause. Moreover, with this view the inescapability of the past is stressed: it is because they cannot forget all the earlier dope periods that the men cannot help being suspicious. We end up with an inextricable web of guilt.[4]

All the characters comment on the fog; it gives a sense of universality to it. Three of them pay only passing attention to it. There is Tyrone's hopeful remark in Act I that the spell of fog "is over now" (40), which draws attention to Mary's earlier spells of morphinism. There is Cathleen's description in Act III of the chauffeur's reckless driving through the fog, which endangered her own and her mistress' lives (98). And there is Jamie's complaint in Act IV that the front steps "took advantage of fog to waylay" him (155). That the misty car ride and Jamie's stumbling on the front steps should be understood symbolically seems clear from Edmund's reference to life as a fog in

[4] The notes for the play show that O'Neill at least originally had this view in mind. There it is made clear that Mary arouses the suspicions of her family simply "by suspecting they have them"; what really happened in the night was this: "she had been frantic—given in—gone to bathroom—spareroom—then, thinking of Edmund, for his sake had conquered craving which was brought on by continual worry about him—at end, she tells Edmund this—he wants believe but can't help suspecting—it is this lack of faith in him, combined with growing fear, which makes her give in—."

which "you stumble on toward nowhere, for no good reason" (153), an echo of Chris' view. Cathleen and Jamie give concrete examples of man's erratic, fumbling, dangerous "journey" through life.

It is Mary and especially Edmund, the nervous and sensitive family members, who react most intensely to the fog and see in it a significance that the others only vaguely sense. Mary's attitude to the fog is at first negative: "Thank heavens, the fog is gone" (17). At the end of Act I she still supports her husband in his claim that the spell of fog is over, but we note that Tyrone only pretends to be "sure" that his prediction is right and that Mary only hopes it is (40). A little later she is sure of the opposite as she, wishing to dismiss two spies, tells Jamie and Tyrone to go out and cut the hedge: "... take advantage of the sunshine before the fog comes back. (*Strangely, as if talking aloud to herself*) Because I know it will" (41). Mary is perhaps contemplating an injection already at this point; the suspicions of the men are hard for her to bear. But it is Edmund's manifest suspicions that break her; she dismisses him with the same advice with which she sent off the others: "It would be much better for you to go out in the fresh air and sunshine" (49). It is as though Mary, feeling the fog closing in on herself, wanted to send her family away to some healthier climate; it is a kind of leave-taking.

In Act II.1 they all discover Mary's relapse. Tyrone admits he has been a bad weather prophet:

TYRONE. ... We're in for another night of fog, I'm afraid.
MARY. Oh, well, I won't mind it tonight.
TYRONE. No, I don't imagine you will, Mary (82).

With the drug in her system Mary will be attuned to the fog. After another shot she not only accepts it but loves it: "It hides you from the world and the world from you. You feel that everything has changed, and nothing is what it seemed to be. No one can find or touch you any more" (98). The fog functions as a protective mask as does the drug; both wipe out the guilty past and the surrounding world reminding you of it. Yet a little later she has come back to her initial dislike:

It's such a dismal, foggy evening (108).

It's very dreary and sad to be here alone in the fog with night falling (112).

Why is it fog makes everything sound so sad and lost, I wonder? (121).

The reason for this change is not hard to find; Mary tells us herself: "I must go upstairs. I haven't taken enough" (107). But she is prevented from taking more by the return of Tyrone and Edmund. With the drug slipping out of her system the old horror of the fog makes itself doubly felt. At her final appearance she significantly makes no comment on the fog, because she is now wholly a part of it.[5]

Edmund, whose illness seems as fatal as the mother's, also changes his attitude toward the fog. But with him the reason for the change is not physiological. It is rather the result of a changed life perspective. As we have seen, life is to him a lonely stumbling through a blinding fog. But this characterization is part of what we might call his spiritual obituary, for Edmund by this time is convinced that he is going to die. He has lived, he finds, only for a few seconds; for the rest he has merely existed. Only rarely has the solitary and miserable wandering through the mist of life been lit up by moments of joy and a sense of belonging. Such is Edmund's past experience of the atmospheric conditions. His present one is somewhat different. Returning from his walk along the beach he declares:

The fog was where I wanted to be. ... Everything looked and sounded unreal. Nothing was what it is. That's what I wanted—to be alone with myself in another world where truth is untrue and life can hide from itself. ... The fog and the sea seemed part of each other. It was like walking on the bottom of the sea. As if I had drowned long ago. As if I was a ghost belonging to the fog, and the fog was the ghost of the sea. It felt damned peaceful to be nothing more than a ghost within a ghost (131).

It is obvious that Edmund is not talking here about the fog as a symbol of life, as a "veil of things" (153); on the contrary, the fog is now opposed to "life as it is" (131), softening, changing or hiding its harsh contours; it is the pipe dream weather. The description resembles to a certain extent the one of his "high spots" (153); again it is a mystic experience connected with the sea, resulting in a peaceful sense of belonging to something outside oneself. But this time the element of death contained in all his earlier revelatory experiences of belonging—Edmund himself declares that he "must always be a little in love with death" (154)—is more pronounced. When he takes his beach walk he knows that the father has virtually condemned him to death for a piece of land. Is it any wonder, then, that he feels as though he "had drowned," that the fog comes to mean death rather than life and that, considering his inherent death longing, he welcomes it?

It will be seen that, depending on whether we include the preceding night or not, we may speak either of a linear development from light to darkness or of a circular progression from foggy night through sunny daylight back into foggy night. I believe O'Neill had both movements in mind when he composed his play. He needed a distinct contrast between hopeful beginning and tragic end; this light development which is the visible one as well as

---

[5] Cf. O'Neill's notes for this act: "Dense fog, black night—M[ary]. exults in it—it is in her—cannot see an instant of future—it is all dream, nothing is what it is—."

the one indicated in the play title is highly suitable to O'Neill's technique in the play, which is that of gradual revelation; it limits itself to the long day of life, to what we know about; and it is a movement of despair. But O'Neill presumably also wanted to suggest that however hopeless our life may seem, it is perhaps only our lack of vision that makes us deem it so. Could we but see what has gone before and what comes after we might judge it otherwise. The circular composition reminds us, in the words of Dowson as quoted by Edmund, that

> They are not long, the days of wine and roses:
> Out of a misty dream
> Our path emerges for a while, then closes
> Within a dream (130).

And Shakespeare, as quoted by Tyrone, says something similar: "We are such stuff as dreams are made on, and our little life is rounded with a sleep" (131). Taken in its widest, cosmic sense the fog, I believe, is O'Neill's visual approximation to Dowson's "misty dream" and Shakespeare's "sleep." Life is only a long day,[6] a "strange interlude" between two periods hidden to our sight as in a fog.

Although the outer light conditions attract the major attention in *Journey,* the interior lighting is by no means unimportant. The light equipment in the Tyrone living room is rather conspicuous: "*At center is a round table with a green shaded reading lamp, the cord plugged in one of the four sockets in the chandelier above*" (12). The comparable stage direction in *Wilderness* for the Miller sitting-room reads almost the same—with one notable difference: there are five sockets in the Miller chandelier (185). The difference may seem a trifle but is not without interest. Since no particular attention is given to the interior lighting in *Wilderness,* it seems likely that O'Neill in his comedy of remembrance was drawing on the actual number of sockets in the chandelier of the O'Neill living room in New London, the model for both settings. The question then arises: why did he change the number to four in *Journey?* The answer is given as we read on in the stage directions for the play: "*Around the table within reading-light range are four chairs, three of them wicker armchairs, the fourth (at right front of table) a varnished oak rocker with leather bottom*" (12). Even when he discusses the furniture arrangement O'Neill is concerned with the lighting—another touch lacking in the *Wilderness* description. There is an obvious correspondence between the four chairs, one of which is singled out from the others, and the four lamps of which, again, one is singled out from the rest.[7] By its position the reading lamp

---

[6] Cf. the words of the sage in *Marco:* "every day is a life in miniature" (402).

[7] In *Wilderness* there are, similarly, five chairs around the table corresponding to the five sockets in the chandelier.

suggests isolation, by its obscure green light dreaminess. In the opening of the final act it is the only light in the room and Tyrone sits close to it, alone, playing solitaire. Midway in the act Edmund's pantheistic experiences at sea—all occurring when he has been separate from others—are rendered vivid by its green light. And at the end of the play, when Mary takes leave of her three men and places herself away from them for her final dreaming aloud, we strongly identify her with the table lamp which is only tenuously connected with the three bulbs up above.

Quite naturally it is not until darkness has fallen that the interior lighting comes into focus. Left alone in the growing darkness, Mary suddenly hears Tyrone and Edmund returning:

TYRONE. Are you there, Mary? (*The light in the hall is turned on and shines through the front parlor to fall on Mary.*)
MARY. (*rises from her chair, her face lighting up lovingly—with excited eagerness*) I'm here, dear. In the living room. I've been waiting for you (108).

With the arrival of the men the darkness around Mary is scattered; and the light from the hall, reflected in Mary's face, establishes a visual rapport between husband and wife supplementing their verbal one; it is the light of love shining through the darkness (cf. the dedication preceding the play).

Tyrone's miserliness ordinarily causes him to use as little electricity as possible. He sticks to the one bulb principle as firmly as to the one dollar rule. And as with the dollar he learned his lesson once and for all as a child, working in a machine shop "where the only light came through two small filthy windows, so on grey days I'd have to sit bent over with my eyes almost touching the files in order to see!" (148). Compared to this the light of even a single lamp appears a luxury. When his wife and sons ridicule him for his stinginess concerning electricity, they are doing far more than criticizing a limited and isolated failing. For his stinginess in this area has its more serious counterparts in others. The reason O'Neill makes much of Tyrone's attempt to save on electricity is that it gives him unusual opportunities to illustrate the father's miserliness theatrically. When Edmund returns home in the final act and hurts his knee in the dark hall, we have an example of how Tyrone's stinginess leads directly to physical suffering. The trivial incident parallels and takes its meaning from Tyrone's decision a few hours earlier to save on Edmund by sending him to a cheap sanatorium where he is almost bound to die. Edmund resents his father's miserliness not only because he is himself made a victim to it but also because it perverts Tyrone's vision. In an attempt to break through to the son and conquer his own greed and distorted vision Tyrone lights the three bulbs in the chandelier and, with the lights on, proceeds to disclose to Edmund what he has "never admitted to anyone before": that his life has been a moral failure. Yet as soon as the revelation has been made, he fears the son's contempt and reverts to the dreamy light of pretense:

The glare from those extra lights hurts my eyes. You don't mind if I turn them out, do you? We don't need them, and there's no use making the Electric Company rich.

    EDMUND. (*controlling a wild impulse to laugh—agreeably*) No, sure not. Turn them out.

    TYRONE. (*gets heavily and a bit waveringly to his feet and gropes uncertainly for the lights—his mind going back to its line of thought*) No, I don't know what the hell it was I wanted to buy. (*He clicks out one bulb.*) On my solemn oath, Edmund, I'd gladly face not having an acre of land to call my own, nor a penny in the bank—(*He clicks out another bulb.*) I'd be willing to have no home but the poorhouse in my old age if I could look back now on having been the fine artist I might have been. (*He turns out the third bulb, so only the reading lamp is on, and sits down again heavily.*) (151).

Since Tyrone's action blatantly contradicts his words without his sensing it, we are given an ironical picture of his inability to distinguish between what he is and what he imagines himself to be, of how completely he is ruled by his past. While his words suggest self-sacrifice, his action shows him as sacrificing the other family members. His past dooms him to assert himself at the expense of others, even those who are close to him; and so he plunges his family into darkness.

Paradoxically, the long day's journey into *night* as far as the interior lighting is concerned is a journey into light: apart from the reading lamp and chandelier in the living room, the five-bulb-chandelier in the front parlor is shining, lit by Mary shortly before the end. The front parlor, as we have noted before, is essentially Mary's room and it has connotations of past happiness to her. It therefore seems reasonable to assume that the five bulbs represent *all* the Tyrones, that is, including Eugene, the dead child who is still very much 'alive' to Mary. Behind the four somewhat dissociated lamps in the living room representing the living present, we see the five 'united' front parlor bulbs reminding us of the harmony that might have been.

Both the exterior and the interior lighting receive great attention in *Electra*. The exterior light sequence is carefully patterned. Part I opens "*shortly before sunset*" (Act I), progresses towards sunset and twilight (Act II) to moonlit night (Act III) and dawn (Act IV). Part II is set on two consecutive moonlit nights. Part III opens "*shortly after sunset*" (Act I), progresses towards black night (Acts II–III) to sunlit "*late afternoon*" (Act IV). It will appear from this, that no act is set in broad daylight, and that the Mannons move from initial sunlight through a nocturnal period back to sunlight. The two glimpses of light in the middle acts—the dawn of Part I.IV and the sunset glow of Part III.I—provide no light for the Mannons; in the former act the closed shutters only permit a little light to enter Ezra's bedroom (58); in the latter Lavinia and Orin do not appear until it has grown dark (132, 137).

The meaning of this light sequence is found in Orin's clairvoyant words: "I hate the daylight. It's like an accusing eye! No, we've renounced the day, in which normal people live—or rather it has renounced us. Perpetual night—darkness of death in life—that's the fitting habitat for guilt" (150). If the middle acts may be said to represent the life-denying puritan mind and the deeds of darkness it gives rise to, the framing sunlight acts may be taken to visualize the sinless, pagan love of Nature embraced by the islanders. On the islands, Brant recalls, the sun is "drowsing in your blood" (24), that is, man experiences God inside him in a kind of Dionysian rapture. A similar drunken, "drowsing" effect seems conveyed in the opening and closing acts by the soft, luminous sunlight *"mist"* (5, 169), which is rejected by the Mannon windows but embraced by Christine in the first and by Lavinia in the last act.[8]

"A house drunk with sun" is precisely what we see at the beginning of Part I.II, where the glow of the setting sun fills Ezra's study (28). Christine's spirit still rules the house; the light is warm; God still seems benevolent. But the light changes: *"As the action progresses this [the glow] becomes brighter, then turns to crimson, which darkens to somberness at the end"* (28). Although O'Neill does not indicate exactly when the light changes occur, the subject matter of the act provides relatively safe indications. Thus the light becomes painfully bright, we may assume, as Lavinia plays the judge to her mother, virtually reducing Christine to a prisoner. It turns crimson as Christine, in revolt against this 'imprisonment,' makes up her mind to kill Ezra and plots the murder with Brant.[9] And it *"darkens to somberness"* as she is left alone, an ageing woman with a deed of darkness on her mind. Thus, ironically, we witness how Christine's struggle for light only brings on the darkness.

Beginning to fall as Christine unwittingly succumbs to the evil Mannon spirit, the darkness grows into night, the "fitting habitat" of the Mannons, as Ezra returns home. Yet Ezra's life of "perpetual night" is soon to be replaced by the light beyond death; he dies at daybreak (58).

In Part II, opening two days after Ezra's death, the moonlight, which earlier seemed romantic and "beautiful" (46 f.) to Christine, so like the warm moon-

[8] The Dionysian nature of Lavinia's sun worship is verbally clarified in the first typewritten version, where she says: "I want a house drunk with the sun so that you forget men's roofs and ceilings and walls and think of the blue sky" (= 170).

[9] Raleigh notes (p. 55) that the crimson sky signifies death. It seems more apt to say that it signifies violent death, murder.

light over the islands (112), she now finds chilly (77) and haunting (73). These remarks prepare for the sharp light division in Part II.V:

The moon has just risen. The right half of the house is in the black shadow cast by the pine trees but the moonlight falls full on the part to the left of the door-way. ...

CHRISTINE *is discovered walking back and forth on the drive before the portico, passing from moonlight into the shadow of the pines and back again. She is in a frightful state of tension, unable to keep still* (117).

On the left, we know, are the innocent life values: the flower garden, the lilac shrubbery. On the right are the guilty death values: the Mannon portraits, the pine grove. The lighting underlines this stage symbolism. In the opening of the trilogy we found Christine an ally of the light. Once her crime was conceived, she became associated with the darkness. Now, when the crime has been executed, we find her torn between the two, no longer belonging in the innocent life realm on the left and fighting desperately against the guilty death realm on the right.[1] Haunted by the island moonlight and the avenging Mannon furies, she can find no peace—until she faces her guilt and thereby frees herself from it. She does it by killing herself before the portrait of her husband-victim, now her judge, in the moonlit study. Death being her atonement she is brought away from the avenging furies; at last she belongs wholly to the light.

Adam, too, finds a death in light. Falling down by the Mannon pine table in the cabin of the "Flying Trades," he dies directly below the skylight letting in the moonlight (109, 114).

More deeply plunged in guilt than their parents, Lavinia and Orin are victims of a more impenetrable darkness:

LAVINIA. It's black as pitch tonight. There isn't a star.
ORIN. (*somberly*) Darkness without a star to guide us! Where are we going, Vinnie? (151).

Ezra and Christine still had the moonlight; Orin's and Lavinia's night is a night without hope.

Like his mother, Orin can see no way out of the darkness but death. O'Neill was here faced with an intricate problem. How could he show that Orin's death, which takes place at night, is as much a journey into light as are those of the other Mannons? To change the lighting in the act was impossible. Thus, since it could not be suggested visually, it had to be done verbally. Awaiting Orin's death Lavinia cries out:

[1] Koischwitz (p. 69) sees the darkness and light as representing the hellish and heavenly powers at war within Christine.

I love everything that grows simply—up toward the sun—everything that's straight and strong! I hate what's warped and twists and eats into itself and dies for a lifetime in shadow. ... I can't bear waiting—waiting and waiting and waiting—! (*There is a muffled shot from the study across the hall.*) (167).

What Lavinia here expresses "*hysterically*" in words, Orin performs off-stage in action. Her anguish is his; he, even more than she, cannot "bear waiting" for the sun. Facing his victim—the mother—in death, his suicide is a recognition of his guilt; the furies are appeased, and as his life ceases, the darkness, we may assume, gives way to the redemptive light.

The final sunlight act parallels and contrasts with the initial one. Christine's struggle for light and air—so the lighting of the opening acts told us—was precarious but not hopeless—until she decided to get what she wanted through murder. After three 'murders' Lavinia's parallel struggle in the final act is doomed from the outset. We see it in her costume, pitch-black like the Mannon night, and in her eyes which, like the windows of the house, reject the sunlight (169 f.), then close it out altogether (171), leaving her soul in the same darkness which she shortly proclaims on the interior of the house by ordering the shutters closed "so no sunlight can ever get in" (178). Since it is "*late afternoon*" (169), we know that the interior darkness will soon be matched by an exterior one. Lavinia, as Orin had predicted, cannot escape the "fitting habitat for guilt"; the rest of her life will be a "perpetual night."

Yet it is significant that while the coming darkness is implied, it is not *visibly* suggested. For on the metaphysical level the trilogy ends in light as it began in light, visualizing man's journey from birth through life to rebirth, from belonging through isolation to renewed belonging. Beyond the strange dark interlude of life, separating us from the eternal, benevolent, divine light, Lavinia too will find, in recompense for her earthly suffering, her islands of light and love.[2] As Hazel tells her: "... I know your conscience will make you do what's right—and God will forgive you" (174).

Orin not only explains the significance of the exterior darkness; he also makes the meaning of the interior light—he is sitting close to a table lamp in his father's old study—emphatically clear:

... I find artificial light more appropriate for my work—man's light, not God's —man's feeble striving to understand himself, to exist for himself in the darkness! It's a symbol of his life—a lamp burning out in a room of waiting shadows! (150).

[2] Cf. Stark Young's review (p. 139) of the original production: "When the play ended, and the last Mannon was gone into the house, the door shut, I felt ... that the Erinyes were appeased, and that the Eumenides, the Gentle Ones, passed over the stage."

A lamp—or a candle. Before Ezra is murdered, he performs a significant illustrative act:

MANNON. We'd better light the light and talk a while.
CHRISTINE. (*with dread*) I don't want to talk! I prefer the dark.
MANNON. I want to see you. (*He takes matches from the stand by the bed and lights the candle on it. ... His face, with the flickering candlelight on its side, has a grim, bitter expression*) You like the dark where you can't see your old man of a husband, is that it? (59).

At the outset of the play, we recall, Christine was linked with the light; while Ezra, when he first appeared, advertized his belonging to the darkness by stopping in the shade (46). Now we find their traditional alliances reversed. Christine, we have already observed, began to move towards the Mannon darkness of hatred and guilt the moment she decided to trap her lover by making him an accomplice in her murder. Ezra, on the other hand, sickened by his professional 'murdering' in the war, has moved from his ancestral death worship towards the light of love and life. There is a stark irony in this reversal of roles, in the fact that Christine, the amateur murderer, kills Ezra, the professional one, precisely when he reveals himself willing to surrender to her original life affirmation.

Ezra has thus come home determined to understand and love Christine (55). But he needs her help to kindle the ashes of their love; together they must "light the light" and make life liveable. Yet it is Ezra alone who lights the candle. The table lamp next to Christine (58 f.) remains unlit. Christine, as Ezra rightly assumes, does not want to understand him; shortly—as the flickering candlelight indicates—she is to blow out his life flame.

Lamp and candles return in the *lit-de-parade* scene (Part II.III). Behind Ezra's corpse, laid out in his study, there are *"two stands of three lighted candles ... at each end of the black marble chimneypiece, throwing their light above on the portrait and below on the dead man"* (93). The six white candles on the black marble chimneypiece clearly correspond to the six white columns of the portico in front of the stone-gray house proper and thus again fatefully remind us of the six human lives to be extinguished by the evil Mannon spirit. Properly, it may seem, there should be three unlit and three lit candles on the mantel, corresponding to the Mannons dead and those still alive. But such an arrangement would obviously have looked both obtrusive and strange. Moreover, it would have obscured the parallel to the outdoor columns. O'Neill was therefore satisfied to suggest the two kinds—the living and the dead—by grouping the candles in two trinities, an arrangement which, of course, also carries Christian connotations.

It could be shown also by other examples how meticulously O'Neill arranges and numbers his light sources. Thus, in the ship's cabin of Part II.IV *"there is a lighted lamp on the sideboard and a ship's lantern, also lighted, at the right end of the table"* (110). The position of the characters in the cabin makes it easy to link the lamp with Christine and the lantern with Brant, the ship's captain.

In Part III the interior lighting, like the exterior one, fights an unsuccessful battle with the Mannon darkness. In the sitting-room scene of Part III.I.2,

PETER *has lighted two candles on the mantel and put the lantern on the table at front. In this dim, spotty light the room is full of shadows. ... In the flickering candlelight the eyes of the Mannon portraits stare with a grim forbiddingness* (139).

The visual symbolism here strongly anticipates Orin's Maeterlinckian words about man's life being "a lamp burning out in a room of waiting shadows." The lantern, although it belongs to the barn, we connect with Brant, and if we take the two candles to represent the other two victims of the family fate, whose deaths we have witnessed—Ezra and Christine—we have in these three light sources an addition, as it were, to the Mannon portrait gallery, a visual indication of how these recently dead ones nourish and give life to the avenging family force.

If Orin is linked with the lamp in the study, Lavinia is connected with the one in the sitting-room. At curtain rise this lamp *"is lighted but turned low"* (157). Seth has informed us that ever since the house was first built in hate, its evil spirit has kept growing (136). Now, in the final interior act we can see how the fateful Mannon darkness predominates. Orin has just made his incestuous proposal, but Lavinia wants to escape him and the Mannons and marry Peter. He is now Ezra, she is Christine and Peter recalls Brant. Entering the room *"in a terrific state of tension,"* Lavinia *"comes to the table and turns up the lamp"* (157). She wants enlightenment. "Show me the way to save him [Orin]," she entreats the portraits. But her act is also an echo of Christine's desperate struggle for life and love, a struggle that ironically is to bring Lavinia, as it did her mother, only closer to the Mannon darkness; in the end we see her entering the darkened house.

All the Mannons, we have found, are at one point or another linked with a light source, symbolizing their struggle for love and belonging in the darkness of life; all the lamps—in the bedroom, study, sitting-room and cabin —are significantly placed on the left side, which we have identified as the 'pagan' or life area. But just as the blessed island can be found only in death, so the true light—God's, not man's—can be found only beyond life. Thus we witness how, with all the Mannons, the "artificial" earthly light gives way to the eternal heavenly one.

Frankly non-illusionistic lighting appears only in a few of O'Neill's plays and most consistently in *Welded*.

It was not until after the early editions of *Welded* were published,[3] that the idea of using spotlights to bring out the theme of separateness and 'weldedness' occured to O'Neill; he also then stylized the play in other ways, eliminating much of the detailed descriptions of sets and characters.[4] In the later versions of the play, then, we have two circles of movable light which,

like auras of egoism emphasize and intensify ELEANOR *and* MICHAEL *throughout the play. There is no other lighting. The two other people and the rooms are distinguishable only by the light of* ELEANOR *and* MICHAEL (443).

The essential meaning of the *"auras of egoism"* is found in the following words by Lazarus: "Cast aside is our pitiable pretense, our immortal egohood, the holy lantern behind which cringed our Fear of the Dark!" (*Lazarus,* 324). This spotlighting of the main characters naturally throws their stage positions into marked relief; their movements toward and away from each other, their merging and separation are by this device given a greater dramatic emphasis. Sitting close beside Eleanor in the harmonious beginning of Act I, Michael draws attention to the meaning of the spotlights: "It began with the splitting of a cell a hundred million years ago into you and me, leaving an eternal yearning to become one life again" (448). As he says this we have a visual illustration of the almost—but not quite—unified cell. A little later, as the Capes embrace passionately, the coalescing light circles symbolize how they have, as it were, become "one life"; again Michael points to the significance of the lighting: "I've become you! You've become me! One heart! One blood! Ours!" (448). But the John intermezzo brings Eleanor away from Michael, and after this event they sit in separate chairs, facing front; the reunification has failed. The act ends with a desperate attempt on Michael's part to force his love upon Eleanor (460), whose growing hatred is expressed by her physical separation from Michael with the concomitant separation of the light circles. With the aid of the lighting, O'Neill tries to give a definite rhythm to the act of alternating separateness and oneness, freedom and dependence, hatred and love, the final note being separateness. The same rhythm is adhered to in the other marital act of the play—Act III—but there the final note is oneness.

The spotlights thus illustrate Michael's romantic, philosophical-biological

---

[3] By Boni and Liveright in April 1924 and Jan. 1925.

[4] In the first two editions Eleanor's *"chaise longue has been pulled up within the circle of light"* shed from a nearby reading lamp. Already here what was later to be compared to an aura of egoism is suggested, but the hint is too slight to be grasped by an audience, particularly since Eleanor could not very well remain on the chaise longue throughout the act for the sake of symbolism.

idea, that man and woman were originally one flesh and that their aim must be to become so again in a spiritual sense.[5] When they cast aside their selfishness and let their love reign supreme, they become again "a whole, a truth" (488), overcoming their former loneliness "in a hundred million years of darkness" and no more fearful of the "black world" (488); in short, they belong.[6]

The action of *Welded* takes place at night. In this respect the play is by no means exceptional. On the contrary, there is a noteworthy number of night scenes in O'Neill's plays—some twenty of them are set wholly or largely at night—indicative of the dramatist's preoccupation with the death-in-life theme.

[5] The idea, as Raleigh indicates (p. 11), is undoubtedly overtaken from Aristophanes' speech in Plato's *Symposium*.

[6] Falk's view (p. 117) that Michael and Eleanor never really escape their "*auras of egoism*" reveals a disregard both for the light symbolism and for the Christian symbolism of the play ending.

III. THE VISUALIZED SOUL

Just as O'Neill designs his scenery and lighting with regard for an inner—psychological and/or metaphysical—reality, so he designs the appearance and actions of his characters with regard for their state of mind and/or their place in a spiritual hierarchy (Gassner, 1954, p. 644). O'Neill, it has been said, "tries to use the physical man as a means of showing us the subconscious man in whom he is chiefly interested" (Lawson, p. 132).

This interest has led to a tendency towards typification that has been noted by several critics. Thus Winther maintains (p. 5) that "the favorite character of an O'Neill play has dreamy eyes." Enlarging upon this indication of stylization Kemelman claims (pp. 95 f.) that the male protagonist of an O'Neill play is always "a sensitive soul with large, dark eyes and a face harrowed by lines of internal struggle," whereas the male antagonist is usually "a thick-set, practical man with small, blue eyes."[1] Koischwitz notes (pp. 77, 79) that similar character descriptions occur in plays very different in subject matter, a circumstance which he ascribes to the fact that O'Neill does not draw after nature but concerns himself with the regions of the soul. Therefore, whenever the same spiritual problems are introduced, they find the same or similar visual expression.

As for the dramatist's reliance on illustrative actions to convey his meaning, we may quote the author himself. Commenting on one of the many striking illustrative actions found in the plays—the lockstep file in *Ape* (217)—O'Neill told Mullett (p. 118): "Some people think even that is an actual custom aboard ship! But it is only symbolic of the regimentation of men who are slaves of machinery. In a larger sense, it applies to all of us, because we all are more or less the slaves of convention, or of discipline, or of a rigid formula of some sort." The example well illustrates the widespread tendency to interpret the actions of the characters on too superficial a level, without regard for their spiritual significance.

---

[1] Kemelman and, after him, Raleigh (p. 293) simplify the picture when they assume that blue eyes are a feature merely of unattractive characters in O'Neill's plays. As a matter of fact there is a preponderance for this eye color in the dramas. Olson in *Voyage,* Marsden in *Interlude,* John in *Days,* Eileen in *Straw,* Sara and Nora in *Poet,* and Josie in *Misbegotten* are some of the likeable characters who have blue eyes.

Character Appearance

O'Neill's concern with his characters' outward appearance is quite noticeable throughout his work. From the beginning we find detailed character descriptions, whose amplitude tends to increase in the late plays. Attention is paid to the characters' age, constitution, complexion, facial traits, hair, costume, voice and manner. But in most cases all these characteristics are not discussed with regard to one and the same character—an indication, perhaps, that O'Neill was not thinking in terms of production when finally shaping the plays for the printer but rather took the approach of a novelist, who is free to limit himself to those visual characteristics he finds important and illuminating and ignore the rest. A director of *Interlude* must obviously find costumes for all the characters in all the acts. But O'Neill, except for Marsden, only incidentally—usually when he finds it symbolically relevant—tells us what the characters wear. In the majority of cases, however, attention is paid to the hair and eyes of the characters. In agreement with traditional symbolism, the hair frequently has connotations of strength and sexuality,[2] while the eyes mirror the souls of the characters.

If the masklike faces in *Electra* establish the puritan male tradition, the women's hair and eyes symbolize the opposing 'pagan' one. The pallor and immobility of the death mask juxtaposed to the living colors of hair and eyes, represent the battle between the stern, life-denying Father God, Jehovah, and the soft, life-affirming Earth Mother.

The significance of the hair was partly outlined in the "Working Notes":

peculiar gold-brown hair exactly alike in Lavinia and her mother—same as hair of the dead woman, Adam's mother, whom Ezra's father and uncle had loved— who started the chain of recurrent love and hatred and revenge—emphasize this motivating fate out of past ... strange, hidden psychic identity of Christine with the dead woman and of Lavinia ... with her mother—(O'Neill, 1931/Frenz, p. 9).

In the play, Christine has *"thick curly hair, partly a copper brown, partly a bronze gold, each shade distinct and yet blending with the other"* (9). Lavinia

---

[2] This is true especially of the women in the plays. Thus, in *Desire*, the grossly sensual (221) Abbie's hair *"tumbles over her shoulders in disarray"* after she has possessed Eben (244). Cybel's hair, similarly, *"hangs down in a great mane over her shoulders,"* when her Mother Earth characteristics are most pronounced (*Brown*, 320). Deborah Harford has *"thick, wavy red-brown hair,"* linking her with Melody's beloved mare (*Poet*, 67). And Josie, in *Misbegotten*, similarly, has *"black hair as coarse as a horse's mane"* (3). Since Josie is another Mother Earth figure, it is interesting to note that "Black Demeter," according to Frazer (p. 471), in Arcadia "was portrayed with the head and mane of a horse on the body of a woman." O'Neill owned the abridged 1925 edition of Frazer's work; his copy, now at C. W. Post College, L.I., is signed and dated "March '26."

"has the same peculiar shade of copper-gold hair" (10).[3] And both Brant and Seth verify that Marie Brantôme had hair of the same unusual kind (22, 44). The richness of the hair points to primitive, vigorous sensuality,[4] the strength of which is further indicated by the metallic references. These also serve the purpose, it would seem, of raising the women above the common run of men,[5] vaguely suggesting their kinship with the royal dynasty of golden Mycenae. But above all, the two colors of the women's hair, distinct from each other yet harmoniously blending, suggest the warm sun (24) and earth (112, 147) of the South Sea islands and the "good spirit—of love" (147) that reigns there.

The eyes of the women further link them with the islands. O'Neill carefully distinguishes between them. We hear of Marie's "big, deep, sad eyes that were blue as the Caribbean Sea" (22). There is no indication that Marie ever acquired the masklike appearance the Mannons have otherwise grown on their wives; on the contrary, the sadness of her eyes suggests that she never hardened herself to life but remained open and vulnerable to it. In this respect she resembles the Chantyman, another former servant of the Mannons, unaffected by their puritanism; his eyes, too, are the *"big round blue"* (102) ones of the sea.

While Christine and Lavinia retain the sea and sky (90) color of Marie's eyes—*"a dark violet blue"* (9 f.)—they are somewhat further removed from its spiritual origin. Christine's eyes are *"deep-set"* and *"alive"* (9) but apparently not especially large; Lavinia's seem to have lost even their depth. The soul-destroying puritan influence can be traced further to Seth and Borden—both long-time servants of the Mannons—with their small, sharp eyes (6, 67). The fact that Ezra's eyes are never described seems significant in this context; symbolically speaking his mask has grown so dominant that he has become virtually eyeless.[6]

One more visual trait bring the three women and the islanders together. Christine, we learn, *"has a fine, voluptuous figure and she moves with a flowing animal grace"* (9). Marie, too, had "something free and wild about her like

---

[3] In the scenario, where the Marie Brantôme figure is missing, Christine's hair is a "dark reddish-brown"—Mary Tyrone's color!—and Lavinia's "a heavy mass of straight black hair." Here O'Neill was still thinking more in terms of the basic moral and religious conflict than of the fated identity; Christine's hair has a burning sensuality, whereas Lavinia's makes her an ally of the straight-laced puritans.

[4] This is true of Brant, too, who wears his hair *"noticeably long"* (21).

[5] Christine's symbolic counterpart in Part II.IV is merely a "yaller-haired wench" (106).

[6] The eye symbolism here may be compared to the one in *Marco*, where the eyes of the Orientals in token of their spirituality are vivid (364), whereas nothing is said about Marco's eyes—his father's are *"small, cunning"* (358)—because symbolically speaking he is eyeless, blind, without a soul.

an animile. Purty she was, too!" (44). And Lavinia, after her return from the islands, looks and moves like her mother (139) and declares that the islands have set her free (147).

The symbolism resembles the one in *Ape.* The naked islanders enjoy the freedom and harmony of animals, and the three women, especially Marie, have retained much, if not all, of their sense of belonging. But in *Electra* the women may also be said to represent man's harmony with life preceding his Fall, while the Mannons, with their strong puritan sin consciousness, illustrate his state of mind after it. Apart from the Darwinian longing to return to animal status and the Christian-puritan yearning for a lost paradise of sinlessness, there is the Freudian longing for the maternal womb. It is all these longings taken together that gives scope and significance to the Mannons' love for their women-islands.

The fated chain of "hidden psychic identity" is established by means of a series of striking parallel situations. In Part I.I Brant tells Lavinia:

You won't meet hair like yours and hers again in a month of Sundays. I only know of one other woman who had it. You'll think it strange when I tell you. It was my mother. ... Yes, she had beautiful hair like your mother's, that hung down to her knees ... (22).

This should not be taken as calculating flattery. It is true that Brant's courting of Lavinia seems largely motivated by his need to keep up appearances and divert suspicions from his adulterous relationship with Christine. Yet this does not explain why he has recently gone as far as kissing the young girl; surely, this was not part of his scheme, far less of Christine's (23). We must assume, that he simply could not resist it. Reminiscing their moonlight romance Brant dreams:

Whenever I remember those islands now, I will always think of you, as you walked beside me that night with your hair blowing in the sea wind and the moonlight in your eyes! (*He tries to take her hand, but at his touch she pulls away and springs to her feet.*) (24).

The free-flowing hair and the eyes belong with the sea, the wind and the islands—especially with the one named Marie Brantôme,[7] the lost paradise which the mother-fixated, guilt-ridden Adam constantly longs for; momentarily, in the dreamy light, she comes alive to him in Lavinia; insofar as Lavinia recalls his mother, she is lovable. Brant would most certainly have fallen in love with her, had she not by the circumstances been an unfit love object and had she not repressed her maternal nature in favor of her Mannon rigidity: she wears her hair *"pulled tightly back, as if to conceal its natural curliness"* (10). Lavinia, on her part, apparently agreed to Brant's kissing her;

[7] Brantôme is the name of a French town (arr. de Périgueux) built on an island.

for all her puritanism, she is not insensitive to the 'pagan' values. Her negative reaction at this point is easily explained by the fact that since the moonlight romance, she has come to suspect that Brant is her mother's lover. Basically, however, it is not Christine's rivalry she fears but Marie's; her outbursts against the "low Canuck nurse girl" (24) reveal most of all her jealousy of the woman Brant truly loves, who partook of the affirmative qualities Lavinia secretly longs for. In this way the scene demonstrates the power of the dead over the living.

In Part I.III there is a similar situation, this time between Ezra and Christine:

MANNON. ... (*Leans toward her, his voice trembling with desire and a feeling of strangeness and awe—touching her hair with an awkward caress*) You're beautiful! You look more beautiful than ever—and strange to me. I don't know you. You're younger. I feel like an old man beside you. Only your hair is the same—your strange beautiful hair I always—
CHRISTINE. (*with a start of repulsion, shrinking from his hand*) Don't! (52).

Brant might have uttered Ezra's last words, a circumstance which in itself motivates Christine's violent reaction. But there is a deeper reason for it. As Ezra's words imply, the situation revives his father Abe's love for the beautiful young stranger Marie Brantôme, a relationship of which Christine undoubtedly is well aware.[8] But Ezra, too, loved Marie. She gave him the maternal tenderness his own "stern" mother withheld from him (44); and as the woman of his childhood, she incarnates a lost paradise to him. To him, as to Brant, Christine is a mother substitute; their love for her is a love by proxy. Of this, too, Christine may intuitively be aware. Again the spirit of the dead woman is evoked.

Twice more the ghost of Marie is called forth. In Part II.II Orin tells Christine:

And do you remember how you used to let me brush your hair and how I loved to? He hated me doing that, too. You've still got the same beautiful hair, Mother. That hasn't changed. (*He reaches up and touches her hair caressingly. She gives a little shudder of repulsion and draws away from him but he is too happy to notice*) (90).

Four identical situations of the past are evoked here. There is Ezra's gesture the night preceding the murder two days earlier. There is Brant's concern with Christine's hair (22). There is the Orin-Christine relationship of the past. And there is Ezra's parallel relationship with Marie, which indicates that his hatred of Orin's hair-brushing is motivated by jealousy at a blissful

---

[8] This is what her reference to Abe's hatred (17) implies.—In the second typewritten version her association was explicit: "Don't touch my hair! Don't look like that! You make me think of your father—" (= 52).

mother-son relationship he had once enjoyed himself but which ended when Marie left him for his uncle (44), just as, later, Christine turned away from him to her son. Ezra's ghost now looms large beside that of Marie.

The final hair-touching scene occurs in Part III.III. Orin tells Lavinia:

There are times now when you don't seem to be my sister, nor Mother, but some stranger with the same beautiful hair— (*He touches her hair caressingly. She pulls violently away. He laughs wildly*) Perhaps you're Marie Brantôme, eh? (165).

Orin's words hark back to the initial Abe-Marie relationship. Again Mannon love for 'paganism' is inextricably connected with sin—adultery in Abe's case, incest in Orin's. The fated chain has come full circle; the sin of the grandfather is visited upon the grandson. The scene also relates to the one between Ezra and Christine just dealt with, for Orin and Lavinia are now virtually identical with their parents (155). Like Ezra's love for Christine, Orin's love for Lavinia, his 'wife,' is one by proxy, is a love for Marie or the qualities she symbolizes.

The psychological pattern of the play has become ever more introverted and complex. From Abe's fairly simple preference of the mistress to the wife, actively dramatized, we have moved to Ezra's inner conflict between two much less contrasting figures: the 'mother' (Marie) and the wife. Finally we reach Orin's desperate struggle with his inner furies, his attempt to reincarnate the mistress and mother qualities associated with the two dead women in his sister, thereby combining true love, freedom and protection. Ironically, this ideal combination can only be found in an incestuous relationship, which is especially abhorred by the puritan part of Orin. It is hard to imagine a more crushing and inevitable fate than the psychological one O'Neill has designed for Orin.

The attentive reader has noticed how, in all the hair-touching scenes, two words are constantly repeated: "strange" and "beautiful."[9] Verbal repetition thus is coordinated with the gestic one to bring out the "strange hidden identity" between the women and between the men. Moreover, both words are frequently used in connection with the islands (24, 89 f., 101, 141). When Lavinia towards the end talks about the "mysterious and beautiful" good spirit of love belonging to the islands (147), she points also to what the hair of the women and the whole figure of Marie Brantôme ultimately represent: the life affirmation and love incarnate which oppose the spirit of hatred and death wish and therefore are worshipped by all the Mannons.

---

[9] It is significant that O'Neill, in the second galley proofs, at one point changed the description of Lavinia's hair from "*strange golden*" to "*strange beautiful*" (154) to keep the recurrent pattern.

Hair and eyes again play an important role in *Journey*. Attention is drawn to Mary's appearance at an early point. Already the opening speeches turn our glances to her figure:

TYRONE. You're a fine armful now, Mary, with those twenty pounds you've gained.
MARY. (*smiles affectionately*) I've gotten too fat, you mean, dear. I really ought to reduce (14).

A little later our eyes are caught by her hands, which move restlessly over the top of the table at center (15). And shortly after that we find ourselves concentrating on her hair and eyes: "(*Her hands flutter up to her hair.*) Is my hair coming down? It's hard for me to do it up properly now. My eyes are getting so bad and I never can find my glasses" (20). Here, in the simultaneity of gesture and speech, hands and hair and eyes are brought together, and we can hardly help paying attention also to what has been emphasized earlier: Mary's figure.

The concern with these four physical elements is kept up in various ways throughout the play. Twice we are reminded of Mary's inability to find her glasses (68, 81), and thus, obliquely, of her bad eyesight. And we continually see her hands nervously fluttering up to her hair (27, 47, 68, 89, 95)—when they do not move in front of her bosom or play on top of the family table.

The four elements have one thing in common, which motivates Mary's excessive concern with them. In her own words: "Poor hands! You'd never believe it, but they were once one of my good points, along with my hair and eyes, and I had a fine figure, too" (103). The hands with *"long, tapering fingers"* are knotted by rheumatism and have *"an ugly crippled look"*; the hair, at fifty-four, is *"pure white"*; the eyes are *"unusually large"* and still *"beautiful"* but, as we have noted, at the same time poor; and the figure is *"graceful"* but *"a trifle plump"* (12). In other words, some of the past beauty is retained but most of it is gone and Mary's good points have become her weak ones. She might have reconciled herself to this sad change if it had merely been a sign of ageing. But the change occurred within a short span of time and in connection with a particular event; says Mary:

But I did truly have beautiful hair once, didn't I, James? ... It was a rare shade of reddish brown and so long it came down below my knees. ... It wasn't until after Edmund was born that I had a single grey hair. Then it began to turn white (28).

Much later she tells Edmund: "I never knew what rheumatism was before you were born!" (116).

Since Mary's appearance visualizes the effects of her addiction, and since all the Tyrones have played a part in bringing her 'illness' about, Mary is something more than the beloved wife and mother, whose health they always worry about, because their own well-being depends upon it; she is also a constant reminder to them of their guilt, made acute when there is a threat of a relapse. Mary's appearance thus demonstrates in a very concrete way her conviction, thoroughly borne out in the play, that "the past is the present" (87).

Once we know the meaning of Mary's physical traits, the frequent references to them naturally take on a greater significance. Her initial talk about reducing (14) ominously suggests either that she has already relapsed into morphinism or that she desires to do so.

Of particular interest is the hair which, as it were, divides Mary's life into two distinct periods. Before Edmund's birth it was of a sensual reddish brown; after that it began to turn into its present pure white. The color change matches her transformation from "health and high spirits and the love of loving" (138) to the detached hiding in "a bank of fog" (139).[1]

When we first see her, the hair is arranged *"with fastidious care"* (13)—a sign of her ambition to appear attractive to her family and, from another point of view, a hint of her over-concern with her guilt-ridden past. When Act II.1 opens she has taken at least one injection, but she is still preoccupied with her hair. She still tries to hide her relapse from her family; she still cares about them. But she has begun to drift away from them: "the only way is to make yourself not care" (60). The hair becomes now an excuse to leave the family—for more injections: "I'm going upstairs for a moment, if you'll excuse me. I have to fix my hair" (75). When Mary appears again, the hair, far from being fixed, has *"a slightly disheveled, lopsided look"* (97)—a visual warning, it appears, of her disarranged, one-sided way of looking at things once the drug is in her system and a reminder to us that she has stopped caring—or rather, that she has begun to care about something quite different. What it is, is revealed in her final appearance, when her hair is *"braided in two pigtails"* (170). Mary is once more the young convent girl; she has reverted beyond the unhappy, conjugal part of her life to the time before any of the Tyrones existed to her.

Mary's bad eyesight has clearly a symbolic purport (cf. Falk, p. 184). Early in the play, shortly after she has refused to 'see' that Edmund is seriously ill, she admits that her eyesight is bad and that she needs new glasses (27). At this point she is apparently still willing to set right her faulty view of reality. But the new glasses are never acquired; Mary's vision is not improved. At the end of the play Jamie, speaking not only for himself but also for Edmund and Tyrone, can truly state with Swinburne:

[1] Cf. Raleigh, p. 151: "Mary Tyrone's white hair ... is emblematic of that white, somnambulist world which finally engulfs all the characters."

> Nay, and though all men seeing had pity on me,
> She would not see (174).

But the desire to acquire new glasses may also be interpreted as an expression of Mary's longing for a faith. Her religious concern is shared by her son. While at sea Edmund has had momentary, pantheistic experiences of oneness with Life: "For a second you see—and seeing the secret, are the secret. For a second there is meaning!" (153). For a second only. For the rest of his life man is doomed to blindness or at least—as with Mary—to bad eyesight. Only momentarily can he overcome his feeling of life's meaninglessness and experience "a saint's vision of beatitude" (153); only briefly can he profoundly believe.

Mary has had a similar revelatory experience. Once when she was praying as a young convent girl, she had "a true vision" that the Virgin was smiling and blessing her intent to become a nun (175). But Mary breaks her promise. By marrying Tyrone she deceives the Virgin. In her attempt to make a good wife she must suppress her former longing to become a nun and with that her faith. Says Tyrone: "She hasn't denied her faith, but she's forgotten it ..." (78). And Mary echoes him: "If I could only find the faith I lost, so I could pray again!" (107). In the final act, no longer aware of her family, she is voicing more intensely what she has been looking for all along: "Something I need terribly. I remember when I had it I was never lonely nor afraid. I can't have lost it forever, I would die if I thought that. Because then there would be no hope" (173). Although she does not mention them, we cannot help thinking of the lost glasses which we have come to see as a symbol of her lost faith, which had once helped her to "a true vision." Her eyes are now *"enormous"* and *"glisten like polished black jewels"* (170)—both far-seeing and unseeing. Her final dreaming aloud makes it clear that she has left the present for the past and recaptured "a saint's vision of beatitude" at the terrible price of her own sanity and of blinding herself to the tragedy of her family.

Unusually strinking is Mary Tyrone's 'mask' at her final appearance:

Her face is paler than ever. ... The uncanny thing is that her face now appears so youthful. Experience seems ironed out of it. It is a marble mask of girlish innocence, the mouth caught in a shy smile (170).

Like Ophelia, to whom Jamie compares her (170), Mary appears out of her mind; she barely recognizes her husband and her sons. And like Ophelia she has 'drowned' herself (174)—in morphine; she is clearly removed from life. Her 'death' occurred when Edmund, her beloved son, hatefully called her a dope fiend; at that moment life drained from her face, *"leaving it with the appearance of a plaster cast"* (120).

But Mary's masklike face tells us not only that she has 'died'; it tells us also that she has regressed to the time before she met Tyrone and was exposed to life. The innocent *"mask"* is not a mask held up to the world to disguise her shortcomings; it is rather a mask grown from within to protect her against an insufferable feeling of guilt and self-hatred, from which she cannot, as a Catholic, free herself by deliberately seeking death. It is because her girlhood represents the innocence she feels so desperately lacking in her, that the mask comes to recreate her as the virginal young woman she once was.

O'Neill's use of masks, as Falk and Waith have demonstrated in different ways, is no easy stunt. Nor is the idea underlying the device limited to mask plays proper. Figuratively speaking, nearly all O'Neill's protagonists wear a mask, hide their true selves from the world and from themselves. The dramatist's *"dogma for the new masked drama"*—"one's outer life passes in a solitude haunted by the masks of others; one's inner life passes in a solitude hounded by the masks of oneself" (O'Neill, Nov. 1932/Cargill et al., p. 117) —applies to a good deal of his non-mask plays as well. For, as Waith points out (p. 30) borrowing a phrase from the playwright himself, the typical O'Neill play is "an exercise in unmasking."

Even as a *visual* idea—our concern at present—the mask is old with O'Neill. In a number of plays the faces of the characters are compared to masks in the stage directions. When this is done, the characters invariably find themselves in a state of fatalism or extreme grief. Thus Mrs. Mayo's face, in *Horizon*, after the death of her husband and the failure of her beloved son Robert to keep the farm and his marriage prospering, *"has lost all character, disintegrated, become a weak mask wearing a helpless, doleful expression of being constantly on the verge of comfortless tears"* (112). Nina Leeds' face, in Act II of *Interlude*, is *"a pale expressionless mask drained of all emotional response to human contacts"* (39); the deaths of her lover and father and the crushing experiences at the army hospital leave her less than alive. Marsden's face, similarly, *"becomes distorted into an ugly mask of grief"* (98) when he thinks of his recently dead mother, to whom he stood in an Oedipal relationship. Hutchins Light's face, in *Dynamo*, *"is a mask of stricken loneliness"* (455) after his wife has died and his son has left him and discarded his religion. In these cases the 'mask' seems to express simply a deathly state of mind.

In other cases its defensive function is more pronounced. When Caleb is rejected by Emma in Act I of *Diff'rent,* his face *"sets in its concealment mask of emotionlessness"* (518), and thirty years later we still find the same masklike expression on his face, belied only by his eyes, which *"cannot conceal an inward struggle"* (535). Clearly, Caleb's masklike expression visualizes not merely the grimness of his fate but also his attempt to cope with it, to harden himself against it. But to harden oneself is to die a little. Thus the *"mask,"* designed to protect against disruptive emotions which would lead to self-annihilation, substitutes death-in-life for death, slow destruction for an instantaneous one. Ephraim Cabot in *Desire*, a stoic like Caleb, *"hardens his face into a stony mask,"* when he learns from Abbie, that the child she has just killed was not his but Eben's; and he explains the significance of the facial change himself when thinking aloud: "I got t' be—like a stone—a rock o' jedgment!" (264).

Wherever O'Neill employs the mask, there is a note of death (cf. Brugger, p. 165). Emma Crosby in *Diff'rent*, finally realizing that she has wasted her own life as well as Caleb's, 'dies' before she takes her life: her face *"is frozen into an expressionless mask, her eyes are red-rimmed, dull and lifeless"* (547). Kukachin in *Marco*, similarly, *"stares ahead stonily,"* her face *"a fatalistic mask of acceptance"* (417), before she voluntarily ends her life.

In *Fountain* Death itself is masked; we see *"a tall woman's figure ... shrouded in long draperies of a blue that is almost black. The face is a pale mask with ... eyes that stare straight ahead with a stony penetration ..."* (438). This description may be compared to the following one of Ruth Mayo in Act III.1 of *Horizon*: *"A heavy shawl is wrapped about her shoulders, half-concealing her dress of deep mourning. ... Her pale, deeply-lined face has the stony lack of expression of one to whom nothing more can ever happen"* (144). What we get in the last description, as the close resemblance to the description of the Death figure bears out, is not the picture of a mourning mother—Ruth is beyond mourning—but of petrified grief, of death in life; although O'Neill does not use the word, it is easy to see that Ruth wears the 'mask' of frozen emotions.

The mask of death is momentarily grown on Eleanor in *Welded* too. In a need to assert herself against her despotic husband, she tells him—dishonestly —that she loves John; her face at this point is *"deathly calm"* (460), a mask of hatred. In Act II.1 we see her arriving at John's place. She is determined to act the part of loving mistress to John out of a desire to revenge herself on Michael, to kill her love for her husband and set herself free. As the actress she is, she is acting a part. But it is not to establish this obvious fact that O'Neill describes her face in terms of a mask. When Eleanor's face *"becomes mask-like, her body rigid, her eyes closed"* under John's kisses (465), it is an altogether truthful expression of her feelings of hatred, self-loathing and spiritual death. Far from representing a pose, the mask is an integral part of her character.

The same holds true, generally, about O'Neill's masked characters. When dealing with the mask-face symbiosis, we should not think so much in terms of surface and depth or persona and shadow as in terms of conflicting impulses of death and life, hatred and love, (Nietzschean) pride and (Christian) humility. The division is not merely psychological; it is also ideological. The characteristic development of the O'Neill hero from pride to humility, from self-love to love is not just a 'case study'; it is a moral prescription, an act of exorcism.

The more conventional idea that we wear masks—pose—to one another appears already in *Servitude,* where Mrs. Frazer tells Roylston about her husband: "He never could see his business in all its hideousness as I came to see it, and I don't think he wore a mask just for my benefit: but you never can tell" (236). Ironically, the remark is truly applicable, not so much to Frazer as to Roylston, who hides an ugly egotism behind his 'mask' of superman, creator and maker of new values. Mrs. Frazer later discovers this. "Your cruel vanity has torn off the mask" (280), she tells him.[2]

From the opening of the fourth scene of *Ape,* O'Neill found in retrospect (Jan. 1933/Cargill et al., p. 119), "where Yank begins to think he enters into a masked world" and in which "even the familiar faces of his mates in the forecastle have become strange and alien," all the faces Yank encounters "should be masked." Actually, Yank's growing alienation from the world is suggested in the play by masklike effects. Thus, the stokers in Scene 4 have a black coal make-up around their eyes, *"giving them a queer, sinister expression"* (226), which they did not have in the opening scene, when Yank still felt not only that he belonged to them but was, in fact, their leader. The *"rouged, calcimined, dyed, overdressed"* Fifth Avenue women (236) are virtually masked.[3] And the I.W.W. Secretary's eye shade (245) modestly approximates a hiding mask.

The genesis of the masks, as used by O'Neill in such plays as *Brown, Electra* and *Days,* may be described as follows. Before man discovered sin, while he still enjoyed primordial unity with the "old God"—Nature—there was no need for hiding, no need to wear 'masks.' When man was separated from nature the situation changed. Unable to return to his harmonious origin, unable likewise to accept his new, painful status, man became divided against

---

[2] The inspiration for this conception of the mask as a façade hiding and prettifying inner ugliness may well have come from *The Portrait of Dorian Gray,* which, O'Neill declared, "made an indelible impression" on him in his youth (Bowen, 1959, p. 125). It may have been overtaken from *Dr. Jekyll and Mr. Hyde,* which is referred to in *Abortion* (155). Or it may have come from *A Doll's House,* where Helmer, in Act I, talks about forgers who are forced to wear masks even before wife and children. Ibsen's play has influenced *Servitude* in several respects (cf. Törnqvist, 1965, pp. 218 f.).

[3] In the original production of the play the Fifth Avenue marionettes actually wore masks (Gelb, pp. 495 f.).

himself, one part of him—the open, naïve, romantic side—longing to return to the lost paradise, the other, rational part of him trying to adjust to the earthly hell. At times one side or the other becomes so predominant that the total character is nearly fused with it. Thus the Mannons are almost identified with the 'mask,' whereas Marie and Christine are closely related to the 'face.' In Lavinia the two are fatefully balanced, as her circular development from 'mask' to 'face' and back to 'mask' illustrates.

On this symbolic level the characters can no longer be viewed as individuals; instead they typify the two dispositions of the human soul just described. The marriage between Ezra and Christine, by the same token, becomes a symbol of the unhappy state of man; her attempt to free herself from him equals man's attempt to free himself from his 'mask'; and her love for Brant, so like the young Ezra, is an ironical illustration of man's inability to escape his 'mask.' The men, similarly, although they long to discard their 'masks' and revert to naked, primordial unity, find life too hard to bear without this protective armor; not until they die, when life's hostility is no longer a threat to them, can they unmask themselves. Moreover, as an alienating effect, the masks help the audience to see that the staged events should not be taken at their realistic—often melodramatic—surface value, that the real drama "takes place on a plane where outer reality is mask of true fated reality" (O'Neill, 1931/Frenz, p. 12).

In *Electra* O'Neill actually prefers masklike faces—the 'mask' consisting of heavy make-up—to masks proper. This device he arrived at after he had tried and discarded both full masks and half-masks.[4] Undoubtedly the masklike faces are better suited to the action in *Electra*. Without breaking the realistic illusion they suggest all that is essential of the underlying reality: the two basic impulses, here identified with 'paganism' and puritanism; the fateful identity between the Mannons; their connection with the house; their isolation from the world; their puritan secretiveness and death-in-life (9).

The 'masks' found on all the Mannons for generations as well as on those long and intimately connected with them—wives, servants—represent a life-denying "fate springing out of the family" (O'Neill, 1931/Frenz, p. 9) and corrupting everyone who comes within its reach. Like the shining portico the 'masks' pretend purity but incarnate only death.

Although the theme of the trilogy necessitates a far-going similarity among all the 'masks,' O'Neill indicates some differences among them as well as changes in them. Thus the masklike look is *"more pronounced"* in Ezra, the

---

[4] The full masks, O'Neill felt, demanded a language akin to that in Greek tragedy, and this he considered himself unable to write (Dec. 1932/Cargill et al., p. 120). The half-masks used in the first typewritten version introduced a "duality-of-character symbolism" outside his purpose in the trilogy (O'Neill, 1931/Frenz, p. 11).

son of Abe (79), than in the others (46);[5] it is virtually a death mask (93). Christine's, on the other hand, is initially *"a wonderfully lifelike pale mask"* (9), a thin, almost transparent veneer, we are asked to imagine, grown on her by the Mannons but foreign to her real nature. The moment she decides to murder Ezra, she ironically succumbs to the very spirit she fights, the Mannon one; her face is transformed into *"a sinister evil mask"* (35). Shortly after the murder, when she is haunted by guilt-feelings but still hoping to escape, we find that *"beneath the mask-like veneer of her face there are deep lines about her mouth, and her eyes burn with a feverish light"* (71). O'Neill is close to the half-mask in this description, which suggests Christine's disintegration, her vacillation between hardened acceptance of her crime and anguished rejection of it, her dwindling hope for escape and growing fear of retribution. As the furies continue to torment her, her desire for life is weakened and the Mannon semblance grows on her. Shortly before her suicide she finds herself "old and ugly and haunted by death" (118), an incarnation of the Mannon spirit and very like the house she tries to escape. A little later her face has become, like Ezra's, *"a tragic death mask"* (122).

In no other play by O'Neill are masks of such a fundamental importance as in *Brown*. As the author himself pointed out, referring to the scene where Brown steals Dion's mask, the mask device enabled him to dramatize the transference of personality.[6]

Most commentators on the play have been inclined to stress the mask-before-the-world idea, but this was not the aspect that concerned O'Neill the most. In a letter to De Casseres (6.22.1927) he states his discontent with the way in which the masks were handled in the original Broadway production:

When you read what I wanted those masks to get across—the abstract drama of the forces behind the people—as it is suggested in the script you will remember more clearly how wrong they were [in the production]. They suggested only the bromidic, hypocritical & defensive double-personality of people in their personal relationships—a thing I never would have needed masks to convey. They became an unnecessary trick. Perhaps I was demanding too much, and it can't be done—but I'm sure with the right masks my meaning would get across, that the play would be mystic instead of confusing....

In his public explanation of the play he also spoke of the "background pattern of conflicting tides in the soul of Man" and made it clear that he regarded *Brown* above all as a 'mystery' play (O'Neill, 1926/Clark, p. 105), describing—to quote his words to Clark—"the mystery of personality and life" (Clark, p. 106). It was the function of the masks to suggest this mystery.

[5] Brugger points out (p. 163): "Bei ihm wird nur von einer Maske gesprochen ohne den Zusatz: *lifelike.*"

[6] Cf. O'Neill's note to the play in the Wilderness edition, 10, p. xi.

Only the four main characters in the play—Dion, Brown, Margaret, Cybel —are masked.[7] The mask scheme for the women is relatively simple. Cybel wears the rouged mask of a hardened prostitute in token of the fact that she is "doomed to segregation as a pariah in a world of unnatural laws." Beneath her mask her face is that of "Cybele, the Earth Mother" (O'Neill, 1926/ Clark, p. 104). When we first see her, she is unmasked, staring with large dreamy eyes, *"forgetting time with an eternal end"* (278). Beside a cheap alarm clock her mask is lying (278). The prostitute, this seems to indicate, is the temporal, perverted counterpart of the eternal, virtuous Earth Mother. By giving her customers a Tart, Cybel explains, she is able to keep her real virtue (284). The mask serves as an armor.

While there is no indication that Cybel's mask ever changes (although her increasing stoutness indicates the growth of the Earth Mother beneath the mask), Margaret's undergoes a certain alteration. In the Prologue it has *"the abstract quality of a Girl instead of the individual,* MARGARET" (262). The mask thus gives her a lifeless, anonymous, stereotype appearance, indicative of Margaret's attempt to conform and adjust to an established social pattern. Yet the difference between her mask and face is minute. After seven years of marriage her face, which she shows only to Dion, has grown worried and hurt (270), while her mask is now that of a *"pretty young matron"* (274), i.e. showing only the biological change she has undergone but revealing none of the sorrows she has suffered. After another seven years her face is care-worn, sad and querulous, while her mask, even more than before, represents *"the brave face she puts on before the world to hide her suffering and disil-lusionment"* (291). Margaret is thus one person to Dion, the artist, and an-other to the world. If the mask means a protective façade, it is not the façade of the obvious hypocrite—Margaret is not trying to appear better than she is—but rather the 'face' demanded by a hedonistic world to which she feels the need of belonging. If it represents a pose, it is one that has become second nature with her. In this she is representative of all the masked characters in the play.

"Dion's mask of Pan which he puts on as a boy," O'Neill explained (1926/ Clark, p. 105), "is not only a defense against the world for the supersensitive painter-poet underneath it, but also an integral part of his character as the

---

[7] In the typewritten version some of the minor characters are also masked. Thus the Brown parents and the draftsmen in Brown's office wear masks which exactly reproduce their facial features. The purpose of these masks, O'Neill indicated, was to give the characters *"an unreal, lifeless appearance"* (= 257). In the play only Margaret (in the Prologue) wears a mask of this transparent type. O'Neill's idea in the type-script seems to have been to illustrate the deadliness of the Brown way of life by means of the masks. In the play he prefers to treat all the minor figures alike, thereby simplifying his scheme and emphasizing their 'choral' background function.

artist." The artist, more sensitive than the average man, has a greater need for the mask. Also, the conflict visualized in the mask-face dichotomy, is a prerequisite for his artistry; it keeps Dion, as Cybel puts it, "alive" (289) —in contrast to Brown. Inner division means life and creativity; inner harmony stands for deathly sterility.

In the case of Dion we are informed of the genesis of his mask. At the impressionable age of four, we learn, he had drawn a picture in the sand. Envious of Dion's artistic faculty, Billy Brown, whom he loved and trusted, destroyed the picture after he had hit Dion. It was an act not unlike Cain's slaying of Abel. Suddenly, Dion recalls,

the good God was disproved in his person and the evil and injustice of Man was born! Everyone called me cry-baby, so I became silent for life and designed a mask of the Bad Boy Pan in which to live and rebel against that other boy's God and protect myself from His cruelty (295).

When the play opens Dion has worn his mask for fourteen years; he is to wear it for another fourteen before he dies. The mask is

a fixed forcing of his own face—dark, spiritual, poetic, passionately supersensitive, helplessly unprotected in its childlike, religious faith in life—into the expression of a mocking, reckless, defiant, gayly scoffing and sensual young Pan (260).[8]

[8] Dion's mask and face have their essential contrasting characteristics already in the original longhand draft, but the mask—*"confident, bold, proud, cynical, hard and ironical"*—is here more perverted than it is at the corresponding stage—the Prologue— in the play. The face expresses no *"religious faith in life"*; the mask does not suggest a *"gayly scoffing and sensual young Pan"*; and Dion Anthony significantly carries an 'ordinary' name: Stanley Keith.

Towards the end of the draft, however, the name Dion begins to appear and here, too, the mask acquires its Pan-like expression. While Dion's mask in the play preserves its demonic look after Brown has overtaken it, in the draft it gradually loses its Mephistophelean traits and becomes first *"a healthy, sensual Silenus,"* then *"a glorified youthful Pan,"* i.e., identical with Dion's mask such as it must have been some time prior to the opening of the play. The idea of having Dion's mask change back from Mephistopheles to Pan after Dion's death is retained even through the galleys. While such a reversion would make Margaret's renewed love for Dion (i.e. Brown) more intelligible, it would not reveal how Brown is haunted by Dion's mask—a much more important matter.

Presumably while working on the original draft O'Neill, in a note, charted the spiritual development of the main characters as follows:

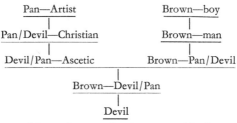

Pan, he noted, represents "the ancient creative harmony with the earth," while Devil

Originally, we must suppose, Dion was undivided, unmasked, in harmony with "the good God," at one with "the deep main current of life-desire" (O'Neill, 1926/Clark, p. 105). Once he was made a victim of an unjust, evil act, he could no longer believe in the benevolence of Man and God. With one part of himself, corresponding to the mask, he sought to protect himself against the lovelessness in the new, callous world he had been initiated into; with another he sought to retain or recreate his old faith in a loving God. Failing both to adjust to the new world and to regress to the old one, Dion experiences how the struggle within him becomes ever more violent, until he is finally (like Dionysus, but in a spiritual way) torn apart. Visually his increasingly disruptive struggle is indicated by the growing polarity between his mask and face, finally established as that between Satan and Saint.

As O'Neill made clear in his comment on the play, Dion's inner struggle is not merely fought within his individual breast; it is an ideological struggle of universal significance. For the split within Dion stems from "the creative pagan acceptance of life" (Dionysus)

fighting eternal war with the masochistic, life-denying spirit of Christianity as represented by St. Anthony—the whole struggle resulting in this modern day in mutual exhaustion—creative joy in life for life's sake frustrated, rendered abortive, distorted by morality from Pan into Satan, into a Mephistopheles mocking himself in order to feel alive; Christianity, once heroic in martyrs for its intense faith now pleading weakly for intense belief in anything, even Godhead itself (O'Neill, 1926/Clark, p. 104).

In other words, in modern civilization neither the pagan sense of harmonious oneness with Life nor the Christian sense of oneness with God are vitally experienced. Deprived of the old sense of belonging to something outside and spiritually more significant than himself, modern man has come to worship—himself. For "the Great God Pan" (267) and for the Christian God he has substituted "the visionless demi-god of our new materialistic myth" (O'Neill, 1926/Clark, p. 105): the Great God Brown.

Yet for the artist, whose mission in life is based on a concern for spiritual values, the materialistic demi-god is not acceptable. Dion Anthony, the painter-poet, is thus caught in the dilemma of having lost touch with the truly life-giving faiths, that would render his art meaningful, and of rejecting the faith that rules his contemporaries, so that he actually belongs nowhere

stands for the "same impulse distorted by civilization striving after a similar harmony with life." The five stages of the chart correspond to the Prologue and four acts of the play. In the case of Brown it suggests a somewhat different development from the one depicted in the play, where Brown's ascetic nature (his face) is as prominent as his devilish one (his mask): like Dion he dies, not as "Devil" but unmasked, as tortured 'martyr.'

(cf. Krutch, 1957, p. 91). As an artist—not to say life artist, for this, at bottom, is what Dion attempts to be—he is an anomaly in the modern world. Like Cybel, he can communicate with it only by prostituting himself, by becoming a utilitarian artist, an architect, instead of adhering to the art for art's sake principle.

In a sense Dion's mask was grown on him the moment he was born. This is the implication in his question: "Why was I born without a skin, O God, that I must wear armor in order to touch or to be touched?" (264 f.). In his mother's womb it was all so different. The mother protected him. She was his skin, his armor, his mask. Dion longs to return to this prenatal harmony, this oneness with something outside himself (comparable to the sensual Dionysian oneness with Life), and dreams of recreating it in a love relationship with Margaret: "She protects me! Her arms are softly around me! She is warmly around me! She is my skin! She is my armor!" (266). By marrying Margaret he hopes to be able to discard his mask and lead a truly creative and affirmative life, protected by her love. But Margaret does not recognize, or wish to recognize, his face. When Dion unmasks himself, she takes protection behind her mask (266, 268); when he replaces his mask, she takes off hers.

It is easy to see the need for this arrangement from a dramaturgical point of view. Dion's mask is to be stolen by Brown, who gains Margaret's love by appearing in it. This idea would not work out if Margaret were to love Dion's face. But there is also a grim psychological point to the fact that the wife, who believes herself in love with her husband, actually does not know him and, like Brown, takes for drunken raving what he says when unmasked (266, 282), while she accepts his masked rhetorics as his truthful emotions (267). Thus Dion's unmasked speeches—serious, tender and poetical—are understood by no one. The world hears only the mocking, abusive, harsh way in which he talks when masked.

Brown, finally, who is "inwardly empty and resourceless, an uncreative creature of superficial preordained social grooves" (O'Neill, 1926/Clark, p. 105), is unmasked in the first half of the play. He is obviously well adjusted to the sterility of modern life. He does not need to wear a mask, because his face *is* a mask, petrified, lifeless. Like the minor figures in the play—unmasked like the choruses in *Electra*—he represents the common run of men leading a deathly, uncreative life.[1]

But midway in the play, after Dion's tortured soul has entered him, Brown comes to suffer from inner division to an even greater extent than Dion did.

---

[1] Cf. Packard, p. 5: "those whose inner selves never differ from what the world takes them to be never wear masks."

He now appears in Dion's mask before Margaret and her children, who never realize the transference of personality that has taken place. Before the world he wears the mask of William A. Brown, the successful business man. Only when alone does he show his own face, *"tortured and distorted by the demon of Dion's mask"* (305). Ironically, Margaret discards her mask shortly after Brown has adopted his. As blind to the real Brown as she was to the real Dion, she apparently experiences a sense of happiness and completeness with the man who partakes of both Dion's and Brown's characteristics. Failing to make Margaret love his true self, Brown is forced to identify himself more and more with the Dion part of him. Through Margaret he comes to hate the successful businessman within him and decides to annihilate him. But this, of course, means killing the part of himself that is accepted by the world and which at the same time is felt to be more truly himself, ugly though it may be. The murder thus comes to mean self-murder. Brown, unable to go on being "not himself to anyone" (O'Neill, 1926/Clark, p. 105), finally must seek protection, like a little boy, in the bosom of Mother Earth. Only before Cybel can he, like Dion, show his naked, tortured and bewildered face and be loved for it.

Despite O'Neill's statement to the contrary, the mask scheme in *Brown* seems not merely "mystic" but also confusing. The confusion stems from the fact that there is no unifying principle underlying the scheme. Or, if there is, no one, including the author himself, has as yet revealed it. Constantly one is struck by what appears to be inconsistencies in the handling of the masks. Not only are some characters masked, while others are not—a fact which, strictly speaking, precludes the idea that we *all* wear masks before one another—but we also find that some masks (Dion's, Margaret's) change, while others (Cybel's, William A. Brown's) do not, and that one mask (Dion's) carries much more complex connotations than the others.

Generally speaking, the masked characters doff their masks, when they are alone or together with someone they love. But even in these situations the *en garde* mechanism cannot wholly be put to rest. Dion, seated in Cybel's parlor, claps on his mask at the mere mention of Brown, the hated rival (285), and again at the horrifying thought of his own impending death and the silence of God (286). At least in the last instance the mask clearly functions as a protection, not against the world but against another impulse—the humble despairing one—within Dion.

That Dion should deliver his long speech about his parents (282) with his mask off is natural, if we consider the imaginative, poetical and non-ironical nature of the speech—qualities which harmonize with Dion's face rather than with his mask. Yet, it remains puzzling why he should at this point unmask himself to Brown, before whom he otherwise always (until his dying moment) wears a mask.[2] The fact that Brown here—unlike Margaret in the Prologue —recognizes also the unmasked Dion, while in the following scene he does not recognize the unmasked Cybel, is another seeming inconsistency or differentiation, which obscures the mask scheme.

In his attempt to get away from the more commonplace connotations aroused by the masks, O'Neill appears to have made them carry a greater weight than they are able to if they are to remain dramatically and theatrically effective. Although the play was successful in the theatre, O'Neill could hardly have felt that the success was due to *his* mask scheme, since, as we have seen, he considered the production exceedingly faulty in carrying out his ideas. The fact that he was never to employ masks again in the same complex way as in *Brown* may perhaps be taken as an indication of his awareness that he had unduly strained the device. The reason may, however, have been a simpler one: his discovery that the mask scheme, even if dramatically valid, did not work out in the theatre. Apart from the difficulty of getting the masks correctly designed—O'Neill's complaint to De Casseres— there was the more fundamental problem of making the masks clearly visible to the audience. In *Brown,* O'Neill told Clark (p. 116) shortly after the play had been put on, he could not know in advance how the scheme would function in the theatre. During rehearsals he discovered that the masks were too realistic, that "sitting way back in the theater you couldn't be sure if the actors had on masks or not. I should have had them twice as large—and conventionalized them, so the audience could get the idea at once" (ibid.).

When this statement was made, O'Neill had already finished the first draft of his next mask drama, *Lazarus,* in which he does employ a "conventionalized" mask scheme and makes use of double-sized masks for the choruses, apparently to keep them distinct from the crowds, which appear in masks of normal size.

Lazarus is the only character in the play who does not wear any mask (274). Having discovered that beyond the grave "there is only life" (279), Lazarus has lost the fear of death which enslaves mankind. He has become an integrated, complete human being, who does not need to hide behind a mask. If all the other characters wear masks, it is because they fear not only death but also life: "Men call life death and fear it. They hide from it in horror. Their lives are spent in hiding" (309).

Although the plot in *Lazarus* does not call for any transference of masks, it would of course have been possible to emphasize the short glimpses of life affirmation, when fear is momentarily gone, by a symbolic unmasking. It

[2] In the typewritten version Dion is masked when he delivers this speech. There O'Neill apparently paid more attention to the presence of Brown than to the nature of the speech.

would even seem logical if the characters were visibly to resemble the un-masked Lazarus,[3] when they ecstatically embrace his joyous gospel, only to relapse again into their masked existence when left alone. Yet O'Neill, if he ever contemplated using removable masks in this manner, refrained from doing so, undoubtedly afraid of complicating his mask scheme the way he had done in *Brown*.

Instead of removable masks, the author now tried another device for sug-gesting duality of character. All the main characters (except Lazarus) wear half-masks, covering the upper part of the face.[4] This type of mask, con-stantly employed in the *commedia dell'arte,* fitted O'Neill's psychological purposes.

With Miriam the half-mask has the *"pure pallor of marble,"* while her own skin is *"sunburned and earth-colored"* and her lips are *"still fresh and young"* (274). The deathly pallor appears secondary with her; basically and originally she shares her husband's healthy, life-affirming color. The half-masks of the three Romans—Caligula, Tiberius, Pompeia—are respectively *"crimson, dark with a purplish tinge"* (299), *"pallid purple blotched with darker color"* (337), *"olive-colored with the red of blood smoldering through"* (336). The purple, being the Roman imperial color, is found also in the dresses and lighting of the Capri scenes. The uneven, unnatural complexion of these masks suggests the sickness of mind that characterizes the Romans, representatives of a decadent human race. Pompeia's half-mask has the char-acteristics of the hardened imperial mistress (336). But beneath the mask, her face with its *"gentle, girlish mouth"* is not altogether unlike Miriam's, al-though the deathly pallor in Pompeia's case belongs to her own skin rather than to her mask. While Miriam still in part retains an affirmative attitude to life (her face), Pompeia's perverted mask has distorted her face and left it with but a ghost of her past innocence. The same is true of Caligula and Tiberius. Like Pompeia, Caligula has a skin *"of an anaemic transparent pallor"* (299). As her mouth is *"girlish,"* his is *"boyish."* But Caligula is even further removed from nature; there is nothing in his face that attracts our sympathy; presumably his mouth, too, once could have appealed to us, but *"long ago,"* as an effect of military life, its innocence was wiped out (299). Tiberius, finally, demonstrates the split between the *"able soldier-statesman"* and the *"healthy old campaigner"* (337) on one hand (face) and the de-bauched old man on the other (mask).

There is thus the suggestion with all these characters not only that they are divided against themselves but also that they have become so gradually, that

---

[3] Lazarus' followers do resemble their master in that they wear *"a LAZARUS mask"* (285).

[4] Raleigh comments on the half-masks on pp. 44 ff.

the masks have grown on them and that the suppression of their natural, original selves has been accomplished in different degrees, Miriam representing one extreme and Caligula another.

While secondary characters wear full masks, which *"broadly reproduce their own characters"* (275, 299, 332), the full masks of the crowds and choruses follow a typological pattern. Years later (Jan. 1933/Cargill et al., p. 120) O'Neill commented on his use of masked crowds in *Lazarus* as follows:

I advocate masks for stage crowds, mobs—wherever a sense of impersonal, collective mob psychology is wanted. This was one reason for such an extensive use of them in *Lazarus Laughed.* In masking the crowds in that play, I was visualizing an effect that, intensified by dramatic lighting, would give an audience visually the sense of the Crowd, not as a random collection of individuals, but as a collective whole, an entity. When the Crowd speaks, I wanted an audience to hear the voice of Crowd mind, Crowd emotion, as one voice of a body composed of, but quite distinct from, its parts.

And, for more practical reasons, I wanted to preserve the different crowds of another time and country from the blighting illusion-shattering recognitions by an audience of the supers on the stage.[5]

Apart from indicating race or nationality—Jewish, Oriental, Greek and Roman —the crowd masks suggest age and psychological type according to the following formula:

Period	Type
(1) Boyhood (Girlhood)	(1) The Simple, Ignorant
(2) Youth	(2) The Happy, Eager
(3) Young Manhood (Womanhood)	(3) The Self-Tortured, Introspective
(4) Manhood (Womanhood)	(4) The Proud, Self-Reliant
(5) Middle Age	(5) The Servile, Hypocritical
(6) Maturity	(6) The Revengeful, Cruel
(7) Old Age	(7) The Sorrowful, Resigned (273).

By scrambling periods and types in various ways O'Neill could compose different kinds of crowds. Thus, whereas the Semitic crowds, mostly, I take it, for expository reasons, contain all seven types and periods, the Greeks are all of Period 3, Type 4 (298); the Roman senators are of Period 5–7, Type 3–7 (312); and the courtesans surrounding Tiberius are of Period 1–3, Type 3 and 5–6 (336).[6]

[5] In *The Theatre of Tomorrow* (p. 275) Macgowan had noted that the mask and the marionette would have their natural place in the theatre of the future, especially in the works of playwrights interested in an unrealistic "drama of group-beings" to be staged in a theatre of Rheinhardtian circus proportions.

[6] Several critics have been skeptical concerning the dramatic effectiveness of the typological scheme which, in the theatre, would certainly detract the attention from the chief characters. Cf. Winther (p. 260), Engel (1953, p. 191), and Lorimer (p. 212).

In contrast to the prolific use of masks in *Lazarus* we find only one masked character in O'Neill's last proper mask drama, *Days*. There is an obvious practical reason for Loving's mask: since John and Loving are not separate individuals but representatives of conflicting impulses within the man John Loving, they must naturally look alike so that the audience immediately can grasp their symbolic nature and intimate connection with each other. Since there are few identical twins in the theatre world, O'Neill had to rely on the mask (or the masklike make-up) to bring about the likeness. Yet, since Loving represents an impulse opposed to that embodied by John, the two could not be visualized as completely identical. Hence, "LOVING'S *face is a mask whose features reproduce exactly the features of* JOHN'S *face—the death mask of a* JOHN *who has died with a sneer of scornful mockery on his lips*" (493 f.).[7] As a child, we learn, John Loving was an integrated person, reared in love. But when he reached the age of fifteen he had a traumatic experience. Despite his ardent prayers to the God of Love, both his parents died. With them his faith in a benevolent God died—or nearly so. He became a disintegrated person. With one part of himself (John) he yearns to return to his childhood faith, with another (Loving) he tries to go on living in an indifferent or malignant world. But without a loving God to trust and to identify oneself with, life is not worth living. Hence Loving, as his death mask indicates, represents that part of John Loving that 'died' when he was fifteen, the part which yearns for annihilation, not only because it is sick of life, but also, perhaps, because in death Loving sees a hope for reunion with the mother; he characteristically speaks of death as "the warm, dark womb of Nothingness" and as a Dream in which John and Elsa, who is clearly a mother substitute, may sleep forever "beyond fear of separation" (562). Psychologically, it is quite possible to see Loving as representing the strong attachment to the mother, the inability to accept any other love but hers, resulting in a desire to revenge oneself on all other loves including Elsa's.[8] Thus viewed, his name seems not merely ironical (cf. Törnqvist, 1966, pp. 370 f.).

In a figurative sense, the conflict between mask and face is everywhere felt in O'Neill's work, which takes for its central theme the inner division of man, his longing for truth and need of illusions. The masklike effect is

[7] The scheme is identical with the one O'Neill recommended for *Faust:* "In producing this play, I would have Mephistopheles wearing the Mephistophelean mask of the face of Faust. For is not the whole of Goethe's truth *for our time* just that Mephistopheles and Faust are one and the same—*are* Faust" (Nov. 1932/Cargill et al., p. 118).

[8] The Mephistophelean Loving has much in common with O'Neill's brother Jamie, whose inability to survive his mother was later dramatized in *Misbegotten*.

gained not merely by means of masks or masklike faces. As I have indicated, it can also be suggested by means of costume. The Fifth Avenue ladies in *Ape*, we noted, are *"overdressed"*; about their counterpart in Scene 2, Mildred's aunt, it is said that she *"is dressed pretentiously, as if afraid her face alone would never indicate her position in life"* (218). Their dresses, in other words, serve to mask their spiritual emptiness. The islanders in *Electra*, by contrast, are "naked and innocent" (147), still living in Paradise.[9]

In some cases there is a significant change of costume, equivalent of an unmasking. Thus Brutus Jones first appears in all his pompous regalia. O'Neill significantly refers to it as his *"make up"* (*Jones*, 175). Gradually he has to rid himself of one piece after another until, at the end, he is practically naked, returned to the aboriginal level, 'unmasked.' Brown, similarly, once he has partaken of Dion's mask is forced to cast off his elegant business suit. Shortly before he dies, we see him *"stripped naked except for a white cloth around his loins,"* rather like a hermit—another St. Anthony—praying to the "Savior of Man" in frank—'unmasked'—anguish (*Brown*, 319). Cornelius Melody in *Poet* returns home from his disruptive experience with the Harfords, an experience which has killed his Major pipe dream and his will to life in the process. We see by his costume that it is both an 'unmasked' and degraded man who comes back: his brilliant *"scarlet uniform is filthy and torn and pulled awry"* (152).

The costumes of O'Neill's characters also have other connotations. In *Electra* it is not surprising that all the major male characters wear uniforms since the play begins on the day the Civil War ends, but the uniforms have a significance beyond the realistic one. At an early point we learn that when Christine fell in love with Ezra[1] "he was handsome in his lieutenant's uniform" (31), and her youthful reaction is repeated in stage action when Lavinia enthusiastically greets Orin as he returns from the war, a first lieutenant and "a hero in blue" (75). But Orin, as he himself surmises (95), is not a true hero; brought up as his mother's baby, his Mannon characteristics have been repressed, and although his father has tried to make a "man" of him at the front, his uniform, upon his return home, is still *"ill-fitting"* and *"baggy"* (74), without the splendor that characterized that of his father.

Adam Brant's uniform links him basically with the Mannon men, yet it

[9] In a letter to George Tyler (6.8.1919) describing his life at Peaked Hill Bar near Provincetown, O'Neill enthusiastically exclaims: "No need to wear clothes—no vestige of the unrefined refinements of civilization—."

[1] Brooks–Heilman err (appendix, p. 3) when stating that Christine, unlike Clytemnestra, "never loved" her husband. Apart from Christine's own words—"I loved him once—before I married him" (31)—which we have no reason to disbelieve, we can rely on O'Neill's assurance in the "Working Notes" (Frenz, p. 5) that Christine "had romantic love for him [Ezra] before marriage."

differs significantly from those of Ezra and Orin. As a *"merchant captain's blue uniform"* (104) it is 'peaceful' and connected with the sea. Ultimately, his blue uniform proclaims his longing to return to his "Garden of Paradise," "set in the blue of the sea" (24).

When he first appears, however, Brant does not wear his uniform. Even so, the *"foppish extravagance"* (21) of his costume links him with Christine, whose *"green satin dress"* is *"smartly cut and expensive"* (9). Both of them are set apart from the Mannons in their plain, severe clothes. Reminiscent of the "colored rags" (145) worn by the South Sea islanders, their costumes establish their sensual, life-affirming, 'pagan' qualities as opposed to the Mannon asceticism.[2] In Part I.III Christine still wears green, but she has changed from the enticing satin to velvet, a material more in agreement with Ezra's puritan notions and less likely to stir his sexual desire.[3] There is a striking costume contrast at the beginning of this act: Lavinia, severely dressed in black, is seated on the steps in the bleak moonlight, while above and to the right of her stands Christine, the light from the hall glowing *"along the edges of the dress and in the color of her hair"* (45). At no other point in the trilogy is the contrast between life-affirming 'paganism' and life-denying puritanism so clearly visualized. The warm light outlining Christine's hair and body suggests the benevolent sun shining over the green islands. Momentarily resembling the Dionysian Lazarus, *"radiant in the halo of his own glowing light"* (*Lazarus*, 307), Christine takes on the majestic proportions of an Earth Mother, celebrating the values denied by her daughter.

The black that Lavinia affects in the greater part of the trilogy has several connotations. There are perfectly commonplace reasons for it in the last two parts, where she mourns her father and brother respectively. But in the first part her choice of costume testifies rather to her spiteful jealousy and hatred of Christine.[4] Throughout the play her black attire is linked with her father's judicial robe, visualized in the portrait in his study. She sternly 'condemns' both her mother and brother to death, acting out her part as the devil's advocate in the mistaken belief that she is wielding justice. Above all, her

---

[2] In the scenario O'Neill noted that Christine's extravagant way of dressing is a source of conflict between her and Ezra: "It goes against his Puritan grain and seems to him an evidence of a sinful strain in her, an inclination toward vanity and worldly pomp."

[3] In the first typewritten version O'Neill, still thinking in Greek terms, designed quite different costumes for Christine: a dress of *"rich brown and gold material"* (Part I.I) harmonizing with her hair, and a gown of *"a deep purplish crimson"* (Part I.III). While these costumes suggest her earthy nature, her sanguinary state of mind, and her affinity to the regal Clytemnestra, they do not clearly link her with the South Sea islands, an infinitely more important matter.

[4] Even in the case of dressing-gowns O'Neill carefully distinguishes between Lavinia's *"dark"* (56) and Christine's *"light-colored"* (58) one.

blackness stands for puritan life denial. Commenting on the trilogy title O'Neill stated: "in old sense of word—it befits—it becomes Electra to mourn —it is her fate,—also, in usual sense (made ironical here), mourning (black) is becoming to her—it is the only color that becomes her destiny" (1931/ Frenz, p. 6).[5] The ultimate reason why mourning becomes Lavinia is simply that she never wanted to be born.[6] This explains the intensity of her hatred for her mother, the person who brought her into this miserable world, the world she renounces at the end, when she decides to spend the rest of her life inside the Mannon "temple of Hate and Death." Orin, too, visualizes the father-judge in the third part. Haunted by the furies—his guilt-ridden con-science—he appears in a *"black suit"* (138).[1] The black suit at once reveals that the South Sea has had no liberating effect on him.[2] Seated below the portrait of the forty-year-old judge, dominated by the father's puritan spirit, he now appoints himself the 'judge' of the family, recording their crimes from the initial one of the grandfather down to his own and Lavinia's.

If Orin is now his father, Lavinia, in the greater part of "The Haunted," is her mother. In the scene with her 'lover,' Peter, she appears in a green satin dress (137, 139). In the scene with her puritan 'husband' and 'son,' Orin, she dresses in the maternal velvet gown (149 f.).[3] It was in California— where Brant had been (15)—that Lavinia discarded her mourning and bought new clothes in her mother's color (153). The change of costume occurred after she had met Wilkins, a ship's officer reminding her of Brant. Her green costume thus advertizes her unconscious love for Brant or for the life-affirming spirit in him, the spirit she later recognizes in Wilkins, in Avahanni, and in all the natives of the green islands.

---

[5] Cf. the second galley proofs, where Lavinia as the only surviving member of the family decides: "I'll never wear anything but mourning again! Life doesn't fit the Mannons! Only death becomes them!" (= 178).

[6] In the second typewritten version Lavinia states explicitly: "I didn't want to be born" (= 57).

[1] The connection between mind and apparel is indicated more clearly in the second galley proofs, where Orin reproaches himself: "I turned against her [Christine] when I should have forgiven her. And to make it blacker, it was all my fault in the first place. Why did I ever let Father and you [Lavinia] drag me into the war when she pleaded with me not to leave her" (= 152).

[2] In the first typewritten version Orin appears at this point in *"clothes of a ship's officer's cut."* While this costume emphasizes his identity with Brant, it gives a false impression of his island experience.

[3] In the first typewritten version her costume, following the pattern set by Christine, is first a *"deep crimson,"* then a *"purplish plum color,"* both reminiscent of Christine's second, sanguinary costume. In the second galley proofs she still has *"a red Indian blanket"* thrown over her chair in the final act, a pagan touch warring with her black costume and reminding us that the Shenandoah of the theme song is not only the name of a river but also of an Indian chief.

One of the first things that especially strikes a spectator of *Journey* is the contrast in costume between husband and wife, all the more apparent since they enter closely together:

She is dressed simply but with a sure sense of what becomes her (12 f.).

He wears a threadbare, ready-made, grey sack suit and shineless black shoes, a collar-less shirt with a thick white handkerchief knotted loosely around his throat. There is nothing picturesquely careless about his get-up. It is commonplace shabby (13).

Tyrone's stinginess proclaims itself in his threadbare suit, and in general his get-up reminds us of his Irish peasant origin of which he is so proud. Mary talks contemptuously of his "filthy old suit" which she has "tried to make him throw away" (43). The contrast between their costumes is one between attractiveness and ugliness, cleanliness and shabbiness. It reveals, on Mary's part, sensitivity to the views of others and, on Tyrone's, indifference to such views.

The remark that his clothes *"do not costume any romantic part"* (13) reminds us that he is an actor, especially successful in romantic parts. It was the romantic actor who conquered Mary's heart: "... he was handsomer than my wildest dream, in his make-up and his nobleman's costume that was so becoming to him. He was different from all ordinary men, like someone from another world. ... I fell in love right then" (105). And she married him in a gown made of

soft, shimmering satin, trimmed with wonderful old duchesse lace, in tiny ruffles around the neck and sleeves, and worked in with the folds that were draped round in a bustle effect at the back. The basque was boned and very tight. I remember I held my breath when it was fitted, so my waist would be as small as possible. My father even let me have duchesse lace on my white satin slippers, and lace with the orange blossoms in my veil. Oh, how I loved that gown! It was so beautiful! (115).

The wedding gown, it would seem, represents the young girl's romantic idea of the happy, beautiful, different marriage in store for her:

That wedding gown was nearly the death of me and the dressmaker, too! (*She laughs.*) I was so particular. It was never quite good enough (114 f.).

But the dream of a marriage different from the ordinary mould could not be realized; the gown was stowed away: "I used to take it out from time to time when I was lonely, but it always made me cry, so finally a long while ago— ... I wonder where I hid it? Probably in one of the old trunks in the attic" (115). The wedding gown is finally brought out from its hiding-place: "*Over one arm, carried neglectfully, trailing on the floor, as if she had forgotten she held it, is an old-fashioned white satin wedding gown, trimmed with duchesse lace"* (170). Mary at this point has reverted to the time before she met Tyrone. The marriage, as her treatment of the gown indicates, no longer has any meaning for her. It still does to Tyrone:

Here, let me take it, dear. You'll only step on it and tear it and get it dirty dragging it on the floor. Then you'd be sorry afterwards. (*She lets him take it, regarding him from somewhere far away within herself, without recognition ...*) (172).

By returning the wedding gown to her worldly bridegroom Mary symbolically divorces herself from him. Wearing *"a sky-blue dressing gown over her nightdress"* (170), she is now not only beyond marriage but also beyond the blinding fog of life itself, at one with the Divine Virgin she has been seeking so anxiously, convinced that "when She sees no one in the world can believe in me even for a moment any more, then She will believe in me, and with Her help it will be so easy" (94). The nightdress recalls the time when Mary "half crazy" had run out of the house and tried to drown herself for lack of morphine (86, 118). At the end we witness another 'drowning' attempt; says Tyrone: "It's the damned poison. But I've never known her to drown herself in it as deep as this" (174).[4]

Like his mother, Edmund is in love with death (154)—and with heaven; her dream of becoming a nun is the more conventional, Catholic version of his poetical dream of being a sea gull (153): both long for freedom from mankind and a celestial sense of belonging. For this reason, perhaps, Mary's sky-blue dressing gown is matched by the *"blue serge suit"* (89)—also reminiscent of his bond with the sea—which Edmund wears from Act II.2 onwards. Set off against these is Tyrone's *"brown dressing gown"* (125), the earthy costume of a man too busy with land speculation to concern himself with heaven.

Illustrative Action

Actions speak louder than words, we say, and the rule certainly holds true in drama. Only by the complex procedure of comparing what a character does with what he says and with what others say about him can we arrive at a reasonably balanced and accurate picture of him. If we tend to set greater store by the actions of a character than by what is said by or about him, it is because we cannot help feeling that actions—or reactions—are usually more spontaneous and therefore more truthful than words. Much of the tension

---

[4] In the first typewritten version the suicide implication is obscured by Tyrone's relative optimism; the relevant lines read: "We've seen her like this before. It's the damned poison. She'll be sane again tomorrow if she gets a good sleep. It isn't often she drowns herself in it like this. She'll be more careful from now on."

and poignancy in O'Neill's plays stems from the contrast between untruthful words and truthful actions. Yet, since O'Neill frequently describes men and women, who have repressed their true selves in favor of some more pleasing image, their actions are by no means always truthful. Often they keep playing a part—not so much to others as to themselves.

Actions are, as a rule, more vague in meaning than words. With regard to drama this is especially true of actions performed at the very beginning of a play, before a word has as yet been uttered. Such initial actions arouse our curiosity and are an effective suspense-creating device. O'Neill uses it skillfully in *Zone, Ile* and *Jones.* His employment of this kind of dumb show is in part motivated by the naturalistic demand for verisimilitude. The characters, alone on the stage, must refrain from soliloquizing and limit themselves to silent acting. Their actions appear altogether plausible and do not strike us as having any significance beyond their realistic meaning. But O'Neill also occasionally resorts to what may properly be termed pantomime: stylized movements or gestures which serve to express emotions of which the characters are not fully aware and which therefore cannot be fully conveyed through words.

Act III of *Welded* begins with an emotionally tense and very complex situation. Husband and wife have returned home after their unsuccessful attempts to kill their love for each other through an act of adultery. The act opens as they confront one another:

For a long, tense moment they remain fixed, staring into each other's eyes with an apprehensive questioning. Then, as if unconsciously, falteringly, with trembling smiles, they come toward each other. Their lips move as if they were trying to speak. When they come close, they instinctively reach out their hands in a strange conflicting gesture of a protective warding off and at the same time a seeking possession. Their hands clasp and they again stop, searching each other's eyes. Finally their lips force out words (480).

Pantomime serves O'Neill's purpose at this point; the impression to be conveyed is that the Capes are *"deeply in love"* (480) and at the same time aware how precarious the situation is. The pantomime is not realistic;[5] as the stylized parallelism and the words *"unconsciously"* and *"instinctively"* suggest, Michael's and Eleanor's actions are intended to visualize the identity of the emotional conflict within each of them.

A stronger note of mystery is struck in the pantomimic passages of *Desire.* Part II.2 reveals the two bedrooms on the top floor of the Cabot house. It is the evening of a hot summer day, two months after Abbie has made her appearance on the farm. Eben is sitting on the bed in his room in undershirt

[5] Cf. O'Neill's remark to Nathan: "the play is about love as a life-force, not as an intellectual conception, and the plausibilities of realism don't apply" (Caputi, p. 449).

and pants. In the other bedroom Abbie and Ephraim *"are sitting side by side on the edge of their bed"* in night shirt and night-dress. Suddenly,

EBEN *gets up and paces up and down distractedly.* ABBIE *hears him. Her eyes fasten on the intervening wall with concentrated attention.* EBEN *stops and stares. Their hot glances seem to meet through the wall. Unconsciously he stretches out his arms for her and she half rises. Then aware, he mutters a curse at himself and flings himself face downward on the bed, his clenched fists above his head, his face buried in the pillow.* ABBIE *relaxes with a faint sigh but her eyes remain fixed on the wall; she listens with all her attention for some movement from* EBEN (236).

The multiple set and the pantomime help to inform the audience of Eben's desire for Abbie, even before he has become fully aware of it himself. This desire was first aroused the moment Eben first saw Abbie from far away arriving at the farm in the buggy. Reporting to his brothers that he can feel—rather than see—that it is Ephraim and Abbie who are in the distant buggy, he *"squirms as if he had the itch"* (219), an indication of his desire for Abbie, for what is the father's property. The description may be compared to the one concerning Abbie's lust for Eben: *"her body squirms desirously"* (229).[6]

In the bedroom scene their mutual desire, under the impact of—or rather corresponding to—the heat of the summer night, has reached a bursting point. The scene testifies to the truth of Abbie's earlier pronouncement that Nature will beat Eben (229). It is starkly ironical in its demonstration of the impenetrable barrier that exists between husband and wife despite their closeness in the matrimonial bed and the lack of such a barrier between the lovers despite the physical wall separating them. After Ephraim has left to seek the warmth his wife denies him among the cows in the barn, the contact between the lovers is firmly established:

EBEN *and* ABBIE *stare at each other through the wall.* EBEN *sighs heavily and* ABBIE *echoes it. Both become terribly nervous, uneasy. Finally* ABBIE *gets up and listens, her ear to the wall. He acts as if he saw every move she was making, he becomes resolutely still. She seems driven into a decision—goes out the door in rear determinedly* (239).

What O'Neill presumably wanted to express here, as generally in the play, is what the characters feel "subconsciously" (O'Neill/Cowley, 1926, p. 21), above all that they are in the grip of a "life-force" stronger than themselves—what

[6] In a letter to Nathan (3.3.1925) O'Neill says: "What I think everyone missed in 'Desire' is the quality in it I set most store by—the attempt to give an epic tinge to New England's inhibited life—but, to make its inexpressiveness practically expressive, to release it" (Goldberg, p. 158). The pantomimes may be considered one of the ways in which the author tried to make the "inexpressiveness practically expressive."

Abbie terms Nature—which makes you "want t' grow—into somethin' else —till ye're jined with it" (229).[7] In a sense the mystical note is merely a result of the playwright's way of *grouping* the characters; obviously, the whole scene gains its meaning and power from the fact that the two lovers are in separate rooms. If the grouping in this instance is a little more conspicuous than what is normal with O'Neill, it is, on the other hand, but one of many examples that could be cited to indicate the playwright's constant attempt to place his characters in significant positions. A few other examples indicate the symbolic possibilities of this the most common of all illustrative actions.

In *Horizon,* Robert's replacement of Andrew as husband and farmer is demonstrated visually in the first interior scene. In the Mayo sitting-room are *"three rockers with crocheted tidies on their backs, and one straight-backed"* (93). The straight-backed chair is apparently singled out. Andrew is at first sitting on it (94), but after he has left, Robert occupies this chair (99). Even before Andrew realizes the situation, Robert has "put [himself] in [Andrew's] place" (110). The uncomfortable and hard chair suits Andrew, the "born farmer" (97), but Robert, as the ensuing action bears out, "wasn't born for it" (136). Also in Act II.1, when Robert still attempts to live up to his farmer's task, he occupies this chair (119). But in the final act when, mortally ill, he expresses a wish to move to the city, he recognizes his defeat by sinking down in one of the rockers (145), half-lying in it with closed eyes, like a corpse. Andrew, similarly, recognizes *his* defeat, when he too *"sinks down"* in one of the rockers (154), now preferring its padded comfort.

Stating that he wants to make his "position clear" (160), Robert asks Andrew to marry Ruth, when he himself is dead (162); as he once replaced Andrew, thereby ruining all their lives, so Andrew must now replace him and recreate the original situation. For the pronouncement of his last wish Robert is, however, placed between Andrew and Ruth. His in-between position is kept after he has died and remains until the end of the play (168). Ruth's and Andrew's position on either side of his dead body coupled with her apathy seem to shut out hope that they shall ever be able to free themselves of the guilty past and join in marriage.

[7] Leech claims (p. 53) that the scene makes sense "on a naturalistic plane," that a desired person can "exercise power through a mere bed-room wall." The latter is not to be denied, but if he does it in the manner O'Neill demonstrates, it is certainly not "in accord with everyday experience" (ibid.).

Winther is more to the point (p. 268) when he regards the similarity between Eben's and Abbie's actions as determined by transference of thought. Yet he oddly rebukes O'Neill for resorting to such an unscientific idea. Surely, O'Neill would be the last to reject the idea of telepathy on the ground that it has no "basis in fact" (ibid.). Suggestions of telepathy occur in many O'Neill plays (cf. Raleigh, pp. 149 f.).

In *Electra* O'Neill very carefully groups his characters with regard to the steps in front of the Mannon house. We first see Christine, the mistress of the house, on top of the steps (8). Shortly afterwards Lavinia *"comes out to the top of the steps where her mother had stood"* (10). By position alone O'Neill thus suggests the basic identity between mother and daughter as well as Lavinia's desire "to steal [Christine's] place" (33).

Shortly after Ezra's homecoming there is a significant grouping: "CHRISTINE *sits on the top step at center; he sits on the middle step at right;* LAVINIA *on the lowest step at left"* (47 f.). Ezra significantly takes the Mannon position to the right. His place between the two women is suggestive. He has long felt closer to the daughter than to the wife; yet now he has come home with long locked-up desire and renewed love for Christine. She can therefore easily dominate him, whereas Lavinia must be satisfied with a humble position removed from the father.

After the murder Christine's strength wanes as the furies of guilt begin their work upon her. She tries to avert Lavinia's suspicions in a long, hysterical speech, delivered from the top of the stairs—Christine's position is outwardly unchanged—to the daughter below on the ground. Finally, however, Christine is unable to stand Lavinia's mocking silence. She rushes down the steps and tries by force to wring an answer out of the daughter (77 f.). Christine, we note, has left her triumphant position. Lavinia and the Mannon furies within herself have brought her low. When we see Christine again at the top of the stairs in the following act, she is *"leaning against a column for support"* (119), and finally—after the news of Adam's death—she *"sinks down on the lowest step"* (121), Lavinia's former place. A moment later she is at ground level, dead on the floor in the study.

The mother's positional downfall is balanced by the daughter's positional ascendancy. In the final act we see Lavinia at the top of the stairs (170). She has stolen the mother's place and is now sole mistress of the house. Yet, since she has meanwhile undergone a change, she now, like the mother, desires to leave the house. In a scene (171 ff.) recalling the mother-daughter battle just referred to, Hazel tells her from below the steps that she cannot escape; trapped, Lavinia sinks down in a chair; again the 'groundling' has brought the triumphant character low. But unlike Christine, Lavinia regains her strength. *"Stiff and square-shouldered"* (179) she stands at the top of the stairs as the play ends, exactly as she did when we first saw her, lonelier and more truly triumphant in her self-punishment, grimly reminding us that she is the last Mannon.

In *Days* the strength of the conflicting desires incarnated by John and Loving is indicated in the grouping. When the play begins, the two are sitting next

O'Neill's sketch of the grouping at the end of *Days,* showing John's and Loving's cross gestures beneath the Cross of the church.

to one another, Loving in the deathly, facing-front position he usually occupies. In other words, the two desires are kept in balance; the end of the novel John Loving is working on, which will demonstrate who is the stronger of the two, is still unwritten. Gradually Loving gains in power. The end is written the way he wants it. When it seems clear that Elsa will die, Loving experiences the apogee of his triumph. At this point we see John lying on a chaise longue in *"a drugged half-sleep,"* much as his dying wife, while Loving stands right behind him, *"staring down at his face"* (556). But once John decides to return to the old church of his childhood to pray before the cross that his wife be saved, the situation changes. Unsuccessfully, Loving tries to bar his way. The demonic figure is forced to retreat until he stands with his head right underneath the foot of the cross. Confronted with the symbol of Love, Loving is forced to surrender:

He slumps forward to the floor and rolls over on his back, dead, his head beneath the foot of the Cross, his arms outflung so that his body forms another cross. JOHN *rises from his knees and stands with arms stretched up and out, so that he, too, is like a cross* (566).

The three crosses—note that O'Neill capitalizes only the one with Christ—recall the ones on Golgotha, and John and Loving may well be likened to the repentant and the hardened sinner on either side of Christ, one condemned, the other blessed.

Less spectacular, but not less effective, is the character grouping in *Journey.* The play opens with Mary's and Tyrone's entrance shortly after breakfast: *"Tyrone's arm is around his wife's waist as they appear from the back parlor. Entering the living room he gives her a playful hug"* (14). Shortly afterwards the two sons enter *"together,"* laughing (19), and as they all sit around the table we have a sense of family unity despite the teasing that goes on. But the tone soon grows more somber. Edmund is disgusted with the father's attack on Jamie and leaves the room (26). The note of discord has been sounded and its reverberations are to grow in volume as the play progresses. We never again see the family sitting down together around the table, and we only briefly see all four together in the room until the very end.

As soon as Tyrone knows that Mary has relapsed into morphinism his attitude towards her changes; this is represented by the positions of the couple, as they enter the living room after lunch:

Mary is the first to enter from the back parlor. Her husband follows. He is not with her as he was in the similar entrance after breakfast at the opening of Act One. He avoids touching her or looking at her (71).

The four family members are now scattered about the room: Mary stands to the left of the table, talking with nervous volubility; Tyrone stares out through the screen door at right; Jamie stands looking through the window at right; Edmund, spiritually closest to the mother, sits by the table, he too turning away from her *"so he does not have to watch her"* (71). The grouping indicates both the disintegration of the family and the men's unwillingness to face a calamity they are all partly responsible for.

Mary's frequent staring through the windows is not only motivated by her need to hide from her family; it is also, I think, meant to represent her turning away from the living room—life—towards "the other shore" (82). It prepares for her final 'leave-taking' of her family, which fittingly takes place as Jamie recites three stanzas from Swinburne's "A Leave-taking." During his recital Mary moves behind each of the men—they all sit around the table— and finally places herself to the left at *"the front end of the sofa beneath the windows ..., facing front, her hands folded in her lap, in a demure school- girlish pose"* (174). The separation could not have been suggested more de- finitely: the position is highly emphatic, for it is the only time anyone sits down away from the family table; Mary's gesture is protectively virginal; and she is turned away from her men in a deathly facing-front position, while they, motionless like corpses, listen to her reverie.

Dancing or dance-like movements occur in many of the plays, usually as an expression of an affirmative attitude to life.[8] When Kublai Kaan in *Marco*

---

[8] For Nietzsche the dance is a symbol of joy and levity; while the average man is weighed down by his spirit of gravity, the superman who has overcome this spirit by his *amor fati* is free to dance (cf. Morgan, p. 312). O'Neill was undoubtedly inspired by Nietzsche's concept of the dance.

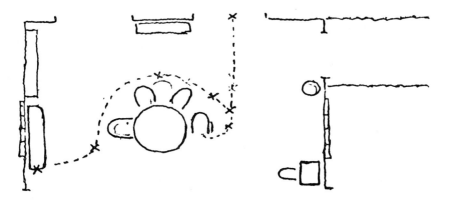

Drawing by O'Neill, showing Mary Tyrone's movements and positions at the end of *Journey*.

admonishes his Commander-in-Chief and his soldiers to go into the ballroom and dance and threatens to revoke his declaration of war on Japan unless Bayan "learn to dance and be silent" (423), he is admonishing those encumbered by the spirit of gravity. The pompous, militant Bayan—an oriental Marco—is contrasted with Kukachin, who incarnates the spirit of love and whose "little feet danced away the stamp of armies" (437). In memory of the dead princess we also witness how a troupe of young girls and boys, forming part of the funeral procession in her honor, move *"in a gliding, interweaving dance pattern"* (433).

Their movements have the same grace as those of Lazarus' followers, who dance in rhythmic *"weaving patterns"* (*Lazarus,* 285), not unlike, one may suppose, the dancers of Greek antiquity; O'Neill at one point significantly compares Lazarus' followers to *"figures in a frieze"* (289). An Orthodox Jew complains that the followers are leaving the farms "to dance and sing" (286), and by the time Lazarus reaches Athens, his dancing crowd is made up of people from a great many different countries, a circumstance which vividly illustrates how his gospel has spread like wildfire.

The life-denying Jews, who oppose Lazarus and his gospel, nevertheless cannot refrain from dance-like movements; but their 'dance' is a grotesque parody of that performed by the followers; it is jerky, mechanical, marionettish and perverted (287, 289). Similarly Caligula, who is in many respects a mob character, never learns to dance properly; his crazy leaps (305) and hopping capers (308) are the characteristic movements of a spiritual *"cripple"* (308). Caligula is, in fact, another hairy ape (299, 308, 311, 360), and his capers— the word is derived from the Latin word for 'he-goat'—visualize his satyric nature, which in turn indicates his not-yet-fully-human status,[9] his crucial position between beast and (super)man as well as his attachment to Lazarus-Dionysus. If O'Neill stresses his apelike rather than goatlike characteristics, it is, I take it, because, since Darwin the ape is a more meaningful symbol than the goat.

We must be aware of ideas like these in order to see the significance of the apelike nature and satyric capers not only of Caligula but also of Dion and Brown. Says Dion in the Prologue of *Brown:* "Seek the monkey in the moon! (*He suddenly cuts a grotesque caper, like a harlequin and darts off, laughing with forced abandon.*)" (262). The monkey, we learn a little later, is the one that "broke loose from Jehovah and ran away to join Charley Darwin's circus" (268). Dion's caper points in two directions. The reader is likely to pay attention to the word "*caper*" and be reminded of Dion's Dionysian origin and nature; when Brown has put on Dion's mask he too begins to cut "*goatish capers*" (313, 317). The spectator, on the other hand, will see Dion's leap and, since it follows immediately after the spoken word "monkey," he will regard it as an apelike movement.

We are not surprised to learn, of course, that Dion "sings and dances so marvelously" (263), whereas the unmasked Brown is "too fat ... to dance" (296). But once Brown has inherited Dion's mask, he designs a capitol with a Silenus dancing on the cupola (312) and finds it hard to avoid dancing himself (318). The fact that the play begins and ends with a graduation ball is undoubtedly in part due to O'Neill's interest in dancing as a symbol of Dionysian life affirmation. When Margaret, in the Epilogue, admonishes her boys to "go in and dance" (325), she is not just dismissing them because she wants to be alone with her memory of Dion; she is also, like Kublai, giving advice as to the proper way of living. In Brown's dying words about the laughter of Man, which will play "in innumerable dancing gales of flame upon the knees of God" (322), it is made plain that dancing and laughter are both manifestations of divinity.

Already in *Desire* O'Neill employs dancing in a symbolic way. When the Cabot brothers first appear, they "*clump heavily along in their clumsy thick-soled boots caked with earth*" (204) as though they were part of, or tied to, the farm—as indeed they are. Their ponderousness goes both with their primitive, bovine natures and with their feeling of being slaves to a life marked by gray monotony and loneliness. Once they get the opportunity to

[9] In the notes it says that the satyrs are "displaced beings—nearer to men than D[ionysus].—half-way creatures between animal & human—speculating wistfully on their being because not wholly understanding themselves & their place in nature."

leave the farm for what they consider the promised land, California, they are
filled with an ecstatic sense of liberation which is expressed visually in the
characteristic Dionysian levity:

> PETER. ... My feet feel itchin' t' walk an' walk—an' jump high over thin's—
> an'....
> SIMEON. Dance? (*A pause.*)
> PETER. (*puzzled*) It's plumb onnateral (220).

They soon give way to these feelings before their astounded father:

> SIMEON. We're free, old man! (*He cuts a caper.*)
> PETER. Free! (*He gives a kick in the air.*)
> SIMEON. (*in a frenzy*) Whoop!
> PETER. Whoop! (*They do an absurd Indian war dance about the old man
> who is petrified between rage and the fear that they are insane.*) (223).

Ephraim, we later learn, has killed Indians in the West in his youth (251).
By identifying themselves with Indians performing a war dance the sons thus
openly side with the father's enemies. The Indians, children of nature roving
across the prairies, are free from the sense of ownership, of worldly cares, that
enslaves the Cabots. They are truly the lilies of the field Simeon and Peter
aim to become (216). With their newly gained freedom and the long, adven-
turous trip that lies before them, Simeon and Peter may feel like Indians.
But what drives them to California is a materialistic desire for gold, quite
alien to the mind of the noble savage, if we may trust O'Neill's description
of the Indians in *Fountain*.

If the ironical aspect of the dance remains obscure at this point, it becomes
quite evident when Ephraim later, in the feast scene, performs the same kind
of dance before all his guests. Ephraim's "*Indian war dance*" (251) has several
connotations. It is, first of all, an expression of his contempt for his soft
neighbors, who are too weak, even though they are much younger than he is,
to dance the way he does. More specifically, it is an attempt to prove to them,
by a feat of vigor, that he is still virile enough to father a child; dancing he
boasts: "Whoop! Here's dancin' fur ye! ... I be the on'y man in the county!"
(251). But through Abbie we have already learnt that it is Eben who is "the
best dancer in the county" (248). Ephraim's dancing, therefore, although
certainly an admirable demonstration of his powerfulness, convinces neither
us nor his guests of his procreative power. It is also ironical—and foreboding
—that Ephraim should identify himself with the people he has been slaying
and, obliquely, with the sons who have left him. Does *he* also long for the
freedom of the natives and is this, ultimately, what his dance expresses?
Should we perhaps understand his earlier killing of Indians symbolically, as
an expression of his attempt to suppress a pagan, joyous, life-accepting ten-

dency within himself? Such a view gains support from his reaction close to the end of the play, where Ephraim, cutting *"a mad caper"* and shouting "Whoop!" (268), expresses the same sense of liberation as his sons had done at the idea of leaving the farm for the golden fields of California.

Such everyday occupations as eating, smoking and drinking all have their special connotations in O'Neill's plays. When Mary and Edmund Tyrone in *Journey* show themselves lacking in appetite, there is a natural reason for it. Both of them are ill. But it would be a mistake to think that this explanation exhausts the meaning, for eating in O'Neill's plays is almost always a sign of materialism. Thus, Mary's and Edmund's lacking appetite is contrasted with Tyrone's and Jamie's hunger (54, 66 ff.). Tyrone's appetite seems a modest indication of his more significant land hunger and concomitant stinginess towards his family; Jamie's seems suggestive of his sexual appetite: he especially relishes women with big breasts and satisfies his desire with Fat Violet in the course of the play.

There is an element of life appetite in this materialism, coarse though it may be. Conversely, it is natural to see Mary's and Edmund's disinterest in food as an expression of their disinterest in the life-supporting powers, as a manifestation of a deep-going sickness of life. Edmund draws attention to this meaning when he tells his brother: "You're in luck to be hungry. The way I feel I don't care if I ever eat again" (54).

The contrast between Edmund and Jamie is found already in *Fog,* where the Poet's hunger is taken away by the thought of the poor woman next to him, who has been crying all night after the death of her child, whereas the Businessman *"greedily"* munches sea biscuits while he explains, *"his mouth full,"* that the Poet takes things too much to heart (93). The briskly callous life appetite of the Businessman is pitted against the melancholy compassion and death longing of the Poet.

Like Edmund Tyrone, Robert Mayo in *Horizon* is a much more avid reader than eater. He is late for lunch, does not care if his food gets cold and eats *"gingerly, without appetite"* (122). The same holds true of Eben Cabot in *Desire,* another transparent self-portrait. Although he is the cook of the household, he keeps *"picking at his food without appetite"* (206). His brothers Simeon and Peter are his antitheses, kinsmen of Jamie. When they hear Eben calling that supper is ready, their beastlike characteristics are at once manifested:

SIMEON. (*startled—smacks his lips*) I air hungry!
PETER. (*sniffing*) I smells bacon!
SIMEON. (*with hungry appreciation*) Bacon's good!
PETER. (*in same tone*) Bacon's bacon!

146

A little later we see them eating, *"as naturally unrestrained as beasts of the field,"* while Eben is glancing at them *"with a tolerant dislike"* (205 f.).[1] Simeon and Peter subscribe to the idea that man should be "eating flesh, and drinking wine" (Isaiah 22: 13)—they later get drunk on whiskey (217)—while his life lasts, a simple, animalistic view of life. Eben's "desire," as his attitude to the food indicates, is not of this primitive order.

The brothers' lustful enjoyment of the bacon is also indicative of their love of the flesh in an erotic sense. Simeon characteristically compares Min, the village prostitute whose graces he, Peter and Ephraim have all relished, to a heifer (210), and Peter tells his father to turn Abbie "in the pen with the other sows" (222). Eben's reasons for making love to Min seem much more complex than theirs: they are a blend of sexual desire, longing for the Earth Mother and, above all, a wish to make what has been the father's his own (cf. 214).

The contrast between Eben and his brothers has a counterpart in *Brown*, in the contrast between Dion, on one hand, and the materialistically inclined Brown and Margaret, on the other. Failing to see that Dion seeks Cybel in her capacity of Earth Mother rather than prostitute, Brown is jealous of what he thinks is Dion's successful "love of the flesh" (287). Margaret shows as little understanding of Dion's true needs. Act I.1 opens with Dion's fundamental spiritual worries—"Come unto me all ye who are heavy laden and I will give you rest," he reads from the New Testament (269)—and ends with the wife's trite, everyday concerns; says Margaret: "Will you stop at the butcher's and have them send two pounds of pork chops?" (273). Beginning with the Word the scene ends with the flesh.

Brown has a kinsman in Marco. When Kublai asks Marco to tell him about his soul, the Babbitt-like representative of western man replies:

I know it's a great honor, sir—but forgetting the soul side of it, I've got to eat.
KUBLAI. (*astonished*) To eat?
MARCO. I mean, I'm ambitious. I've got to succeed, and— (*Suddenly blurts out*) What can you pay me? (*Marco,* 380).

Here, explicitly, appetite is used as an image of selfish greed.

Kukachin long believes that Marco has a soul but finally gives up the idea. Sarcastically she asks her intended husband, the King of Persia, to give an immense feast in honor of Marco "as a fitting tribute to his character": "Let there be food in tremendous amounts! He is an exquisite judge of quantity. Let him be urged to eat and drink until he can hold no more, until he becomes his own ideal figure, an idol of stuffed self-satisfaction!" (418). The

---

[1] The longhand draft puts it more strongly; there Eben reacts with *"disgusted resentment."*

"immense feast" takes place a year later as the Polos return to Venice. Enormous platters with *"whole pigs, fowl of all varieties, roasts, vegetables, salads, fruits, nuts, dozens of bottles of wine"* are carried in by servants and arranged on the table until it resembles *"the front of a pretentious delicatessen store"* (428). The *"whole pigs"* are, of course, fitting attributes for the Polos and their guests, whose voices are *"muffled by roast pig"* (431). Kukachin sees Marco as a "pig of a Christian" (416, 419) and his girl friend Donata as a "sow" (416). The food is piled so high that only the faces of the *"substantial bourgeois"* guests (427) can be seen above the dishes. When Marco, with American easy-goingness, tells them to pick a chair and sit down, they disappear *"with one motion"* behind the heaps of food (431). What can come closer to a wallowing in food, in flesh? Kublai, witnessing the scene in his crystal, explains the meaning of the action: "The Word became their flesh, they say. Now all is flesh! And can their flesh become the Word again?" (432). The Epilogue, showing how Marco-the-theatre-goer *"with a satisfied sigh at the sheer comfort of it all, resumes his life"* (439), gives little hope that the flesh will ever become the Word again in the West.

Smoking is illustrative of certain moral principles, or lack of the same, in *Wilderness*. In the Miller family it is strictly a man's business: Nat and Sid smoke cigars, Arthur a pipe; the prudish McComber is, significantly, a nonsmoker (201); cigarette smoking is particularly wicked and decadent, a habit for chorus girls (239, 283). More suggestive is Sam Evan's pipe smoking in Act IV of *Interlude*: *"He smokes a pipe, which he is always relighting whether it needs it or not, and which he bites and shifts about and pulls in and out and puffs at nervously"* (66 f.). Sam feels downhearted. Ignorant both of Nina's pregnancy and of her abortion, forbidden to sleep with her, he feels uncreative both physically and mentally and fears that he will

get fired ... sterile ... (*With a guilty terror*) in more ways than one, I guess! ... (*He springs to his feet as if this idea were a pin stuck in him—lighting his already lighted pipe, walks up and down again, forcing his thoughts into other channels*) (67; O'Neill's dots).

Sam's pulling his pipe in and out of his mouth seems to be an illustration of what is evidently on his mind: sexual intercourse. In line with his own doubts concerning his sexual potency are Darrell's and, in particular, Nina's as she thinks: "How weak he is! ... he'll never do anything ... never give me my desire ... if he'd only fall in love with someone else ... go away ..." (69; O'Neill's dots). Sam's repetitive and nervous act of lighting the pipe signifies, I take it, his attempt to overcome his own lack of passion and imagined sterility.[2] But his action is really superfluous: the pipe is already lighted, just as his passion, at least to a degree, and his procreative ability are already there.

Of even greater significance is the drinking that many O'Neill characters devote themselves to. As they succumb to drunkenness, their defense mechanisms give way and their semi-conscious or unconscious desires come to the fore. What they have to say when affected by alcohol is, in Jamie's words, "not drunken bull, but 'in vino veritas' stuff" (*Journey*, 165). Thus with the help of liquor, as Whitman observes (Gassner, 1964, pp. 160 f.; cf. Mårtensson, p. 119), O'Neill is able, especially in his last plays, to depict quite naturally the dichotomy in man between his 'mask'—his sober façade—and his 'face.'

The drinking that goes on in O'Neill's plays in addition to this psychological significance sometimes has a religious implication. Thus, in *Lazarus* the rebirth of Lazarus is properly celebrated with the drinking of wine (278), for Lazarus is "*Dionysus in his middle period ..., the soul ... of the wine of life stirring forever in the sap and blood and loam of things*" (307). In *Christie,* a play rich in Christ symbolism, as McAleer has shown, it is meaningful that Anna, at the end of Act I (24), "begins her redemption by drinking a toast not in her usual whiskey but in wine—the sacramental symbol of Christ's sacrifice" (McAleer, p. 393). Harry Hope's birthday party in *Iceman,* as Day has demonstrated (1958, p. 7), in many ways resembles the Last Supper. Grouped more or less as the disciples in Leonardo da Vinci's painting, the inmates eat birthday cake, i.e. bread, and drink wine, which Hickey, the Savior figure of the play, has brought to their nocturnal meal. At the Holy Supper Jesus, raising his cup, told his disciples that he would not drink wine again "until that day when I drink it new with you in my Father's kingdom" (Mat. 26: 29). Hickey, whose soberness has shocked everybody, who is soon to be arrested and, presumably, executed, similarly drinks for "the beginning of a new life of peace and contentment" (659).

Recurrent throughout O'Neill's work is the game image. It appears first in *Abortion,* where the baseball game in which the hero is victorious is explicitly said to represent "the game of life" (149), the usual meaning of the game image with O'Neill. For obvious reasons the game is never visualized on the stage. In *Man,* on the other hand, we are at least indirectly witnessing

---

[2] Sam at this point very strongly feels that he is a poor substitute for Gordon, who was evidently of a passionate nature. To Nina there is a direct link between her refusal to quench Gordon's flaming passion and his death in flames. The first typewritten version is explicit on this point; there Nina says: "He was never mine! He flew up to the sky and came down in flames, his love consuming him in flames, his flaming passion destroying him because I had refused!" (= 19).

a game: *"Through the open windows on the right come the shouts of children playing.* MARTHA's *voice joins in with theirs"* (576). Martha, whose *"strenuous life in the open has kept her young and fresh"* (553), remains true to the out-of-doors. We can hear how she is enjoying playing hide-and-seek with Bigelow's children. The little scene serves to emphasize her love of children, her longing for a child, for soon this will be pitted against her husband's intellectual and religious ambition; her "first man"—the son to be—will be contrasted with his: the oldest man, man's origin.[3] *"With a trace of annoyance"* Curtis abstains from joining Bigelow at the window, claiming that he can see "well enough" from where he is (576). Bigelow reports: "Ah, Eddy discovered her behind the tree. Isn't he tickled now" (577).

The game seems connected with the illustrative action with which the act closes, after the secrets have been revealed:

> CURTIS. ... I love you— You are me and I am you! ... (*He kisses her fiercely. They look into each other's eyes for a second—then instinctively fall back from one another.*)
> MARTHA. (*in a whisper*) Yes, you love me. But who am I? You don't know. ... (*They continue to be held by each other's fearfully questioning eyes.*) (588).

Curtis' and Martha's marriage is like a game of hide-and-seek, a serious play with masks, with identities. Curtis, unlike Eddy, it is implied, has never discovered Martha, because, self-centered as he is, he has never cared to look properly for her true self: the child-desiring woman rather than the helpful assistant.

In *Chillun* life is seen either as a square game between friendly partners or as a fight between hostile antagonists. The play begins with a tableau suggesting both. In the foreground four white and four black children play marbles together; behind them are two streets, one filled with white people, the other with black. The symbolism is quite obvious: unlike the grown-ups the children know no racial segregation; they play the game of life *"with concentrated attention"* (301), considering black and white as equal partners, concerned only with "the human race" (336). Or, to be precise, they do so *"for a while,"* long enough to imprint on our brains a picture of what life could be like. As soon as they begin to talk, we realize that they are, in fact, already tainted by the racial thinking and pugnacious spirit of their parents. With one exception: Ella. She genuinely loves Jim and wants to swap colors with him. It is because Ella supports him that Jim can win the marble game;

---

[3] *The Oldest Man* was the original title of the play. In the notes O'Neill draws attention to the double meaning of the title he finally settled for: "Perhaps lay emphasis on The First Man as symbol of all Curt's work means to him spiritually— in his defense to her [.] Martha—'He will be our First Man, Curt [.]'"

her love gives him the self-respect he needs to play, i.e. live, successfully in a white society.

Nine years later (Act I.2) life has turned into a hostile struggle. With Ella's support Mickey, the white boy who earlier lost his marbles to Jim, has become a successful, bullying prizefighter. Without her support Jim fails to pass his school examination (307). Another five years pass (Act I.3) and now neither Mickey nor Jim enjoy Ella's support. Both of them fail. Mickey faces his defeat in the ring, and it is made clear, that it is the girls he has wronged, especially Ella, who cause his downfall by giving spiritual support to his antagonist (313). Jim faces his defeat in the classroom, made nervous by "all the white faces" looking at him (316). Thus blackness of the soul and of the skin both prove self-destructive.

We see this also in Jim's and Ella's marriage. Both of them being by this time seriously damaged in their self-respect feel an acute need to assert themselves; being black-skinned Jim must prove to himself that his soul is 'white'; feeling black-souled Ella must take pride in her white skin. Finally, the struggle is resolved in Ella's insanity. Forgetting her past, she forgets her guilt; and the guilt feeling gone, Ella is again ready to accept blackness and swap faces with Jim: "Pretend you're Painty Face and I'm Jim Crow. Come and play!" (342). The struggle is over. Life is again a friendly children's game—beyond sanity and on the threshold of death.

Various aspects of the game symbol are brought together in *Hughie.* The hero, Erie Smith, has once been in "the big bucks" but is now reduced to "*a small fry gambler*" (9). Moreover, once he lost his faithful listener Hughie, he also lost his self-confidence and his luck (35). "By way of obit" he has presented the dead friend with a grotesque funeral decoration:

A big horseshoe of red roses! I knew Hughie'd want a horseshoe because that made it look like he'd been a horse player. And around the top printed in forget-me-nots was "Good-by, Old Pal." Hughie liked to kid himself he was my pal (31).

Erie's gift is even more appropriate than he himself appears to realize. It is hardly accidental that his "*red and blue silk handkerchief*" and "*red and blue foulard tie*" (9)[4] match the red and blue of the funeral wreath; these attributes visually tie Erie to the dead friend. The horseshoe form also links them, for Erie is a horse player (15) and horses seemed to be the only things in the world he and Hughie truly loved and admired (21). Finally, the horseshoe illustrates Erie-the-gambler's conviction that Hughie has "got all the luck"

[4] In the second typewritten version the latter is "*white and blue.*"

(33) at last in death, the luck that is denied his surviving pal; in this latter sense the gift is thus an indication of Erie's death wish.

A loser in all real games, in the Game of Life, Erie has no longer the consolation of being the winner in make-believe games, for he no longer has anyone to play these games with. Unable to accept death-in-life as a *modus vivendi* he is, when the play opens, faced with the alternative of finding another 'playmate' or of ending his life. Although his suicidal leanings are nowhere made explicit, they are strongly suggested. With reference to himself Erie declares that "there's guys who'd feel easier if he wasn't around no more" (11).[5] Erie knows that up in his hotel room his feeling of loneliness may cause him to commit suicide. Associated as it is with death, the hotel room both attracts and repels Erie. Whenever he realizes his failure of establishing any contact with the clerk, he approaches the elevator that will take him to his room. And throughout the major part of the play he keeps playing with his room key *"as if it were a fetish which might set him free"* (28) from the imprisonment of life. Yet his death fear proves the stronger; it keeps him glued to the desk, clinging to life.

If life is a game—as Erie says it is (18)—then all men are players. Both Hughie and Charlie, despite their initial hesitation, turn out to be interested in gambling. "Night after night" Erie played crap with Hughie and told him his tall tales. He calls this giving the clerk "some interest in life." The story-telling and the game-playing had the same effect: they stimulated Hughie's imagination and gave a thrill to his monotonous life. In short, they gave him a sense of being alive. In the case of Charlie we actually witness how he comes to life during the play. When it opens he is as close to a corpse as a human being could possibly be: he looks cadaverous, is immobile, stares *"at nothing," "is not thinking"* (7). After Erie has entered he begins to think a little, mostly to protect himself from getting involved in the guest's life problems. Concerned at first only with himself, he eventually begins to identify himself with people who hold more active occupations. His thinking is now dialogistic and dramatic. But it still lacks real engagement; it is *"without curiosity"* (26), *"disinterested"* (27). The change comes when the clerk is able to connect his idol, Arnold Rothstein, with Erie. His pipe dreaming, which has become increasingly imaginative, active and violent, is now conceived in the same spirit and form as Erie's speeches (32); it concerns gambling and the clerk plays the same heroic part in his dream tale as Erie does in his spoken ones. Finally we see the clerk engaged in the crap game *"with an excited dead-pan expression he hopes resembles Arnold Rothstein's"* (38). Slowly life and pipe dreaming—the two are inseparable—have been

[5] The second typewritten version adds: "on the bottom of the Hudson with a weight tied to him."

evoked. The clerk has found his exciting dope. As with Hughie, Erie has given him "some interest in life." Likewise, the clerk has given Erie a reason to go on living.[6]

The play thus illustrates how the 'dead' men, vacillating between death fear and death longing, eventually find a *modus vivendi* and experience a sense of togetherness by accepting and supporting each other's pipe dreams. The final crap game (38) is a ritual, re-establishing the myth Hughie and Erie once shared.

[6] Falk's claim (p. 202) that Erie, at the final curtain, "is gambling with death" seems to me a misinterpretation of the ending.

IV. WHERE WORDS FAIL

In a memorandum to director, designer and cast concerning *Dynamo* O'Neill commented generally on the importance of sound in his plays:

... I have always used sound in plays as a structural part of them. Tried to use, I mean—for I've never got what the script called for (even in "Jones"), not because what I specified couldn't be done but because I was never able to over-come the slip-shod, old-fashioned disregard of our modern theatre for what ought to be one of its superior opportunities (contrasted with the medium of the novel, for example) in expressing the essential rhythm of our lives today (Simon-son, p. 118).

As this statement indicates, O'Neill's interest in sound effects is partly due to the greatly increased possibilities in the modern theatre of reproducing sound. Much more important, however, is the fact that O'Neill apparently had an instinctive feeling for the sound pattern of his plays, 'sound' taken in its widest possible sense:

J—— once said that the difference between my plays and other contemporary work was that I always wrote primarily by ear for the ear, that most of my plays, even down to the rhythm of the dialogue, had the definite structural quality of a musical composition. This hits the nail on the head. It is not that I consciously strive after this but that, willy nilly, my stuff takes that form (Simonson, p. 117).

In the ensuing discussion I shall mainly be concerned with sound effects in the ordinary, narrow sense of the term. Only incidentally shall I deal with sound in the wider sense indicated by O'Neill in the second quotation. When discussing the songs in the plays I shall deal not only with the music but also with the words, since it is obviously artificial to separate the two.

Mechanical Sounds

O'Neill's first important play, *Cardiff,* is also the first to employ sound effects in a "structural" and not merely incidental way. The most obvious aural effect is an off-stage mechanical sound: "*At regular intervals of a minute or so the blast of the steamer's whistle can be heard above all the other sounds*" (477). The whistle, which is the audible sign that the ship is surrounded by fog, is the only continuous sound in the play.

154

Inside the forecastle, where Yank lies dying in his bunk, there is a variety of sounds, arranged in a meaningful pattern. When the play begins we hear, apart from the ever-present whistle, the soft playing of *"some folk-song on a battered accordion"* (477). In response to Cocky's yarn there are bursts of laughter, increasing in volume, so that Yank is finally wakened and starts groaning. Immediately there is *"a hushed silence"* (478). For a while the sailors had forgotten that they had a dying man in their midst; now they are reminded and feel a bit ashamed of their thoughtlessness; the conversation, which now concerns Yank, is toned down. Yet, as the topic changes to the rotten food on board, their anger makes them forgetful of Yank; *"unconsciously"* they raise their voices (481). Another groan from Yank causes Driscoll to order the accordion player, Paul, to put his instrument away: "Is that banshee schreechin' fit music for a sick man?" (481). Driscoll's concern with what he wants to deny—death—is revealed in his choice of metaphor. For a banshee, according to popular Irish belief, is a supernatural being, who takes the shape of an old woman, foretelling death by mournful singing or wailing. The accordion sound ceases, but instead, as an illustration of Driscoll's inability to fight death, *"the steamer's whistle sounds particularly loud in the silence"* (481). The true banshee, apparently, is the whistle.[1] One of the sailors, Olson, complains that he can't sleep "when weestle blow." Yet, a moment later, he is *"fast asleep and snoring"* (481). Ironical with regard to himself, Olson's remark holds true with regard to Yank, to whom the whistle speaks of approaching death (cf. Engel, 1953, p. 14) and who is not going to 'sleep' until the fog has dissolved and the whistle has stopped.

Soon Yank weakly begins to speak. He realizes that he is going to die. But Driscoll rejects the idea:

Don't be thinkin' such things! (*The ship's bell is heard heavily tolling eight times. From the forecastle head above the voice of the lookout rises in a long wail:* Aaall's welll. *The men look uncertainly at* YANK *as if undecided whether to say good-by or not.*) (482).

The tolling and the wail suggest burial, the burial at sea Yank wants to escape. The lookout's cry—on the realistic level the catchword for the men who are to relieve their comrades on deck—seems ironical in content when sounded in the presence of a dying man (cf. Koischwitz, p. 104).

When the men leave for the deck everything quiets down. Yank's death struggle is fought to the accompaniment of the intermittent blowing of the whistle outside and to the snoring of the relieved mates around him. Yank

---

[1] It is characteristic that Driscoll, in the longhand draft, talks about the whistle as "shriekin'" (=481), i.e. producing about the same sound as the "schreechin'" accordion.

pairs the two sounds off: "Why should it be a rotten night like this with that damned whistle blowin' and people snorin' all round?" (489). As Yank's fear of death finds aural expression in the mournful whistle, so his sickness of life is nourished by the various sounds inside the forecastle—the accordion playing, the laughter, the snoring—which have one thing in common: they illustrate his mates' indifference to his fate, an indifference which is not due to any dislike of Yank but is an illustration of the unconsciously selfish way of the world. Their indifference dramatizes Yank's complaint that his life has been spent "without no one to care whether you're alive or dead" (486).

The play ends quietly. The moment Yank dies, we must suppose, the whistle ceases. The fog has lifted; the struggle is over. The rest is—relative—silence: a sob from Driscoll at the loss of his best friend, a hushed whisper from Cocky in recognition of Yank's death. Along with Yank we have journeyed from the everyday sounds of life to the stillness of death.

The steamer's whistle in *Cardiff* anticipates the tom-tom in *Jones* (Pellizzi, p. 354). The most dominant sound effect in any O'Neill play, the impact of the tom-tom in the theatre is quite overpowering. If we have difficulties identifying ourselves with Jones as a man, we can at least, thanks to the tom-tom, be affected by his agitation.[2]

On the realistic level, the beating of the drum is part of the "war dance" (184), which the insurgent natives perform to get up their courage to pursue Jones, whom they believe to possess strong magical powers; by beating the tom-tom they work a counterspell. The moment Jones first hears it, it comes like an ominous answer to his culminating boast displaying his utter contempt for the "trash niggers" (184); the sound strikes the first note of fear in him —"*a strange look of apprehension creeps into his face*" (184)—and as the drum beat grows faster and louder his fear mounts.

In one sense the tom-tom may be seen as only an outer excuse for the inner sound that O'Neill was anxious to reproduce: that of Jones' throbbing heart:

It starts at a rate exactly corresponding to normal pulse beat—72 to the minute —and continues at a gradually accelerating rate from this point uninterruptedly to the very end of the play (184).

When Jones' heart finally ceases to beat, the sound of the tom-tom "*abruptly ceases*" (203).[3] To indicate further that the drum beat represents essentially an inner fate, O'Neill makes it grow and accelerate after each shot from

---

[2] The tom-tom, Quinn notes (2, p. 179) is a unifying force in its establishment of a primitive emotion which character and audience can share.

[3] The indication in the longhand draft that Jones has been shot in the heart further corroborates the identity between the two sounds.

Jones' revolver, for as Jones realizes that by firing he has exposed himself to his pursuers, he experiences them as being nearer and his fear mounts.

Yet, since what is heard by Jones is heard also by us, the fate is at the same time experienced as an outer, "supernatural menace" (O'Neill, Dec. 1932/Cargill et al., p. 119); or rather, we vacillate between regarding the sound as an internal and an external reality as our minds fluctuate between the rational and the irrational, reason and emotion. O'Neill realized the necessity of satisfying both demands, of combining plausibility with mystery, to make his play something more than a case study in fear.

Constituting both an outer and inner fate, the tom-tom governs, it seems, the other sound effects in the play, which, taken together, reveal a similar escalating pattern.[4]

Throughout the play the reports from Jones' revolver, like the tom-tom, have an important unifying function: they climactically end each forest scene except one—the slave ship scene—where instead a similar effect is gained by Jones' voice rising to *"the highest pitch of sorrow, of desolation"* as the scene ends (199). His wail carries over to the following Congo scene, thereby binding the two together. Similarly, the Witch Doctor's shrills of *"furious exultation"* as he demands Jones' sacrifice (202) are echoed in the *"savage, exultant yells"* (203) of the natives as they kill Jones in the final scene; here the parallel sounds help to suggest the mysterious identity of Jones' killers and of his 'deaths.'

In Scene 2, O'Neill calls for a *"brooding, implacable silence"* (187), the fateful 'sound' of the Great Forest, broken only by (apart from the pervasive drum) the moaning of the wind (187) and the *"mocking laughter like a rustling of leaves"* of the Little Formless Fears (190). The animistic description of the sounds is an adequate expression of Jones' primitive belief—of all our beliefs, in fact, when we are under the pressure of guilt-ridden fear. But there is still a natural explanation for each sound; Jones' fear is not yet desperate. A director must therefore aim at making the wind sound both like a realistic, recognizable wind and like a moaning spirit, i.e. he must strike a key in between and aim at a super-naturalistic effect. Similarly, the clicking sound in Scene 3 should be such that it can be mistaken for a realistic forest sound; for we do not immediately see Jeff (191) and can therefore not at once identify the sound as coming from his throwing of the dice. We thus go through precisely the same mental process as does Jones a little later, and must, along with him, admit that what is hallucinatory is also, paradoxically, what is real. In this manner the sound effects contribute to

---

[4] The crescendo arrangement, as Carpenter notes (p. 91), is rather like that of Ravel's *Bolero.*

establish the dictum of the play: that what man takes to be reality is only a surface, underneath of which inscrutable forces—exterior and interior—are at work, just as the *"brilliant"* and *"unruffled"* surface of the Congo river (199) is found to hide the horrifying Crocodile God.

Scenes 4 and 5 represent a mediatory stage; the reality of the visions is no longer doubted by Jones; he himself becomes a part of them. Yet they retain something unreal in their absence of sound. The convicts move silently, the prison guard *"cracks his whip—noiselessly"* (194), the planters and dandies make their remarks *"in silence,"* and the auctioneer's description of Jones-the-slave (197) is made in dumb show.

In the last two visions the "ha'nts" are not only seen but are also heard, and they are heard as plaintive human beings. Jones joins them in their high-pitched wail, which seems to express suffering and which reaches an *"unbearably acute"* pitch until it is succeeded by *"silence"* (199)—death. Jones' fate appears vocalized in this; he is now completely at one with his hallucinatory ghosts, whose sounds are direct expressions of his fear. Thus the Witch Doctor's croon *"rising to intensity"* and *"punctuated by shrill cries"* (201) is clearly a recapitulation of the two continuous sound effects, both expressions of Jones' fear—the growing sound of the tom-tom punctuated by the revolver shots—just as his dance is a retelling of Jones' flight through the forest.[5] By joining in both Jones recognizes the religious significance of his fate; and this recognition gives meaning to his sacrifice.

With special reference to *Dynamo* O'Neill declared in 1928: "This is a machine age which one would like to express as a background for lives in plays in overtones of characteristic, impelling and governing mechanical sound and rhythm—" (Simonson, p. 118).

Already in *Ape* O'Neill tried to give aural expression to the machine age (cf. Kaucher, p. 131). Like *Dynamo,* the play describes "the death of the old God and the failure of science and materialism to give any satisfying new one for the surviving primitive religious instinct to find a meaning for life in, and to comfort its fears of death with" (O'Neill/Nathan, 1929, p. 119). The symbol of "science and materialism," the new 'God,' in *Ape* is the steel. Those who complain that the play is incoherent, because Yank in the later scenes fights successive antagonists (Adams, p. 174), forget that these antagonists are only manifestations of this 'God,' of the materialistic spirit of our age which Yank tries to fight by pitting against it his own materialism. O'Neill recognized this symbolic unity of the play when he described Yank's struggle as being "with his own fate" (Cargill et al., p. 111).

[5] Zeller suggests (p. 110) that the dance is a mimetic expression of Jones evil living, but the stage directions hardly support such a reading.

We are reminded of the supernatural function of the steel already toward the end of the opening scene, when Yank by identifying himself with it virtually raises himself to the level of a thundering Lucifer:

... I'm steel—steel—steel! ... (*As he says this he pounds with his fist against the steel bunks. All the men, roused to a pitch of frenzied self-glorification by his speech, do likewise. There is a deafening metallic roar through which* YANK'S *voice can be heard bellowing*) Slaves, hell! We run de whole woiks (216).

It is important that Yank is pounding and bellowing simultaneously; by merging his voice with the metallic roar O'Neill produces the desired effect of identification, the impression that Yank is steel. But Yank's action has an ironic duplicity. Its full meaning we realize as we later see and listen to Yank's rattling of the bars of his prison cell (240, 244) and his pounding against the rail of the gorilla cage (253). O'Neill, in fact, forewarns us by drawing attention to the cagelike aspect of the forecastle: "*The lines of bunks, the uprights supporting them, cross each other like the steel framework of a cage*" (207). Like modern man, Yank ironically substitutes himself for God by the very things—science and materialism, here symbolized by the steel—which enslave him and turn him into a beast.

It is in the third, stokehole scene that the sound effects are most predominant. Fire, engines and steel here contribute to create a dissonant, yet rhythmic, 'music' of the modern machine age. Unobtrusively, by means of sound effects, O'Neill warns us of the forthcoming conflict; we hear "*the brazen clang of the furnace doors as they are flung open or slammed shut, the grating, teeth-gritting grind of steel against steel, of crunching coal*" (223).[6] If the powers still seem balanced in this description, another mechanical sound soon deprives Yank of his view that the subrace alone partakes of the steely strength: "*A whistle is blown—a thin, shrill note from somewhere overhead in the darkness*" (223). Yank has earlier claimed that he is "factory whistles" (216), but this whistle belongs to his superior, the second engineer. The spatial arrangement seems, however, not merely an illustration of social injustice, of the superrace enslaving the subrace; rather, since the superrace, too, is enslaved by the steel, the "*inexorable*" and "*peremptory*"

---

[6] From a realistic point of view the stoking, as Carless Jones points out (p. 228), is altogether incorrect. No engineer would allow the stokers to open all the fire-doors at the same time; O'Neill omits the part of the work known as slicing, i.e. breaking up the clinkers with a steel bar; and the break-neck speed makes no sense, since time must be allowed for the coal to burn or it will all go up in smoke. O'Neill knew enough about stoking to be able to describe it accurately. The point is, of course, that what interested him was not how stokers work but what they, as symbols of mankind, feel. Commenting on the scene O'Neill told Mullett (p. 118): "Stokers do not really shovel coal that way. But it is done in the play in order to contribute to the rhythm. For rhythm is a powerful factor in making anything expressive."

whistle (224 f.) from the darkness above suggests modern man's enslavement by the steel idol of materialism, his struggle with "his own fate"; it is significant that Yank's anger is first directed towards an *invisible* antagonist; mere sound becomes expressive of inner fate. Four times the whistle is heard and each time Yank reacts more violently against it. The scene ends with a clear sound demonstration of *"steel against steel"* (223); insulted by Mildred, the steel magnate's daughter, Yank hurls his steel shovel after her towards the iron door, which has just clung shut, imprisoning Yank, as it were, in his cage; the shovel *"hits the steel bulkhead with a clang and falls clattering on the steel floor. From overhead the whistle sounds again in a long, angry, insistent command"* (226). Yank's attempt to fight steel with steel, the world's materialism with his own, is doomed to fail.

Two more scenes end on a note of steel made audible. Multiplied, the domineering whistle appears again in the Fifth Avenue scene, here supplemented by another metallic sound, literally signifying Yank's loss of freedom:

Many police whistles shrill out ... and a whole platoon of policemen rush in on YANK *from all sides. He tries to fight but is clubbed to the pavement and fallen upon. ... The clanging gong of the patrol wagon approaches with a clamoring din* (239).

In the prison scene Yank's breaking out of his cell is opposed by 'the steel'; from the hose, turned on full pressure, *"there is a splattering smash as the stream of water hits the steel of* YANK's *cell"* (245). It is characteristic that the curtain drops before we see Yank escape; symbolically he remains imprisoned.

Not only mechanical sounds but also the human voice is employed to illustrate how the steel has affected man. In the second forecastle scene, where Yank's groping struggle against the steel begins, a machine-like stoker chorus with voices that have *"a brazen, metallic quality as if their throats were phonograph horns"* spits out its monosyllables: "think," "love," "law," "God" —useless, empty words in a materialistic world, worthy only of *"hard, barking laughter"* (227 ff.).

Street noises play an important part in *Hughie.* The play is set in midtown Manhattan between 3 and 4 a.m. of a summer's night, i.e. in the dead of the night. Its two characters—Erie and Charlie Hughes, the Night Clerk—have a *"pasty, perspiry night-life complexion"* (8), for to them life is a long, nocturnal 'death struggle,' the painful intermediate stage between true life and death.

The Night Clerk at first seems well beyond any struggle; he looks cadaverous and is almost mute—characteristics of his occupational disease which is also the human disease: left alone in a sleeping city, having no one to communicate with, he has turned into a living corpse. But not quite. Deep down in him there is still a will to live, nourished by the sounds in the street outside. It may seem strange that the clerk should be more interested in these everynight sounds than in Erie's story, which is new to him. But he knows that *"The Guest's Story of His Life"* (14) is invariably a tale of human suffering and so he automatically defends himself against it. The outside sounds give his mind an opportunity to escape from the tiresome guest; they are also attractive in their own right for two quite opposite reasons, under- standable to us if we retain the idea that the clerk is a man whose life is a 'death struggle.' On one hand they are signs of life in an otherwise dead city, evidence that he is not alone in the night. On the other, since he *"can tell time by sounds in the street"* (8), they indicate that *"the night recedes"* (19), that death approaches.

The same vacillation between life and death desire we find with regard to individual sounds. When the slamming of the garbage cans is heard, the clerk dreams: *"A job I'd like. I'd bang those cans louder than they do! I'd wake up the whole damned city!"* (17). Ironically, the clerk is as anxious to make the city react to him as Erie is to make the clerk react; they share a basic desire to make themselves heard as individuals. The sound of the El train has both a metaphysical and a psychological meaning:

Its approach is pleasantly like a memory of hope; then it roars and rocks and rattles past the nearby corner, and the noise pleasantly deafens memory; then it recedes and dies, and there is something melancholy about that (19).

Here man's, especially Hughie's, life journey seems outlined. But the sound pattern appears also equivalent of Erie's and Charlie's shared need to make actions—performed or imagined—speak so loudly that they keep one from melancholy thinking. In quite another sense the sound is a sign of life:

Only so many El trains pass in one night, and each one passing leaves one less to pass, so the night recedes, too, until at last it must die and join all the other long nights in Nirvana, the Big Night of Nights. And that's life (19).

In other words, the El trains measure the age of the night as the nights meas- ure the length of life. The clerk's longing for the dawn, when his night shift ends and he is allowed to rest symbolizes, I take it, his longing for the death that is to succeed his weary life: *"Is daybreak coming now? No, too early yet. He can tell by the sound of that surface car. It is still lost in the night. Flat wheeled and tired. Distant the carbarn, and far away the sleep"* (24 f.). The clerk is apparently identifying himself with the surface car performing its nightly job; he thinks of its wheels, because his feet are aching (13); for him too, as we have noted, sleep, i.e. death, and daybreak coincide.

"The footfalls of the cop on the beat" make him dream of violent action: *"If he'd only shoot it out with a gunman some night! Nothing exciting has happened in any night I've ever lived through!"* (24). Excitement and death are characteristically combined. When the clanging of an ambulance is heard, the clerk explicitly reveals his death longing by asking the imaginary doctor: *"Will he die, Doctor, or isn't he lucky?"* (26).

The final sound comes from the siren of a fire engine; it causes the clerk to wish for *"a real good"* fire, *"big enough to burn down the whole damn city"* (27).

As the sounds have grown increasingly loud, the siren forming a climax, the clerk's destructive tendency has grown stronger; in the case of the garbage cans he desired to wake up the city, make it come alive and react to him; now he wants to destroy it—and himself. The wail of the siren is followed by *"a rare and threatening pause of silence"* (29) reminiscent of death, which works an ironic peripety. So far we have seen the clerk give vent to an ever greater death wish; now when death seems at hand, he desperately tries to escape it; death longing is found to be no more than a pipe dream to console one's fear of life with. It was fear of silence, loneliness and death that kept Erie glued to the Night Clerk's desk, endlessly talking, attempting to establish a contact. It is the same fear that finally makes the clerk respond. Human contacts and human speech, O'Neill seems to say, are ultimately based on a need to escape the thought of death and its auditory symbol: the silence.

The foghorn in *Journey,* it might be held, is O'Neill's counterpart of the more or less supernatural beings—soothsayers, sorcerers, witches—in Greek and Elizabethan tragedy who prophesy the fate of the hero; for in its capacity of ominous herald a foghorn is a close, mechanical equivalent of these demonic figures.

As such it is at once more and less effective than its human counterparts. It is more effective in creating an intense mood of portentous foreboding but less effective in its inability to indicate the nature of this foreboding. In short, we are more worried, but we do not know what we worry about. Such would be the case if O'Neill had used the foghorn early in his play without having the characters comment on it. As it is, he saves the sound until he has had them clarify its meaning; so that when we hear it, the plaintiveness of the sound itself is reinforced by what we know it represents.

The first reference to the foghorn occurs early in Act I:

MARY. ... I wasn't able to get much sleep with that awful foghorn going all night long.

TYRONE. Yes, it's like having a sick whale in the back yard. It kept me awake, too.

MARY. (*affectionately amused*) Did it? You had a strange way of showing your restlessness. You were snoring so hard I couldn't tell which was the foghorn! (*She comes to him, laughing, and pats his cheek playfully.*) Ten foghorns couldn't disturb you. You haven't a nerve in you. You've never had (17).

Tyrone's reference to the sick whale—a natural enough remark in a whaling port like New London—sounds prodigious. It links the sound with the two family members who are soon found to be seriously wanting in health: Mary and Edmund. Mary, however, compares it to Tyrone's and, later, to Jamie's snoring (20)—another awful sound which, she claims, has been driving her crazy during the night (47). Snoring, Cathleen informs us, is a sign of health and sanity (99), and we may suspect that this is why Mary finds it unbearable: for she knows that her own frail health, as well as Edmund's, is on the decline. She is at once jealous and contemptuous of her husband's ability to sleep soundly with a sick son nearby, of his non-caring attitude—this is what the snoring ultimately seems to represent—which makes life so much easier for him and so much harder for his environment.

Tyrone's and Mary's different 'interpretations' of the foghorn in Act I have a counterpart in the opening of Act III, for Cathleen's view here might easily have been Tyrone's:

MARY. ... That foghorn! Isn't it awful, Cathleen?
CATHLEEN. ... It is indeed, Ma'am. It's like a banshee (98).

Superstitiously Irish, Cathleen refers to that supernatural being in Gaelic folklore who forebodes death by her mournful wailing. While we still thought Mary healthy and Edmund harmlessly ill, the foghorn warned about sickness; now when we suspect that they are both seriously ill, it warns about death. But Mary does not mind this. To her it is an "ugly sound" for precisely the opposite reason, because "it won't let you alone. It keeps reminding you, and warning you, and calling you back" (99). The sound, it would seem, expresses Mary's acute sense of guilt, warning her not to forget her responsibility, calling her back to life.

The women's remarks are preceded by the first moan of the foghorn; O'Neill gives the following description of the sound: "*From a lighthouse beyond the harbor's mouth, a foghorn is heard at regular intervals, moaning like a mournful whale in labor*" (97). This somewhat curious stage direction indicates that O'Neill was less concerned with the sound itself than with its meaning. We have already noted the connection between the "sick whale" and the sick Mary. Now we hear that the whale is "*in labor*"—like a woman. And the whale, we recall, was placed by Tyrone "in the back yard," hidden away, as it were, in the spatial equivalent of the past. If the first whale metaphor connects the foghorn with Mary and Edmund, the second links it with a particular event in their lives: it was the *"labor"* of giving birth to Edmund that broke Mary's health (87), and it was to ease her pain during the sickness following his birth that she was first offered morphine, the drug that was to make the rest of her life fogbound. Thus, when Mary talks about how the foghorn reminds her and calls her back, how its sound is "ugly" like her hands (99, 104), how it resembles the nerveless snoring of her husband, who is in part responsible for her addiction, she is referring not so much to the past in general as to the particular traumatic events surrounding Edmund's birth which marked a decisive break with her healthy past and launched her on her tragic, nightbound journey.

Laughter

Although O'Neill naturally employs the whole range of human sounds—laughter, weeping, sobbing, snoring, yawning, not to mention his frequent indications of vocal pitch, volume, etc.—I shall limit myself to the first of these sounds—laughter—which, unlike most of the other sounds, is frequently used in an unrealistic and perhaps somewhat puzzling manner.[7]

In *Ape* the stokers and prisoners express their hatred and cynicism through *"hard, barking laughter"* (210, 212, 227 ff., 240), and the Cabots in *Desire*, who lead an equally bleak slave existence on their rocky, puritan farm, are just as incapable of joyous laughter. Ephraim might laugh "fur once in his life," his son Simeon imagines, when he hears that Eben considers himself owner of the farm. And, as though imitating Ephraim's laughter, Simeon and Peter laugh *"one single mirthless bark"*: "Ha!" (208). They use the same abrupt "Ha!" when implying adultery on the part of Eben's mother (207) and of Eben (214). Eben uses it when announcing Ephraim's marriage to the brothers (212) and when spiting his father (254). Ephraim, finally, adopts it at the end of the play (268) when he is hardening himself to his lonely existence on the rockbound farm, after he has found himself deprived of his sons, his wives, and even the money that could have taken him to richer and softer soil. The joyless, monosyllabic 'hawing' suits the life-denying Cabots; it is as though their laughter was fenced in. It is significant that not until Simeon and Peter are about to leave the farm can they break into something like joyful laughter:

[7] There can be little doubt that it is especially Nietzsche's evaluation of laughter as the outward sign of the superman's affirmative attitude to life that has inspired O'Neill to his frequent employment of this sound. "Learn to laugh at yourselves, as one must laugh," says Zarathustra in the section of *Thus Spake Zarathustra* entitled "Of Higher Man." The statement appears among the excerpts O'Neill made from the Tille translation.

SIMEON. (*grinning*) I feel like raisin' fun. I feel light in my head an' feet.
PETER. Me, too. I feel like laffin' till I'd split up the middle (220).

It is made quite clear that the liquor they have been drinking is not primarily responsible for this change. It is their new-won sense of freedom that results in an ecstatic feeling of release.

Eben and Abbie also experience a sense of liberation and rapture at the close of the play, more dignified, to be sure, but not altogether different from that of the brothers. Eben's sardonic 'hawing' and Abbie's sensual, *"humid"* laughter (229) here give way to the trembling smiles (267) of purified, sacrificial love and joyous acceptance of suffering.

In *Welded* the gospel of laughter is fittingly put in the mouth of the *"bovine"* Mother Earth figure, who tells Michael: "You got to laugh, ain't you? You got to loin to like it [life]!" (478). The prostitute's simple wisdom makes a profound impression on the playwright, who significantly expounds it in Nietzschean, yea-saying terms:

Yes! That's it! That's exactly it! That goes deeper than wisdom. To learn to love life—to accept it and be exalted—that's the one faith left to us! (*Then with a tremulous smile*) Good-by. I've joined your church (478).

In accordance with this we witness how Eleanor's and Michael's harsh, hateful and revengeful laughter in the middle scenes gives way to tender smiles and a *"tearful gaiety"* (489) at the end, expressive of their determination to accept life—even the painful part of it—with joy.

A mystical note is struck in *Marco*, where, in the Prologue, the dead Kukachin comes to life under the sacred tree in Persia:

A sound of tender laughter, of an intoxicating, supernatural gaiety, comes from her lips and is taken up in chorus in the branches of the tree as if every harp-leaf were laughing in music with her. The laughter recedes heavenward and dies as the halo of light about her face fades and noonday rushes back in a blaze of baking pain (352).

The miracle is a fulfillment of Kublai's words to the corpse of his granddaughter at the end of the play: "Open your eyes and laugh! Laugh now that the game is over" (438). Kukachin laughs Lazarus' Dionysian laughter; like him she has discovered that there is no death, only life and love. Paradoxically, she is more alive in death than she ever was in life, when her lips drooped "even in smiling" (385).

It is hardly surprising that Dion in *Brown* should declare himself a lover of laughter (264). Yet Dion, forced to live in a joyless and valueless time, deprived of a life-giving faith, cannot laugh the pure, affirmative, Dionysian laughter. His laughter has turned into an ironic grin; it is *"forced"* (262) and bitter (267). Shortly before he dies, he raises himself to his full height, looks upward *"defiantly,"* spiting Heaven, and says: "Nothing more—but Man's last gesture—by which he conquers—to laugh! Ha—" (299). Deprived of his earlier belief in a benevolent god, man must turn himself into a god and laugh a proud, self-assertive laughter. But there is no more joy in this laughter than in Ephraim Cabot's grim 'hawing' or in the *"mocking laugh"* Yank, hauling himself to his feet, produces in his cage just before he dies (*Ape,* 254). Dion cannot keep up his Mephistophelean gesture. Kneeling and kissing Brown's feet—an act indicative of his "abject contrition" (O'Neill, 1926/Clark, p. 105) and sudden change to Christian meekness—he reveals his desperate need for belief in a godhead outside himself.

Up to this point Brown, although good-natured, never laughs. But once Dion's demon enters him, he gives vent to an even more strident laughter than Dion. Psychologically, his laughter is that of a man "on the verge of a breakdown" (315). Brown is in a desperate dilemma. He wants to be loved by Margaret—as he can when appearing as Dion. But he also wants to retain his uncreative, unloved Brown self. The tension between these conflicting desires results in a laughter which grows increasingly neurotic. His laughter is thus a sign of inner suffering.

However, the inner tension Brown has come to experience is a sign of life and as such something to rejoice in, despite the pain it involves. To the world, which sees without seeing and which "can't believe in joy ... except by the bottle," Brown's merriment is taken as a sign that he is "soused all the time" (315). In a sense he is. But his intoxication is not produced by alcohol. A truly Dionysian 'drunkenness,' it is an effect of intense living, of being part of "the deep main current of life-desire" (O'Neill, 1926/Clark, p. 105).

The true, affirmative laughter appears neither to the individual who has never suffered (the early Brown), nor to him who suffers without under· standing the significance of his suffering (Dion). It is when he mystically divines a meaning in his adversity, that man can embrace it with an *amor fati* and see existence as profoundly joyful. Thus, in his dying moment Brown arrives at the insight that "only he that has wept can laugh," a discovery that significantly is not accompanied by any laughter but is spoken *"with ecstasy"* (322). Unlike Dion, Brown dies on a note of affirmative joy: "The laughter of Heaven sows earth with a rain of tears, and out of earth's transfigured birth-pain the laughter of Man returns to bless and play again in innumerable dancing gales of flame upon the knees of God!" (322). The reasoning behind this mystical passage seems to be that God in His love for man (His laughter) makes him suffer, because He knows that only suffering can lead to that deep sense of life which alone can be profoundly joyful. And Man, once he sees this, is able to love God in return.

The most pervasive use of laughter is found, of course, in *Lazarus Laughed*;[8] there is hardly a page in the play which does not, in dialogue or stage directions, refer to it. Despite the central role played by the laughter, there has been singularly little comment on it.[9] In a letter to Quinn (May 1927/Quinn, 2, pp. 252 f.) O'Neill himself has, however, explained the significance of the laughter; it reads:

The fear of death is the root of all evil, the cause of all man's blundering unhappiness. Lazarus knows there is no death, there is only change. He is reborn without that fear. Therefore he is the first and only man who is able to laugh affirmatively. His laughter is a triumphant Yes to life in its entirety and its eternity. His laughter affirms God, it is too noble to desire personal immortality, it wills its own extinction, it gives its life for the sake of Eternal Life (patriotism carried to its logical ultimate). His laughter is the direct expression of joy in the Dionysian sense, the joy of a celebrant who is at the same time a sacrifice in the eternal process of change and growth and transmutation which is life, of which his life is an insignificant manifestation, soon to be reabsorbed. And life itself is the self-affirmative joyous laughter of God.

The Dionysian laughter, then, does not so much signify acceptance of one's individual life on earth as of existence *per se*. Since it is not related to the happy or unhappy state of human affairs, Lazarus' laughter is heard also at moments which seem tragic, such as the death of his nearest relatives; it says Yes also to suffering. It laughs at such transient phenomena as death and man in its affirmation of Eternal Life and Man.

Lazarus' laughter, as described by O'Neill, is so pregnant with meaning and so different from what we normally think of as laughter, that it is hard to see how any actor could possibly convey even a fraction of the overtones suggested by the author.[1] It is not the result of any humorousness (in the

---

[8] The title, O'Neill explained (Gelb, p. 599), is derived from the biblical "Jesus wept" (John 11: 35), the first words of the play.

[9] Winther (p. 95), Skinner (p. 185), and Engel (1953, p. 180) recognize the Zarathustrian nature of Lazarus' laughter but do not discuss it.

[1] In May 1926, O'Neill confessed to Macgowan that he knew of no one who could play the lead: "Who can we get to laugh as one would laugh who had completely lost, even from the depths of the unconscious, all traces of the Fear of Death?" (Gelb, p. 601). A year later he wrote De Casseres (6.22.1927) that he could imagine Chaliapin doing the part, an opinion he repeated in 1944 to Clark (p. 148), adding that Chaliapin could "give speech the quality of music—and that's exactly what Lazarus must do." In a letter (9.11.1927) to his wife Agnes he says that he contemplates Paul Robeson for the part: "He's the only actor who can do the laughter."

ordinary sense) on the part of the character; Lazarus is no Falstaff. Even less is his laughter motivated by the humorousness of others.[2]

Lazarus' laughter is one of love; the most frequent adjectives used with regard to it are 'soft,' 'affectionate' and 'gentle.'[3] His first laughter, according to an eyewitness, was that of "a man in love with God" (277), and his first laughter on the stage is similarly "*infectious with love*" (280). It is not a pitying laughter, for Lazarus knows that men are but all too prone to be pitied. It can even at times become "*gaily mocking*" (306, 341), a laughter *at* death and individuation. Due to his dual role of Christian and Dionysian-Zarathustrian savior, Lazarus laughs a laughter which expresses both love of one's neighbor and, more emphatically, love of the farthest. His laughter is significantly often directed upward, to the sky, to God (318, 349). At the same time it is itself "like a god's" (341). Before he appears in the Athens scene, his laughter "*comes ringing through the air like a command from the sky*" (305). This reciprocity may be seen as an expression of Lazarus' power to "believe in the laughing god" within himself (360), in his identity with God.

Unlike the laughter of men, Lazarus' laughter is "*so full of a complete acceptance of life, a profound assertion of joy in living, so devoid of all self-consciousness of fear, that it is like a great bird song triumphant in depths of sky, proud and powerful ...*" (279 f.). Its musicality is constantly pointed out (307, 318, 324), and this is hardly accidental, for Lazarus' laughter is an expression of the Dionysian music (cf. Nietzsche, 1909, section 2). The Jew who reports about Lazarus' laughter immediately after his rebirth also assures: "Such a laugh I never heard!" And he further clarifies its Dionysian character: "It made my ears drunk! It was like wine!" (277). At one point Lazarus' laughter mingles with "*the sound of singing and the music of flutes and cymbals*" (318), the characteristic Dionysian instruments.[4] As befits a laughter denying death and celebrating eternal change it is spirited, vigorous, dynamic, changing in pitch and volume (279, 318, 333). It is also of a metaphysical, all-embracing order, expressing a cosmic harmony. The laughter Lazarus laughs can rarely, and perhaps never fully, be laughed by any of his followers, but it has its counterpart in nature:

---

[2] For these reasons O'Neill had little to gain from Bergson's and Freud's theories of laughter (cf. Gelb, p. 600). Also Sherwood Anderson's primitivistic concept of laughter in *Dark Laughter* (1925) is rather removed from O'Neill's idea in *Lazarus*. Apart from Nietzsche, Whitman with his dynamic life affirmation may have been a source of inspiration; a 1900 edition of *Leaves of Grass* belonged to O'Neill's library (copy now at C. W. Post College).

[3] It is characteristic that in the notes the second type in the typological scheme for the crowds is given as "Happy laughing [,] loving & lovable."

[4] In the notes O'Neill remarks: "Dionysus inspires & rules over all music of reed as Apollo over strings." Cf. Frazer, p. 389.

The wind laughs!
The sea laughs!
Spring laughs from the earth!
Summer laughs in the air!
Lazarus laughs!

Thus the Jews chant *"in a great, full-throated pæan"* (280). The laughter is heard not only in nature but also in the universe; says Lazarus: "Millions of laughing stars there are around me! And laughing dust, born once of woman on this earth, now freed to dance!" (348). Man, in other words, does not die. He is transformed into "laughing dust," and as dust he can give birth to new stars (348). What we term death is merely change and, indeed, a happy change, since it means that man finally becomes attuned to the harmony of the universe. The cosmic aspect of the laughter is especially pronounced in Act II.2, playing immediately inside the walls of Rome. Here *"terrific flashes of lightning and crashes of thunder seem a responsive accompaniment from the heavens to [the] laughter of thousands which throbs in beating waves of sound in the air"* (318).[5] The combination of the laughter of thousands, inspired by Lazarus' laughter, and the thundering 'laughter' of heaven confirms Lazarus' monistic view of the universe; as he exultantly tells God: "I am Your laughter—and You are mine!" (324).

It is noteworthy how death in the play is invariably met with the clear, accepting, Dionysian laughter—even with those who have not earlier been capable of such a laughter. Thus Marcellus, sent by Tiberius to murder Lazarus, is converted by the Dionysian laughter and ends instead by killing himself:

(*trying to laugh*) Ha-ha— Yes! (*He stabs himself and falls. Suddenly his laughter is released*) I laugh! You are a fool, Caligula! There is no death! (*He dies, laughing up at the sky.*) (334).

This is the first time Marcellus laughs; and it is characteristic that his laughter is not wholly natural until he is face to face with death, *"released"* from life.

Tiberius, we learn, "never laughs" (294). This is not strictly correct, for he

---

[5] Cf. the scenario where Lazarus says: "Beyond the grave ..., tuned to the pulsing throbbing beat of space, the musical rise and fall of eternal laughter, I danced...." This again may be compared to the following passage in Angus (p. x) referring to the same period as is dealt with in *Lazarus:* "Never was there an age which heard so distinctly and responded so willingly to the call of the *Cosmos* to its inhabitants. The unity of all Life, the mysterious harmony of the least and nearest with the greatest and most remote, the conviction that the life of the Universe pulsated in all its parts, were as familiar to that ancient cosmic consciousness as to modern biology and psychology."—Angus' book belonged to O'Neill's library (copy now at C. W. Post College); in the notes for *Lazarus* there are several excerpts from it.

does laugh the cold, guilty, self-conscious "hyena laughter" of men, "howling its hungry fear of life" (289), the antithesis of the Dionysian laughter. But he is incapable of true, innocent, unselfish laughter—until just before he dies (368). Pompeia's cruel laughter, similarly, is transformed into clear, passionate laughter as she voluntarily throws herself into the flames which consume Lazarus (367). Lazarus' followers kill themselves "laughing, in one another's arms"—the position indicates the end of individuation they have found; their laughter, like that of Lazarus, is a laughter at death: "it seemed it was not they who died but death itself they killed!" (321).[6] Even the debauched Roman youths surrounding Tiberius laughingly appeal: "Let us die, Lazarus!" (349).

Moreover, as a proof that "there is no death," laughter is heard once from beyond the grave, as it were. Miriam never laughs (319), because she cannot forget Lazarus' death (331) and the death of her children (317), and because she is too earthbound, too concerned with the suffering of mortals, to grasp Lazarus' lofty love of the universe.[7] Yet, when she has bitten into the poisoned peach and feels death approaching, she too can laugh *"a queer, vague little inward laugh"* (346), and call the deathly fruit "mellow" and "sweet" (347). And after her body has been immobile for some time, indicating that she has indeed died, she confirms, much as Kukachin, *"in a voice of unearthly sweetness"* that "there is only life" and laughs her first true laughter (348).

For the *spectator* Lazarus' final laughter may also seem to emanate from beyond death. When he is pierced by Caligula's spear, his laughter ceases—a sign, it would seem, that he has died. During most of Caligula's long soliloquy there is no sign of life from Lazarus, but towards the end of it his laughing voice is heard again, assuring Caligula that "there is no death" (371). By describing this sound as a *"faint dying note of laughter,"* O'Neill suggests to the *reader* of the play that Lazarus is not yet dead, but in the theatre this meaning would not be clear.

Lazarus is not the bringer of a new gospel to mankind. His divine laughter has been sounded before. Once, Lazarus says, men did not fear, did not believe in death. Once they lived joyfully. "They must be taught to laugh again!" (310). That Lazarus refers to the time when faith in Dionysus was a living reality appears from the Greeks' hailing him as the reborn Dionysus (310), who will give them back their "lost laughter" (303). But the age of harmony and innocence in the history of mankind has a counterpart in the life cycle

---

[6] For a motivation of the happy suicides, see Day, 1960, p. 302. Cf. the chapter of *Zarathustra* entitled "On Free Death."

[7] In the notes O'Neill remarks that Miriam is sad "with the aged sadness of her race" and cannot laugh, "because of her memory of the grief when he [Lazarus] was dead and her fear of his dying again."

of every man; thus Tiberius recognizes that when he was a child or youth he could laugh somewhat like Lazarus (339).

The effect of Lazarus' laughter is overpowering, since the will to affirm Life, the desire towards primordial unity, is found in all men. The Jews, the Greeks, the Romans—all are affected by it. Yet, lacking courage and nobility, the crowds are only gradually converted and the moment Lazarus' laughter ceases to goad them, they relapse into their old fear of life and death. A good example of the typical reaction is found already in the initial scene. Here Lazarus' first laughter arouses wondering awe (279). His second, more exultant laughter begins to affect the crowd positively—they smile self-consciously— but, *"holding themselves in for fear of what the next one will think,"* they do not dare to respond (280). The chorus does respond but in a murmuring way, without conviction. Only after Lazarus has added a note *"of compelling exultation,"* does the chorus respond in his vein and gradually, *"joining in by groups or one by one,"* it begins to laugh, harshly and discordantly (280 f.) but with a groping towards that freedom which Lazarus has attained. The scene thus ends on a climactic note of powerful laughter.

The following scene witnesses a different sound progression. Beginning with singing laughter from Lazarus' followers inside his house and discordant laughter from the Orthodox and Nazarene crowds outside it, it moves towards a climax as Lazarus converts them all to laugh with him. But as soon as he leaves, the laughter falters and the scene ends with a hopeless wail. The final scene, similarly, demonstrates how the crowd is swayed from hostile, mocking laughter against Lazarus (364) to *"liberated"* laughter with him (368). But again: the moment Lazarus' laughter ceases, *"the laughter of the crowd turns to a wail of fear and lamentation"* (369). As Lazarus observes elsewhere: "They forget! It is too soon for laughter!" (360).

Caligula, who comes closest of the main characters to being a symbol of man, reveals the same longing and difficulty as the mob characters to laugh Lazarus' laughter. The reason for his inability to laugh affirmatively, he explains, is that he finds men—and he does not exclude himself—neither lovable nor loving, hence awful in both senses of the word (358 f.) and there-fore fit to be killed. Caligula's way of laughing reveals his divided mind. When he does not smile twistedly (311, 331), he laughs *"gratingly"* (357 f.). Often his laughter breaks into whimpering or fearful silence (324, 338, 358). At one point his *"fanatically cruel and savage"* laughter *"fights to overcome"* that of Lazarus, which has attained *"the most exultant heights of spiritual affirmation"* (319 f.). It is the sound of the brute pitted against that of the god, and the effect is not without its irony, for Caligula has just declared, that *his* laughter is that of "gods and Caesars." Naturally he cannot keep it up; his laughter turns into a fearful sobbing; the would-be god becomes a whimpering baby. Highly ironical, too, is Caligula's attempt to laugh at the end of the Athens scene. Left alone in the square he

snatches up his sword defensively, glancing over his shoulder and whirling around as if he expected someone to stab him in the back. Then, forcing a twisted grin of self-contempt—harshly) Coward! What do I fear—if there is no death? (*As if he had to cut something, he snatches up a handful of flowers— desperately)* You must laugh, Caligula! (*He starts to lop off the flowers from their stems with a savage intentness)* Laugh! Laugh! Laugh! (*Finally, impatiently, he cuts off all the remaining with one stroke)* Laugh! (*He grinds the petals under his feet and breaks out into a terrible hysterical giggle)* Ha-ha— (311 f.).

To an extent Caligula's laughter is a genuine, groping attempt to join in Lazarus' Dionysian laughter, which has affected him as well as everyone else in the scene. Yet, as his action reveals, he is completely unable to affirm life: the flowers which Lazarus' followers have scattered around[8]—like Lazarus' laughter symbols of innocence and beauty—are cruelly destroyed. Thus we witness how Caligula, longing to laugh, actually murders laughter.

The little tableau relates to the end of the play, where Caligula again is found alone, whirling around in fear of *"imaginary foes"* (370). He has declared his love for Lazarus; he has even been able to laugh his Dionysian laughter (338, 360). Yet, unable to share Lazarus' lofty idealism for any length of time and therefore experiencing the Dionysian laughter as a plagueing mockery, reminding him of his own moral frailty, he ends by killing Lazarus—as he had formerly destroyed his flowers. His final speech reveals an even greater state of bewilderment than the one at the end of the Athens scene. Caligula is torn between longing, pride, meekness and self-contempt, a brute desiring to believe in the laughing god in his breast but lacking power by himself to do so, a picture of man in his utter spiritual confusion.

A structural employment of laughter is apparent in *Days*. The ending of each of the first three acts shows John and Loving alone. Act I ends with Loving's taunting remark that John is not responsible for his adultery, for when he committed it he was possessed by "some evil spirit." The remark is followed by *"a mocking laugh"* (513). Act II ends with Loving's admonishment that John kill himself, followed by *"a low, sinister laugh"* (531). Act III closes with John's prayer to God that He shall not let Elsa die, followed by Loving's sarcastic wish that John would hear God's mocking laughter in answer to his prayer. Loving's God, in whose image he is created, is a "malignant Spirit hiding behind life," a mysterious "Something," which kills men

---

[8] Cf. Frazer, p. 387: "One of his [Dionysus'] titles was 'teeming' or 'bursting' (as of sap or blossoms); and there was a Flowery Dionysus in Attica. . . ."

for Its sport and laughs "with mocking scorn" (535). Not only Loving but also John, Lucy and Elsa come under the influence of this God of Vengeance as their bitter, hard or hysterical laughter testify (517, 537, 550).

The peripety occurs at the end of the final act. Father Baird enters the church, where John has just refound his childhood faith in a God of Love and has become integrated as John Loving. The priest tells him that Elsa's life is saved. Again there are two live characters on the stage, but Loving, the Mephistophelean figure, has been replaced by Father Baird, the benevolent, godly one. The inner division is gone, and John Loving, "*he, who had been only* JOHN," can for the first time express what amounts to an affirmative, verbal laughter; the closing line reads: "Life laughs with God's love again! Life laughs with love!" (566 f.).[9]

Music and Songs

The high frequency of musical effects in O'Neill's plays is, in part, due to the unusual power of music to speak directly to our emotions. Far from being an alienating effect, music is used by O'Neill as an integral, mood-sustaining part of the plays. Behind his predilection for popular songs one divines the Romantic idea that folk song represents "original melody," a musical mirroring of the cosmos (Nietzsche, 1909, section 6; cf. Törnqvist, Aug. 1968, pp. 108 ff.).

Already in *Thirst* this metaphysical meaning of music is apparent. There are two major 'sounds' in the play: the absolute silence of sky and sea, and the crooning of the Mulatto on the life raft. The two are not, as one might suppose, contrasted. On the contrary, the chant is completely attuned to the silence. The play opens with the crooning and with comments on the silence, and the first half of it oscillates between chant and silence; the Gentleman significantly finds that the singing only makes him feel the silence more keenly (16) and that the song is only slightly preferable to "dead silence" (8).

The Mulatto explains that the song is a charm by which he hopes to keep the sharks at bay. But O'Neill hardly meant us to understand it merely as such. It is the Dancer's description of the song that suggests its true meaning:

A queer monotonous song it was—more of a dirge than a song. I have heard many songs in many languages in the places I have played, but never a song like that before (6 f.).

---

[9] In the first typewritten version Loving furthermore laughs a liberated Zarathustrian laughter of "*joyful self-mockery*" as he dies—a manner of dying which harks back to the laughing deaths in *Lazarus*.

What a song! There is no tune to it and I can understand no words. I wonder what it means (7).

Monotonous, mournful and incomprehensible, the chant, like the "dead silence," seems a musical mirroring of the cosmos. It is hardly accidental that it is intoned by a West Indian Mulatto, who explains that the charm is a song of his people (7). The silence and the chant both tell us, not merely that death awaits the three on the raft, but, more significantly, that life is an incomprehensible, maddening mystery. The play is, essentially, not a naturalistic piece but a parable of man's plight, his shipwrecked existence, his little life (the life raft) drifting across an enormous ocean hiding unfathomed depths, under an infinite sky. The "great silence" (9), like the "*great angry eye of God*" (3), is a manifestation of a world order that appears malignant in its inscrutability. As long as he feels a victim of this world order, the Mulatto devotes himself to his sorrowful crooning; when, at the end, he sees a hope for survival, his tune changes to "*a happy Negro melody that mocks the great silence*" (31)—a hubris for which he immediately has to pay with his life.

Smitty, the sailor in *Caribbees,* is another gentleman who has been "gazing at the sea too long and listening to the great silence" (*Thirst,* 9). The play is a mood piece and the mood it strikes is determined largely by a visual effect —the moonlight—and by a sound effect: the "*melancholy Negro chant*," which, "*faint and far off, drifts, crooning, over the water*" (455). Although the chant is continuous, it is heard only intermittently, when the noise from the sailors on board quiets down.

The whole play is a tapestry of sounds. It begins with a low murmuring conversation between the sailors, followed by silence in which the chant is heard. Next there is conversation in normal voice followed by a storm of groans and laughter. The ship's bell strikes three. Then there is silence, "*broken only by the mournful singing of the Negroes on shore*" (459), soon drowned in the men's singing of a sea chanty. The voices grow loud, disputatious, but quiet down again as the native women appear and start to distribute their rum. Then, after everyone except Smitty and the Donkeyman has disappeared into the forecastle, "*the mournful cadence of the song*" (466) is heard in the silence. Soon the men and women come pouring out on deck again, drunkenly laughing and singing. The noise grows louder. The sound of an accordion is heard. There is dancing, soon turning into a wild fight between seamen and firemen, witnessed by the shrieking native women and ending with "*a loud yell of pain*" (472) from the knifed Paddy. The arrival of the first mate causes most of the men to disappear inside the forecastle again. As Driscoll and Yank bend over Paddy's still body, there is silence and *"the mournful chant from the shore creeps slowly out to the ship"* (472). Paddy is carried away. The women leave the ship. Smitty and the Donkey-man are again left alone with the stillness and *"the melancholy song"* (473). Smitty half-sobs. The ship's bell strikes four. He leaves for the forecastle. Only the old "Donk" remains: *"There is silence for a second or so, broken only by the haunted, saddened voice of that brooding music, faint and far-off, like the mood of the moonlight made audible"* (474).

It is obvious that O'Neill has tried to create a meaningful rhythm in his play by this contrast between the faint eternal background chant and the boisterous, varied, momentary sounds in the foreground. From the beginning the chant attracts our attention. By opening the play with the low murmur of the sailors and by then letting this murmur cease abruptly and be followed by a complete silence on board, in which the chant *"can be plainly heard"* (456), O'Neill emphatically punctuates the singing.[1]

None of the sailors seem unaffected by the chant.[2] But their reactions differ. Three attitudes may be distinguished. Driscoll, who acts as the leader of the crew, represents the majority opinion when he *"irritably"* connects the singing with "keenin'" (456): "the divil take their cryin'. It's enough to give a man the jigs listenin' to 'em" (457). The sailors ask Driscoll to sing a chanty, so that they will not hear "dot yelling" (459). Smitty shares the majority view that the chant is haunting. It reminds him of the past—"the beastly memories"—and makes him think of the devil (466). But he is more deeply affected by the chant than any of the others; and, unlike the majority, he does not find it "bad music." The most positive view is held by the Donkeyman, who finds the song "nice an' sleepy-like": "Tain't sich bad music, is it? Sounds kinder pretty to me—low an' mournful—same as listenin' to the organ outside o' church of a Sunday" (466).

The Donkeyman, it should be noticed, is the only character who remains on the stage throughout the play; like the chant, he is ever-present. Twice—midway in the play (466) and at the very end of it (474)—we see him alone as the singing is heard plainly. Placidly he remains sitting in the background, puffing his pipe, undisturbed by the drinking, love-making and fighting that surrounds him, *"an old gray-headed man with a kindly, wrinkled face"* (458), a representative of the "ancient ... life" (*Ape*, 205), when man belonged.

In line with Smitty's double function as individual and symbol of man, the chant can be interpreted in different ways. As a gentleman Smitty is more sensitive, more romantic than the rest of the sailors. Largely because of

[1] Kaucher (p. 130) mistakenly takes the first reference to the chant (455), which merely serves as a general description, as an indication that the play opens with this sound.

[2] I disagree with Engel (1953, p. 11) on this point.

a tragic experience in the past—he has apparently been rejected by a woman he loved because of his predilection for the bottle (467; *Zone,* 531 f.)— Smitty is filled with self-contempt. The moonlight and the chant, we may assume, call forth romantic memories of the love he had once known, so different from the prostitution that goes on around him. But Smitty cannot think of this love without being reminded of the fact that it is a thing of the past, and that he has himself worked its destruction. The romantic memories are thus transformed into "beastly memories." Eagerly turned away from the boisterous life activities on the deck towards the deathly shore (456, 466)— the *"white"* coral beach[3] from which the *"mournful"* singing comes—Smitty may well be contemplating suicide. But his fear of death finally proves stronger than his sickness of life. He leaves the deck to escape the haunting chant and to seek oblivion, temporary 'death,' in the alcohol served in the forecastle.

In the parabolic context the chant has the same meaning as in *Thirst.* Here too man is afloat on the sea of life, awaiting death, faced with the mystery of existence. The majority of men, like the majority of the mates, escape the maddening thoughts of the ultimate meaning of life through loud living. The old Donkeyman has a simple, firm religion which helps him to accept the world order as it is. Smitty can share neither the mates' unthinking vegetative existence nor the Donkeyman's quietism. Demanding more from existence than they do, feeling himself damned "from here to eternity" (467), he is the only one who suffers from an unquenchable metaphysical thirst;[4] this, I take it, is the true cause of his alcoholism; as he himself explains, he is "drinking to stop thinking" (468).

"Like the movement of a ship on an ocean swell," O'Neill thought (Cowley, 1957, p. 44), is the refrain of "Blow the Man Down," the chanty sung by the sailors to drown the disturbing chant. The words are not irrelevant in the play context:

[3] Cf. Act I of *Gold,* where *"the white coral beach"* is *"contrasting with"* the *"vivid blue"* of the sea (623).

[4] The brooding chant, it might be held, is an expression of Smitty's *Weltschmerz* Agnes Boulton interestingly indicates a possible source of inspiration for the chant when reporting (p. 64) that O'Neill sent her two stanzas from a poem by Richard Middleton along with the finished play; the poem is entitled "The Artist," and the relevant stanzas read (Middleton, pp. 98 f.):

> I am only a dream that sings
> In a strange, large place.
> And beats with impotent wings
> Against God's Face.
>
> No more than a dream that sings
> In the streets of space;
> Ah, would that my soul had wings,
> Or a resting place!

Blow the man down, boys, oh, blow the man down!
Wa-a-ay, blow the man down!
A pretty young maiden I chanced for to meet.
Give us some time to blow the man down! (460).

A pretty young maiden is, of course, what the sailors are looking forward to after Driscoll has informed them of the arrival of the native women. But the line has special relevance for Smitty, whose "beastly memories" are connected with a young maiden in the past and with the weakness he has shown in this relationship. When the chanty is sung, Cocky has come *"down to the deck, leaving* SMITTY *alone"* (459) on the forecastle head. The grouping thus underlines the contrast between the gentleman up above and the crowd below. While the Donkeyman, like a good seaman, is used to hitting the women he loves "a whack on the ear" (468), Smitty, being a gentleman, does not "hit women" (468). Instead, he receives a wallop by Pearl, the *"youngest and best-looking"* (464) of the native women, who has tried to make love to him. The Pearl-Smitty relationship seems to dramatize Smitty's relationship to the woman in his past. Smitty is the man who has been blown down.

In *Ape* all the songs occur in the first scene. They serve primarily to characterize Yank and to foreshadow his future fate. It is noteworthy that the lines following each song are always given to Yank; the songs function as reaction pieces for him.

The first one—an anonymous stoker's "Beer, beer, glorious beer!" (209)—causes Yank to declare his preference for whisky, "somep'n wit a kick to it"; in this unobtrusive way Yank's worship of and identification with strength is first established. Due to Yank's disapproval, the singing immediately stops and the acquiescent stokers instead ask Paddy to sing something more appropriate, a "whisky song." But Yank reacts just as negatively to this, for "Whisky Johnny" (210) is a chanty, a product of the sailing ship era, and Yank, belonging (as he imagines) exclusively to the modern world, wants none of the "ancient ... life." The two stanzas state that while "whisky is the life of man," it also "drove my old man mad." The idea that man lives by what destroys him is fundamental in many O'Neill plays. We need only substitute steel for whisky—both symbols of strength—to see that the chanty, rather than merely expressing the singer's or the stokers' miserable plight, foreshadows Yank's destruction by the very thing he identifies himself with.

As the chanty expresses Paddy's longing for the past—he sings it *"in a thin, nasal, doleful tone"* (210)—so the third song (211), again presented by an anonymous stoker, expresses the sailor's age-old longing for a home and a woman. To Yank, who has never had a real home and considers all women "tarts," this is meaningless sentimentality; the ship is a sailor's true home, and a sailor should depend on no one but himself. Yank's hubris is ridiculed by Paddy in his mocking laughter and good-natured singing of the first lines of "The Miller of Dee":

> I care for nobody, no, not I,
> And nobody cares for me (216).

The same kind of paradoxical juxtaposition that we recognized in "Whisky Johnny" applies here. Concerned only with the first line, which echoes his own gospel of recklessness, Yank falsely assumes that Paddy is converting to his own egotism. Actually, Paddy is fully aware of the at once ludicrous and tragic disproportion between Yank's imagined and real self; his song forebodes the conflict of the play: Yank's recklessness pitted against that of the world. Yank's development may be described as his increasing awareness of the second line; when he is crushed by the gorilla, its literal truth is fulfilled and the play reaches a logical conclusion.

In *Electra* singing is an expression of life affirmation. Marie Brantôme, we learn, used to be "laughin' and singin'—frisky and full of life" (44). And her nature, tempered by puritanism, is retained in the good, healthy Hazel, whose "sweet and clear and pure" singing—as reminisced by Orin in the battlefield —is like a hymn to life rising above the grim 'music' of war: "the screams of the dying" (83).

More discernibly Dionysian is the combined singing and drinking of Seth, the Chantyman and Joe Silva, a Portuguese fishing captain and member of the final chorus of old men. O'Neill carefully differentiates between their voices. The Chantyman's is a *"good tenor"* (103), Silva's *"a hoarse bass"* (129) and Seth's *"the wraith of what must once have been a good baritone"* (6). The pitch and quality of the voices seem to illustrate their different attitudes to life as symbolized by the sea. Obviously Silva is prosaically, the Chantyman poetically related to it; while Seth, too long under the influence of life-hostile 'Mannonism' to be able fully to keep up the Dionysian spirit of music, is detached from it.

Like the Greeks, O'Neill opens his play with music:

In the distance, from the town, a band is heard playing "John Brown's Body." Borne on the light puffs of wind this music is at times quite loud, then sinks into faintness as the wind dies.

From the left rear, a man's voice is heard singing the chanty "Shenandoah"— a song that more than any other holds in it the brooding rhythm of the sea. The voice grows quickly nearer. It is thin and aged, the wraith of what must once have been a good baritone (5 f.).

Just as the stage picture visually presents the theme and conflict of the trilogy, so the two intermingling tunes aurally suggest its combating forces:

178

land and sea, war and peace, death and life. For here regular-beat, martial brass music is pitted against a melodious sea chanty sung by a frail human voice.

The band-playing is motivated by the fact that Lee's surrender is a matter of hours; it is the music of the victorious Union army. Although we do not hear the words of "John Brown's Body," the idea of slavery and the notion of souls who "go marching on" after death are relevant to the play,[5] and O'Neill presumably took for granted that some of the most familiar lines were known to the audience. The foreground-background arrangement of the songs has a counterpart in the presence-absence of the characters: while we associate the distant war music with Ezra and Orin,[6] we connect the sea chanty with Christine's primeval yearning for life in the full—represented by the "rolling river" of Shenandoah—a yearning which, to be sure, is shared by the Mannons, although it is repressed by their militant puritanism.

"Shenandoah" is the theme song in the play. Occuring six times in the trilogy (twice in each part and always at the beginning or end of the acts), interspersed with and commenting on the action,[7] the chanty may be regarded as an equivalent of the choral songs in Greek tragedy. With the exception of the ship's scene (Part II.IV), where it is sung by chantymen, it is always Seth, the 'chorus leader' and therefore the proper commentator on the action, who intones the chanty.

The first time it is heard (6), its importance is largely atmospheric. By the third act, the sea longing seems especially relevant to Christine and Brant, who hope to be "bound away" for their island of love once Ezra is killed, whereas the two lines of the second stanza added here—

> Oh, Shenandoah, I love your daughter
> A-way, my rolling river (43).

—suggest not only Brant's but all the Mannons' love for their life-affirming women.

In the ship's scene we have a division resemblant of the one in the opening act of the trilogy; O'Neill's phrasing helps to indicate this:

[5] Cf. Dion's singing in Brown (294): "William Brown's soul lies moldering in the crib but his body goes marching on!"—In a letter to Michael Gold, written in late 1923 or early 1924, O'Neill, in reply to Gold's plans of writing a play about John Brown, states: "I've always argued that John Brown was one of the few historical Americans who demanded a real play to be done of him."

[6] In the second galley proofs the band is part of a parade in honor of Ezra, the victorious brigadier-general. It starts from the town square, eventually arrives at the Mannon residence, the participants cheer for General Mannon and return to town (= 18). Since Ezra has not yet returned home, this counterpart of the Greek *parodos* seems somewhat contrived.

[7] In the "Working Notes" it says (O'Neill, 1931/Frenz, p. 9): "even the stupid words have striking meaning when considered in relation to tragic events in play—."

Borne on the wind the melancholy refrain of the capstan chanty "Shenandoah,"
sung by a chantyman with the crew coming in on the chorus, drifts over the
water from a ship that is weighing anchor in the harbor. Half in and half out of
the shadow of the warehouse, the CHANTYMAN *lies sprawled on his back, snoring*
in a drunken slumber. The sound of the singing seems to strike a responsive
chord in his brain.... He begins to sing in a surprisingly good tenor voice, a
bit blurry with booze now and sentimentally mournful to a degree, but still
managing to get full value out of the chanty (102 f.).

Again there is a house and a singer in the foreground and a chorus—rather
than a band—in the background. But this time songs and characters do not
noticeably clash. Yet there is a contrast in situation. For while one chanty
is sung at sea in its completely appropriate context[1]—is the sea made audible
—the other comes, drunkenly, from land, where it does not properly belong.
Once we see that the Chantyman is not only resemblant of Seth but also, and
much more so, of Brant, the meaning of this division becomes clear. After the
cowardly murder of Ezra, Brant feels defiled and believes that a return to a
meaningful life—life at sea—is impossible, that the sea, which "hates a
coward," is through with him (112). The Chantyman's mournful singing and
position on "dry land" (105) bear out Brant's feeling of death-in-life as a
consequence of his separation from the sea as well as his forebodings of
death.[2]

The Chantyman's singing not only expresses Brant's feelings of disloyalty
to the sea, for which retribution awaits him; it also establishes the nature of
this disloyalty:

> Oh, they call me Hanging Johnny
> Away—ay—i—oh!
> They says I hangs for money
> Oh, hang, boys, hang!
>
> They say I hanged my mother
> Away—ay—i—oh!
> They say I hanged my mother
> Oh, hang, boys, hang! (106 f.).

This is obviously a description of Brant, who was partially responsible for
his mother's death (26)—a crime he has never been able to forget—and who
was bribed into killing Ezra for the love of his property (ship and wife).[3]

---

[1] "Shenandoah" is an anchor weighing chanty; see Linscott under song title.

[2] In his review of the original production (p. 134), Stark Young notes that the
chanty establishes a "mood of longing, futility, land-chains and the sea's invitation
and memory."

[3] In the first typewritten version Brant says: "It's I who may be the Johnny!"
(= 107). He also repeats the seventh line to himself *"mournfully in a low voice"*
(= 107). This line relates not only to Brant but also to Orin and Lavinia (their
'matricide').

When Seth intones "Shenandoah" in the following act, we know that death is near at hand. But O'Neill surprises us just the same by allowing no time lapse between the two: Christine's suicide occurs even before Seth has finished the song; the *"sharp report"* replaces the "Missouri" of the chanty as death takes the place of life (123). But Seth, adding a new line to the song, takes away the grimness of death by assuring us that Christine is at peace "far across the stormy water" of life (124).

As we approach the end of the trilogy, the tension between the two meanings of the key words of the chanty makes itself more strongly felt. When the chanty is first heard (169), Orin has just been buried; he too is "bound away" for the mother in death. But Lavinia still hopes to be "bound away" for life. She believes she can escape the Mannons by marrying Peter —until, finally, she too is forced to face her fate: "I'm bound here—to the Mannon dead!" (178). Although Lavinia alone has the strength to accept the punishment of staying alive, her tragic insight does not differ from that of the other Mannons. All of them discover that the only alternative to being "bound here" for the "stormy water" of life is to be "bound away" for death; that they "can't get near" the beautifully rolling Shenandoah river—cannot attain harmonious oneness with life—until they have *crossed* the Missouri; that death will then—and this is their final, consoling faith—reveal itself as a beautiful mother island.

Silence

Any discussion of the 'score' in O'Neill's plays would be incomplete without reference to the dramatist's use of silence.[4] For silence is a sound effect of sorts, and it is the alternation of sound and silence that gives rhythm and meaning to the aural fabric of the plays; we have already noted the importance of the prolonged pause in such plays as *Thirst, Caribbees, Jones* and *Hughie.*

The continuous 'sound effect' in *Ile,* as in *Thirst,* is the silence of nature, of the universe. The play opens with *"a moment of intense silence"* (535), an extension, as it were, of the 365 days of endless silence Mrs. Keeney has endured in the Arctic seas. From the Steward we learn that the silence—"so thick you're afraid to hear your own voice" (538)—has had the same detrimental effect on Mrs. Keeney as on the Dancer in *Thirst:* "she's near lost

---

[4] Kaucher (pp. 136 f.) pays brief attention to O'Neill's use of pauses.—It is interesting to note that O'Neill's own way of speaking was marked by frequent, often long, silences between speeches (cf. Mullett, p. 112; Boulton, p. 60; Gelb, pp. 152, 259).

her mind" (538). This is corroborated by Mrs. Keeney's outburst against "the ice all around, and the silence" (545), followed, for emphasis, by a prolonged pause—and by her explicit remark: "I can hear the silence threatening me— day after gray day and every day the same. I can't bear it" (549).

In the cabin there is a small organ, which the Captain has bought for his wife, "thinkin' it might be soothin' to ye to be playin' it times when they was calms and things was dull-like" (546). Ironically, the religious instrument only aggravates Mrs. Keeney's precarious state of mind; she says, "I hate the organ. It puts me in mind of home" (540).

When Keeney finally reveals his lovelessness towards her by rejecting her wish that the ship return home immediately, his wife sits down by the organ and *"starts to play wildly an old hymn"* (551), showing by her behavior that the impending insanity has broken out:

Her whole attention seems centered in the organ. She sits with half-closed eyes, her body swaying a little from side to side to the rhythm of the hymn. Her fingers move faster and faster and she is playing wildly and discordantly as the curtain falls (552).

The organ recital demonstrates that Mrs. Keeney has regressed to the past, when she was a hymn-singing, organ-playing schoolteacher in puritan Home-port. In its discordant quality of mock-prayer the recital seems, however, to signify a rejection both of this past and of the God she had faith in then. It is a protest against the brutal, implacable silence of the universe, a desperate attempt to crush it, to assert oneself against it.[5]

In *Welded,* more than in any other play, O'Neill relies on the dramatic pause to convey his meaning. That it is a very conscious device appears from the author's comment on the original production:

The actors did about as well as they could, but the whole point of the play was lost in the production. The most significant thing in the last act was the silences between the speeches. What was actually spoken should have served to a great extent just to punctuate the meaningful pauses. The actors didn't get that (Clark, p. 91).

The pauses in the last act may be the most important ones but they do not stand alone: of some eighty indicated pauses (absolute exactness is impossible),

---

[5] This interpretation seems corroborated by the longhand draft, where Mrs. Keeney not only plays the organ but also sings *"in a loud mocking voice"*:

On the other side of Jordan
In the green fields of Eden
There is rest for the weary (repeated twice)
There is rest for you.

This is ultimately the "home" Mrs. Keeney is longing for.

not counting brief pauses indicated by hyphens, about twenty-three fall in
Act I, twenty-five in Act II and thirty-two in Act III. The interesting thing
about the pauses is that they are not evenly spread out over the play but
come in clusters. Thus, in Act I there are three such clusters, and in the
remaining acts/scenes there is one in each. Especially in the brief last act
the contrast between the first six pages, containing thirty-two pauses, and the
last three, containing none, is conspicuous.

To determine the significance of the pauses we must see them in their
context and decide whether the subject matter and emotional situation in the
parts rich in pauses differ from those in the pauseless parts. This can best be
done in the form of a schematized survey.

Act I

One pause. Man and wife have been apart for some time. The long initial pause,
accompanied by their looking into each other's eyes, is, as their speeches later
indicate, motivated by love and jealousy: Has he forgotten me for his work?
Has she forgotten me for someone else? (444).
No pauses. Love and harmony reign supreme (445).
Pauses. Her jealousy of his work, his jealousy of her premarital past begin to
appear (446 f.).
No pauses. Reminiscences of their past together. Love and harmony (448 f.).
Pauses. John's visit. Strained everyday conversation. Michael's jealousy aroused
by the late visit of the man to whom Eleanor has once offered herself (450–
52).
No pauses. Audible thinking. Thoughts flow on without interruption. Two long
pauses mark the beginning and end of this part and set it off against the
dialogue (452–54).
Pauses. Michael's jealousy growing; sarcastic references to Eleanor's premarital
past (454–56).
No pauses. Growing mutual hatred culminating in physical violence (457–61).

Act II.1

Few pauses. Relative harmony between Eleanor and John; both believe that she
has come to stay (462–65).
Pauses. After Eleanor's hallucinatory vision of Michael, she and John realize that
she still loves her husband (466–69).
No pauses. Friendship and harmony restored (470).

Act II.2

Pauses. Mutual need and distrust between Michael and the Woman. The pauses
frequently occur within the Woman's speeches as though she was waiting in vain
for Michael to say something (471 f.).
Few pauses. Michael reveals his hatred of the Woman; then, because of her
reactions, he is seized by a compassion bordering on love (473–78).

One pause. This long pause, opening the act, is *"an apprehensive questioning"*: What has happened since they separated a few hours earlier? Has the other dragged their ideal "in the gutter"? This pause clearly echoes the one opening Act I (480).

Pauses. Both have made the same discovery: that they cannot be unfaithful to one another, that their love 'welds' them. At the same time both fear that the other has been unfaithful and that they cannot make the other believe the truth. This emotionally complex situation calls for groping, hesitant speech, filled with pauses (480–86).

No pauses. A moment of anguished crisis: Eleanor appears determined to leave. Then she returns. Love and harmony restored (487–89).

Among the pauseless parts can be distinguished three different types of mental states: (1) audible thinking or—more properly—feeling, (2) exultant love, and (3) violent hatred. What these three types have in common is, clearly, the free flow of emotions. The pause-filled sections, on the other hand, reveal the spontaneous emotions in conflict with counter-emotions within the characters. The pauses may be described as thinking made audible, the thinking being a result of painful inner tension.

Both Michael and Eleanor are divided individuals, part thinkers and part dreamers. He has *"the forehead of a thinker, the eyes of a dreamer"* (443). She has *"passionate, blue-gray eyes, restrained by a high forehead"* (443). After their separation both are haunted by thoughts. Acting the part of doctor, John tells the feverish Eleanor: "don't think" (464). Speaking to himself in the prostitute's bedroom Michael says: "Stop thinking, damn you!" (472). And in the beginning of Act III we find the following criticism of rational thinking:

CAPE. (*bitterly*) Now—we must begin to think—to continue going on, getting lost—
ELEANOR. (*sadly*) It was happy to forget. Let's not think—yet.
CAPE. (*grimly*) We've begun. (*Then with a harsh laugh*) Thinking explains. It eliminates the unexplainable—by which we live.
ELEANOR. (*warningly*) By which we love. Sssh! (481).

Thinking is thus contrasted with an emotional experience which alone can 'explain' "the unexplainable" (cf. Alexander, 1959, p. 311). As dreaming and thinking, love and hatred, 'life' and 'death' alternate, so pauseless and pause-filled sections, being the outer expression of these mental states, alternate, giving an audible rhythm to the play corresponding to the one created by the coalescing and separating light circles.

V. THE VERBALIZED SOUL

O'Neill has often been criticized for lacking the power of language.[1] Yet there has been little consensus as to the nature of its defects or, for that matter, of its possible virtues. Most critics have found that the plays act better than they read (e.g. Clurman, p. 214, Atkinson, p. 132), but sometimes the opposite view has been voiced (Nathan, Jan. 1925, p. 119).[2] Fairly widespread is the opinion that O'Neill wrote reasonably good dialogue when he dealt with some kind of vernacular (New York lingo, New England dialect, sailor jargon), but was at a loss when he attempted to catch ordinary middle-class language or soaring poetical speech (Wilson, pp. 464 ff.). At times O'Neill's theatrical skill and imagination has been viewed as little more than a compensation for his deficiencies at language (Nicoll, p. 881); unable to "put flowers in his language," he "had to put some real ones on the stage" (Asselineau, p. 149).[3]

The author may seem to agree with his detractors when admitting, in a letter to Quinn, that when composing *Electra* he was incapable of writing the "great language" the trilogy needed "to lift it beyond itself" (Quinn, 2, p. 258). But unlike most of the critics commenting on his language, O'Neill was not, when stating this, thinking of his own work in relation to that of other modern dramatists; rather, he was measuring it against the dramatic masterpieces of the past, especially the *Oresteia*; the letter continues:

... by way of self-consolation, I don't think, from the evidence of all that is being written today, that great language is possible for anyone living in the discordant, broken, faithless rhythm of our time. The best one can do is to be pathetically eloquent by one's moving, dramatic inarticulations! (Quinn, 2, p. 258).

That this is precisely what O'Neill is attempting in his dialogue and that he considered himself utterly misunderstood by the critics in this endeavor appears from an earlier letter to Quinn where he says: "... where I feel myself

---

[1] For a survey of the attitude to O'Neill's language among the critics, see Cargill et al., pp. 11 ff.

[2] Bentley (1955, p. 9) seems to hold the view that the plays are as poor on the stage as they are in the study.

[3] In all fairness it should be pointed out that Asselineau's remark concerns merely *Electra* and that he accepts O'Neill's view that it seems impossible for any modern dramatist to "put flowers in his language."

most neglected is just where I set most store by myself—as a bit of a poet, who has labored with the spoken word to evolve original rhythms of beauty, where beauty apparently isn't—*Jones, Ape, God's Chillun, Desire,* etc." (Quinn, 2, p. 199).

It has rightly been said that "a play which communicates to the audience only those passions or thoughts which the characters can communicate naturally to each other is in danger of becoming either superficial or colourless" (Ellis-Fermor, p. 97). In his dialogue O'Neill, as we shall see, tries to circumvent these dangers. If the language of his characters often seems awkward, it is not, I would suggest, because O'Neill was insensitive to idiomatic speech. Rather, the awkwardness stems from his disinterest in surface reality and concern with the underlying reality.[4]

Attempting to write a language that "is dramatic and isn't just conversation" (O'Neill/Gelb, p. 698), O'Neill tried to make his characters express their deeper, at times unconscious needs. About the dialogue in *Desire* he once stated:

I never intended that the language of the play should be a record of what the characters actually said. I wanted to express what they felt subconsciously. And I was trying to write a synthetic dialogue which should be, in a way, the distilled essence of New England ... (Cowley, 1926, p. 21).

When commenting on *Brown* he went even further. The play, he said, was meant to convey "a pattern of conflicting tides in the soul of Man," a pattern suggested by the use of "mysterious words, symbols, actions they [the characters] do not themselves comprehend" (O'Neill, 1926/Clark, p. 105 f.).

The author's intention with the dialogue in these two plays seems to underlie many of his other plays as well. We must now proceed to see what formal means O'Neill employs in his endeavor to suggest the more profound levels of the human mind in his dialogue. Here we are faced with a great variety of devices ranging from seemingly altogether realistic effects to provocative, non-realistic ones.

Diction

With regard to his diction the typical O'Neill character, being part individual, part symbol, displays a characteristic fusion of realistic and stylized language. Paddy's monologue in the opening scene of *Ape,* although it has a decidedly

---

[4] In a letter to Nathan (6.19.1942) O'Neill points out that when writing the speeches for Erie in *Hughie,* he had tried "to stick to the type's enduring lingo, and not use stuff current only in 1928 but soon discarded. Being too meticulously timely is not worth the trouble and defeats its purpose, anyway."

realistic flavor, reads like a prose poem; to bring out its prosody I reproduce part of it as it might have been rendered in the play:[5]

> Oh, to be back in the fine days of my youth, ochone!
> Oh, there was fine beautiful ships them days—
> clippers wid tall masts touching the sky—
> fine strong men in them—men that was sons of the sea
> as if 'twas the mother that bore them.
> Oh, the clean skins of them, and the clear eyes,
> the straight backs and full chests of them!
> Brave men they was, and bold men surely!
> We'd be sailing out, bound down round the Horn maybe.
> We'd be making sail in the dawn, with a fair breeze,
> singing a chanty song wid no care to it.
> And astern the land would be sinking low
> and dying out,
> but we'd give it no heed but a laugh,
> and never a look behind.
> For the day that was, was enough,
> for we was free men—
> and I'm thinking 'tis only slaves
> do be giving heed to the day that's gone
> or the day to come—until they're old like me (213 f.).

It is obvious that O'Neill has labored with this speech in order to evoke, through the melodiously ordered rhythm of Paddy's audible dreaming, the era of the beautiful sailing ships and their harmonious riding of the seas, the "ancient ... life" of the play's subtitle. The lines describing this glorious past are fittingly rendered in the form of poetical prose. Note how O'Neill suggests the slow sinking of the land below the horizon, the disappearance of a weary life ashore before the release of the sea, by the slow "and dying out" before the faster, gayer tempo of the next line.

But rhythm is not the only stylistic measure employed. In addition, O'Neill makes use of frequent word repetitions ("days," "fine," "men," "them," "was," "day"). Note especially the final return to the initial repetition of "days"; since the first and the last lines are also very similar metrically, the two lines seem to balance each other and harmoniously round off the speech. Note also the three anaphoric oh's, expressive of Paddy's regretful awareness of the never-more of the wondrous clipper life. The ample alliterations help to give the speech its musicality. There is even an occasional aural rhyme ("bound down round") and a sparse but effective use of imagery, as in the first lines, where the clipper sailor is shown to be in

---

[5] The idea of writing a play in verse to be printed in prose form was not alien to O'Neill around this time; he originally intended to write *Fountain* in this manner (Gelb, p. 468).

harmonious touch both with heaven, "the sky," and earth, "the sea," a natural child of the cosmos. This imagery relates by contrast to Yank's painful realization at the end of the play of the modern stoker's—modern man's—chaotic dilemma: "I ain't on oith and I ain't in heaven, get me? I'm in de middle tryin' to separate 'em, takin' all de woist punches from bot' of 'em. Maybe dat's what dey call hell, huh?" (253).

There is not a word in Paddy's speech that rings false; and yet O'Neill has not strained after colloquialisms or 'Irishisms'—apart from the initial "ochone." Words and clauses flow on as naturally as the life they depict. Seen in relation to their visual context they gain a meaning beyond the immediate one. Thus the catalogue of adjectives glorifying the past in the opening of the speech becomes dramatic and meaningful when related to the misery of the present that surrounds the 'bard'; while Paddy lets his inner eye dwell on "clean skins" and "straight backs" of men working in the open air, we see him as part of a crowd of bent, broken, dirty, drunken stokers encaged in a cramped forecastle.

As Paddy's speech reflects his infatuation with a poetical past, an age still in harmony with nature, so Yank's speeches reflect what *he* claims to belong to and even to incarnate: the modern machine age. Rendered in the form of free verse one of his pæans reads:

> He's old and don't belong no more.
> But me, I'm young!
> I'm in de pink!
> I move wit it.
> It, get me!
> I mean de ting dat's de guts of all dis.
>
> It ploughs trou all de tripe he's been sayin'.
> It blows dat up!
> It knocks dat dead!
> It slams dat offen de face of de oith!
> It, get me!
> De engines and de coal and de smoke and all de rest of it! (215).

In place of Paddy's emotive adjectives, suggestive of his subjective experience of the world, we find in Yank's speech a hard-boiled concentration on nouns and verbs, indicative of his rudimentary nature (a child would favor the same verbal forms), his materialistic outlook and emphasis on action and movement. The frequent use of plosives, the predominance of monosyllables (only four words do not fall into this category) and of short sentences contribute to express the hectic tempo of modern life, adequately reproduced also in the abrupt, staccato-like, irregular rhythm. The use of slang ("in de pink," "guts," "tripe") and vulgar pronunciation ("de," "trou," "offen," "oith") further qualify Yank's speech as that of a second Neanderthal age, devoid of poetical and spiritual values. There is to be sure a certain symmetry also in Yank's speech, as my division of it into two stanzas indicates: each ends with a line longer than the preceding ones and contains a kind of definition of what the mystical "it" stands for, each includes an identical line (the fifth), and each makes frequent use of anaphora. But the order this suggests is completely outbalanced by the rhythmical disorder; the total effect is barren dissonance, a dissonance that we may ascribe to the fact that Yank is not as well in tune with modern life as he himself believes.

The fullest expression of Yank's illusory feeling of belonging is found in his stokehole working chant, which, again, I reproduce in verse form:

> One—two—tree—
> ...
> Dat's de stuff!
> Let her have it!
> All togedder now!
> Sling it into her!
> Let her ride!
> Shoot de piece now!
> Call de toin on her!
> Drive her into it!
> Feel her move!
> Watch her smoke! (224).

The regular beat suggests the monotonous throbbing of the steamer engines Yank is in the process of feeding; he has just declared himself satisfied to be "a flesh and blood wheel of the engines" (214), and the working chant shows him up as just that. In a more general sense the regular beat expresses, of course, the mechanized rhythm of an industrial era. Yank's modern 'sea chanty' is the verbal counterpart of the *"mechanical regulated recurrence"* (223) with which the furnace doors are flung open and slammed shut; the sequence of short, imperative exclamations expresses the spirit of the steel made verbal. At the same time, as Yank's words make plain, the rhythm has a sexual connotation; the lustful energy with which Yank feeds the engines of the ship is that of a man making love to his woman; by appealing directly to our senses O'Neill thus 'explains' Yank's feelings for the ship and for the modern world.

The *lapsus linguæ,* the slip of the tongue, has been used with great effectiveness by dramatists long before Freud paid attention to its psychological significance.[6] In a narrow sense the *lapsus linguæ* may be defined as the intro-

---

[6] Freud himself (1947, pp. 107 ff.) provides examples from Schiller and Shakespeare.

duction of a word or phrase which is contradictory to the speaker's conscious intention as established by the context; it may therefore be interpreted as the expression of a repressed wish.

We have an early example of what might be called a slip in *Cardiff*:

COCKY. (*after a pause*) Yank was a good shipmate, pore beggar. Lend me four bob in Noo Yark, 'e did.
DRISCOLL. (*warmly*) A good shipmate he was and is, none betther (480).

With its past tense—"was"—Cocky's statement sounds like a necrologue and a very blunt one at that, since the juxtaposition of his two statements gives us the impression that Yank's claim to goodness lies solely in the fact that he once lent Cocky money. True to his name, Cocky never realizes that he has slipped. It is characteristically Driscoll, Yank's closest friend, who draws attention to Cocky's insensitive statement by a meaningful rephrasing of it. The slip, of course, suggests the truth: Yank is indeed going to die. But only a man who does not care whether Yank is alive or dead can voice it in the way Cocky does.

Cocky's slip may be compared to Marsden's comment in *Interlude* on the seriously ill Sam Evans: "poor Sam! ... he was ... I mean he is my friend..." (183; O'Neill's dots). Marsden experiences Sam as an obstacle; he wants Nina for himself. But unlike the rough sailor, the frustrated, introspective novelist slips only in his thoughts and discovers the slip before it has reached the conscious level of speech.

In *Electra*, Orin slips in the opposite direction when, insensitive to the fact that Ezra is dead, he jealously tells Hazel that Lavinia is "always coddling Father and he likes it." Shuddering, Christine draws attention to his slip: "Orin! You're talking as if he were—alive!" (81). Superficially Orin makes a mistake; in reality his slip draws attention to a basic truth: that the father is alive in all their minds and that he is still being coddled by Lavinia, who sees it as her duty to revenge him.

The most profound and dramatically effective example of the *lapsus linguae* occurs in the final act of *Electra*. Throughout the act Lavinia is under an extraordinary emotional and moral pressure. Not only does she feel that she has driven her brother to suicide; she is also informed by Hazel that she will ruin Peter's life if she marries him. When Peter arrives she is torn between her feeling that she should leave him alone and her desire to escape with him, at least for some time, from the Mannon dead. Her hysterical flow of words expresses her inner tension and her attempt to cling to the sound and healthy Peter at any cost; this constitutes her more or less conscious attitude. But as her senses are stirred she begins to identify Peter with Adam Brant:

(She kisses him with desperate passion) Kiss me! Hold me close! Want me! Want me so much you'd murder anyone to have me! I did that—for you! Take me in this house of the dead and love me! Our love will drive the dead away! It will shame them back into death! (176).

The passage is deeply ironical. While expressing the belief that she and Peter will be able to lay the dead to rest, Lavinia revives them by demanding the same from him that Christine and Adam demanded from one another; the conscious attempt is thwarted by an upsurge of unconscious desires. As though by natural association, the reference to "the dead" is followed by the fatal slip:

(At the topmost pitch of desperate, frantic abandonment) Want me! Take me, Adam! *(She is brought back to herself with a start by this name escaping her— bewilderedly, laughing idiotically)* Adam? Why did I call you Adam? I never even heard that name before—outside of the Bible! *(Then suddenly with a hopeless, dead finality)* Always the dead between! It's no good trying any more! (176 f.).

The slip comes as a climax not only at the end of the crescendo speech in which it occurs but also at the end of the final part of the trilogy. Through nine acts we have witnessed Lavinia's love for Adam Brant, implied already in Part I.I. We have seen her follow him to the "Blessed Isles," dress in the green he relished, find substitutes for him. But Lavinia herself has never realized the significance of these actions. She has always repressed her love for Adam, because the puritan Mannon part of her demands that she had Adam killed not out of jealousy—as is the case—but out of justice; once she admits to herself that she loved him, she must accept the painful consequence of this admission: that her retribution has not been that of divine justice but of selfish desire. This is why it is so necessary for Lavinia to repress her love for Adam. The revelation comes in the form of a slip which, as O'Neill is anxious to make clear, means a great surprise to her. She is depicted as a victim of an unconscious passion, of an illusion; and her tragic stature lies in the fact that although she might have claimed in her defense that her crimes were founded on an illusion she could not be held responsible for, she does not do so; on the contrary, she is ready to punish herself even more severely than she had punished the other Mannons.

Although O'Neill motivates Lavinia's slip by building a speech which contains a logical, associative line of thought ("the dead"—"Adam") and by throwing Lavinia into a despair bordering on insanity, a state of mind which would naturally release her repressed desires, the slip holds true primarily on a deeper, symbolic level. Lavinia's reference to the biblical archetype indicates that Adam to her is man before the Fall. Adam Brant himself relates in Part I.I how he has lived on the "Blessed Isles" in a "Garden of Paradise before sin was discovered" (24). With her deeply rooted puritan sense of sin, increased recently after the death of Orin, there is nothing Lavinia longs for more intensely than sinlessness, the sinlessness she still enjoyed when she first met Adam and which was most seriously violated when she had him, whom she really loved, killed. Her slip is a manifestation of a deep, repressed need not only for love but also for purity, for the Adam of the "Blessed Isles."

Patterned Language

One of the most conspicuous characteristics of O'Neill's dialogue is its consistent employment of verbal repetition. In each play a few key words, which relate closely to the theme of the play are repeated a great number of times. Often priority is given to one particular word, which may be included in the play title. Thus "home" is the key word in *The Long Voyage Home;* "diff'-rent" is the key word in *Diff'rent;* "laughter," "desire" and "end" are key words in *Lazarus Laughed, Desire Under the Elms,* and *Days Without End* respectively.[7]

The verbal repetition is most apparent, of course, when it occurs within a single speech. Cybel's final pæan in *Brown* brings out the eternal seasonal rhythm of life through an insistence on "always" and "again":

Always spring comes again bearing life! Always again! Always, always forever again!—Spring again!—life again! summer and fall and death and peace again! —(*With agonized sorrow*)—but always, always, love and conception and birth and pain again—spring bearing the intolerable chalice of life again!— (*Then with agonized exultance*)—bearing the glorious, blazing crown of life again! (*She stands like an idol of Earth, her eyes staring out over the world.*) (322 f.).

To condemn this speech for being repetitious and argue that its meaning could be expressed more briefly (Raleigh, p. 218), is to misjudge its function. The speech is longer and more repetitious than it rationally need to be precisely because O'Neill wanted us to *feel,* not merely recognize, the eternal recurrence of the love and pain that make up the essence of life.

Critics have often found the verbal repetitions superfluous.[8] O'Neill, they have felt, is so anxious to clarify his points that he makes them too clear, i.e. repeats them too many times; he underestimates the intelligence of his audience. Even Lawrence Langner, who otherwise belongs to O'Neill's most

---

[7] For the significance of "desire," see Downer, pp. 470 f. For further examples, see Raleigh, pp. 213 f.

[8] Stark Young (p. 139) is one of the few critics who praises O'Neill for understanding "the depth and subtlety that lie in repetition and variation on the same design." For a positive evaluation, see also Raleigh, pp. 175 ff.

ardent defenders, saw fit to complain to the playwright that a certain point in *Iceman* is repeated eighteen times. O'Neill laconically answered: "I *intended* it to be repeated eighteen times!" (Langner, p. 405).[9] The basis for this criticism is the assumption that O'Neill is trying to pound home intellectual ideas when in fact his intention, as Doris Alexander rightly observes (1962, p. 261), is "to affect his audience emotionally, to speak directly to the unconscious."

Far from making the issues too clear (as the critics would have it), the verbal repetitions may, on the contrary, be said to contribute to their mystifying complexity. For when we witness how one and the same word is used by several, often contrasting, characters in different situations and referring to different things, we experience how the meaning of the word expands as the play develops until, finally, it has become so complex as to seem mysterious.

O'Neill's ability to give significant connotations to the words and speeches of his characters has been noted by several commentators (Koischwitz, p. 58; Dietrich, p. 200). Sometimes these connotations appear from the immediate context. Frequently, however, they emerge only when seen against a larger canvas. A word or passage, which in its immediate context appears flat may, when related to other passages in the play, suddenly seem meaningful. With regard to the unobtrusive, repetitive key words, we normally find their superficial meaning established in the beginning of the plays. Only gradually is this meaning superseded by a more significant one, which may well, however, have been implied from the first. This suggests that the key words are not aimlessly spread out over the plays, but that they are subordinated to a certain design or *pattern,* nebulous though it may be.

In *Horizon* there is a noteworthy emphasis on the word 'go.' When old Mayo is forced to face the fact that Andrew is leaving the farm for the sea, he reacts in a surprisingly violent way: "Yes—go!—go!— You're no son o' mine—no son o' mine! You can go to hell if you want to!" (108). Mayo's curse on Andrew is obviously motivated by the fact that he feels deceived by the son, who is very like himself and in whom he has had much confidence

---

[9] It is interesting to compare the contrasting views of two directors of the play. To Bentley's rationalistic mind the repetitions seem superfluous (1955, p. 223): "One can cut a good many of Larry's speeches since he is forever rephrasing a pessimism that is by no means hard to understand the first time." José Quintero, on the other hand, views the repetitions in much the same way as O'Neill did himself (cf. p. 154). *Iceman,* Quintero finds (p. 28), "resembles a complex musical form, with themes repeating themselves with slight variations, as melodies do in a symphony. It is a valid device, though O'Neill has often been criticized for it by those who do not see the strength and depth of meaning the repetition achieves." It is not surprising that Quintero's production was far more successful than Bentley's.

(97). Without Andrew he sees no hope that the farm will ever become "one of the slickest, best-payin' farms in the state" (97). His materialistic dream crushed, his life has lost all meaning:

MAYO. (*incoherently*) I'm goin'—to bed, Katey. It's late, Katey—it's late. (*He goes out.*) (108).

These are Mayo's final words in the play. A year later, before the opening of the next act, he is dead.

Mayo's curse, amounting to a death wish, is echoed in Act II.1 by Ruth, who hatefully tells Robert: "I do love Andy. ... And he loves me! ... So go! Go if you want to!" (128). Everything in the scene suggests that Ruth wants Robert dead. But she is afraid to make this clear—even to herself. On the surface she merely asks him to leave the farm.

In the opening of the following scene Robert picks up her thought, when he asks his little daughter: "Would you like Dada to go away?—far, far away?" (129). The child's answer is violently negative. Robert finds that he must stay alive. At the end of Act III.1 Ruth, returning from Robert's bedroom, calls:

... *trembling with fright*) Andy! Andy! He's gone!
ANDREW. (*misunderstanding her—his face pale with dread*) He's not—
RUTH. (*interrupting him—hysterically*) He's gone! The bed's empty (166).

For a moment both Andrew and the audience equate 'going' with 'dying.'

When Robert finally dies, he picks up the word again: "And this time I'm going! It isn't the end. It's a free beginning—the start of my voyage! I've won to my trip—the right of release—beyond the horizon!" (168). Robert's death is a fulfillment of two promises stated in Act I. One is the promise he made to himself as a child, that "when [he] grew up and was strong," he would follow the road, and it and he "would find the sea together" (89). Dying by the roadside, he has taken the first steps on the road leading to the sea; he has begun his "voyage." The other, hypothetical promise was made to his brother. About to leave the farm Andrew says in Act I.2:

You love her too, Rob. Put yourself in my place, and remember I haven't stopped loving her, and couldn't if I was to stay. Would that be fair to you or her? Put yourself in my place. ... What'd you do then? Tell me the truth! You love her. What'd you do?
ROBERT. (*chokingly*) I'd—I'd go, Andy! (*He buries his face in his hands with a shuddering sob*) God! (110).

The emotional intensity of this passage should, I think, be seen in the light of the play ending. The advice which Robert here gives Andrew he finally obeys himself. In the belief that Ruth still loves Andrew, he reverses the earlier situation: he 'goes' and asks Andrew to marry Ruth (162).

The theme of the play, it appears from the above, is to a great extent designed around the parallel between sea traveling and dying, both of which meanings are contained in the word 'go.' At first only the former meaning is clear to us and, presumably, to Robert; gradually the latter is unravelled. The longing for the "far-off sea," which Robert harbored already as a child (89), is at bottom a death impulse.

"It will give satisfaction to those who once complained of O'Neill's profanity to know that the earliest of his surviving plays opens with 'Gawd! What a night!'" (Clark, pp. 49 f.). Clark, who has little praise for O'Neill's dialogue, seems to agree with the plaintiffs. His comment on *Web* misses the point largely because he sees Rose's speech in isolation. Had he examined the play more closely, he would have discovered that it is but the first of many references to God, all of them made by Rose, and that it relates directly to her final speech. Rose's opening speech reads in full:

(*Listening to the rain—throws the cigarette wearily on the table*) Gawd! What a night! (*Laughing bitterly*) What a chance I got! (*She has a sudden fit of coughing; then gets up and goes over to the bed and bending down gently kisses the sleeping child on the forehead. She turns away with a sob and murmurs*) What a life! Poor kid! (36).

The soliloquy reveals Rose's awareness that she stands little chance of finding a customer and of improving her health in the dreary night (38). At a deeper level, understood only in retrospect, the soliloquy reveals her infinitesimal chances for a decent life in a dark, cruel world. Whether we believe that she is totally unaware of the deeper meaning of her words or that she is dimly conscious of it, we can agree that the spiritual action of the playlet consists in her gradual awareness of the workings of an ironic life force.

It soon becomes clear that "Gawd" is more than an oath to Rose:

Gimme a couple of dollars and let me go to the doc's and git some medicine. Please, Steve, for Gawd's sake! (38).

Please, Steve, for the love of Gawd lemme keep her [the baby]! (40).

Reform? Take it from me it can't be done. They [all the righteous people] won't let yuh do it, and that's Gawd's truth (45).

TIM. ... Yuh swear yuh won't squeal on me?
ROSE. I won't, so help me Gawd! (47).

As the "Gawd" expressions gradually lose their flavor of careless jargon, their religious meaning is strengthened; in the last example there is no longer any doubt that Rose acknowledges the existence of a supernatural power.

There is a glimpse of hope, when she meets Tim, another basically innocent outcast in society, but the hope is brutally crushed when he is killed by Steve. Rose immediately seems to sense the supernatural significance of the event: *"She stares straight before her and repeats in tones of horrible monotony)* Dead. Oh Gawd, Gawd, Gawd!" (51). When accused of the murder she appeals to the dead Tim: "For the love of Gawd speak to 'em. (*Weeping and sobbing bitterly)* Oh Gawd, why don't yuh speak, why don't yuh speak?" (52). Since Rose's concern with God has by this time been established, the "yuh" may refer to God as well as to Tim. Shortly after these words she

seems to be aware of something in the room which none of the others can see— perhaps the personification of the ironic life force that has crushed her)
> FIRST PLAIN-CLOTHES MAN. Your kid?
> ROSE. (*to the unseen presence in the room*) Yes. I suppose yuh'll take her too? (53).

Now the "yuh" refers to God rather than to the police. Rose's final speech is the only one in which she explicitly directs herself to God:

(To the air) That's right. Make a good job of me. (*Suddenly she stretches both arms above her head and cries bitterly, mournfully, out of the depths of her desolation)* Gawd! Gawd! Why d'yuh hate me so? (53).

The desperate question, which was latent in her initial soliloquy, has become fully phrased.

Another playlet included in the debut collection, *Thirst,* also begins and ends with references to God, a god who is visualized in the sun which scorches the three shipwrecked characters on the life raft and who finally makes them victims of the sharks. The play opens with the following speech:

DANCER. (*raising herself to a sitting posture and turning piteously to the* GENTLE-MAN) My God! My God! This silence is driving me mad! Why do you not speak to me? (4).

We note the double meaning of the "you"; that the Gentleman does not speak to her is relatively unimportant; that God is silent is the real tragedy. The Dancer's despair is akin to that of the Crucified, who also suffered from thirst and who cried out: "My God, my God, why hast thou forsaken me?" (Mat. 27: 46). When a little later the Gentleman exclaims: "God! God! How my eyes ache! How my throat burns!" (5), O'Neill suggests to the spectator what the reader of the play has already learned in the stage directions: that *"the sun glares down ... like a great angry eye of God"* (3). A seemingly casual phrase like the Gentleman's "God knows we are all in the same pitiful plight" (9) seems a disguised protest against the Divine Power who "knows" the misery of mankind, yet does not pity it. A little later the protest is made explicitly:

GENTLEMAN. ... I, too, might whine a prayer of protest: Oh God, God! ... Is this the meaning of all my years of labor? Is this the end, oh God? So I might wail with equal justice. But the blind sky will not answer your appeals or mine (18).

The final speech of the play, spoken just before the two men fall into the water, is the Gentleman's protest: "No! No! No! Good God, not that!" (31). But, as though contradicting his insistence on a benign god, the sun, as in the beginning, *"glares down like a great angry eye of God"* (32).

The frequent references to God in these plays serve to indicate the mysterious fate of which all the characters are victims. Since this fate is only gradually recognized by them, there are no explicit references to it until the latter part of the plays. If the early references appear more realistic than the later ones, it is merely because they are more implicit; and they are more implicit, because the action O'Neill wants to present is that of an inner revelation, of emotions or ideas at first unconscious or dimly experienced which, under the pressure of crucial situations, become more real to the characters and are therefore faced directly and explicitly.

When the reiterated word or phrase is somewhat unusual, we naturally notice it more easily. In *Christie* nobody can help paying attention to Chris Christopherson's reiterative complaint about "dat ole davil, sea"; whenever Chris uses the word "davil" he refers to the sea. The only other character who uses the phrase (once) is Marthy (17), who has obviously been influenced by Chris. When the other characters use the word 'devil' they frequently refer to Chris. Larry calls him "the old divil" (5). Johnny-the-Priest welcomes him with: "Speak of the devil" (6). Mat Burke finds that he is "a divil to be making a power of trouble" (46). The only time Anna uses the word she does it emphatically. "You're like a devil, you are!" she tells Chris (54).

This difference in usage illustrates the fact that whereas Chris attributes the misery of his life to the sea, symbol of a baleful fate (cf. O'Neill 12.18. 1921, 6, p. 1), the others attribute it to his own weakness. It may seem as though the majority would represent a more objective and truthful view and in a sense they do: Chris is partly to blame. But not altogether. In the end Mat comes around to Chris' fatalism, and Anna, who has earlier incidentally echoed her father's resigned belief, also reveals that she is affected by it. Chris' belief in a malign fate proves justified even if his attitude to this fate does not; "dat ole davil, sea" exists but it is man's task to fight it, not to run away from it.

In almost any drama there is one verbal category which is automatically subject to repetition: the words by which the characters address or refer to each other. By arranging such words in a meaningful way the dramatist can tell us much about the characters' relations to one another.

In Act III of *Interlude* Mrs. Evans consistently refers to her son as "Sammy" —he is still her little boy—while Nina naturally calls him "Sam"; at this point she respects him and even loves him in his capacity of father to her child. After the abortion, when Nina has fallen in love with Darrell and become pregnant by him, she significantly adopts the possessive maternal address and calls her husband "Sammy" (109, 113). When her power within the marriage has waned she reverts to the earlier "Sam" (154 ff.).

The change of climate between two people as mirrored by their way of addressing each other can be seen also in *Hughie*. Erie, anxious to establish a contact with the Night Clerk, inserts a "Pal" or "Brother" in almost all his speeches. This is not accidental. As Erie reveals late in the play: "Hughie liked to kid himself he was my pal. (*He adds sadly.*) And so he was, at that —even if he was a sucker" (31). In other words, the address illustrates how Erie tries to see a substitute for the dead Hughie in the Night Clerk.

But the Night Clerk is not interested in any contact. He calls Erie "Mr. Smith" even after he has been told to say "Erie," and late in the play he still makes the slip: "I beg your pardon, Mr.—Erie ..." (32). As soon as he begins to connect Erie with his idol, Arnold Rothstein, and with gambling, he starts to take an interest in him and from this point he addresses him as "Erie."

Frankly non-realistic addresses appear in *Brown*. Thus Dion consistently addresses Brown in the third person ("Billy," "Brown," "the Great God Mr. Brown," "Almighty Brown," etc.) until his dying moment, when he, un-masked, switches to a normal, personal address: "May Margaret love you! May you design the Temple of Man's Soul!" (299). Dion also repeatedly addresses his wife in the third person; for example:

I love Margaret! Her blindness surpasseth all understanding! (271).

So my wife thinks it behooves me to settle down ... (271).

Margaret addresses Brown in the same way in Act I.2:

... Billy is doing so wonderfully well, everyone says (274).

Dion certainly draws well, Billy Brown was saying? (275).

The pattern is set at the very beginning of the play by Mrs. Brown who, in the presence of her son, states that "Billy used to draw houses when he was little" and asks him: "How would Billy like to be an architect? (*She does not look at him.*)" (259). Mrs. Brown, although most of her speeches concern her son's future, always speaks either "*to the air,*" as though she was thinking aloud, or to her husband. In either case it reveals a domineering mother's refusal to let her son decide for himself and shape his own life, her selfish view of Billy as a means to the realization of her own success dream.

As Leech has noted (pp. 65 f.), the effect of the third person addresses is one of unreality and lack of contact between the characters. Strictly speaking, they do not address each other at all when using these forms; rather, they refer to each other. In this way the author could give a mystical note to the dialogue and suggest that the characters are separated, isolated from each other. It is significant that Dion and Margaret use the third person addresses only when they are masked.[1] The sarcastic tone that goes with this form of address contrasts markedly with the humble, loving tone in which Dion finally arrives at an unmasked you-relationship with Margaret (292) and with Brown.

Audible Thinking

In view of O'Neill's later concern with audible thinking as an integral part of dramatic dialogue it seems premonitory that the first two literary lines from his hand we know of should read:

> Weary am I of the tumult, sick of the staring crowd,
> Pining for wild sea places where the soul may think aloud
> (O'Neill, 1912/Sanborn–Clark, pp. 111 f.).

Audible thinking will here be used as a general term for all speeches which are not—or not exclusively—directed to any character on the stage (except the speaker himself) and which therefore often transcend real-life plausibility. All other speeches will be considered elements of the *dialogue,* the term used in a narrow sense. In certain cases it is easy to differentiate between the two, but frequently the question whether a speech is primarily, partly, or not at all addressed to some other character cannot be answered with any certainty. This does not mean that the question is meaningless. The actor, who has to learn a speech, must certainly interpret it and decide for himself, whether it should be spoken with a dreamy stare in a far-away voice by a man who momentarily is concerned only with his own thinking; or whether it should be spoken distinctly and matter-of-factly, with a concentrated look at the listener by a man who is confessing something *to* someone else and is more aware of the reactions of the person he is addressing than of the story he has to tell; or whether some middle way can be found between these extremes, suggesting

---

[1] Cf. *Interlude* where Darrell, hiding his desire for Nina behind the *"mask of a doctor,"* impersonally addresses her as "Sam's wife," when he advises her in the name of science to commit adultery (85 f.). The third person address here indicates how Darrell deludes both himself and Nina as to the objectivity of his device.

that the speaker is half dreaming aloud, half aware of the presence of whomever he is talking to. A careful examination both of what the speaker says and *how* he says it will often help us to decide in favor of one of these alternatives.

Further distinctions may be made among five different types of audible thinking in O'Neill's work: soliloquy, pseudo-soliloquy, pseudo-monologue, monologue, and thought aside.[2]

By *soliloquy* I mean a speech by a person, who is the only awake, flesh-and-blood character on the stage or who believes himself to be so. Ever since naturalism made its slice-of-life demand that soliloquies must seem 'natural,' i.e. that they must be motivated by a special state of mind of the speaker—drunkenness, delirium, anguish, senility, insanity, etc.—dramatists who have at all been in touch with this literary tradition have labored to justify their characters' soliloquies. O'Neill is one of them. Only in a few plays does he completely disregard the demand for outward plausibility. One is his first play, *Wife*; here the inclusion of the soliloquies—they comprise about one sixth of the play—is clearly determined by the fact that the playwright was unable to present his information in a genuinely dramatic way. And even in later plays the soliloquies may at times seem too obviously expository. Thus Abraham Bentley's initial soliloquy in *Rope* (578 f.), although made plausible by his senility, is inserted primarily to inform us that there is a secret known only to Bentley attached to the rope; it prepares for the surprise at the end of the play. In *Electra* Christine's soliloquy "I've got to see Adam! I've got to warn him!" (92) provides a strong curtain for Part I.II and points forward to the following act; from a naturalistic point of view it is hardly a well-motivated soliloquy. Yet, since the speech is brief, since Christine is definitely upset, and since the style of the play does not call for meticulous realism, the soliloquy does not disturb us. In *Brown* the non-illusionistic style of the play itself may be said to motivate the soliloquies, and the same is true of the thought soliloquies in *Interlude*; the very term indicates that we deal with a frank break with realism; its rules do not apply. More startling is Richard's thought soliloquy in Act IV.2 of *Wilderness,* for it breaks with the realistic style of the play as a whole. But this must have been precisely O'Neill's intention: the scene of youthful love should be set off from the other scenes in the play; it should strike one like the unstripping of a mask. It is done partly through a marked change of setting and lighting but also through a change from realistic dialogue to stylized audible dreaming, from outer to inner reality.

Usually, as Macgowan has shown (1929, pp. 449 f.), the audible thinking

---

[2] The conventional type of aside, the *à part* speech, is exceedingly rare with O'Neill and has, when it appears, usually a purely expository function. See, for example, *Wife* (219) and *Kid* (610).

of O'Neill's characters is realistically motivated. Thus the long soliloquies by Captain Bartlett in *Gold* (681 f.) and by Ella Harris in *Chillun* (330 f.) are justified by the mental confusion of these characters, and the Chantyman's soliloquy in *Electra* (103 f.) is made probable by his drunkenness. Bartlett is not only talking to himself; he is actually reliving past experiences; we hear him addressing Silas Horne—the boatswain who is supposed to return with the gold—Abel and Butler, the murdered members of the crew, and Sarah, his wife, who has died prematurely as a result of his obsession; it is plain that these ghosts are exceedingly real to him, that they are part of his daily company. The soliloquy thus confirms that Bartlett is indeed insane, but more important is its indication of what constitutes his insanity. Had he limited himself to addressing Horne, his madness would be merely a sign of an intense longing for gold, of a wish-thinking so potent that it has affected his reason. Such an opinion does not seem altogether untenable in view of Bartlett's earlier admission that he has been dreaming of gold all his life (638). But no such limitation is made. And Abel, Butler and Sarah, the innocent victims of Bartlett's obsession, are at least as real to him as Horne. From this we may conclude that Bartlett is victimized by two painfully combined and therefore overpowering feelings: a life-long desire and an intense guilt related to this desire; he cannot think of the gold without recalling his crimes and vice versa. The soliloquy thus demonstrates not only how but why Bartlett is imprisoned in his past.

Ella Harris' problem is somewhat different and is also worked out in another way. In Act II.1 O'Neill was faced with the problem of how to express Ella's beginning disintegration, how to make it clear that it hinged on her need to compensate her feelings of inferiority and that it is this need for compensation that makes her pay attention to her 'superior' skin. He accomplished this by creating a crucial situation and by giving a long soliloquy to her, in which the split is revealed. From her window Ella regards the all-black street below her; suddenly she discovers Shorty, the white pimp; she calls him but receives no answer. Her arguments for and against the likelihood that he has heard her (330) might have been printed thus:

No, he didn't hear you.

> Yes, he did, too! He must have! I yelled so loud you could hear me in Jersey!

No, what are you talking about? How would he hear with all the kids yelling down there? He never heard a word, I tell you!

> He did, too! He didn't want to hear you!

As indicated, two voices are clearly discernible in this soliloquy: the consoling voice of illusion (to the left) and the cruel voice of truth (to the right). Both voices insist on being heard. Eventually, however, the latter proves victorious:

<blockquote>He's afraid it'd get him in wrong with the old gang.</blockquote>

Why?

<blockquote>You know well enough! Because you married a—a—a—well, I won't say it, but you know without my mentioning names!</blockquote>

<blockquote>(ELLA *springs to her feet in horror and shakes off her obsession with a frantic effort*) Stop! (*Then wimpering like a frightened child*) Jim! Jim! Jim! Where are you? I want you, Jim! (*She runs out of the room as the curtain falls.*) (331).</blockquote>

The audible thinking significantly ceases as Ella comes to the taboo word 'nigger'; her periphrasis indicates that she tries but cannot fully repress the word and the idea that goes with it. At this point the censoring superego intervenes; the thought process is interrupted. And with a characteristic transference of thought, as though to condone for the imagined word 'nigger,' she calls appealingly for Jim. This represents a third voice, an attempt to resolve the conflict by reverting to childhood, to the time when she could "want" Jim in a simple, honest way and was not affected by what the world thinks. Though soliloquies are often held to be unsuitable even for non-illusionistic drama on the ground that they are undramatic and this may be true in the sense that they necessitate an interruption of the outer action, Ella's soliloquy illustrates how O'Neill has arranged her thoughts—or emotions, rather—in such a way that the speech gives a vivid picture of the intense inner division she is subject to.

The *pseudo-soliloquy* occurs, when a character who is not physically alone clearly reveals in his speech that he is not aware of the world surrounding him but is actually engrossed with another reality. Thus Rose, at the end of *Web*, is "*aware of something in the room which none of the others can see— perhaps the personification of the ironic life force that has crushed her*" (53). And it is to this life force that her last two speeches are directed. The Dancer in *Thirst* (28 f.) and Mary Tyrone in her curtain speech (*Journey*, 175 f.) reveal that they have completely recreated their past, seeking protection there from the unbearable present. And a host of other characters—Eben in *Desire,* Orin and Lavinia in *Electra* to mention a few—momentarily direct themselves to their dear departed as though they were visible to them.

When the addressee is non-human (or 'dead') and is visible to the audience I term the speeches *pseudo-monologues.* Included in this category would be Captain Bartlett's speeches to the drowned sailors in *Cross,* Brutus Jones' addresses to his "ha'nts," Ella Harris' directing herself to the Congo mask, as though it were alive, Brown's addressing his own mask, Reuben's prayer to the dynamo, and Lavinia's discourses with the Mannon portraits.

The impact on an audience of a pseudo-soliloquy is not quite the same as that of a pseudo-monologue; the character who addresses ghosts invisible to us is not the same as the character who addresses ghosts that we can see. The mere fact that we also see them gives them and, obliquely, the speeches directed to them a normalcy we deny speeches directed to supernatural phenomena that are invisible to us. Rationally, in other words, the ghosts in *Cross* may be experienced as an inner, psychological fate; emotionally, they appear to us as an outer, metaphysical one; and the speeches addressed to them are, in line with this, experienced as part soliloquy, part dialogue. Our empathy with the characters is of course far stronger with the pseudo-monologue than with the pseudo-soliloquy, a fact which explains why O'Neill often resorts to this type when describing mentally disordered characters. Captain Bartlett in *Gold* clearly runs the risk of being seen only as a mental case, but we do not worry over the normalcy of his namesake in *Cross* or the sanity of Brutus Jones, of Yank (in *Ape*), or of Dion and Brown. Shared insanity is no insanity.

Although the term *monologue* is sometimes used as a synonym for soliloquy, more often it is defined as a prolonged speech by one character addressed to one or several others present on the stage. I use it here to refer to a speech (not necessarily long) by one character, which on the surface is addressed to one or several other characters present on the stage but which in reality is a thinking aloud. As part soliloquy, part dialogue it comes close to the pseudo-monologue but differs from this with respect to the nature of the addressee, who is a flesh-and-blood character.

It follows from this that the monologue is more difficult to distinguish from the dialogue than are the other types of audible thinking. Frequently an O'Neill character will begin his speech as straight dialogue, then drift into a dreamy talking to himself without obtrusively revealing the change; on the surface the speech remains a piece of dialogue. In these cases the speaker is not wholly unaware of his listeners; but he is too preoccupied with his own inner problems to pay more than casual attention to them.

Subtle psychological effects can be gained from this procedure of trans-ference; as a character slips into monologue, we may assume that he is talking about matters of the utmost concern to himself. In *Electra* Orin begins by telling Lavinia about his war experiences in straight dialogue: "I'll tell you the joke about that heroic deed." But very soon, when he relates how he killed an enemy, his voice sinks *"lower and lower, as if he were talking to himself"* (94 f.); after the words about how the enemy's eyes "dimmed and went out" there is a pause, signifying death. As Orin touches on a traumatic memory—traumatic because to Orin each killed enemy represents himself, each murder is a symbolic self-murder—his speech turns first into a monologue, then into silence.

Even such a seemingly direct speech as Nat Miller's in *Wilderness* just after he has read some of the 'indecent' poems Richard has provided for his virtuous girl friend has an element of monologue in it:

(*an irrepressible boyish grin coming to his face*) Hell and hallelujah! Just picture old Dave digesting that for the first time! Gosh, I'd give a lot to have seen his face! (*Then a trace of shocked reproof showing in his voice*) But it's no joking matter. That stuff *is* warm—too damned warm, if you ask me! I don't like this a damned bit, Sid. That's no kind of thing to be sending a decent girl (205).

The speech reveals two completely different sides of Nat: the natural, irre-sponsible, *"boyish"* one as opposed to the socially oriented, responsible, grown-up one. The former is fittingly presented in Nat's spontaneous outburst, the latter in his serious afterthought. It is highly characteristic of O'Neill's tech-nique that the transition, so violent as to amount to a reversal of viewpoint, occurs within one and the same speech. The fact that Nat thus, *unaided by the outward world,* rejects his former viewpoint, tells us of his inner conflict, moderate though it may be. Moreover, the transition parallels his son's change from boyish revengefulness to grown-up acceptance of the social mores—the main theme of the play—and thus reveals father and son to be basically alike; the difference between them, due to the age difference, is one in degree only. Miller's speech illustrates the essential meaning of the O'Neill monologue: to reveal inner division and to establish the basic sameness of the human soul.

Whether a speech is an element of dialogue or an expression of audible thinking is determined not solely by the speaker's state of mind but also by the non-speaker's attitude. Thus, in a few of his plays O'Neill adopts a dialogue technique, determined by modern psychological insights, which may be described as a fusion of two theatrical conventions: the soliloquy and the aside. The theatrical fiction, coinciding with that of the aside, consists in the fact that certain speeches are supposed to be heard only by the speaker and the audience but not by the other characters on the stage; like the traditional soliloquy these speeches represent the speaker's private thoughts or emotions,[3] and we may therefore use O'Neill's own term, *thought asides* (1931/Frenz, p. 10), for them.[4]

The technique of thought asides, which meant a decisive break with realism, did not spring full-grown from O'Neill's brain at the time he was working on *Interlude*. Already in *Kid* (621 f.) there is an approximation to the *Interlude* technique in the use of counterpoint to bring out the contrast between what Dreamy is and what his grandmother takes him to be. The characters do not listen to one another, they merely record occasional words, which, robbed of their context, may be interpreted in quite a different way from that intended by the speaker. Each plays his own melody, ironically contrasting with that of the other.

Much closer to the *Interlude* technique, as Engel notes (1953, p. 111), is a passage in Act I of *Welded*. Eleanor and Michael, in separate chairs, sit motionless facing front:

They speak, ostensibly to the other, but showing by their tone it is a thinking aloud to oneself, and neither appears to hear what the other has said.
CAPE. (*after a long pause*) More and more frequently. There's always some knock at the door, some reminder of the life outside which calls you away from me.
ELEANOR. It's so beautiful—and then—suddenly I'm being crushed. I feel a cruel presence in you paralyzing me, creeping over my body, possessing it so it's no longer my body—then grasping at some last inmost thing which makes me me—my soul—demanding to have that, too! I have to rebel with all my strength—seize any pretext! (452 f.).

It is sufficient to quote the beginning of Eleanor's and Michael's audible thoughts (which cover about one page and amount to three speeches by each of them) to give an idea of the style. The speeches are neatly balanced to fulfill their double function of being both dialogue and thought aside. Each one may be related either to the preceding speech by the other character (dialogue) or to the preceding speech by the same character (thought aside). O'Neill's suggestion in the stage directions that the speeches are constructed as dialogue but will appear as audible thinking due to the special intonation used by the characters is thus a simplification of the matter.

[3] The thought asides are often said to represent the characters' subconscious minds. This is a simplification of their function. As we shall see, it is more correct to say that they represent both the characters' more or less conscious thoughts and their more or less unconscious emotions.
[4] Block (p. 163) rightly observes that while the traditional aside serves to reveal what is hidden in a very factual sense, O'Neill's thought asides, much closer to the Shakespearean soliloquy in spirit, serve to reveal inner processes.

The style is rather removed from what we may term dramatic realism, i.e. real-life speech qualified by dramatic conditions. Both speak figuratively; Michael compares the intrusion of life outside to a knock on the door; Eleanor describes his spiritual possession of her as a brutal rape. This too helps to set the speeches off from the ordinary dialogue, to define them as a thinking aloud. The difference in style is, however, not very marked. As expressions of audible thinking the speeches are syntactically quite coherent. And naturally it could not be otherwise, since, by O'Neill's decision, they should still retain the outward appearance of being dialogue. Not until he threw off all the fetters of realistic demands for plausibility and treated the thought asides as markedly different from the dialogue, could he also contrast their styles; could the strained style of *Welded* give way to the two styles of *Interlude*.

What position and intonation do in *Welded* to set the audible thinking off from the dialogue, is done also by means of masks in *Brown*. In the Prologue Billy, unmasked, proposes to Margaret and Margaret dreamingly 'proposes' to Dion, whose name she lovingly repeats seventeen times, the mask in her hands (262 ff.). What we have here is really one long piece of dialogue (by Billy) juxtaposed to one long dreaming aloud (by Margaret); by making them similar in content (each being a love declaration), and by cutting each into pieces, O'Neill closely intertwined the two speeches; the discrepancy between the blunt, prosaic Billy and the shy, sensitive Dion (as described in Margaret's speeches) becomes more dramatic and more ironic by this arrangement. When Billy has worked himself up to a pitch of agony, Margaret finally hears him, but before she can answer him she must put on her mask.

After the wary and very incidental attempt in *Kid* to juxtapose the thoughts of two characters, after the more daring and obvious attempt to do so in *Welded,* after the employment of alternating masked and unmasked faces in *Brown*, O'Neill had almost inevitably arrived at the formal split between dialogue and thought asides which constitutes the *Interlude* technique.

The thought asides in *Interlude* serve two different, even conflicting, purposes, one dramaturgical, the other psychological. Beyond these a third, metaphysical purpose may be distinguished. The dramaturgical aspect indirectly throws light on the limitations of the psychological one. The antithesis between the two is obvious and amounts to a contrast between theatre and life. In real, waking life we are all continuous thinkers. A play based on the technique of audible thinking would therefore, realistically presented, mean continuous, simultaneous thought-speeches, hardly distinguishable from and mingling with the ordinary speeches. The result would be cacophony, and a play thus presented would most likely be a theatrical nightmare.

To satisfy dramaturgical and theatrical demands O'Neill was forced to depart from real-life-psychology in several respects: The thoughts and emotions are presented not simultaneously but sequentially, separately from one another and from the speeches. Only a small part of what the characters, viewed as real-life figures, think or feel is reproduced, and the dramatist has felt quite free to decide both the distribution and the nature of their thinking. For the sake of clarity and dramatic tightness the thoughts or feelings reproduced are fairly distinctly and briefly formulated. The fact that the asides are frequently used for expository and preparatory purposes (Lawson, p. 137; Kaucher, p. 139) further necessitates a certain clarity and orderliness.[5] In short, because they are elements of a play structure the thoughts and emotions of the characters cannot be presented as realistically as in a novel.[6]

It is obvious, however, that O'Neill would never have resorted to the use of thought asides unless he had felt that they offered certain possibilities denied a conventional dialogue technique. Langner has indicated (p. 236) a purely practical reason. O'Neill once told him that he invented his technique of asides, because the majority of actors would be unable to see the deeper significance of the speeches unless it was explained to them. By providing a running commentary pointing up the disguised meaning of the speeches, the dramatist would considerably limit the risk of misinterpretation on the part of the actors. This practical consideration was certainly not foreign to O'Neill; his ample stage directions indicate the same anxiousness to safeguard the dramatist against misinterpretation. But it would be absurd to claim that the aside technique was evolved solely or even primarily on the basis of such practical considerations.

Far from being an extraneous addition (as such a view implies) the asides, in conjunction with the regular speeches, are the logical formal expression of a basic tenet in the play: that words do not convey but hide the truth; as Nina has it: "How we poor monkeys hide from ourselves behind the sounds called words!" (39 f.). Nina's negative attitude to verbal communication is obvious: words serve to disguise the painful truth that spiritually we have developed little beyond the animal stage. Nina is not primarily concerned with the lying we do to each other; this is relatively unimportant compared to the

[5] Each of the first seven acts begins with one or several long thought asides—or better: thought soliloquies—which serve to inform us of what has happened before the act. A good example of the preparatory function is found at the end of Act I in Professor Leeds' premonition of his death (23).

[6] Hardly anywhere do the thought asides in *Interlude* amount to a (seemingly) incoherent stream of consciousness of the Molly Bloom type (cf. Engel, 1953, p. 226). O'Neill may, however, well have been inspired to his thought asides by Joyce's *Ulysses,* which he apparently read shortly after its appearance in 1922 (Gelb, p. 475), and which he gave to Carlotta while *Interlude* was in rehearsal; his dedication in the book, now at Yale, is dated 12.1.1927.

lying we do to ourselves. Moreover, her criticism implies that *all* words are, in a sense, lies, that verbal communication as such is self-delusive. Nina seems to argue as follows: Man is no more than an animal; yet he has the faculty of speech, which gives him the illusion that he is superior to other animals; hence, the faculty of speech as well as what is communicated through speech must be considered an expression of self-delusion.

Speech functions as a human 'mask' covering the animal 'face' underneath. The 'mask' is a prettified version of the 'face,' a lie. As a distortion we hate it and want to rid ourselves of it. Yet it represents also what is specifically human, that which differentiates us from the animals and makes human coexistence possible. And for this reason we need it. By and large, we would conclude from the foregoing, the speeches represent a seemingly rational superstructure hiding a welter of instinctual desires. A few examples will illustrate the dichotomy (most of the dots in the following are O'Neill's; they indicate that the speeches are thought asides).

Marsden, worried about his mother's health, thinks: "... she's sixty-eight ... I can't help fearing ... no! ...." When Evans refers to her old age, Marsden protests, assuring him that she is "still under sixty-five." The speech is followed by a self-reproaching afterthought: "Why did I lie to him about her age? ... I must be on edge ..." (73 f.). Marsden's lie is clearly not intended for Evans; it is meant for himself. By speaking aloud what Marsden himself has been thinking, Evans increases Marsden's fear unbearably; the lie is a desperate attempt to counteract this growing fear; by making the beloved mother younger, Marsden removes her from the fatal age, thereby assuring himself that he will not yet be deprived of her.

The same type of lie occurs when Nina tells Darrell that Madeline, her rival for Gordon's love, is "hardly even pretty." Yet a little earlier she has been thinking: "how I've come to detest her pretty face!" (168). The thought aside represents the truth; that Madeline *is* pretty is corroborated by the stage directions (159), by Darrel (168), and by Marsden (175). The speech represents a distorting fusion of the two facts suggested in the aside—Madeline is pretty; Nina hates her—resulting in a seemingly objective, factual statement. Nina's lie, like Marsden's, is primarily an expression of wish-thinking, an attempt to convince herself, not Darrell, that Madeline is not the dangerous rival Nina at heart knows she is.

Again, Darrell reveals himself to be a victim of the same need for self-delusion. He tells Marsden that he has returned to America because of his father's death but immediately thinks: "Lie ... Father's death just gave me an excuse to myself ... wouldn't have come back for that ... came back because I love her! ..." (125). It is true that Darrell has a legitimate reason to keep Marsden off the true track; the novelist must not know about his adulterous relationship with Nina. Yet the spoken lie expresses far more than a momentary attempt to avert Marsden's suspicions. Rather, the lie comes so easily to Darrell because, as the aside indicates, he has been living with it for a long time, trying to repress his love for Nina.

Like Nina's hatred of Madeline, practically all expressions of undisguised aggression belong to the thought sections. "I'm glad he's dead," Professor Leeds thinks about Gordon (16). "Let Sam die," Nina thinks, and Darrell echoes her: "to hell with Sam!" (97). Yet, in the following act, after Darrell has betrayed her, Nina is ready to reverse her former thought: "I'll promise to love Sam if he kills him [Darrell]" (108). Marsden, sensing the love relationship between Nina and Darrell, jealously thinks: "if only God would strike them dead!" (129). Gordon, revealing his Oedipal disposition, thinks about Darrell, his father: "I was hoping he'd died!" (138).

But the death wish can be directed also against oneself. When it becomes clear that Nina will leave him, Professor Leeds significantly begins to think of his own death. The fear of a life in loneliness results in an increase of his latent death instinct (23). Sam, feeling spiritually and sexually unproductive, contemplates suicide (92). Nina, once her passion is spent, longs for death as Marsden has always done. Her observation that "we're always desiring death for ourselves or others" (170) is thus fully borne out in the play.

It is possible to argue that Nina's thought about Madeline and Darrell's about his reason for returning to the U.S. are somewhat superfluous. Even without the asides we would guess Darrell's repressed reason for returning to Nina and Nina's jealousy of Madeline. Their inclusion may be ascribed to O'Neill's anxiety to bring out the theme of the lying words in the play. But there are other examples of a more subtle use of the aside technique. Sam's first speech in Act VI reads: "(*turning over a page of his paper*) There's going to be the biggest boom before long this country has ever known, or I miss my guess, Nina" (113). A little later he thinks: "Charlie's mother must have hoarded up a half million ... he'll let it rot in government bonds ... wonder what he'd say if I proposed that he back me?" (113). Without the informative aside we might have taken Sam's remark about the financial situation in the country as coincidental, merely suggested by something he has been reading in the paper. By including the aside O'Neill strongly suggests that Sam selects this particular topic because, consciously or unconsciously, he feels that it may eventually satisfy his materialistic greed; before long he asks Marsden to become his partner, i.e. to lend him a large sum of money (121). Moreover, the aside throws light on his earlier implication that Marsden's mother has reached a fragile age (73). At the time this statement was made it seemed merely an indifferent remark. Now, because of the aside, we are inclined to see it as a disguised desire that the rich mother would die and leave Marsden her money. Then Sam could come to possess it, as he also does.

Similarly, an aside helps to make it clear that Marsden's seemingly objective information to Nina that Darrell has come home to see about his estate (126) is motivated by jealousy and a desire to hurt her. And it is, again, an aside by Darrell that explains why he confesses to Nina that he has had a mistress (127): by this admission he hopes to test her feelings for him, to see if she can still be jealous.

These examples may suffice to refute the opinion that the thought asides are superfluous and that the play would fare much better without them (Langner, p. 233; Fraser, p. 49). We need only ask ourselves how Sam in the example just mentioned could suggest in any conventional way—through intonation, mimicry or gesture—that he is talking about big business because he wants Marsden's money, to realize that the aside, being much more explicit than any of these methods of presentation, has a legitimate function.

In the examples discussed so far the discrepancy between speech and thought has been a dominant feature. But O'Neill also occasionally makes use of parallels between what is spoken and what is thought. For example, Nina returns home to her recently dead father with the laconic remark, spoken *"in queer flat tones"*: "He's dead, Mary says. ... It's too bad." There is a contrast between the words, implying Nina's regret of the father's death and the indifference with which she utters them. Obviously Nina does not find the loss of the father so "bad" as she wants Marsden to believe. But in addition to her speech O'Neill gives Nina an explanatory aside which ends "... and now I feel nothing ... it's too bad ..." (26 f.). The repetition in the aside of the words uttered in the speech ("it's too bad") give the latter a new and deeper meaning. We now realize that her speech is a monologue expressing the same idea in lapidaric form that is later enlarged upon in her thought aside. The discrepancy is thus not between her speech and thought but between the meaning of her speech and our initial understanding of it. Again we are reminded of the duplicity of verbal communication.

The parallel may also concern the thought of one person and the speech of another. Thus Marsden, jealously wishing to separate Nina and Darrell, thinks: "I must get her away from him ... get her to marry Evans! ..." (36). A little later Darrell says: "There's only one way I can see. Get her to marry Sam Evans" (37). Darrell's suggestion is an altruistic echo of Marsden's egoistic thought; the verbal identity ironically points up how the same decision may have radically different motivations. The identity between Marsden's thought and Darrell's speech may be seen, however, also in another light. Before he voices his thought, Marsden has revealed that he nourishes a secret hope of becoming Nina's lover, once she is married to the weak Evans. We know that

Darrell has felt attracted to Nina. Later he is to play the role desired by Marsden as Nina's lover. But at this point he rejects the idea of love and of being tied to a woman. Is it not conceivable, in view of all this, that his unconscious reason for marrying Nina off to Sam is quite similar to what is implied in Marsden's aside: a secret hope to be her lover, of satisfying his desire while remaining independent?

As indicated in Nina's use of "too bad," the division between speech and thought is not as clear-cut as the typography suggests. A thought may take the form of a speech and, conversely, a speech may be an audible thinking. In Act II Nina has an aside that reads in part: "I'm sorry, Father! ... you see you've been dead for me a long time ... when Gordon died, all men died ... what did you feel for me then? ..." (27). The direct discourse here serves to indicate that the dead father, despite Nina's statement to the contrary, is a living reality to her.

To distinguish monologue from regular speech is a more delicate task; there is, as we have noted earlier, no absolute dividing line between the two. Early in the play O'Neill draws attention to the phenomenon by preceding one of Nina's speeches with a direction to the actress: "*her thoughts breaking through*" (18). Nina is in a state of high tension and this motivates her speaking her thoughts directly. Again, the following speech by Nina has all the characteristics of an aside:

(*in a queer flat voice*) Yes, he's dead—my father whose passion created me—who began me—he is ended. There is only his end living—his death. It lives now to draw nearer me, to draw me nearer, to become my end! (39).

This speech is characterized by the honesty we have found typical of the asides; it differs markedly from most of the other speeches in the play; and it is significantly followed by her criticism of the lying words. Even Marsden, the most frustrated character in the play, has his moment of honesty, when he speaks his thoughts in a flow of words (174 ff.). Here O'Neill uses the device, frequently resorted to in the later plays, of getting Marsden drunk, thereby breaking down his inhibition.

So far we have dealt with the relationship between speech and thought. While startling and refined effects are sometimes gained from this interrelationship, it must be admitted that many of these effects could be conveyed less conspicuously by means of a conventional dialogue technique through voice modulations, changes of tempo, use of pauses, and so on; it is questionable whether the gain has outbalanced the loss.

When we turn exclusively to the thought asides the picture changes. Much of what is suggested here could not possibly be conveyed in a conventional play. For the asides do not gain dramatic life solely from their symbiosis with the speeches; they also lead a restless life of their own. Thus Professor Leeds' thinking reveals how he tries to fight his own feeling of guilt concerning his destruction of Nina's happiness (11). Marsden's thinking reveals his emotional division between Nina and the mother (75) and, later, his desire both to forget and to remember the dead mother (112 f.). Often the asides indicate how a primitive, aggressive instinct is superseded by a more 'cultivated' thought:

NINA. ... if he'd disappear ... leave me free ... if he'd die ... (*Checking herself—remorsefully*) I must stop such thoughts ... I don't mean it ... poor Sam! (69).

DARRELL. ... Is her husband dead ... at last? ... (*Then with a shudder at his thoughts*) No! ... I don't hope! ... I don't! ... (183).

MARSDEN. ... I will not have long to wait now! ... (*Then ashamed*) How can I think such things ... poor Sam! ... (183).

All three wish Sam dead, yet none of them reveal their thoughts in speech.

At times this censorship is so severe that the primitive impulse is repressed even at the thought level. Thus Marsden's way of imagining himself as Nina's lover is illuminating; he thinks: "... if she were married to this simpleton would she be faithful? ... and then I? ... what a vile thought! ... I don't mean that! ..." (33). The thought is violently rejected even before it has become clearly formulated. It is not merely the moral of the *ménage à trois*, which is banned here; it is the idea of sex itself.

To regard the conflicting ideas within a character's thought aside as an expression of a wholly conscious arguing of the mind is obviously to misjudge O'Neill's intention. The simple, laconic way in which the asides are phrased bears the stamp, not of rational discourse, but of highly charged emotions. The 'thought' conflicts may therefore, as I have indicated, better be seen as an illustration of how emotions on different levels of consciousness are in combat within the characters.

Marsden's reaction in the last example is directly related to a fundamental negative sexual experience he has had at the age of sixteen. Suffering from the ridicule of his comrades, he then tried to prove himself a man in their eyes by sleeping with an ugly Italian prostitute. The incident has left him wounded for the rest of his life; it has resulted in a traumatic neurosis.

Nina, too, suffers from a traumatic experience but in her case the cause of it is the very opposite of the one that applies to Marsden. Nina and Gordon were truly in love with one another. Yet she did not let him sleep with her. She can never forgive herself for her sexual abstinence and punishes herself for it by sleeping with the most seriously wounded soldiers (i.e. the ones who come closest to the dead Gordon) she can find in the army hospital where she nurses.

Although Nina and Marsden like one another, their antithetical traumas provide an insurmountable barrier between them. Marsden is identified in Nina's mind with her own, former prudish self: the "silly virgin." Similarly, whenever Nina devotes herself to sinful sexual love, such as her prostitution at the army hospital and her adulterous love for Darrell, she is associated in Marsden's thoughts with the Italian prostitute. It is significantly when they have both reached an age of weakened sexual desire that the traumatic experiences lose their grip on them, enabling them to reestablish the mutual sympathy of the past.

Up to the very end of the play Nina and Marsden are governed by their youthful experiences; these constitute their psychological fate. The cause of Nina's trauma is clear to others from the very beginning, but the reason for Marsden's is never revealed; only we, the audience, learn about it in his asides. But both find themselves in circumstances which revive their traumatic experiences. Thus Nina's callousness in Act II immediately brings back to Marsden the Italian prostitute of his youth (25, 40). When Darrell talks about the danger that she might "dive for the gutter," Marsden reacts in a way that reveals that, again, he has been painfully reminded of what he tries to repress: "(*With apprehensive terror*) Gutter ... has she ... I wish he wouldn't tell me! ..." (35). When Nina tells him of her promiscuity at the hospital he thinks of her in turns as "the little filth," "the dirty little trollop" and "this little whore" (44 f.); the gradation is significant; Marsden uses the strongest, the most repressed, word last, when it stands clear to him that Nina's prostitution is a direct consequence of her love for Gordon, for Marsden's jealousy culminates at this point.

The Italian prostitute turns up in his mind again as he senses the lustful desire between Darrell and Nina (100) and, presumably, as he thinks of them as "a harlot and a pimp" (129). Even in one of his last speeches (not a thought aside), he harks back to the traumatic experience when claiming that the meaning of life is that man scrapes his soul clean of "impure flesh" (199), the implication being that all flesh is impure; Marsden's youthful experience has brought him to the position of an ascetic and mystic.

In the same way Nina several times relives, as it were, the moment when her father told her that Gordon had been killed. Thus, before Mrs. Evans tells her that she must have an abortion, she experiences the same "sick dead feeling" she had before she received the message about Gordon (57). When Mrs. Evans begins to tell her she again associates with Gordon's airplane crash: "Out of a blue sky ... black!" (58).

So far we have held that the thought asides represent the true feelings of the characters as opposed to the masked feelings appearing in the dialogue. But sometimes the characters lie to themselves also in their thoughts. In Act

V, set in the Evans home in a suburb near New York, where Nina and Sam have moved from her father's New England house, the reasons for the moving are given in Nina's thoughts:

> ... I had to sell my father's home to get money so we could move near his job ... and then he lost his job! ... now he's depending on Ned to help him get another! ... my love! ... how shameless! ... (*Then contritely*) Oh, I'm unjust ... poor Sam doesn't know about Ned ... and it was I who wanted to sell the place ... I was lonely there ... I wanted to be near Ned ... (93).

If the first reason had been given in the dialogue Nina would have been consciously lying; as it is she seems to be doing it only unconsciously; she has talked herself into believing that she has suggested that they move for Sam's sake; only momentarily, to make up for some gross injustice towards Sam, does she admit the truth to herself.

Similarly, Mrs. Evans, determined to tell Nina that she must have an abortion, first argues in her thoughts that her reason for telling Nina about the family insanity is that she wants her beloved son to be happy (56). Later, however, she reveals a less noble reason: "(*Thinking fiercely—even with satisfaction*) Tell her! ... make her suffer what I was made to suffer! ... I've been too lonely! ...*" (58). Mrs. Evans has ample reasons for telling Nina about the family curse and there is, from a dramaturgical point of view, no need for the second, egoistic thought. But O'Neill apparently did not want to make Mrs. Evans a heroic martyr. Like all the other characters she too must be shown to nourish a secret selfishness; her motives, like those of the others, must be revealed as a mixture of egoistic and altruistic tendencies, self-assertive instincts checked by the restraints of civilization.

A mutual repression of truthful emotions explains why Nina and Darrell, neither of whom reveals what we would term a deceitful nature, can betray the husband/friend Sam. Nina thinks: "This doctor is nothing to me but a healthy male ... when he was Ned he once kissed me ... but I cared nothing about him ... so that's all right, isn't it, Sam's Mother?" (85). She ignores the fact that *now* she desires Darrell; she has "*put on her best dress, arranged her hair, rouged,*" and she has identified him with Gordon: "Strong hands like Gordon's ... take hold of you ... not like Sam's" (79). It is clear that Nina is merely trying to ease her conscience by telling herself that she is indifferent to Darrell and only desires a healthy child from him to give to Sam. Darrell, similarly, tries to repress his desire for Nina, arguing that he will agree to the adultery only because he wants to help his friend Sam get a healthy child; at the end of the act, however, when his sexual desire has been aroused, he thinks frankly egoistically: "I shall be happy for a while!" (89).

By making the thoughts of different characters very similar O'Neill strikes a mystical note, which widens the perspective of the play and makes it a description not only of lives but also of Life. Thus, in Act VIII, Nina and Darrell sum up their lives in surprisingly similar ways:

DARRELL. (*thinking with melancholy interest*) And now? ... what? ... I can look into her eyes ... strange eyes that will never grow old ... without desire or jealousy or bitterness ... was she ever my mistress? ... can she be the mother of my child? ... is there such a person as my son? ... I can't think of these things as real any more ... they must have happened in another life....

NINA. (*thinking sadly*) My old lover ... how well and young he looks ... now we no longer love each other at all ... our account with God the Father is settled ... afternoons of happiness paid for with years of pain ... love, passion, ecstasy ... in what a far-off life were they alive! ... the only living life is in the past and future ... the present is an interlude ... strange interlude in which we call on past and future to bear witness we are living! ... (165).

The thought asides are parallel up to a point: both establish Darrell's and Nina's experience of the present as unreal. But whereas Darrell, the scientist, limits himself to observations concerning his own experience of life, Nina, the all-embracing mother, sees her private experience as archetypal. And we, having partaken of their identical feelings, tend to agree with her.

That Darrell's thought of the present as unreal and Nina's thought of it as a "strange interlude"—the implication that the present represents life, as she later explains (199), can be sensed in her words—should appear in thought asides, whose parallelism is itself a sign of unreality and strangeness, is deeply meaningful. It is likely that it was, among other things, this mystical, metaphysical aspect of the aside technique, relating to the play title, which O'Neill had in mind, when he later referred to his occasional attempts to probe below the "immediate subsurfaces" (Dec. 1932/Cargill et al., p. 119). Unfortunately, as he himself remarked, the attempts are not altogether successful; the metaphysical aspect is too incidental and remains too much in the background to attract enough attention.

O'Neill was to use the *Interlude* technique again in *Dynamo* but with considerably less success. Up through the second draft of *Electra* he also used thought asides but then decided to discard them (O'Neill, 1931/Frenz, p. 10). At one stage he contemplated using the *Interlude* technique for the scene between Elsa and Lucy in *Days* to bring out Loving's infidelity and Elsa's dawning suspicions.[7] And he employed it again, and quite efficiently, in Act II.3 of *Mansions*, when depicting the "neurotic, disintegrated" (O'Neill, 1931/Frenz, p. 10) souls of Simon, Sara, and Deborah. He gave, as we have noted, a thought soliloquy to Richard Miller in Act IV.2 of *Wilderness*. In either case the audible thinking appears, however, more coherent, hence more

---

[7] This appears from the notes for the play.

conscious, than in *Interlude.* In *Mansions* the thinking of the characters serves to illustrate how each of them spies on the others and tries to keep a powerful middle position. In *Wilderness* Richard's thinking serves to reveal him as the innocent and romantic boy he is, a youthful Dion without his mask looking into the beautiful moonlight, feeling part of the nature around him.

O'Neill also tried variations of the *Interlude* technique. In the play called *The Life of Bessie Bowen,* begun after *Wilderness* but never finished, only the protagonist speaks her thoughts aloud (Gelb, p. 770). And in *Hughie* we have the opposite situation: a long speech by the protagonist, Erie, occasionally interrupted by the Night Clerk's thought asides.[8]

[8] Unlike the thought asides in *Interlude,* those of the Night Clerk are printed as part of the stage directions. This has resulted in different interpretations of O'Neill's purpose with them. In the original Stockholm performance they were left out of the play; in American performances they have been spoken aloud in *Interlude* fashion.

O'Neill himself seems to have been hesitant about the production method. According to the Gelbs (p. 844) he contemplated using "a filmed background and sound track" for the play. In a letter to Nathan (6.19.1942), quoted on p. 25, he shows little interest in the drama as a stage play.

VI. "LIFE IN TERMS OF LIVES"

O'Neill's primary concern was never the depiction of men and women but the depiction of forces at work within men and women. This is what he indicated, when he told Mollan in 1922, that it was just life "as a thing in itself" that interested him (Clark, p. 163), and when he wrote Quinn (2, p. 199) a few years later, that he was "always trying to interpret Life in terms of lives, never just lives in terms of character." What mattered most to him was not whether individual characters were depicted in a truthful or engaging way, although this was certainly important, but whether the plays evoked a sense of beauty, truth, fate and mystery, whether they constituted "a poetical interpretation and symbolical celebration of life," as he stated in January, 1933 (Cargill et al., p. 121). About one of his characters O'Neill once said, that her tragedy consisted in the fact that she could not see the "Oneness of Mankind" (Bird, p. 60); in this she differed from her creator, who constantly stresses the essential oneness of the human race.[1]

This oneness is suggested in two different ways. First, there is the oneness between characters and audience. As we have noted earlier (cf. p. 14), O'Neill strove to make us feel our "ennobling identity with the tragic figures on the stage." To this end he created characters who on the surface are flesh-and-blood individuals found in their specific situations (for we cannot identify ourselves with abstractions suspended in a void) but whose problems at closer inspection have universal application. Hence, underneath the stoker Yank, the playwright Cape, and the architect Brown we discover Man.

The second aspect will concern us in this chapter: the oneness between the characters themselves. The struggle between opposing desires, O'Neill sought to show, is fought within most human beings, and the same impulses can be detected in seemingly utterly different characters. Practically, this means that the characters are closely related to one another either because they share similar characteristics, in which case we shall speak of *parallel characters,* or because they find themselves in similar circumstances, in which case we shall speak of *parallel situations.* The two are naturally closely interrelated and cannot be wholly kept apart.

[1] The view that all men are essentially the same may be considered part of O'Neill's tragic vision (cf. Myers, p. 40).

Blatant or disguised antitheses can be found in any play, and critics have usually paid much attention to the polar aspect and what it enfolds. But whereas contrast, pure and simple, belongs to the black-and-white world of melodrama, higher forms of drama prefer to have it operate in close conjunction with parallelism. This is perhaps most apparent in the Shakespearean subplot, which both contrasts with and parallels the main action. Just as, in this case, the contrast is immediately recognizable and represents a surface level, whereas the parallel holds true on a much deeper level, never discovered, we may rest assured, by the multitude of Shakespeare's audience, so, with O'Neill, the parallels tend to operate on a deeper, more obscure level than the contrasts.

Parallel Characters

It may seem as though the townsfolk choruses in *Electra* present only a striking contrast to the Mannons (cf. Leech, pp. 87 f.); intellectually, morally and socially they are of a lower station, as is indicated by their size: except Seth, who may be called a half-Mannon, they are never tall like the Mannons, who constantly walk on buskins, so to speak. Resembling in some ways the choruses in the Old Comedy (Ellis-Fermor, p. 102),[2] they reveal definite Dionysian traits in dialogue, action and appearance: the men are revellers both in liquor (7, 129) and in women (7, 71, 130); Seth wears *"earth-stained clothes"* (6),[3] Small a *"goat's beard"* (129).

Though the contrast is too obvious to be denied, this should not blind us to the parallel that also exists. Thus the weakness for liquor is found in Adam, too, and lasciviousness is a characteristic also of Ezra and Orin. Lavinia shows the same prudishness and hatred of Christine as Louisa Ames and Emma Borden. Minnie, like Christine, is forty and foreign to the neighborhood—outward signs, it seems, of their deeper, spiritual relationship: both possess the 'pagan' Mother Earth qualities. Abner Small, like Orin, unsuccessfully attempts to live with the ghosts in the Mannon house. When the townsfolk hide behind the lilac shrubbery and from there spy at the Mannons, they are imitating the Mannon attitude to life, their hiding from it behind a 'mask.' Or, rather, they reveal themselves as victims of the same fateful tradi-

[2] O'Neill's notes for rewriting suggest that he had the grotesque Greek comedy choruses in mind; of the townsfolk he writes: "their characteristics and peculiarities as types should be obviously accentuated in the acting, as well as in costume and facial make-up, even to the extreme point where they lose most of their humanity and take on the nature of people at a masquerade or carnival, a bit clownish and unnatural.'

[3] Falk (p. 131) rightly compares Seth to Silenus.

tion. The conflict between 'paganism' and puritanism is found with them too.

The choruses, O'Neill decided, represent "the world outside which always sees without really seeing or understanding" (1931/Frenz, p. 12). This is brought out with sharp irony in the conversation between the townspeople, who usually mistake appearances for reality. But in this they are not essentially different from the Mannons. Ezra and Orin are fooled by Christine's pretense. Christine and Adam falsely believe that murder will set them free. Lavinia does not until the very end realize her guilt. And all of them are mistaken about the true nature of their love.[4]

Citizens in the town dominated by the Mannons for centuries, the chorus members, much like the Shakespearean subplot characters, in their lower sphere mirror the traits and weaknesses of their masters and help thereby to universalize the drama of the Mannons. As one of them, drawing attention to the parallel, correctly observes: "The Mannons got skeletons in their closets same as others! Worse ones" (9).

Just as the contrast between the Mannons and the townsfolk is more apparent than the similarity between them, so the relationship between Mildred, the enfeebled, refined capitalist in *Ape,* and Yank, the strong, primitive proletarian may seem at first to be merely one of antithesis (cf. Raleigh, pp. 125 f.); actually, it constitutes a striking parallel, which underlines the theme of the play.

For all their outward dissimilarity Yank and Mildred have a basic trait in common, revealed in his *"superior strength"* (208) and her *"disdainful superiority"* (217): both have a strong sense of pride. About Mildred we learn that she is a young American woman of simple origin; her great-grandmother smoked a clay pipe (218) and her grandfather, a self-made man, was originally a puddler, who "played with boiling steel" (221). It is understood that he was still close enough to nature to retain strength, vitality, and integrity, but these traits have later, with the accumulation of money, been lost, and Mildred considers her existence artificial and meaningless: "I would like to be some use in the world. Is it my fault I don't know how? I would like to be sincere, to touch life somewhere" (219). If the Yank who belongs—or thinks he belongs—(Scenes 1–3) resembles Mildred's grandfather, the Yank who seeks to re-establish his lost sense of belonging (Scenes 4–8) is more akin to Mildred herself. As she finds herself to be "a waste product in the Bessemer process" (219), he likens himself to "a busted Ingersoll" (250), another wasted

---

[4] Failing to see the parallel, Stamm (p. 245) not surprisingly finds no more than "the superficial gossip of average people" in the conversation of the chorus characters.

product of industrialized society. Another image provides a closer affinity; referring to herself, Mildred says:

When a leopard complains of its spots, it must sound rather grotesque. (*In a mocking tone*) Purr, little leopard. Purr, scratch, tear, kill, gorge yourself and be happy—only stay in the jungle where your spots are camouflage. In a cage they make you conspicuous (220).

Mildred is the leopard, which has been removed from the jungle, her grandfather's creative life, to the cage of modern, stereotyped comfort, still retaining the spots of the wild animal but with "none of the energy, none of the strength" (219) that should go with them—a hybrid creature, that does not belong in the cage and longs for the wilderness of the past.

The image is transferred visually to Yank. After he has been degraded to a "filthy beast," he "*has not washed either face or body*" and appears "*a blackened, brooding figure*" (226), a visual presentation of his feeling that Mildred has done him "doit." The fellow stokers admonish him to wash off the dirt or it will make spots on him "like a leopard" (227); there is thus but a step from filthiness to beastliness. Yank does not wash; the black spots remain with him and get under his skin as he feels rejected by evermore powerful groups. Sitting in his prison 'cage,' his face is "*spotted with black and blue bruises*" (239). Approximating a leopard, Yank has exchanged his initial purring for a wild desire to "scratch, tear, kill." Closer to nature than Mildred, he tries to practice jungle morals—physical violence and revolutionary anarchism—in a 'cage society'; his situation and desperation are identical with those of a caged wild beast. Mildred and Yank, superrace and subrace, are thus found to be in basically the same dilemma, a dilemma arising from their removal from nature and their inability to attain spiritual stature.

They also attempt similar solutions to their dilemma. Just as Yank's decision to visit the Zoo and let out the gorilla is determined both by his genuine concern for the caged animal and hatred of society and by his need to "go back," to identify himself with the unthinking animal and thus regain his feeling of belonging, so Mildred's decision to visit the stokehole is an expression less of philanthropic concern than of a longing to regain the life energy and primitive sense of belonging that her grandparents still enjoyed. The confrontations between Mildred and Yank (Scene 3) and Yank and the gorilla (Scene 8) are clearly designed as counterparts:

... *she has listened, paralyzed with horror, terror, her whole personality crushed, beaten in, collapsed, by the terrific impact of this unknown, abysmal brutality, naked and shameless. As she looks at his gorilla face, as his eyes bore into hers, she utters a low, choking cry and shrinks away from him, putting both hands up before her eyes to shut out the sight of his face, to protect her own. ... She faints. They carry her quickly back, disappearing in the darkness at the left rear. An iron door clangs shut* (225 f.).

The gorilla scrambles gingerly out of his cage. Goes to YANK *and stands looking at him. ... With a spring he wraps his huge arms around* YANK *in a murderous hug. There is a crackling snap of crushed ribs—a gasping cry, still mocking, from* YANK. *... The gorilla lets the crushed body slip to the floor; stands over it uncertainly, considering; then picks it up, throws it in the cage, shuts the door, and shuffles off menacingly into the darkness at left. ... Then* YANK *moves, groaning, opening his eyes.... He slips in a heap on the floor and dies* (254).

The mirroring of the self in the beast, the mental shock described in terms of physical violence, the cry of painful recognition, the closing of the eyes before the horrible truth, her fainting as compared to his dying, the implacable shutting of the iron door—everything suggests a fundamental similarity between the two situations. Yank repeats Mildred's experience on a lower and more universal level; as he tells the anthropoid: "I was you to her" (252). He mirrors her origin and self as the gorilla mirrors his, for, as we have observed, to Mildred Yank is not only a revolting animal, he is also associated with her puddler grandfather, whose life energy and strength she envies. It is this combination, I take it, that works the shock; at once Mildred realizes the impossibility of going back; she is trapped in her artificial, deadly life, a tamed animal unsuited for the hardship of the free life in the jungle. Degraded in his own eyes, Yank, too, from this moment feels imprisoned. While this confrontation thus leads to a double encaging, the final scene establishes, rather, a double release: the gorilla is let loose and Yank is liberated from his encaged life through death.

An extreme example of character parallelism is found in *Hughie,* where the deceased night clerk, from whom the play takes its title, and Charlie Hughes, the new night clerk, are identical in nearly every respect—so much so that O'Neill seems, in fact, to have slipped in a few, insignificant differences between them only to guard against any misinterpretation that Charlie is a hallucinatory figure, a ghost of the dead night clerk.

It may be argued that the close parallel motivates Erie's lingering in the lobby. About his first meeting with Hughie Erie reports:

At first, he wouldn't open up. Not that he was cagey about gabbin' too much. But like he couldn't think of nothin' about himself worth saying. But after he'd seen me roll in here the last one every night, and I'd stop to kid him along and tell him the tale of what I'd win that day, he got friendly and talked (23).

Finding himself confronted with a night clerk closely resembling Hughie, Erie not surprisingly expects him to react much like the former one; eventually, he believes, Charlie too will "open up."

More importantly, by making the two night clerks identical, O'Neill infinitely widens the scope of his play. The fifteen-year relationship between Hughie and Erie throws light on the new relationship between Erie and Charlie; it extends, as it were, their final game-playing into the distant future. Moreover, the Erie-Charlie relationship sheds light on the earlier one; Hughie is recreated not only through Erie's tales but also, by implication, through Charlie's thoughts. And the parallel underlines the fact that Hughie, no more than Charlie, has admired Erie in his own right, as Erie likes to think; to each of them he is the friend of their "dream guy" and gains his stature from this fact; in Charlie's case the idol is named Rothstein, in Hughie's Legs Diamond (29), that is the only difference. The parallel thus establishes the ironical discrepancy between the way Erie views Hughie's attitude to him and what this attitude was really like. With tragic pathos O'Neill demonstrates the frailty and egocentricity inherent even in life-long friendships and the need of the pipe dream to blind us to this cruel truth.[5]

How parallels help to unify a play both thematically and structurally may be seen in *Wilderness*. When Nat Miller, towards the end of the play, concludes that he and his wife are "completely surrounded by love" (292), he points to the major theme in the play and the common denominator of its characters. Love in various forms is the issue in the Nat-Essie marriage, in the Sid-Lily relationship, in the Richard-Muriel-Belle triangle, in Arthur's courting of Elsie, in Mildred's concern with "her latest" boyfriend, in Norah's good-natured sensuousness and in the Salesman's cynical trading.

Essentially, we are confronted with three loving couples; in order of importance they are: Richard-Muriel, Sid-Lily, and Nat-Essie. The last couple, living in frugal harmony, make poor dramatic material; hence, Nat and Essie function more as parents than as partners. The second couple is more dramatic, because their relationship is less stable; but since the instability has lasted for sixteen years, we cannot expect any drastic changes in this relationship either. Only the first couple fulfills the necessary demands: a love relationship of as yet short duration between partners at an early and transient stage in life, still under strong influence of their parents. At the end of the play it is clear that nothing essential has happened to Nat and Essie as far as their marriage is concerned; that Sid and Lily have again come to the conclusion that they cannot

[5] Ignoring the parallel, Raleigh (pp. 28, 30) sees the end merely as an establishment of a bond between two human beings. Consequently he comes to the conclusion that *Hughie* is one of O'Neill's "most optimistic plays."

get married; and that Richard and Muriel have arrived at the opposite conclusion.

The contrasting love relationships of the grownups serve to illustrate the alternatives open to Richard, who resembles both his father (Adler, p. 283) and his uncle. When he believes himself rejected by Muriel, he identifies himself with Sid and acts accordingly, adopting a posing attitude. When he discovers that Muriel loves and accepts him, he becomes his innocent, natural self, more like Nat.

The Richard-Sid parallel is the more prominent. When the play opens Richard considers himself engaged to Muriel (207). With her letter of dismissal the engagement is broken. Sixteen years earlier—the year Richard was born!—Lily broke her engagement with Sid. The reason in Richard's case is that he has sent Muriel 'indecent' poems, in Sid's that he had mixed with indecent women (213). When he believes himself rejected by Muriel, Richard follows the pattern set by his uncle. Like Sid he adopts a protective 'mask,' not the kidding comic one, to be sure, but that of the tragically misunderstood and lonely one; it is significantly said about both of them that they "ought to be on the stage" (216, 223). Richard spends his time getting drunk with a tart in a hotel of doubtful reputation, where Sid has obviously been a customer (267). Both men feel remorseful for their slips. Sid *begins to sob like a sick little boy,* claiming that he is "a dirty, rotten drunk" who ought to kill himself (258). Richard, very drunk and about to vomit, *"calls to his mother appealingly, like a sick little boy)* Ma! I feel—rotten!" (261 f.). The feeling of nausea, we may feel certain, is not merely physiological.

Even more alike than the men are the women. Both Lily and Muriel are virtuous, romantic and faithful to the one they love and disgusted with the men's drunkenness and dealings with "bad women." To Richard Lily is obviously another Muriel: "It's Aunt Lily's fault, Uncle Sid's going to ruin. It's all because he loves her, and she keeps him dangling after her, and eggs him on and ruins his life—like all women love to ruin men's lives!" (235). In a similar way, he later (286) tries to defend his own behavior and blame Muriel.

Dramaturgically, the Sid-Lily story functions as a somber foil to the Richard-Muriel one. Yet Richard's follies are more modest, more incidental, and more excusable than Sid's; his slip is based on a misunderstanding and besides he is never really unfaithful to Muriel and can therefore be forgiven. The experience with Belle has in fact only helped him to discover the depth of his love for Muriel; the fling has made him grow up mentally. Sid, on the other hand, has slipped not once but a thousand times and he has done so, not because of any misunderstandings, but because of an inherent moral weakness; like Mildred, he does not "understand what love means" (274); at the end of the play he is still, unlike Richard, mentally an adolescent.

As a means to play up a theme on a large scale, O'Neill makes ample use of parallel couples in *Iceman,* where Hickey's love-hatred for Evelyn has its counterpart in Parritt's for his mother, in Larry's for Rosa, in Hope's for Bessie, in Jimmy's for Marjorie, and in the relationships of Chuck and Cora, Rocky and Pearl/Margie, Mosher and McGloin, Wetjoen and Lewis. In most of these relationships the hatred is hidden, as with Hickey, under a layer of love and sympathy.

A parable concerning the plight of mankind (Muchnic, p. 432), the play presents a motley collection of down-and-outers, whose predilection for pipe dreams is their common denominator. Thus, although they have led widely different lives and hold radically different views, they appear strikingly alike in their inability to face the grim present and their tendency to dote upon a glorious past or hope for a promising future. The stories they have to tell— and the way they tell them—bear out Larry's conviction, stated at an early point, that "the lie of a pipe dream is what gives life to the whole misbegotten mad lot of us, drunk or sober" (578). This statement is the key to an understanding of the play; that all the inmates—i.e. all men—are misbegotten and mad, O'Neill keeps reminding us by having his characters address each other as "old bastard" or "fool." The madness is the pipe dreaming curative for the misbegottenness; in an insane world only the fool can be happy and the barflies are "contented men" (594); in Larry's words: "It'll be a great day for them, tomorrow—the Feast of All Fools ..." (578). The universal implication of Larry's words about the inmates and their pipe dreams warns the reader that the play should not, despite its naturalistic touches, be understood as a slice-of-life drama, and that the decadence of the characters should not be taken as a social issue.[6]

To give focus and a sense of unity to his play O'Neill gives pre-eminence to two unusually complex 'lives'—Hickey's and Parritt's—leading to unusually drastic actions: murder and treason. But these actions differ only in degree from those of the other saloon dwellers, whose tendency to murder and betray is clearly revealed. Conversely, the need for pipe dreams is felt also by Hickey and Parritt. Considering this, it appears to be more than a structural peculiarity that accounts for the fact that no real protagonist appears in the play;[7] it underscores the democratic-pessimistic view—a sardonic comment on the spirit of the American Revolution—that all men are born equal in their need for illusions.

[6] In a letter to Nathan (8.2.1940) O'Neill points out that "the play is not 'timely' and has no sociological significance, as such significance is defined nowadays."

[7] In the forementioned letter O'Neill writes: "a travelling salesman is the character around which the play develops, but there is no 'lead' in the usual sense."

Hickey's and Parritt's stories are spread out over the entire play and account for most of the suspense; their secrets are revealed step by step:

	HICKEY	PARRITT
Act I:	Has ceased drinking.	By treason his mother, an Anarchist leader, has been put in jail.
Act II:	His wife is dead.	The traitor is Parritt himself, who claims he has acted out of patriotism.
Act III:	She was killed.	Desire for money motivated his treason.
Act IV:	Hickey himself is the murderer, hatred his motive.	Hatred of the mother was his true reason.

A similar step-by-step revelation could be charted for most of the characters; we may thus talk not only of parallel situations and characters but also of parallel actions in this play. Hickey's story affects all the inmates; Parritt's story affects Larry alone, to whom it is told in a whispering voice. The composition somewhat resembles a *concerto grosso* with its alternating *tutti* and *concertino* passages.

Throughout the play O'Neill points to the resemblance between Hickey and Parritt. In Act I they are set off from the rest by their soberness (586, 620), which Larry later explains as resulting from a fear that booze will make them talk about matters they are afraid to touch on—and yet are dying to tell (638). Both men visit Hope's saloon partly to avoid meeting their normal acquaintances (586). And Hickey explicitly draws attention to the parallel by telling Parritt: "We're members of the same lodge—in some way" (624). In Act II his intuition tells him that what they have in common is the experience of suffering for the sake of a woman (642 f.), and towards the end of this act it is clear that both have been 'unfaithful' to the woman they love (591, 663). Hickey's disclosure of his wife's death opens Parritt's eyes to the resemblance of their fate: "I don't know why, but it started me thinking about Mother—as if she was dead" (666). The real shock comes with the revelation that Evelyn was killed:

LARRY. (*shakenly*) Then she—was murdered.
PARRITT. (*springs to his feet—stammers defensively*) You're a liar, Larry! You must be crazy to say that to me! You know she's still alive! (694).

We realize how haunted Parritt is by his guilt; his "crazy" reaction suggests that he is indeed his mother's 'murderer.' His 'confession' foreshadows Hickey's final revelation. Also later Parritt's confession to Larry follows and goes beyond Hickey's to the crowd:

HICKEY. ... I loved Evelyn. ...

PARRITT. I loved Mother, Larry! (709).

HICKEY. ... I always carry her picture. ... No, I'm forgetting I tore it up—afterwards. I didn't need it any more. ...

PARRITT. (*to* LARRY *in a low insistent tone*) I burnt up Mother's picture, Larry. Her eyes followed me all the time. They seemed to be wishing I was dead! (714).

HICKEY. ... I remember I stood by the bed and suddenly I had to laugh. I couldn't help it, and I knew Evelyn would forgive me. I remember I heard myself speaking to her, as if it was something I'd always wanted to say: "Well, you know what you can do with your pipe dream now, you damned bitch!" (716).

PARRITT. ... I can't kid myself like Hickey, that she's at peace. As long as she lives, she'll never be able to forget what I've done to her even in her sleep. ... And I'm not putting up any bluff, either, that I was crazy afterwards when I laughed to myself and thought, "You know what you can do with your freedom pipe dream now, don't you, you damned old bitch!" (720).

Two crucial points are made in these antiphonally arranged confessions: Although Evelyn and Rosa have earlier been depicted as antitheses, they have evidently affected Hickey and Parritt in a similar, negative way. Furthermore, when face to face with the grim truth of their crimes Hickey and Parritt react differently; the former pleads innocent, the latter guilty.

Rosa is a forceful woman, whose commitment to anarchism and freedom is—much like Hugo's—only a pretty façade hiding a tyrannizing selfishness, "a marble temple," to use Larry's image, covering up "a mixture of mud and manure" (590). Her habit of taking one lover after the other, while neglecting her son, is less an expression of anarchist firmness of principle—as Rosa no doubt likes to believe—than a proof of her emotional sterility and greed. When Parritt betrays her and the Movement—the two are inseparable—it is in revenge of the many times she has betrayed him with the Movement or with other men; it is an act of jealousy.

Like Rosa, Evelyn considers it her mission to clean up the world; both are reformers—one politically, the other religiously—sharing an optimistic belief in the ultimate goodness and nobility of man. But there the resemblance ends. For whereas Evelyn proves in her own person that man can be good and noble, Rosa is unable to do so. Hence Larry's conviction that man's goodness is a pipe dream as opposed to Hickey's belief that it is a reality.

Rosa represents the secular savior, who believes that one can save the world without, in the first place, having saved one's own soul—a belief that is rejected by Larry. Evelyn typifies the religious savior. Sprung from a strict Methodist family (710) she keeps everything in her home, including herself, "spotless and clean" (713). When he first met her, Hickey, rejected by everyone as "a no-good tramp" (709), met with compassion from Evelyn alone:

No one could convince her I was no good. Evelyn was stubborn as all hell once she'd made up her mind. Even when I'd admit things and ask her forgiveness, she'd make excuses for me and defend me against myself. She'd kiss me and say she knew I didn't mean it and I wouldn't do it again (710).

This surely is a love that passeth understanding. Set off against her purity, Hickey's sinfulness appears all the more conspicuous; he begins to hate himself and to love-hate her moral superiority. Even as his sins against her grow worse, her compassion for him remains:

I suppose you think I'm a liar, that no woman could have stood all she stood and still loved me so much—that it isn't human for any woman to be so pitying and forgiving. Well, I'm not lying, and if you'd ever seen her, you'd realize I wasn't. It was written all over her face, sweetness and love and pity and forgiveness (714).

Evelyn is almost superhuman. Like Christ, she is immaculate, yet shows limitless faith in the poorest sinner and love for the lonely and rejected. Like Christ, she is killed because, in Hickey's words, "there's a limit to the guilt you can feel and the forgiveness and the pity you can take" (715). Man's pride—his faith in himself—admits of no interfering helper; man will always be an anarchist and a revolutionary when it comes to destroying the higher man.[8]

Parritt's and Hickey's cases may appear radically antithetical. Parritt feels that his mother shows far less love and understanding for him than he deserves; Hickey, by contrast, feels that his maternal wife shows far more than he deserves. But in either case we may talk about a disproportion between the self-evaluation (which must necessarily be experienced as the true evaluation) and the evaluation made by the person to whom the men feel closely attached. For contrary reasons Parritt and Hickey are both wounded in their pride and must take their revenge, fatal though it is for themselves.

The close parallel between Hickey and Parritt points up their different reactions to their crime. When the play begins both men are victims of pipe dreams. Parritt wants to believe that he betrayed his mother out of patriotism or for money; Hickey wants to believe that he killed Evelyn out of love. The difference between them at this point is one of degree; Hickey seems the more deluded, for he openly boasts of having rid himself of all pipe dreams, whereas Parritt's false excuses do not appear to ring true even to himself. As

[8] O'Neill himself saw Evelyn as representing Hickey's conscience (Gelb, p. 832). Driver (pp. 117 f.) interestingly analyzes the Hickey-Evelyn relationship in Freudian terms: "Hickey (Ego) desires death unconsciously. His sensual nature (Id) desires unbridled life and convinces Hickey he could live more successfully if his wife Evelyn (Super-Ego) were removed. Hickey yields, ostensibly to find peace but actually because he knows that this peace will be the prelude to permanent peace (death). The Ego-instincts, said Freud, are death-instincts."

a result of this, Hickey feels a strong desire to influence others in a way Parritt does not; Hickey judges, Parritt wants to be judged. At the end of the play Parritt, with Hickey's assistance, has rid himself of all illusions and faces the grim truth about himself. So does Hickey momentarily. But he hastens back to the consoling world of pipe dreams. The ironical implication of his reaction is obvious enough: he who has held himself up as an example of a man freed from illusions is the most enslaved by them. Instead of disproving Larry's dictum that men cannot live without illusions, Hickey becomes the prime illustration of its validity, for he cannot even die without them.

Hickey does not plead insanity—in this consists his pipe dream—because he is afraid to die; he has called the police before he confesses (708), and he explicitly states that he wants to go to the Chair (718 f.); his suicidal longing is as great as Parritt's. The point is that Hickey fears to die *guilt-laden* (cf. Törnqvist, 1965, p. 230). As a child he was brought up by his father-minister in a Fundamentalist faith. His marriage to an all-forgiving, Methodist woman was an escape from the stern father to a loving 'mother.' But although he believes that his father's "religious bunk" never affected him, the truth is that it made an indelible impression upon him. His reform wave in Hope's saloon testifies to this: it is performed in his father's spirit. The father, we are told, would alternatively "sell those Hoosier hayseeds building lots along the Golden Street" (622) and scare them with "hell fire" (709). Hickey uses the same alternating method—now caressing, now whipping—in his attempt to force the habitués to leave, as he describes it, the hellish pipe dreams for the blessed truth.

At the same time, however, he has been influenced by Evelyn's love gospel, which has caused him to see his murder as an act solely of mercy. When he suddenly realizes that it is not, that he is therefore guilty of a horrible crime, for which the punishment is "hell fire," he is naturally terrified. Furthermore, Hickey explains that Evelyn "was the only thing on God's earth [he] ever loved" (719). His love for her was the only thing that gave meaning and justification to his life. If this love has been an illusion, then his life has been absolutely devoid of meaning. Thus, again, Hickey's reaction bears out Larry's dictum: the pipe dreams are life-giving because they give meaning to life in a meaningless world.

As we have noted, the Hickey-Evelyn story is only the most conspicuous one in the richly woven tapestry; around it and mirroring it are all the other life stories; each character is depicted with his pride, his pipe dreams, his love and his hatred. Thus the sameness of human life can be distinguished beneath its seeming variations. *Iceman* is O'Neill's fullest attempt to describe "Life in terms of lives."

That a conflict within the protagonist is illustrated by means of other characters, who incarnate his hidden traits, is an old dramatic device.[9] But it has special importance in modern, 'plotless,' psychological drama, for which Strindberg set the pattern with his *To Damascus* (cf. Sokel, pp. 34 ff.).

O'Neill early made use of such symbolic figures. Already in *Servitude* we have an example. When the gardener, Weson, in Act II mistakes Benton, the butler, for Roylston, his master (253), his excuse is his near-sightedness, for the two are utterly unlike each other. Yet the implied identity holds good on the inner plane, as is made clear a little later by Weson's remark about Roylston's foxiness (255), for Benton's marked trait is his *"sly villainy"* (227). Roylston himself alludes to the parallel when remarking: "When I outgrew a governess they gave me Benton. I thought it was a change for the better but it wasn't. I have never been able to outgrow him. He won't let me" (278). Benton significantly is the one who handles Roylston's extramarital affairs. We begin to realize the meaning of the homonymous name endings: Benton is Roylston's evil servant, his Mephistopheles, just as Mrs. Roylston is his angelic one, his Marguerite. How much a part of Roylston's self he is, appears when Roylston gives vent to his cynical treatment of young admiring women and when Mrs. Frazer accuses him of in-sightedness (279), the visual symbol of which we find, not in Roylston's appearance, but in Benton's cross-eyedness (227). Benton thus seems to represent those Mephistophelean traits in Roylston's character that we are only gradually made aware of and which the playwright's handsome appearance gives little hint of. Master and servant forebode the double protagonist of *Days*.

A more obviously symbolic figure is Mrs. Bartlett in *Gold*. Captain Isaiah Barlett is described as *"a tall, huge-framed figure of a man"* with an

immense strength in his heavy-muscled body. His head is massive, thickly covered with tangled, iron-gray hair. His face is large, bony, and leather-tanned, with a long aquiline nose and a gash of a mouth shadowed by a bristling gray mustache. His broad jaw sticks out at an angle of implacable stubbornness. Bushy gray brows overhang the obsessed glare of his somber dark eyes (627).

Six months later he is marked by guilt for the murder he has sanctioned:

His hair has turned white. There are deep hollows under his cheek-bones. His jaw and tight-lipped mouth express defiant determination, as if he were fighting back some weakness inside himself, a weakness found in his eyes, which have something in them of fear, of a wishing to avoid other eyes (639).

---

[9] See, for example, Schroeter's discussion (pp. 131 ff.) of the Messenger, the Herdsman, Teiresias and Creon in *Oedipus Tyrannus* as projections of different mental levels within Oedipus, and Heilman's view (pp. 34 ff.) of the children in *King Lear* as representatives of elements in conflict within the fathers.

His wife

is a slight, slender little woman of fifty. Sickness, or the inroads of a premature old age, have bowed her shoulders, whitened her hair, and forced her to walk feebly with the aid of a cane. A resolute spirit still flashes from her eyes, however, and there is a look of fixed determination on her face (642).

There is a certain resemblance between husband and wife: the white hair, the determined face. But on the whole the two seem complementary. His strength, rebellious and self-willed, is centered in jaw, mouth and body; his weakness is apparent in the eyes. Mrs. Bartlett's strength, by contrast, is expressed solely through the eyes; physically she is exceedingly weak. The reason for these complementary traits is undoubtedly that Mrs. Bartlett represents the Captain's conscience (Engel, 1953, p. 25). Once we realize this, it becomes clear why she turned sick the night she learnt about her husband's crime, why she is now enfeebled, why she keeps hounding him and insisting that she see him alone, why the Captain considers her a good woman, whose maiden name—rather than the defiled name of Bartlett—he wants for his schooner, and why he both needs her and shuns her. When commenting on her husband's moving away from her to the boatshed, Mrs. Bartlett draws attention to her symbolic role: "It wasn't me you ran away from, Isaiah. You ran away from your own self—the conscience God put in you that you think you can fool with lies" (652). O'Neill could hardly put it more plainly. In obedience to her role, Mrs. Bartlett speaks the words of the Captain's conscience: "Confess your sin, Isaiah! Confess to God and men, and make your peace and take your punishment" (654).

The struggle between the two reaches a climax as Bartlett sees the schooner, which was to take him to the treasure island, sail away without him. Predisposed as he is to see himself as a victim of a malign fate, Bartlett's fury is directed, not against the man who has thwarted his plan, but against God:

(Shaking his clenched fist at the sky as if visualizing the fate he feels in all of this) Curse ye! Curse ye! *(He subsides weakly, his strength spent, his hand falls limply at his side.)* (673).

Apparently there is something within him that opposes his rebellious act. This suppressed part of the Captain's self immediately appears in the guise of Mrs. Bartlett:

(turning accusing eyes on him—with a sort of fanatical triumph) ... God's curse on the wicked sinfulness o' men. ... *(She has raised her hand as if calling down retribution on the schooner she can dimly see.)* (673).

The nearly identical gestures couple the two and indicate that they represent antithetical impulses within the Captain. The tormenting inner struggle he undergoes at this point is represented in outward action:

BARTLETT. (*starting toward his wife in an insane yell of fury*) Stop it, I tell ye! (*He towers over her with upraised fist as if to crush her.*) (673).

The struggle ends in defeat for Mrs. Bartlett; she collapses and is carried into the house; before long she dies. This does not mean that the voice of the conscience in the Captain is killed; it continues to live on as a haunting ghost—in the final act Bartlett addresses his wife as though she were alive (682)—and finally it proves victorious: Bartlett confesses, destroys the symbol of his obsession, the island map, "*seeming to grow weaker and weaker as he does so*" (692), and dies, "*an expression of strange[1] peace*" on his face.[2]

Mrs. Bartlett has a counterpart in Luis de Alvaredo in *Fountain*. Like the protagonist, Juan Ponce de Leon, Luis is a Spanish noble. O'Neill indicates their intimacy in various ways.[3] Thus, in the first scene Luis is drunk, while Juan is slightly tipsy. When one of the nobles says he would wager that Luis would not go with Columbus to the Indies, the answer comes:

LUIS. You would lose.
JUAN. I'm planning to go (385).[4]

Notice the complete agreement between the two; the lines could equally well have been spoken by one character.

Juan, we learn, is "*a romantic dreamer governed by the ambitious thinker in him*" (377). Nevertheless, the suppressed dreamer appears symbolically in the figure of Luis, intoxicating himself with wine and poetry. It is he who sings the fountain song and who translates the Moor's chant about the Fountain of Youth. It is because he wants to find this Fountain that Luis decides to join Columbus. Juan, on the other hand, wants to extend the glory of

---

[1] The longhand draft has "*infinite.*"

[2] This interpretation is in agreement with Skinner's view (p. 74) that Bartlett's death represents a "final spiritual triumph." Polemizing against Skinner, Engel (1953, pp. 28 f.) lists four reasons why Bartlett's death should rather be seen as "a hollow victory," none of them tenable to my mind. The first postulates O'Neill's negative view of Mrs. Bartlett's religious ardor. The second claims that because "peace was purchased at the exorbitant prize of death itself," it cannot signify a spiritual triumph —a queer argument. The third is equally absurd: "the expression of peace ... could be discerned only by the reader, since the phenomenon is mentioned in the acting directions alone." The fourth reads: "Sue's reaction to her father's death ... was scarcely that of a person who recognized the justice of God's ways." No, O'Neill could not go that far, so he implied the "spiritual triumph" instead.

[3] Juan bears a close similarity to O'Neill himself, while the Luis of Scene 1 seems modelled after his brother Jamie; cf. *Fountain* (381) and *Journey* (19). "We know his only love is his old mother," Juan says about Luis (384), an obvious allusion to Jamie.

[4] The longhand draft still put it realistically:
LUIS. You would lose. He has agreed to take me.
JUAN. I also plan to go.

231

Spain, a desire which seems rooted in his *"ambitious thinker"* and "soldier of iron" (381) self.

Twenty years later we find Luis a Dominican monk, Juan a Governor. When Juan mockingly calls his friend "reverend Father" (397), it is of course an acknowledgement of his clerical robe. But the expression is perhaps also meant to convey the idea that Luis is a father figure to Juan. The older one of the two (381), Luis keeps giving friendly advice to Juan (403, 421). And he significantly refers to Juan as "a sulky child" (397), sulky in his ridicule of the religion Luis has come to embrace.

Juan has now arrived at the point where Luis was in the opening scene. Luis' description of his own past self—"an aimless, posing rake, neither poet nor soldier, without place nor peace" (398)—fits the present Juan, who is tired of being a "soldier of iron" and romantically dreams of the Fountain of Youth, the Fountain Luis now rejects in favor of the true Fountain, God. Only to the chosen ones, the legend runs, does the Fountain reveal itself. Having seen the Fountain they "go back to life ... with hearts purified" and untroubled by "the old discords" (387). Luis has arrived at this desirable stage already in Scene 3: his face *"has achieved a calm, peaceful expression as if he were at last in harmony with himself"* (397). He has found the key to the Fountain: "You must renounce in order to possess" (398).

Much later Juan too is to identify the Fountain with God (442). And he too recognizes renunciation, sacrifice, as the key to life: "One must accept, absorb, give back, become oneself a symbol!" (448). His face by now *"has gained an entirely new quality, the calm of a deep spiritual serenity"* (444). Luis is fittingly the only one present as Juan dies, kneeling beside his body (448 f.).

Luis thus, because he corresponds to that part of Juan which is constantly in ascendancy and which finally becomes dominant, is seen to anticipate Juan's development throughout the play. In the final scene the two are brought exceedingly close together, although they are not wholly identified: while Luis as a Dominican monk has allied himself with Catholicism, Juan's religion remains a mystical pantheism.[5]

---

[5] Juan and Luis may be compared to other intimately connected, partly complementary male couples in O'Neill's plays. Robert and Andrew Mayo in *Horizon* immediately come to mind. So do the more antithetical couples Dion–Brown in *Brown* and John–Loving in *Days*. Skinner in passing observes (p. 168) that Dion and Brown "are really one person," an idea which has been developed by other critics (Berkelman, pp. 609 ff.; Waith, p. 37). It is significant that O'Neill felt that "Dion in first half and Brown in rest of play should be played by same actor" (letter 7.6.1925 to John Barrymore). Also *Welded* is of interest in this respect. In the early editions the names of the male characters preceding the speeches are given as "CAPE" and "DARNTON"; in later editions the latter has been changed to "JOHN." The Gelbs

The most consistent employment of characters who correspond to mental states within the protagonist is found in *Jones*—not surprisingly, since the monodramatic form invalidates conventional characterization. Thus, the initial sequence between the native old woman and Smithers, far from being "an unnecessary scene" (Shand, p. 25), not only belongs organically to the play but contains, in fact, *in nuce* the story of it. Just as in the forest scenes Jones is confronted with two hostile forces, the natives that hunt him and the visions that haunt him, so in the little play-before-the-play the woman is in a similar dilemma, caught between Jones, the feared black man, and Smithers, the feared white man.

The parallel between the woman and Jones is indicated in several ways. She is a *"Negro woman"* (173); he is a *"full-blooded Negro"* (175). She wears *"a red bandana handkerchief"* about her head (173); he wears *"bright red"* pants (175) and mops his face with *"a bandana handkerchief"* (187). She is bare-footed; so is Jones when he reaches her slave status (196). Smithers levels the two of them off by referring to her as "birdie" (174) and to Jones as "bird" (182). And Jones, although he expresses his contempt for superstitious "ole woman's talk" in Scene 1 (185), falls a victim to it himself in the jungle. Her actions, similarly, foreshadow Jones' behavior in the forest. Fleeing from the Emperor, she *"hesitates"* by the doorway leading to his sleeping quarters, *"peering back as if in extreme dread of being discovered,"* then moves towards the doorway at rear (173); in the same way Jones looks worriedly back when arriving at the *"wall"* of the forest to see if he is being pursued (189), *"hesitates"* there, but finally plunges into the forest (190). The woman struggles with Smithers as Jones struggles with his "ha'nts." She cowers when Smithers threatens to hit her with his whip, as Jones cowers when he is whipped by the white Prison Guard (194). She sinks to the ground embracing Smithers' knees, as Jones is brought to *"a kneeling, devotional posture"* before the Congo altar (200). Referring to Jones as "Great Father," she *"touches her forehead to the floor"* (175); similarly, Jones appeals to the "Lawd" as *"he beats his forehead abjectly to the ground"* (201).

But Smithers too is like Jones. Both are tall, middle-aged, have cunning, dishonest eyes, are fully costumed in a somewhat military fashion. The dialogue reveals both of them to be greedy and reckless materialists, who have spent ten years 'trading' (178 f.)—Jones with white people, Smithers with black—and some time in jail (177, 181). Moreover, there is, as Engel observes

claim (p. 518) that O'Neill borrowed the name Cape from his English publisher, Jonathan Cape. Is it not conceivable that also the name John was inspired by the publisher's first name? And that O'Neill's seemingly inconsistent way of naming the characters in the later editions serves to bring out the spiritual closeness of John and Cape—as do the comparable names John and Loving in *Days*?

(1953, p. 49), a certain levelling of their racial characteristics: Smithers' shiftlessness (179) reflects the stereotype of the black race, Jones' *"strength of will"* and *"hardy, self-reliant confidence in himself"* (175) are traits belonging to the white 'master race.'

When the play begins Jones feels contempt both for Smithers and for the suppressed natives, represented by the old woman. Each of them appears to correspond to one aspect of the Negro Emperor: Smithers to his sinful, rational white veneer; the native woman to his old innocent, irrational "nigger" self. And the physical struggle between the two may be taken to represent the struggle that goes on within the guilt-ridden Jones. Although Smithers seems the superior one in this struggle—just as the Emperor part of Jones predominates in Scene 1—it is actually the woman who emerges as the victor, for she finally manages to escape the white man; so too Jones, after his long struggle with his hardened white 'mask,' finally manages to separate himself from it and return to his original "nigger" state of innocence and belonging.

In the final scene Smithers again represents the rational white part of the self, while Lem—old like the woman—corresponds to the irrational "nigger" part. The contrast is underlined by their costumes: Smithers appears, as before, fully costumed in his dirty white riding suit; Lem is dressed only in a loin cloth, which leaves most of his black body naked. Jones starts out from his white palace fully costumed in his imperial uniform; he returns to his black people with only *"a breech cloth"* (198) left of it. His dramatic change of costume is a change from Smithers' white 'mask' to Lem's black nakedness.

While we do not expect such seemingly realistic characters to embody traits which are found also in Jones, we are inclined to anticipate it with regard to the visionary figures of the forest scenes, since these are obviously to be regarded as emanations of Jones' terrified mind. The first vision is that of the Little Formless Fears:

They are black, shapeless, only their glittering little eyes can be seen. If they have any describable form at all it is that of a grubworm about the size of a creeping child. They move noiselessly, but with deliberate, painful effort, striving to raise themselves on end, failing and sinking prone again (189).

This seems to be a representation of Jones' as yet *"shapeless,"* baby-sized fear: he is not inside the forest yet. Significantly, this first vision could still almost be taken for an external reality, and this is also what Jones does (190). The blackness and evil eyes of the Formless Fears link them with Jones. And their failure to raise themselves prepares for his failure to do so when, twelve hours later, he finds himself in roughly the same spot, squirming on his belly towards the crocodile, which has the same *"glittering"* (201) little eyes as the Formless Fears—and as Jones (175); his fear and guilt have by the time he fully

234

realizes his own evil nature found their horrifying and full-grown shape.[6] In his attempt to calm himself down by rationalizing his hallucinatory experience, Jones tells himself that the Formless Fears are "little wild pigs," which, furthermore, have rooted up and eaten his food (190). Absurd though it is—for how could the pigs eat his canned food?—the idea is a measure of Jones' fearful and guilt-ridden way of thinking, according to which it would be only natural, if, after his "big stealin'," he would retributively be deprived of the necessities of life.

The second vision is that of Jeff, the Negro Jones had killed "in an argument ... ovah a crap game" (181): "*He is middle-aged, thin, brown in color, is dressed in a Pullman porter's uniform and cap*" (191). Jeff, I take it, is an image of Jones himself as a Pullman porter, affected by the "white quality talk," a gambler loading his dice (196, cf. 178) to cheat others. Jeff's color is important; neither black nor white, it is a blend of the two, a true representation of Jones' in-between position. Jones has tried to believe "dat black is white" (185), but this has only resulted in making him a confused hybrid, excluded from both races, a lonely 'brown' man in a world that is either black or white. His second 'murder' of Jeff is therefore not to be dismissed as merely representing Jones' repression of his guilt. It is also, from another point of view, a punishment of the evil within himself—the cheating gambler; hence an act of expurgation.

The next vision is that of the Negro convicts and the white Prison Guard. This scene is the only one that breaks the regressive order of Jones' visions, for in reality he had killed the Prison Guard after he killed Jeff (181). There is, however, as Leech points out (p. 39), a psychological justification for this transposition of scenes, for the killing of the white man represents a worse crime—hence a crime more deeply repressed—than the murder of the Negro one. Moreover, since this scene identifies Jones with the black prisoners and revolting against the white man, it belongs, racially and psychologically, to an earlier phase in his life. It represents Jones' personal experience of 'slavery' and prepares naturally for the first racial vision: the slave market scene.

As I have already indicated, the Prison Guard is another Smithers: each is white, wears a kind of uniform, a weapon and a whip, which is used in an emblematic way, demonstrating the power of the white superrace. But this is only saying that the Prison Guard corresponds to Jones' 'white mask,' his brutal and criminal side. Of Jones' uniform only the pants are left at this stage—he is thus visibly a considerably blacker man by now—and its stripes

---

[6] The significance of the development seems indicated in the following passage in *Lazarus*: "Men are too cowardly to understand! And so the worms of their little fears eat them and grow fat and terrible and become their jealous gods they must appease with lies!" (352).

(175) now link him with the Negroes in their *"striped convict suits"* (194). The scene demonstrates thus, more clearly than the former one, the cleavage within Jones between his role of oppressor and oppressed. And he now solves the conflict more unequivocally by rejecting the "white debil" within him (195).

Essentially the same pattern is followed in the slave market scene. Jones is here grouped and identified with the Negro slaves and must suffer the pain he has let his black subjects suffer during his 'white' régime. He now kills two middle-aged white traders-in-human-lives, the *"spruce, authoritative"* auctioneer (196) and the planter-buyer—incarnations, it would seem, of himself and Smithers.

In the slave ship scene there is no longer any visible suggestion of white supremacy, but it still makes itself painfully felt in the wail of the Negro slaves, and so this vision too has a retributive meaning for Jones, whose costume now makes him look identical with the Negro slaves in their loin cloths (198 f.).

The scene prepares for the final forest scene, where the white dominance has been replaced by a black one. The Congo Witch Doctor bears, however, a striking resemblance to Jones-the-Emperor: he is stained *"bright red"* (200), the color of Jones' pants; he wears *"glass beads and bone ornaments ... about his neck, ears, wrists, and ankles,* as Jones wore *"brass buttons, heavy gold chevrons on his shoulders, gold braid on the collar, cuffs, etc."* (175); he carries a bone rattle in one hand—we think of Jones' dinner bell (182)—and *"a charm stick with a bunch of white cockatoo feathers tied to the end"* in the other—a cross between Smithers' subjugating whip and Jones' *"long-barreled, pearl-handled revolver,"* which is indeed his charm stick.

The parallel is highly ironic in its suggestion that Jones, as Emperor and god image, has held an office comparable to that of the Witch Doctor (cf. 185), and that he has, in fact, been closest to this aborigine—most blood-stained and superstitious—when he thought himself most removed from him. Jones has sacrificed his own people to himself by means of his witchcraft legend; now in retributive justice he is himself sacrificed by his racial ancestor and counterpart. The Witch Doctor calls to *"some God"* in the depths of the river:

A huge head of a crocodile appears over the bank and its eyes, glittering greenly, fasten upon JONES. *He stares into them fascinatedly. ...* JONES *squirms on his belly nearer and nearer, moaning continually. ... The crocodile heaves more of his enormous hulk onto the land.* JONES *squirms toward him. ... He fires at the green eyes in front of him. The head of the crocodile sinks back behind the river bank ...* (201 f.).

The crocodile is an embodiment of *"the forces of evil"* (201), more specifically the evil within Jones. O'Neill indicates their resemblance by making the crocodile masculine and by making Jones crawl on the ground in crocodile fashion and be in rapport with the animal's eyes, glittering like the silver bullet (cf. 179), and like his own *"keen, cunning"* eyes (175).

That a crocodile be worshipped as a god may seem a grotesquely primitive idea exclusively belonging to the aborigenes of the Congo. Yet the point is that such a worship has taken place on Jones' island; and it is Jones who has acted the part of Crocodile God. His perpetual boasting, in Scene 1, of his cleverness, intelligence and rational foresight, his assurance that he has laid "Jesus on de shelf for de time bein'" (185), informs us that Jones is blind to his own limitations, that in his hubris, nourished by the abject worship of the natives (175, 179), he has come to regard himself as a god. In reality he has behaved like a beast and devil, determined to get as much money out of the natives as he can and then make his get-away. O'Neill consistently stresses Jones' greed; the job of Emperor is largely a means to get the money (177), a way of accomplishing "big stealin'" (178). The crocodile symbolizes not only Jones' hubris but also his greed.[7] Referring to dollar bills Jones has earlier assured Smithers: "De long green, dat's me every time!" (177). Now Jones is to be swallowed up by "de long green" crocodile, by his own greed; it is an eye for an eye. He seemingly escapes this nemesis by killing the crocodile with his silver bullet.

The silver bullet plays a central role.[8] Jones shows the greatest admiration for it; he does not allow Smithers to touch it; and he refers to it as his "rabbit's foot" (179 f.). This is not surprising, for his imperial power is founded on it; well knowing that silver cannot be found on the island, he has made the natives believe that only a silver bullet—the one he owns himself —can kill him (178): "I has de silver bullet moulded and I tells 'em when de time comes I kills myself wid it" (179). Jones *is* killed by a silver bullet, made from coins, as his own undoubtedly was. Literally, it is the natives who kill him. In a deeper sense, however, the murderous silver bullet—like the crocodile a symbol of his greed and 'white' pride (cf. Skinner, p. 88)—is the one he has moulded for himself as Emperor.[9] Symbolically, Jones' death is a suicidal act of expurgation (cf. Falk, p. 69); having disposed of the silver bullet —of the greed and pride—Jones *"lies with his face to the ground, his arms outstretched, whimpering with fear ..."* (202). Once feared as a god, Jones

---

[7] I cannot agree with Carpenter's view (pp. 91 f.) that it is an image of "his innermost self" or of "his primitive fears."

[8] Its importance is evident from the fact that O'Neill originally entitled his play *The Silver Bullet* (Glaspell, p. 233).

[9] It is not explicitly stated that Jones is killed by *one* silver bullet, but we cannot help feeling that this is so, that the legend must be borne out. The longhand draft is explicit: *"There is a little reddish-purple hole under his left breast"* (= 204).

dies as a fearful and lowly beast. But not quite. For he dies in the costume and position of the Crucified; by humbling himself to animal level, he has elevated himself to the level of God; through suffering and sacrifice he wins enlightenment and the hope of resurrection: he dies at daybreak and, once dead, he is carried out of his black forest. Smithers unwittingly 'interprets' Jones' double-note death in the closing lines: "Dead as a 'erring! (*Mockingly*) Where's yer 'igh an' mighty airs now, yer bloomin' Majesty? ... Gawd blimey, but yer died in the 'eight o' style, any'ow!" (204). Symbolically a victim of the fish-eating crocodile, Jones has died in the sign of the *ichtys*.[1] And Smithers is not unlike those who mocked the Crucified, "the King of Israel," who could not save himself from death (Mat. 27: 42).

When considering the visions, critics have usually stressed the difference between the earlier ones, related to Jones' *personal* unconscious, and the later ones, related to his—in the Jungian sense—*collective* unconscious. My examination has revealed, however, that the later visions can also be related to Jones' own life and that the unifying factor in all the visions is that they painfully remind Jones of his personal sins. Beginning vaguely with the Formless Fears, interpreted by Jones in terms of materialism, the visions continue to reveal to him his murder of Jeff, pointing to his greed, and his killing of the Prison Guard, suggesting his pride, until, in the last three visions, he is symbolically confronted with his despotism, greed and pride as such; fittingly we move from partly excusable crimes against individuals to much more serious ones against a whole people and his own at that. It is no wonder that Jones' terror rises to a climactic point at the end and that he finds 'suicide' the only possible expiation.

The racial visions also provide a kind of motivation for Jones' crimes; as in *Electra,* O'Neill depicts a "fate springing out of the family" (O'Neill, 1931/ Frenz, p. 9), the family in this case being the race. For Jones' crimes and evaluation of whiteness must be seen against the fact that he started out in life as a proud and intelligent member of a suppressed race. His need to raise himself, i.e. to adjust to the white superrace, is ultimately a need to justify himself in his own eyes. Ironically, since the white values are rotten, Jones' social rise means a moral decline; in gaining the world he sells his soul. When he discovers what has happened, he starts out on his circular *via dolorosa,* which cleanses him of his sins and brings him back dead to his own people.

---

[1] Carpenter's claim (pp. 92 f.) that Jones never drops his 'mask' and dies as confused as he had lived reveals a disregard for the visual suggestion of the ending. Falk's view (pp. 69 f.) that Jones' finds integration in death is correct as far as it goes but needlessly limited to the psychological sphere—as is usual with this critic.

In a tightly composed, structurally conventional play like *Journey*, we find several parallel characters appearing only in the dialogue. Thus, during the long talk between Edmund and Tyrone in the final act both cannot help drawing attention to painful parallel cases. "Booze and consumption" killed Dowson (135) and Mary's father (137)—as it may Edmund. And Dante Gabriel Rossetti "was a dope fiend" (135)—like Mary. The very things that should not be mentioned *are* mentioned, because the characters cannot get away from themselves; even when talking about other things, they keep thinking about their own fate; and the slips are illustrations of their spiritual isolation; in a minor figure they parallel the more serious blows the Tyrones deal to one another, for rightly considered these too are slips, illustrative of their inability to transcend their isolation and their past. These parallels, together with others (the suicide of Tyrone's grandfather as compared to the suicide attempts of Edmund and Mary; Cathleen's uncle, who drank himself to death as Jamie doubtless will do), provide a dark, fateful backdrop for the drama of the Tyrones and widen its scope; they turn, as it were, the domestic drama into a universal tragedy.

Other parallels, more amply dealt with in the play, have meanings beyond this basic one. Here again we are confronted with figures symbolizing tendencies within the pivotal character, Mary Tyrone. There is, for example, the somewhat surprising resemblance between Mary and Fat Violet, the prostitute at whose breast Jamie seeks consolation. The obvious and glaring contrast between Violet and Mary, the whore and the 'virgin,' the woman of all men and the woman of no man (for this is what Mary's name and dream of becoming a nun amount to), is levelled out by a more basic similarity.[2] Thus, in her first speech Mary points out that she has "gotten too fat" (14), and it is pointed out that Jamie likes fat women (134, 160) but that he finds Violet too fat (160). Both women play the piano. Violet has been "on drunks" lately (159), as Mary has relapsed into morphinism; and Jamie brings the two together in his remark that before he discovered his mother's addiction, he could not imagine "that any women but whores took dope" (163); in a sense, his mother thus appears as a whore to him; by not loving him enough, by hiding in her dope world, she betrays him, makes him forever hunger for love. Yet Mary too hungers for love; and so does Violet. Both feel lonely, unpopular; Mary lacks friends; customers do not fall for Vi. Both hope to be loved despite their deformities, Violet despite her fatness, Mary despite her deficiencies as a wife and mother. As soon as Jamie knows that the beloved mother has left him forever, he goes to sleep with Violet. He believes that he selects

[2] 'Mary Ellen,' the names of O'Neill's mother, is actually the term for an amateur prostitute; as the Gelbs indicate (p. 167), O'Neill was familiar with this expression.

her out of consideration for a fellow bum. What he does not see is that his concern for Violet is motivated by her resemblance to Mary, that she functions as an admittedly unsuccessful mother substitute. Thus Jamie's visit to Mamie Burns' brothel becomes a pathetic illustration of his inability to get away from the mother; his love will follow her still.

Even closer is the parallel between Mary and Bridget, the cook.[3] The fog affects Bridget's rheumatism as it does Mary's (41, 99). And she appears to be as much of a whiskey addict as Mary is a "dope fiend." Their desperation, made acute—or rather symbolized—by their bodily pain, stems, as in the case of Violet, from an intense feeling of loneliness. In Act I Bridget, who needs company, keeps Mary in the kitchen for a long while with "lies about her relations" (102). In Act II Mary keeps Cathleen in the living room with memories of her own happy past which, according to Tyrone, must be taken "with a grain of salt" (137). She too needs a listener.

Cathleen describes Bridget as little better than a maniac, who cannot stand being left alone:

... she's like a raging divil. She'll bite my head off (99).

If she don't get something to quiet her temper, she'll be after me with a cleaver (106).

If we are reminded here of Ella Harris in *Chillun,* the association is apt, for Ella, like Mary, seems modelled to a great extent on O'Neill's mother. Hence Bridget, being another Ella, is seen to be another Mary. Never appearing but always (since we are constantly reminded of her presence in the dialogue and in the exits to the kitchen) lurking in the background, she comes to personify the reckless, destructive impulse within Mary, which finally 'kills' her three men. Mary says:

It's no use finding fault with Bridget. She doesn't listen. I can't threaten her, or she'd threaten she'd leave. And she does do her best at times. It's too bad they seem to be just the times you're sure to be late, James. Well, there's this consolation: it's difficult to tell from her cooking whether she's doing her best or her worst (71 f.).

This is no doubt a disguised self-portrait and a speech of defense. In her marriage Mary claims to have "done the best [she] could—under the circumstances" (114). She is no more suited for it than Bridget is for cooking. And besides, Tyrone has never given her much of a chance; he has never really understood that just as you cannot expect the food to taste good if you are late for it, so you can't expect a woman to be a good wife unless you give her a proper environment, which she can delight in. Such is Mary's defensive

---

[3] It is interesting to note that Mary Ellen's mother—O'Neill's grandmother—was named Bridget (Gelb, p. 12).

view; hidden beneath it is her other, more deeply felt view that she is herself to blame. It is precisely because she feels so guilty that Mary cannot accept any blame; she refutes it, like Bridget, by not listening and by eventually 'leaving' her family.

Parallel Situations

In *Journey* O'Neill has inserted what to a casual observer may seem a digression out of tune with the serious mood of the play and completely unrelated to it. I refer to the Harker-Shaughnessy episode, which fascinated O'Neill to the extent that he used it again and more extensively in *Misbegotten*.

Shaughnessy is a poor Irish tenant on a farm owned by Tyrone. This farm borders on the estate belonging to Harker, a Yankee Standard Oil millionaire. Edmund has just met Shaughnessy and he is reporting what the tenant has told him:

(*grins at his father provocatively*) Well, you remember, Papa, the ice pond on Harker's estate is right next to the farm, and you remember Shaughnessy keeps pigs. Well, it seems there's a break in the fence and the pigs have been bathing in the millionaire's ice pond, and Harker's foreman told him he was sure Shaughnessy had broken the fence on purpose to give his pigs a free wallow (23).

But when Harker came to rebuke Shaughnessy, the Irishman

accused Harker of making his foreman break down the fence to entice the pigs into the ice pond in order to destroy them. The poor pigs, Shaughnessy yelled, had caught their death of cold. Many of them were dying of pneumonia, and several others had been taken down with cholera from drinking the poisoned water (24).

This anecdote obviously helps to characterize the Tyrones in the sense that their reactions to it reveal something about their natures. Tyrone's reaction is especially illuminating; while he spontaneously sides with Shaughnessy, he gives some half-hearted support to Harker. But the story is also, I would suggest, the story of the Tyrone family in disguise. Thus the poor farm bordering on the rich estate illustrates Tyrone's transition from poverty to wealth. It is clear that he shares characteristics with both combatants—hence his divided sympathies. He is of humble Irish origin like Shaughnessy, who nevertheless claims that he would be a "King of Ireland" (24), if he had his rights, a claim that would not be foreign to Tyrone, judging by his name (Törnqvist, 1966, p. 372) and pride in the old country. Like Harker, he is a well-to-do 'businessman' and landowner; Harker is ironically referred to as a "king of America" (23), and Tyrone has acquired a similar position as a nation-wide matinée idol.[4] While accumulating his wealth and rising in society Tyrone has declined from "King" to "king," from Ireland to America, from Shakespeare to Monte Cristo, from artist to businessman. Like the pigs, he has run away from the poor farm to the rich estate, but in the process he has fatally poisoned himself. Mary too has moved outside her fenced-in, innocent childhood environment with the same result. Both of them find that they can no longer call their souls their own.

Many of the pigs, we learn, die of pneumonia after they have caught cold. Edmund is, for a long time, thought to suffer from a summer cold—until it is disclosed that he is affected by a far more fatal disease: consumption.[5] Other pigs die from drinking the poisoned ice water. Tyrone's father died by, perhaps deliberately, mistaking "rat poison for flour" (147).[6] Tyrone himself early began poisoning his sons by giving them whiskey as medicine, thereby laying a foundation for future alcoholism. During the long day we actually see the three men "wallow" in whiskey and ice water to make life bearable and short. Mary was poisoned by the quack who first gave her morphine; Tyrone constantly refers to the morphine as "the poison" (78, 111, 123, 139, 142, 174). Jamie jealously 'poisoned' Eugene with measles (from which the baby died) and Edmund with "worldly wisdom"—hard drinking and Broadway tarts—when he was merely a boy (34).

Although it is never made completely clear, it is strongly implied that it was Shaughnessy who broke down the fence. Poor as he is, he wants to give his pigs "a free wallow" at the expense of the hated Yankee millionaire; thus we may construe his motives. But the cheap bath has, as we have seen, consequences unforeseen by the tenant. In the same way Tyrone, unable to unlearn his childhood lesson of "the value of a dollar," tries to get everything second hand and as a result works destruction on his family. It was the cheap quack he sent Mary to that got her started on morphine. And it is a cheap sanatorium, "endowed by a group of millionaire factory owners, for the benefit of their workers" (149), to which he finally decides to send Edmund; and the son evidently stands as slim a chance of survival there as do the pigs in Harker's ice pond. The choice the-poor-Irish-boy-in-Tyrone makes is the choice Shaughnessy would have made; it is motivated not merely by an excessive money consciousness but also by a wish to benefit, for once, from the

[4] According to the Gelbs (p. 220) James O'Neill was worth between $100,000 and $200,000 in cash and real estate around 1912. Much earlier, in 1882, he had been the actor-manager of a play called *The American King* (Alexander, 1962, p. 51). Beginning with this play of little merit, James gave up his artistic demands and began to look at plays from a business point of view (cf. *Journey*, 149 f.).

[5] According to the death verdict, Jamie died of pneumonia (Gelb, p. 532).

[6] It may be noted that "rat poison" is a term for bad liquor in *Iceman* (619).

242

plutocrats, who had treated Tyrone and his family as little better than slaves; Tyrone's sanatorium plan is thus in a sense another battle fought against the Yankees.

Shaughnessy's violent attack on Harker, blaming him for what he himself has most likely done, may be seen as a grotesque and simplified version of the way each of the Tyrones react with regard to the major 'crimes' committed in the past. It is precisely when they feel most guilty that they blame others, applying Shaughnessy's technique of attacking before being attacked; he who evokes their guilt-feelings immediately turns into an enemy against whom they must defend themselves; their attacks thus stem primarily from a need to relieve themselves from an acute self-hatred.

Yet the fact that the question 'Who broke down the fence that opened the way for the pigs' destruction?' is not unequivocally answered is of some significance. No doubt O'Neill was unwilling to provide a clear answer because he was aware that the question foreshadows the much larger one we ask ourselves at the end of the play: 'Who is to blame for the destruction of the Tyrone family?' The whole play, in a sense, is devoted to answering this question. The web of guilt is so complex, is distributed to so many hands and stretches so far back in time that, although we realize that all the Tyrones have their share in it, and Tyrone perhaps most of all, we are ultimately left with Mary's philosophy that life, rather than any one of them, must carry the heaviest responsibility.

Structurally, the pig story springs naturally from the form chosen by O'Neill for his play. The technique of gradual revelation strictly adhered to in *Journey* prevents overt references to the family fate in the early acts; the play structure itself is designed as a long journey into the dark interior of the family and its individual members. The dramatist is obviously presented with a problem here. For the sake of dramatic suspense he is forced to make his characters withhold important information, while for the sake of structural unity he is forced to make them deliver it. He must therefore make the dialogue in the early acts function on (at least) two levels. Even if we do not—and, in fact, often cannot—grasp its more profound meaning at a first reading/hearing, we frequently sense that what the characters are saying is of a greater significance than it appears to be at the moment when it is presented; and we axiomatically assume that some of it will be made clear in the process of the play. This awareness of as of yet unintelligible levels creates a feeling of suspense, which piques our interest before it has been stirred by the human drama before us.

The parallel includes a marked contrast in *tone* between the anecdote and the ensuing action, which illustrates its meaning. The Tyrones can laugh at the Shaughnessy episode precisely because they do not realize that it is their own story in disguise. Had it been told at the end of the long day they—and we—would doubtless view it differently. Thus, by changing the perspective, O'Neill illustrates how life, depending on our degree of involvement, can be seen either as a farce or as a tragedy.

The pigs-in-the-ice-pond episode appears again—and more emphatically—in *Misbegotten*, where Phil Hogan plays the same trick on Harder that Shaughnessy does on Harker in *Journey*. Phil and Josie, as their surname indicates, are not unlike their pigs. When the play opens Hogan is down by the pigpen —"where he belongs, the old hog," his hostile son comments (4), and Phil's appearance bears him out:

He has a thick neck, lumpy, sloping shoulders, a barrel-like trunk, stumpy legs, and big feet. His arms are short and muscular, with large hairy hands. His head is round with thinning sandy hair. His face is fat with a snub nose, long upper lip, big mouth, and little blue eyes with bleached lashes and eyebrows that remind one of a white pig's (11).

Josie's outward appearance—she weighs "*around one hundred and eighty*" (3)—and her boast that she has slept with every man in the neighborhood make her seemingly a 'pig' of a woman. When Phil proudly calls his pigs "fine ambitious American-born pigs," which "don't miss any opportunities" (50), he is actually describing himself and his daughter, "two of a kind" (5), constantly scheming against the Yankees. As they doctor up a sick pig "to look good for a day or two" (8)—long enough to be sold at a good price—so they are in the habit of dressing Josie up to look good to soften the landlord, when he comes around to demand his rent (24, 36). And as Phil helps his pigs to stroll into the millionaire's grounds, where they can "wallow happily along the shores of the ice pond" (50), so he also attempts to help Josie exchange the "lousy farm" for Jim Tyrone's estate, where she could live "in ease and comfort" (175).

Josie at one point—the early part of Act III—attempts to perform the action of the pigs. Believing that Jim has been treacherous and intends to sell the farm to the hated neighbor, she is prepared to defend her home and blackmail Jim by offering him her body and then to force him to marry her and in this manner 'enter' his estate. But it is clear from the beginning that the role does not fit her: the low scheme is not hers but her 'virtuous' brother's; she has the best excuse possible for prostituting herself at this point: not only is it a matter of saving her own and her father's home and of taking revenge on one who has not kept his word; apart from and despite all this, Josie is in love with Jim—hence, sleeping with him is her heart's desire. The scheming role is repugnant to her, and it is significant that she

244

cannot force herself to kiss Jim *"passionately"* until this role has been dropped and love alone motivates her actions (133). Thus Josie, even when attempting the 'pig' role, is shown to fail miserably in adopting it. For a brief, blissful moment she believes that she and Jim can find love and happiness together. Then she discovers that he is 'dead,' that the little part of him that is still living is haunted by the memory of the mother and of the sin he has committed against her. She gives him the night of tender, innocent, maternal love he asks for, a self-sacrificing love, "the greatest of all," she remarks, "because it costs so much" (142). Josie thus runs the gamut from (partly) calculating, prostitute-like love through genuine passion to spiritualized love and servitude. Her pig-like characteristics, it turns out, are merely the outward 'mask' protecting her romantic, virginal soul. The moment Jim admits his genuine love for her, she drops this 'mask' (136). Never acting like a 'pig,' her fate is quite the opposite of that of the animals. When dawn comes she is still a virgin, still unpoisoned, facing a new day of hard work on the poor farm rather than the deathly "ease and comfort" of the rich estate. Phil, too, is capable of a tender, unselfish love beneath his rough, materialistic surface. His true reason for bringing Jim and Josie together is not so much land hunger as a desire to see his daughter happily married to a man he likes; as Phil expresses it: "I'm not a pig that has no other thought but eating!" (174).

The true counterpart of the pigs is the prostitute Jim slept with on the train carrying his mother's corpse eastwards; he significantly always refers to her as the "pig" (122, 129, 138, 149 f.); finds her come-on smile "as cold as a polar bear's feet" (149)—a simile that relates her to the ice pond; and gets "a bad taste" in his mouth, when he thinks of his experience with her a year earlier (129), just as Harder is said to deplore "the taste of pig in next summer's ice water" (51). The pigs, which stroll into the estate, happily wallow along the shores of the ice pond (50), and then die of cold or cholera from the "dirty water" (62), have their human parallel in this "fat blonde pig" (122) who, wallowing in bed with Jim Tyrone, heir to an estate, "for fifty bucks a night" (149), is already frozen and poisoned to death by a life devoid of love. Outwardly resembling Josie, she is actually her antithesis: as Josie incarnates the life force, so the prostitute represents death-in-life. Unable to feel anything for the dead mother, Jim concluded that he too had 'died,' the inference being that he could not survive the loss of maternal love. He logically proceeds to seek the company of someone who is as damned and 'dead' as he is, a whore with "parlor house written all over her" and "a face like an overgrown doll's" (149)—heavily made up, that is, and artificially young-looking like the dead mother. In the prostitute he seeks at once a mother substitute and revenge on the mother for deserting him (149 f.), both love and "the suicide of love" to use Michael Cape's definition of the prostitute in *Welded* (475), both life and death.[7]

More common in O'Neill's plays than such narrative parallels is the parallel situation which in stage action shows the characters in the same circumstances in which they themselves or their forebears have earlier found themselves. The most striking examples of such significant recurrences are found in *Electra,* the whole third part of which is an extended parallel to the first, Orin and Lavinia here repeating the behavior pattern set by their parents. How deliberate a device this was appears from the "Working Notes," where it says: "Repetition of the same scene—in its essential spirit, sometimes even in its exact words, but between different characters—following plays as development of fate—theme demands this repetition—" (O'Neill, 1931/Frenz, p. 12). The repetitions, in other words, serve to give a mystical sense of how everything recurs, a feeling which evokes at once a sense of universality and of inscrutable fate. This is the effect of the recurrent hair-touching scenes, linking three generations, which were discussed earlier (pp. 112 ff.). Of the many recurrences in the play, none is perhaps more emphatic for the spectator than Lavinia's return, at the end of the trilogy, to the situation in which she found herself when it began. Again she is in mourning, again she is a Mannon, stiff and square-shouldered, again she stands at the top of the stairs of the family tomb (179). The circle is completed. Lavinia's attempt to break loose from the paternal tradition has failed. She is trapped.

The pattern of recurring situations is employed also in *Desire,* where in

---

[7] Josephson's interpretation (1953, p. 240) of the prostitute as symbolizing spiritual death seems correct despite O'Neill's denial. Michael's words to the prostitute in *Welded* apply: "You're the perfect death" (476). The train whore in *Misbegotten* clearly corresponds to the prostitute in Dowson's poem "Non Sum Qualis Eram Bonae Sub Regno Cynarae (*The Poems and Prose of Ernest Dowson* (1919) belonged to O'Neill's library; his copy is now at C. W. Post College; the poem is found on p. 39.) When Jim Tyrone remarks that he could not forget the mother "even in that pig's arms" (150), he implies that the dead mother corresponds to the Cynara of the poem. In the draft Josie calls Cynara "a beautiful lady" and observes that "it's a name for death—and the dead" (= Act IV); in the play Jim finds his dead mother "young and pretty. ... Practically a stranger" (147). In the draft Josie prays at the end of Act IV: "May she [Cynara] come soon in answer to your prayers, Jim darlin'—in her arms the final forgiveness—the end and the peace." The forgiveness Jim seeks is that of the mother; it can be found only in death.

In the play the symbolic Cynara figure is fused with the dead mother; the name nowhere appears, only the phrase "in my fashion" (118, 161, 169 f.) and lines four and five of the second stanza about the "old passion" for Cynara and the grayness of the dawn (165). As a result, Jim's death longing is more strongly felt to be a longing for the mother. The dead mother haunts his mind as he sleeps with the train whore and again as he rests in Josie's maternal bosom; both he and Josie sense the mother in the beautiful, deathly moonlight, whose "breath" is "shed" upon Jim's soul. In the moon Cynara and the mother come together.

nearly every scene one or two characters deliver speeches of similar content by or near the gate in front of the house. Thus the play opens with Eben's appearance at the end of the porch calling his brothers to the evening meal:

he puts his hands on his hips and stares up at the sky. He sighs with a puzzled awe and blurts out with halting appreciation.

EBEN. God! Purty! (*His eyes fall and he stares about him frowningly. ...*
He spits on the ground with intense disgust, turns and goes back into the house (203).

The significance of Eben's appreciation of the sunset and curse of the ground can only be understood in retrospect, when we have been informed about his situation. We then learn that his father has married his mother not out of love, but because he was land-hungry and desired the farm she owned; and that he slaved her to death, while he hid from her the money gained from farming. He thus not only deprived her of what was rightly hers but actually victimized her with it. It is Eben who informs us about these matters; such is his view of the father.

After the mother's death Eben has taken over her chores; it is now his turn to be enslaved; Ephraim always insists on the basic similarity between mother and son, their unendurable weakness. Eben sees himself as defender of the wronged mother and as rightful inheritor of the farm that was stolen from her. Basically, he thus desires the farm. Yet as long as it belongs to his father, he must hate it, both because it is a living reminder to him that he has not yet revenged his mother and because he is chained to it (unlike his brothers) by his very determination to get it back from his father. The beauty for Eben at this point lies beyond the farm; he is longing to be released from it, because he sees no way of obtaining his goal; the temptation to leave must be particularly strong for Eben who is the only one who knows where the money is hidden and who is therefore the only one who has the means to go.

Once he has possessed Min and made himself sole heir to the farm by buying his brothers out of their shares, his desire for it can be expressed in positive terms; stopping by the gate in the sunrise of the following day he

stares around him with glowing possessive eyes. He takes in the whole farm with his embracing glance of desire.)

EBEN. It's purty! It's damned purty! It's mine! (*He suddenly throws his head back boldly and glares with hard, defiant eyes at the sky*) Mine, d'ye hear? Mine! (217).

The sky is "purty" no more; as soon as the farm can be regarded as his own it becomes attractive; but, as Eben unwittingly implies ("damned"), the beauty that stems from materialistic greed is a devil's invention.

Eben's brothers, now ready to leave the farm for California, naturally cannot share his evaluation:

They stare up at the sky with a numbed appreciation.)
PETER. Purty!
SIMEON. Ay-eh. Gold's t' the East now.
PETER. Sun's startin' with us fur the Golden West (218).

These speeches are followed by Simeon's bitter reflections on their long suffering on the farm.

Ephraim adds yet another aspect to the earth-sky dichotomy. Also for the old man the sky is "purty"; as for his sons, it promises release from a loveless drudgery on the stony farm, a release from life itself. But instead of cursing the farm he transposes it, as it were, into heaven: "Feels like a wa'm field up thar" (231). Ephraim cannot face the fact that he will ever part with the farm he has created with his own hands.

Already at this point Ephraim feels rejected by Abbie: he complains that it is "lonesome cold" in the house. This feeling is to grow on him. In the next scene we see him on his way from the matrimonial bed to the warm cows in the barn; stopping by the gate he calls in vain to God. On his way back the next morning he meets Eben by the gate:

EBEN. *(jovially)* Mornin', Paw. Star-gazin' in daylight?
CABOT. Purty, hain't it?
EBEN. *(looking around him possessively)* It's a durned purty farm.
CABOT. I mean the sky (245).

Ephraim's concern with the next world has only increased; Abbie makes him feel old and discarded. Eben, on the other hand, is surer of himself than ever; he has just possessed Abbie—a tremendous triumph for him and an assurance that he will soon possess the farm, too.

After the child has been killed, Ephraim appears alone by the gate; staring up at the sky, as though seeking consolation from God in his utter loneliness, he murmurs: "God A'mighty, I be lonesomer'n ever!" (265). A little later Abbie and Eben for the first time appear together by the gate on their way to the prison; and the play is concluded:

EBEN (... *points to the sunrise sky)* Sun's a-rizin'. Purty, hain't it?
ABBIE. Ay-eh! *(They both stand for a moment looking up raptly in attitudes strangely aloof and devout.)*
SHERIFF. *(looking around at the farm enviously—to his companions)* It's a jim-dandy farm, no denyin'. Wished I owned it! (269).

The scene echoes the initial one. Again Eben finds the sky "purty," again he longs to be released from the farm. But his motives are altogether different. In the initial scene, as his curse of the farm indicated, the longing for what was beyond the horizon was based mainly on the fact that he saw little chances of acquiring the farm he desired. In the ending scene he desires the farm no longer; he significantly makes no reference to it; at last he is completely freed from it, seeing only the rising sun, the grace of God, the hope of resurrection. Like Robert Mayo he has, through love and suffering, won "the right of release—beyond the horizon" (*Horizon*, 168). The Sheriff's speech ironically echoes Eben's initial enviousness, thereby measuring Eben's spiritual growth and reminding us of man's innate selfishness: we get the impression that the whole tragic cycle might start again, that the desire characterizing Abbie and the Cabots is a universal trait.[8]

The idea of having the end of a play echo the beginning, while hardly O'Neill's invention,[9] is highly characteristic of his dramatic method. Already in *Thirst* we have a suggestion of it in the reference to the sun, glaring down "*like a great angry eye of God,*" which is given both at the beginning (3) and at the end (32) of the play. The double reference creates the impression of an eternal, implacable fate to which the characters have succumbed.

In the early part of *Voyage* Driscoll orders Irish whiskey for himself and his sailor comrades (497), and then Olson, left behind by his friends, is served a drink which leaves him drugged; in store for him, it is implied, is a fateful voyage ending in death. When Driscoll returns at the end of the play and again orders Irish whiskey, we have a feeling that Olson's fate may be his. By closing the playlet in this manner O'Neill at once rounds it off and suggests that what has befallen Olson has a significance beyond his individual fate.

In *Christie,* Chris' early reference to the "dirty vedder—yust fog, fog, fog, all bloody time" (7) is echoed in his—and the play's—closing speech: "Fog, fog, fog, all bloody time. You can't see vhere you vas going, no" (78). Chris' fatalism is given the first and the last word, as it were. The references also suggest a circular movement from fog through brief sunshine (Act III) back into fog, a movement which also, as we have noted, characterizes *Journey,* where it has obvious metaphysical connotations.

Iceman begins rather harmoniously; the denizens of Hope's saloon have passed out and even after they wake up they contentedly go on pipe-dreaming. With Hickey's entrance it radically changes into the somber bleakness that

---

[8] I do not think, as Krutch does (1952, p. 161), that O'Neill wished to suggest that the Sheriff is a figure whose concept of ownership is wholly different from that of the main characters. But, admittedly, his single speech in the play makes poor material for arguments.

[9] The prime example in modern drama of an artful employment of a circular recurrence technique is Strindberg's *To Damascus* (cf. Brandell, 1950, pp. 247 f.).

comes of a life without illusions—and liquor. But once Hickey has been judged insane and has left, back comes the initial mood: the play ends with a cacophonous chorus, indicating that everyone is *"just a few drinks ahead of the passing-out stage"* (727). The movement is thus from happy sleep (illusions) through a painful awakening to life's realities and back into happy sleep. It is characteristic that those who do not return to sleep and pipe-dreaming—Hickey, Parritt, Larry—are the converts to death. *Hughie* sets a similar pattern, although here the happy mood—Erie's delusive relationship to Hughie—belongs to a period preceding the opening of the play; at the end the Night Clerk has become precisely what Hughie was.

The joking, farcical, workaday tone opening and ending *Misbegotten* sets off Josie's and Jim's poetical and nightly romance and, as it were, singles it out as the unique thing it is. There is a noteworthy parallel in the situations opening and closing the play. In the opening scene Josie helps her brother Mike to escape the father's "slave-driving." It is not really Mike she helps but "the little boy [he] used to be that [she] had to mother" (11):

I'm sorry to see you go, but it's the best thing for you. That's why I'm helping you, the same as I helped Thomas and John. ... I wish you all the luck in the world, Mike. I know you'll get on—and God bless you. (*Her voice has softened, and she blinks back tears. She kisses him—*(7).

Before the father turns up, Mike has disappeared in the woods at right-rear (10). In the closing scene Josie tells Jim to return to the Inn; they exchange a "Good-bye, and God bless you" and kiss, after which Jim *"walks quickly down the road off left without looking back. She stands, watching him go, for a moment, then she puts her hands over her face, her head bent, and sobs"* (174).

Mike and Jim are obvious contrasts: the bigoted teetotaler vs. the licentious drunkard. But their situation is not altogether different: Mike flees from his father's tyranny as Jim seeks to escape the guilt-ridden memory of his mother. Conversely, the father keeps watching Mike, never allowing him "a minute's rest" (4), as the mother's ghost keeps haunting Tyrone. It is characteristic, of course, that the shallow Mike is plagued only in an outward sense; unlike Jim he lacks a soul that can torment him. Josie, forgiving and mothering both men, helps them to their freedom in the way suitable to each of them; Mike takes the road leading to the world, where, Josie ironically notes, he will doubtless be a success; Jim departs the opposite way, for death, the only possible release for him. And Josie, who tolerantly helps one to life, another to death, grows to become an all-forgiving, all-loving Earth Mother.

In many plays there is a psychological reason for the circular movement. The characters feel an urgent need to restore an earlier, trusting, innocent attitude to life, a lost sense of belonging. Ella Harris in *Chillun*, unable to cope with the harshness of grown-up life and her own acute sense of guilt, reverts to the time—childhood—when she still was innocent and loved Jim in a natural, genuine way. Mary Tyrone in *Journey*, for similar reasons, regresses to the time when she still lived a protected convent life away from the turmoil of the world. Her closing line is a pathetic remembrance of the crucial dividing line—which is also the high point—in her life: her first, romantic love for her prospective husband. *Interlude* ends with Nina's decision to return to her father's home, where we first saw her in Act I. Marsden will play the role of father to her. "It will be a comfort to get home," she sighs, "to be old and to be home again at last" (200). After her long, tiring life interlude she has finally come round to her father's and Marsden's life-weariness, seeking protection in the monastic quietude of the paternal home among the memories of childhood. In *Days* John Loving's ideological development again has the form of a circuit. From a trusting childhood faith in a beneficent God he turns to atheism, anarchism, Nietzscheanism, Marxism, oriental religion, Greek philosophy, evolutionism, faith in earthly love (502 ff.) and, at last, back to a trusting faith in a God of Love. His road, as Father Baird prophesies, eventually turns "back toward home" (504): in the final scene he reverts to his childhood faith in the very church where he used to pray and believe (562).

The regressive movement can also extend to generations beyond that of the reverting individual. Thus, at the end of *Poet* Con Melody gives up all gentlemanly pretensions and returns to his parental origin (cf. Raleigh, p. 20). Recognizing that he is no more than a simple shebeen keeper, he prepares to dismiss his bartender and "tend the bar [him]self, like [his] father's son ought to" (174). The upward struggle has ceased—and so, we are given to understand, has in effect Melody's life.

Of greater universal and symbolic significance are the regressions of Brutus Jones and Yank (*Ape*). Jones' circular movement through the black forest is a journey back to his racial 'childhood,' motivated by the same longing for innocence that characterizes the backward journeys of Ella Harris and Mary Tyrone. Less flawed than Jones, Yank makes the same error of judgement: he too mistakenly believes that he controls both the world and his own mind, that he is both rational and powerful. For his hubris he is soon punished with humiliation. In the attempt to restore his lost sense of belonging he retrogresses even further than Jones; in the closing scene he faces his own harmonious origin: the anthropoid. The circle is not completed, for Yank finds that he cannot go back to the simian stage. Yet the thread between beginning and end is tied just the same, for the chattering of the apes around Yank is identical with the *"inchoate uproar"* of the 'Neanderthal men' in the initial forecastle scene. Thus it may be argued that Yank has, in a sense, returned to the forecastle, now seeing it in its true light: as a cage filled with monkeys.[1]

The purpose of having the end echo the beginning may also be that the dramatist wishes to give a sense of timelessness, hence universality, to his play. A striking example is found in *Brown,* where the Epilogue echoes the Prologue in a number of ways (cf. Kaucher, pp. 126 f.). Playing eighteen years later, it reveals the same locale, the same lighting, the same situation. Only the roles have changed. Margaret is no longer a young girl romantically in love, but a mother of young boys who are romantically in love. Her remark that "the nights now are so much colder than they used to be" (324) echoes the remarks of the mothers in the Prologue (259, 261), thereby extending the frame of the play: we sense, by analogy, that Mrs. Brown and Mrs. Anthony have once been like the young girl Margaret; that the Prologue is, as it were, their Epilogue; that the Anthony boys in the future will make the same remarks to their sons and daughters, etc. In short, the repetition renders the situation archetypal, timeless and, in a sense, fated.

A more abstract reason may be given for the inner resemblance between the beginning and the end of *Lazarus.* When the play opens, Lazarus has just been reborn from death; when it closes, he suffers a 'death' which is actually a rebirth to a new form of existence. The parallel is a kind of verification of Lazarus' gospel that there is no death, that there is only change—his version of Nietzsche's "eternal recurrence" (cf. Day, 1960, p. 301).

There is, of course, an esthetic reason for O'Neill's predilection for the circular composition. Framing the plays as they do, the parallels between beginning and end give a sense of unity and harmonious completeness to the dramas, a satisfying impression that the plays have, as we say, come full circle, and that the endings follow with artistic inevitability. But besides this esthetic reason, there are others which no doubt seemed weightier to O'Neill. We have observed how, in the late plays, this composition is closely related to O'Neill's theme: no man can live wholly without illusions. At other times the circular composition is motivated by the characters' need to return in their own footsteps, so to speak, to free themselves of accumulated guilt and experience a sense of belonging. We have also noted how the reiteration helps to suggest inevitability and fate, and this aspect must have been of primary importance to a tragedian, who was constantly attempting to find a modern equivalent for the Greek sense of fate. Finally, we have seen how the parallel situations are a means for the playwright to universalize his themes. Especially when similar scenes are repeated between different characters, are we given a strong impression of the fact that O'Neill's plays occur outside time and place and concern themselves with Life rather than lives.

[1] In his first conception of the play O'Neill actually had Yank return to his ship deprived of his initial faith in himself (Gelb, p. 489).

VII. CONCLUDING REMARKS

Although he did not use the term until 1924, O'Neill was always in spirit a super-naturalistic playwright, a playwright who, due to his keen religious and psychological concerns, was constantly striving to express profound inner experiences. At the same time, however, he always attempted to retain a realistic surface layer in order to make his plays dramatic in an immediate, elementary way and to enable the reader and spectator to empathize with the characters. This is true even of *Brown* and *Lazarus,* his least illusionistic dramas.

Because of this amalgam technique, O'Neill's work is open to interpretation on different levels. Much of the controversy regarding its meaning and quality—and opinions have been, and are still, very divided on these issues —is clearly due to completely different ideas of what the author is trying to communicate. Some commentators have limited themselves to a consideration of the realistic surface layer or have read into the plays a topical meaning never intended by the dramatist. Others have been sensitive to the universal implications and super-naturalistic overtones of the dramas. Literary interpreters often tend to regard the stage directions as extraneous parts of little significance. Directors, similarly, are frequently inclined to subscribe to the widespread view that a first-rate dramatist—and, as ever, Shakespeare is used as a paragon—needs no or few stage directions. O'Neill, in accordance with this view, is considered a major dramatist despite rather than because of his extensive stage directions. Even those directors who take a more positive view of O'Neill's efforts and make a serious attempt to realize the author's ideas on the stage, often find that it cannot be done, simply because their resources do not meet the playwright's demands. Hence the problem arises: if both the literary and the theatrical experts neglect a substantial and integral part of the plays, who is going to be concerned with the dramas as the playwright conceived of them, when he wrote them for his "dream theatre"? My examination has, I hope, in some measure contributed to clarify the significance of the stage directions in O'Neill's plays.

In his endeavor to create a *Gesamtkunstwerk* in which the correspondences between the different play elements, no less than these elements themselves, serve to express those spiritual values that concerned him, O'Neill mobilized all the resources of the modern theatre. Scenery and lighting, properties and costumes are called upon to play their parts. Facial traits, bearings and positions, gestures and movements are entrusted to tell us about the nature of the human souls that people O'Neill's stage. Sound effects of various kinds are employed not only for their emotional but also for their symbolic value. In the dialogue, depth and scope are attempted in different ways: through characterizing diction, through a repetitive use of key words, through an employment of—often disguised—audible thinking.

To this enumeration of areas in which O'Neill has made his super-naturalistic technique operative must be added a device of which he makes regular use and which may properly be considered the fundamental characteristic of his technique. I refer to his preference for parallelisms and significant recurrences. A line, a scene, a costume, a character, a setting, a property, a light or sound effect is repeated in a new context and thereby gains a new meaning, yet retains (part of) the old one. In this way O'Neill could give a high degree of complexity to his plays. The characters achieve but a partial individuality. The basic sameness of mankind is demonstrated. Moreover, the recurrences are a direct expression of O'Neill's primarily fatalistic concept of life. Mary Tyrone's words "The past is the present, isn't it? It's the future, too" (*Journey*, 87) are at the bottom of all his plays and are decisive in the shaping of them.

The primary aim of the present study has been to shed light on a problem of central importance to O'Neill: the problem of how to give expression, in a dramatically and theatrically arresting way, to the depths of personality and to "the inscrutable forces" that can be divined behind life. In his attempt to dramatize these "hidden" phenomena, O'Neill constantly, though in different degrees, tried to transcend the limitations imposed upon drama by the naturalistic demands for a verisimilitude of appearances.

Methodically, I have approached the texts in a manner which has as of yet been relatively sparingly used in dramatic criticism. In this respect the present study is therefore to be regarded as a somewhat tentative endeavor to indicate one way in which an examination of the technique practiced by O'Neill— and not by him alone!—may be pursued.

Unlike many other playwrights who adhere to one dramatic method which they gradually refine, O'Neill restlessly tried new forms. His incessant experimentation may be ascribed to his concern with what he termed the "behind-life," the metaphysical and psychological mysteries of life. His aim as a dramatist, it would seem, was to find an adequate way of expressing the almost inexpressible, to overcome his "stammering" as Edmund Tyrone puts it (*Journey*, 154). The success with which O'Neill overcame his 'stammering,' most critics would agree, varied considerably. To speak of any linear development, in the sense of esthetic achievement, throughout his work is hardly possible, even though many critics would be inclined to see an artistic summit in such late plays as *Iceman* and *Journey*.

The variety of his work has struck many commentators. Equally striking, however, is the homogeneity found below the many-faceted surface. By studying O'Neill's *oeuvre* as a unity—the approach attempted in the present study —we are made aware of this homogeneity. Blurred details in the vast fresco of his work emerge more clearly when related to other parts of the mural showing a similar but more distinct pattern. Plays which are artistic lightweights take on interest, as we can see the same creative mind working in them as in the esthetically more substantial dramas.

It is a characteristic of the great artist, that even in his most flawed works the hand of the master can be sensed. O'Neill is an artist of this rare stature. If his failures seem more inspiring than the successes of lesser spirits, it is because they are indirect signs of how high he was aiming. Perhaps he was attempting the impossible, when he tried to create a true "drama of souls." Yet to O'Neill nothing but the impossible was really worth while. To attempt the impossible was always his ambition; as he wrote Sisk (8.28.1930): "I am always trying to do a big thing. It's only the joy of that attempt that keeps me writing plays. Otherwise I would quit for I really have little interest or enthusiasm for the modern theatre, and to write for success or notoriety, or even to write merely good plays wouldn't keep me on the job a minute. Shooting at a star may be hopeless in my case, time will tell, but it gives one a rich zest in being alive in oneself and putting up a battle about something or other. And so it is important to me, if to no one else."

O'Neill's 'work method,' as this statement reveals, was inextricably connected with his credo as a tragedian; the play he felt completely satisfied with was always—had to be—"beyond the horizon," for, in his own words (2.13.1921/Cargill et al., p. 104), "only through the unattainable does man achieve a hope worth living and dying for—and so attain himself. He with a spiritual guerdon of a hope in hopelessness, is nearest to the stars and the rainbow's foot."

CHRONOLOGY OF O'NEILL'S PLAYS

Although chronological tables of O'Neill's plays have been provided in several earlier works,[1] the addition of yet another one is legitimate for at least two reasons.

In the first place, my chronology is more complete with regard to the dates of composition than any of the preceding ones. It covers all recorded plays (including some that did not develop beyond the stage of first draft), whether published or unpublished, preserved or destroyed. It does not include plays which did not develop beyond the outline/scenario stage. Since some dates and sources are less reliable than others, I have seen fit to provide the chronology with detailed source references; such references have on the whole been lacking in earlier lists. The literature about O'Neill abounds in controversial and inaccurate information even with regard to such factual matters as dates. I have limited myself to correcting a few mistakes in Clark's standard work.

Secondly, my chronology differs from those of earlier bibliographers—except from the one O'Neill made for Skinner—in that it attempts to give an outline of the growth of the plays. O'Neill's list is helpful so far as it goes, but it omits many of the early plays, considered inferior by the playwright, and ends with the year 1933. It is thus a torso in need of completion.

A general dating problem is presented by O'Neill's work method; as the dramatist pointed out in his letter to Skinner (p. vii): "Of course some plays were written in one year, and rewritten into their publication and stage-produced forms in a later year—usually, this meant only a condensation, without any change in essentials." Also, as Mrs. O'Neill has remarked in an interview, "O'Neill was always working on three or four plays at a time" (Peck, p. 94). To trace the growth of the plays in detail would, judging by these statements, amount to an examination of O'Neill's daily work over the years.

[1] The basic chronology concerning dates of composition is the one made by O'Neill at the request of Skinner; it is found in Skinner, pp. viii–x. Dates and places of composition are also given by O'Neill in the notes attached to the plays included in the Wilderness edition (1934–35). A careful collation of all published O'Neill texts and their dates of publication up to and including *Dynamo* is found in Sanborn-Clark. Lists of productions and publications are also included in Clark's biography, pp. 165–69. An alphabetical check list including unpublished plays and listing dates of composition, first production and first publication and a chronology of first productions appear in Cargill et al., pp. 479–86. Miller (1962, pp. 107–65) provides a chronology of composition, copyright and domestic publication and a list of major productions of O'Neill's plays with details about casts, number of performances, etc.

Apart from the fact that a chronology based on such meticulous first-hand knowledge would be extremely cumbersome and show more of the trees than of the forest, it is at present not possible to present such a detailed list, since the document of paramount interest in this respect, O'Neill's work diary 1924 –43 in the O'Neill Collection at Yale University Library, is not yet accessible to scholars.

The plays which did not develop beyond the outline/scenario stage and which are therefore not included in the subsequent chronology are the following:[2]

The Reckoning[3]   ca. 1917
S.O.S.[4]   ca. 1918
It Cannot Be Mad[5]   ca. 1928
Sea Mother's Son[6]   ca. 1928

projects probably belonging to the period 1933–39:

A sequel to *Ah, Wilderness!*
A play about Robespierre
A play about Aeschylus
A play about Shih Huang Ti
A play about Don Juan of Austria and Philip II
Gag's End
The Visit of Malatesta

five plays in the nine-play Cycle entitled *A Tale of Possessors Self-Dispossessed*:

The Calms of Capricorn[7]
The Earth's the Limit[7]
Nothing is Lost Save Honor[7]
The Man on Iron Horseback[7]
The Hair of the Dog[7]

and:

By Way of Obit[8]   ca. 1941
The Last Conquest or *The Thirteenth Apostle*[9]   ca. 1942

[2] This list will undoubtedly be extended when all the material in the O'Neill Collection at Yale is made available. At present about one third of the items are restricted.

[3] The typed scenario ends: "Eugene G. O'Neill, P'[rovince]town, Mass." The initial reveals that the scenario is early but it cannot date further back than 1916, O'Neill's first year in Provincetown.

[4] The typed scenario is 'dated': "West Point Pleasant, N.J." O'Neill stayed at this place from Nov. 1918 to mid-May 1919 (Gelb, pp. 386, 392).

[5] Cf. Josephson (1962, p. 535). The third part of a projected trilogy of which *Dynamo* was meant to be the first part and *Days Without End* the second; the plan was discarded. From a letter to De Casseres (9.15.1928) it appears that O'Neill planned to give the prospective trilogy the Nietzschean-sounding title "God is Dead! Long Live—What?"

[6] Gelb, pp. 671, 679.

[7] Cf. Gallup's information in Falk, pp. 205 f.

[8] "A series of one-acters which will include 7, 8 or 9 plays," O'Neill wrote under this title on the typewritten version of the first draft of *Hughie*, the only play in the series which was completed.

[9] Clark, p. 147.

In the subsequent list, covering plays which were either completed or which received definite dramatic shape in the form of first drafts, seasons are indicated by the following abbreviations: S(pring), Su(mmer), F(all), W(inter). The plays are numbered at their final stage of conception. Published plays are in italics. Destroyed plays are within brackets. In the drafts, referred to in the notes, there are two types of dates: (1) dates made at the time of writing; these dates usually appear at the end and presumably indicate when the drafts were finished; (2) dates appearing on the title pages; these dates were obviously made when the drafts were sent to the various libraries, that is, years after they were written.

Date of composition	Title	First production	Copyright (C) and publication (P)
1913 S	1. *A Wife for a Life*[10]	—	8.15.1913 (C), 1950 (P)
F	2. *The Web*[10]	—	Aug. 1914 (P)
F	3. *Thirst*[11]	Su 1916	Aug. 1914 (P)
F	4. *Recklessness*[12]	—	Aug. 1914 (P)
F	5. *Warnings*[12]	—	Aug. 1914 (P)
1914 W	6. *Fog*[12]	Jan. 1917	Aug. 1914 (P)
S	7. Bread and Butter[13]	—	5.2.1914 (C)

[10] On the title page of the longhand draft of *The Web* O'Neill has written: "Original script of 'The Web' (first *play* I ever wrote—original title 'The Cough'—written Fall of 1913 at our home in New London, Conn. To be scrupulously exact, for the record, 'The Web' is *not* the first thing I wrote *for the stage*. I had some time before dashed off in one night a ten minute vaudeville skit, afterwards destroyed. But this was not a play. In fact, my friends in vaudeville crudely asserted it was not a vaudeville skit, either! It was nothing. And 'The Web' *is* the first *play* I ever wrote.)"

The dramatist here refers to *A Wife for a Life* which, by 1944, when he penned his note, he apparently had forgotten had been copyrighted. It was later published together with four other early plays in an unauthorized volume, their copyright having expired. Clark (p. 49) claims that *A Wife for a Life* was written shortly after O'Neill left Gaylord sanatorium on June 3, 1913, while Alexander (1962, p. 181), who appears to be better informed, indicates that it was composed in May, while he was still there . Cf. also Gelb, p. 231. For the dramatist's earliest attempts at playwriting, see further p. 28, note 8.

[11] On the title page of the original longhand draft of the play O'Neill has written: "To Armina [Langner]: On her birthday, this original script of the 2nd play I ever wrote—with love and gratitude. Gene." The play title is followed by the date: "(1913) (New London, Conn. Fall.)" Cf. note 12.

[12] Revised, handwritten scripts of *Thirst*, *Warnings* and *Recklessness* are contained in a hardcover ledger. *Warnings* is dated "1913," *Recklessness* "11/25/13." The order of composition between *Warnings*, *Recklessness* and *Fog* is uncertain. In the chronology made for Skinner O'Neill dated all five plays in the *Thirst* volume to the fall and winter of 1913–14.

[13] Gelb, p. 253. Cf. note 14.

Date of composition		Title	First production	Copyright (C) and publication (P)
	S	8. *Bound East for Cardiff* (first called Children of the Sea)	Su 1916	5.14.1914 (C), Nov. 1916 (P)
	S	9. *Abortion*[14]	10.27.1959	5.19.1914 (C), 1950 (P)
	S	10. *The Movie Man*[15]	10.27.1959	7.1.1914 (C), 1950 (P)
	Su	11. *Servitude*[14]	—	9.23.1914 (C), 1950 (P)
1915	S	12. [The Dear Doctor][16]	—	—
	S	13. The Personal Equation (first called The Second Engineer)[17]	—	—
	S	14. *The Sniper*[17]	2.16.1917	5.13.1915 (C), 1950 (P)
	S	15. [A Knock at the Door][17]	—	—
	S	16. [Belshazzar][18]	—	—
1916	Su	17. *Before Breakfast*	12.1.1916	Dec. 1916 (P)
	Su	Ile (notes)[19]		
		18. [Atrocity][17]	—	—
		19. [The G.A.N. or The G.A.M.][17]	—	—
1917	W	20. Now I Ask You[20]	—	5.23.1917 (C)
	W	21. *In the Zone*[21]	10.31.1917	June 1919 (P)
	W	22. *Ile*[21]	11.30.1917	May 1918 (P)
	W	23. *The Long Voyage Home*[21]	11.2.1917	Oct. 1917 (P)
	W	24. *The Moon of the Caribbees*[21]	12.20.1918	Aug. 1918 (P)

[14] According to Clark (p. 54) O'Neill told him that *Bound East for Cardiff* "was followed by *Abortion*." In a letter (New London, Conn., 7.16.1914) O'Neill wrote George Pierce Baker: "Less than a year ago I seriously determined to become a dramatist and since that time I have written one long play—four acts—and seven one-act plays" (Cargill et al., p. 19). The four-act play was *Bread and Butter*. *Servitude*, in three acts, was apparently still unwritten at this time. Clark's statement (p. 54) that *Abortion* was produced in 1916 is incorrect.

[15] Clark (p. 54) mistakenly dates *The Movie Man* to 1916.

[16] Clark (p. 54) dates *The Dear Doctor* to 1915, Cargill et al. (p. 480) date it to 1914. Miller (1962) omits it. It is possible that the play—an adaptation—was written already during O'Neill's first term at Harvard, i.e. in the fall of 1914.

[17] Clark, p. 54.

[18] This play was written in collaboration with a classmate, Colin Ford. Cf. Clark, p. 54.

[19] Gelb. p. 314.

[20] Clark (p. 54) claims that this play was written in 1916, and Alexander (1962, p. 220) assures us that O'Neill was working on it in the summer of 1916, while in Provincetown. The Yale typescript is undated but signed "Eugene G. O'Neill, Provincetown, Mass." The Harvard typescript is dated 1917. Possibly O'Neill wrote a first draft of the play in 1916, which he revised in 1917 before having it copyrighted.

[21] The order of composition between the four sea plays written in 1917 is uncertain. The longhand drafts give the date "1917, Winter" for all of them. Only *The Moon of the Caribbees* is also given a more specific date: "3/20/17." I have followed the order suggested by O'Neill in his list to Skinner.

Date of composition		Title	First production	Copyright (C) and publication (P)
	Su	The Hairy Ape (idea)[22]		
	Su	Beyond the Horizon (idea)[22]		
1918	W	25. *The Rope*[23]	4.26.1918	June 1919 (P)
	W	26. *Beyond the Horizon*[22]	2.2.1920	6.7.1918 (C), 8.5.1918 (C), March 1920 (P)
	Su	27. *The Dreamy Kid*[24]	10.31.1919	Jan. 1920 (P)
	F	28. *Where the Cross Is Made*[25]	11.22.1918	June 1919 (P)
		29. [Till We Meet][26]	—	—
		30. Shell Shock[26]	—	1918 (C)
		The Emperor Jones (idea)[27]		
	F	The Straw (1st draft)[28]		
1919	W	The Straw (1st draft)[28]		
	W	Chris Christopherson[22]		
	S	31. *The Straw*	11.10.1921	11.19.1919 (C), April 1921 (P)
	Su	32. Chris Christopherson (rewritten)	3.18.1920	6.5.1919 (C)
		33. [Honor Among the Bradleys][26]	—	—
		34. [The Trumpet][26]	—	—
		35. [Exorcism][26]	3.26.1920	1919 (C)
1920	W	36. *Gold*[29]	6.1.1921	7.27.1920 (C), Sept. 1921 (P)
	Su	37. *Anna Christie*[30]	11.2.1921	11.29.1920 (C), July 1922 (P)
	F	38. *The Emperor Jones*[31]	11.3.1920	Jan. 1921 (P)
	F	39. *Diff'rent*[32]	12.27.1920	April 1921 (P)
1921	W	40. *The First Man*[33]	3.4.1922	10.13.1921 (C), July 1922 (P)
		Marco Millions (idea)[34]		

[22] O'Neill to Skinner.
[23] The longhand draft is dated "1918, winter" and, at the end, "3/1/18."
[24] The longhand draft is dated "1918, summer."
[25] The longhand draft is dated "1918, fall."
[26] Clark, p. 55.
[27] Mullett, p. 118.
[28] The longhand draft is dated "(1918–19) fall—winter" on the title page.
[29] The longhand draft is dated "(1920) (winter)" on the title page.
[30] Copyrighted as *The Ole Devil*. On the title page of the longhand draft O'Neill has remarked that the second title of the play was "The Ole Davil." The draft was finished 9.18.1920.
[31] The longhand draft is dated "Peaked Hill Bar—P'town, Oct. 2, 1920" at the end.
[32] The longhand draft is dated "P[eaked]. H[ill]. B[ar].—P'town, Oct. 19, 1920."
[33] Copyrighted as *The Oldest Man*. The longhand draft is dated "3/16/21" at the end.
[34] Clark, p. 107.

Date of composition		Title	First production	Copyright (C) and publication (P)
S/Su		The Fountain (1st draft)[35]		
F	41.	*The Hairy Ape*[36]	3.9.1922	July 1922 (P)
1922 Su	42.	*The Fountain*[35]	12.10.1925	10.13.1921 (C), March 1926 (P)
		The Great God Brown (idea)[37]		
		All God's Chillun Got Wings (idea)[37]		
F		Welded (half of it)[38]		
1923 W	43.	*Welded*[38]	3.17.1924	5.2.1923 (C), April 1924 (P)
Su		Marco Millions (outline and one scene)[39]		
F	44.	*All God's Chillun Got Wings*[40]	5.15.1924	Feb. 1924 (P)
F		Strange Interlude (notes)[41]		
		Desire Under the Elms (idea)[37]		
	45.	*The Ancient Mariner* (adaptation)[42]	4.6.1924	Oct. 1960 (P)
1924 W	46.	The Revelation of John the Divine (adaptation; 1st draft)[42]		
W/S	47.	*Desire Under the Elms*[43]	11.11.1924	8.29.1924 (C), Jan. 1925 (P)
Su		Marco Millions[44]		
1925 W	48.	*Marco Millions*[45]	1.9.1928	1.28.1925 (C), April 1927 (P)
W	49.	*The Great God Brown*[46]	1.23.1926	1.2.1925 (C), March 1926 (P)
Su		Lazarus Laughed (scenario)[47]		

[35] O'Neill to Skinner. The longhand draft is dated "(1921—'22) summer—summer" on the title page.

[36] O'Neill to Skinner: "Late Fall (written in three weeks)." At the end of the longhand script O'Neill has written: "Begun Dec. 7—finished Dec. 23, 1921."

[37] Dated note, Yale University Library.

[38] O'Neill to Skinner. The "longhand first draft with revisions" is dated "(1922–23)" on the title page and "3/16/23 4/7/23" at the end. Of the later dates the first probably indicates the completion of the uncorrected draft, the second the completion of the revised draft.

[39] O'Neill to Skinner. Cf. Gelb, p. 528.

[40] The longhand draft is dated "Peaked Hill—fall 1923."

[41] Lewis, pp. 14 f.

[42] Gallup, 1960, p. 61.

[43] O'Neill to Skinner. The scenario is dated "Ridgefield—Jan. 1924."

[44] O'Neill to Skinner with the comment: "Finished 'Marco Millions' in its original two part two-play form, each play short full length."

[45] O'Neill to Skinner with the comment: "Final draft of 'Marco Millions' condensed into one play."

[46] The longhand draft is dated " 'Campsea,' Bermuda. March 22, 1925" at the end.

[47] Gelb, p. 589.

Date of composition		Title	First production	Copyright (C) and publication (P)
	Su	Strange Interlude (scenario)[48]		
	F	Lazarus Laughed (half of 1st draft)[49]		
1926	W/S	50. *Lazarus Laughed*[50]	4.9.1928	6.23.1926 (C), 11.12.1927 (P)
		Dynamo (idea)[51]		
	S	Mourning Becomes Electra (idea)[52]		
	S/Su	Strange Interlude (first half)[49]		
1927	W/S/Su	51. *Strange Interlude*[53]	1.30.1928	7.1.1927 (C), Feb. 1928 (P)
	Su	Days Without End (scenario)[54]		
1928	S/Su	52. *Dynamo*[55]	2.11.1929	10.4.1928 (C), Oct. 1929 (P)
	F	Mourning Becomes Electra (idea)[52]		
1929	S/Su	Mourning Becomes Electra (notes, scenarios)[56]		
	F	Mourning Becomes Electra (1st draft)[57]		
1930	W	Mourning Becomes Electra (1st draft)[57]		
	S/Su	Mourning Becomes Electra (2nd draft)[58]		
	Su/F	Mourning Becomes Electra (1st and 2nd rewrite)[59]		
1931	W/S/F	53. *Mourning Becomes Electra*[60]	10.26.1931	5.12.1931 (C), Nov. 1931 (P)

[48] Lewis, p. 16.
[49] O'Neill to Skinner.
[50] O'Neill to Skinner. Act I was published already in Sept. 1927 (cf. Sanborn-Clark, p. [67]).
[51] Dated note in Yale University Library. The Gelbs claim (p. 561) that O'Neill was making notes for *Dynamo* already in the summer of 1924. I take this to be an erroneous dating.
[52] O'Neill, 1931/Frenz, p. 3.
[53] O'Neill to Skinner. The first draft was apparently finished in February, 1927. Cf. Lewis, p. 16.
[54] On the title page for the notes of this play O'Neill has remarked that the scenario was written "in notebook four years previously (1927)."
[55] O'Neill to Skinner. The notes and drawings for the play are dated "Guéthary, B. P. France. Sept. 9, 1928."
[56] O'Neill, 1931/Frenz, pp. 4 ff.
[57] O'Neill, 1931/Frenz, p. 7.
[58] O'Neill, 1931/Frenz, p. 9
[59] O'Neill, 1931/Frenz, pp. 9 ff.
[60] O'Neill, 1931/Frenz, pp. 13 ff.

Date of composition	Title	First production	Copyright (C) and publication (P)
Su/F	Days Without End (notes)[61]		
1932 S/Su	Days Without End (1st and 2nd drafts)[62]		
F	54. *Ah, Wilderness!*[63]	10.2.1933	8.8.1933 (C), Oct. 1933 (P)
F	Days Without End (3rd draft)[62]		
1933 W/S	Days Without End (4th draft)[62]		
Su/F	55. *Days Without End*[64]	12.27.1933	7.20.1933 (C), Feb. 1934 (P)
1934	56. [The Life of Bessie Bowen or The Career of Bessie Bolan (later incorporated in the final play of the Cycle, The Hair of the Dog)][65]		
1935 W	More Stately Mansions (notes)[66] The Cycle: A Tale of Possessors Self-Dispossessed (notes, scenarios, etc.)[67]		
1936	The Hair of the Dog (original title for A Touch of the Poet)[68]		
1937	57. [And Give Me Death (1st draft)][69]		

[61] The notes are dated "Northport, L.I. (Beacon Farm, July, 1931)," "Sea Island Beach, Georgia Nov. 26, '31," "Sea Island Beach—Nov. 29th 1931," and "Sea Island, Dec. 6, '31."

[62] O'Neill to Skinner.

[63] In the list to Skinner O'Neill dates this play to September, 1932. The first typewritten version is dated "Sea Island, Georgia. September 6, 1932" on the title page and "Sept. 27, 1932" at the end.

[64] I have followed the simplified version O'Neill furnished Skinner with. The draft material shows, as Falk notes (p. 145), that O'Neill counted up to eight drafts of this play while working on it. The first completed version, termed the fourth draft by O'Neill, is dated "Sea Island, Ga. Nov. 30, 1932." The second completed version, i.e. the fifth draft, is dated "Sea Island March 31, 1933" at the end.

[65] Gelb, p. 770, Miller, 1962, p. 131, and Cargill et al., p. 481.

[66] In his prefatory note to *More Stately Mansions* Gallup provides the following timetable (p. x): First notes (Feb. 1935), 1st draft (finished 9.8.1938), 2nd draft (finished 1.1.1939), 3rd draft (finished 1.20.1939), revisions (1940 and 1941). As published, the play is less than half of O'Neill's complete typed script (p. xii). The shortening of the script was undertaken by Dr. Karl Ragnar Gierow, Director of the Royal Dramatic Theatre in Stockholm at the time the play received its world première there.

[67] In a letter to Sisk (7.3.1935) O'Neill states that he has written scenarios for three Cycle plays and is at work on a scenario for a fourth and an outline for a fifth.

[68] Cf. Gallup's information in the prefatory note to *More Stately Mansions* (p. vii) and in Falk (p. 206). Lest anyone should assume, from Clark's quotation of an O'Neill letter (p. 147), that *A Touch of the Poet* was written in 1928, it should be pointed out that the year mentioned by O'Neill was no doubt 1828, the time of action in the play.

[69] The dating is inferred from Gallup's information to Falk (p. 206) that the completed Cycle plays were written in the following order: (1) *A Touch of the Poet*, (2) *And Give Me Death*, (3) *The Greed of the Meek*, (4) *More Stately Mansions*. Nos. (2) and (3) could have been written also in the spring of 1938.

Date of composition		Title	First production	Copyright (C) and publication (P)
		58. [The Greed of the Meek (1st draft)][70]		
1938		More Stately Mansions (1st and 2nd drafts)[71]		
1939	W	More Stately Mansions (3rd draft)[71]		
	S	A Touch of the Poet[72]		
	Su	The Iceman Cometh (notes)[73]		
	Su	Long Day's Journey Into Night (notes)[74]		
	F	59. *The Iceman Cometh*[75]	9.2.1946	2.12.1940 (C), Oct. 1946 (P)
1940		More Stately Mansions (revisions)[71]		
		Long Day's Journey Into Night (1st and 2nd drafts)[76]		
1941		60. *More Stately Mansions*[71]	11.9.1962	1964 (P)
		61. *Long Day's Journey Into Night*[77]	2.2.1956	1955 (C), 2.20.1956 (P)
	S	62. *Hughie*[78]	9.18.1958	Feb. 1959 (P)
	F	A Moon for the Misbegotten (notes)[79]		
1942	W	A Moon for the Misbegotten (1st draft)[80]		
		63. *A Touch of the Poet*[81]	3.29.1957	1.4.1946 (C), Sept. 1957 (P)
1943		64. *A Moon for the Misbegotten*[82]	2.20.1947	1945 (C), 1952 (P)

[70] Cf. note 69.

[71] Cf. note 66.

[72] The typescript is dated "Tao House, May 20, 1939" at the end of Act I.

[73] The notes are dated "June '39."

[74] The notes are dated "June '39." Cf. Peck, p. 92, and Gelb, p. 6.

[75] The first typewritten version is dated "Tao House, December 1939."

[76] The longhand draft is dated "Tao House Sept. 20th 1940" at the end.

[77] The second typewritten version is dated "Tao House Sept. 20th '41."

[78] In a letter to Nathan (6.19.1942) O'Neill states that he finished *Hughie* "a little over a year ago."

[79] The notes for the play are dated "Oct. '41."

[80] In a letter to Sisk (4.24.1942) O'Neill writes that he had finished a first draft of the play in January.

[81] Notes for reconstruction are dated "Feb. 16th '42." The first typewritten version is dated at the end of Act III "Oct. 2, 1942," at the end of Act IV "Tao House, Nov. 13, 1942 (Friday!)."

[82] Cf. Gelb, p. 847, and Mrs. O'Neill's statement to Peck (p. 93) which indicates that O'Neill, because of his poor physical condition, notably the tremor in his hands, actually ceased writing in 1943. O'Neill's dedication to his wife on the published play clarifies that he considered *A Moon for the Misbegotten* his last play, dating it back to 1944 (O'Neill, 1960). In a note preceding the published play O'Neill states, however, that it was completed in 1943. The second longhand draft is dated "May 17, '43" at the end.

The place of composition will appear from the following list:

Play no.	Written at:
1–11	New London, Connecticut
12–16	Cambridge, Massachusetts
17–42	Provincetown, Massachusetts[83]
43–47	Ridgefield, Connecticut
48	Ridgefield, Connecticut and Bermuda
49–50	Bermuda
51	Bermuda and Maine
52	Guéthary, France
53	St. Antoine du Rocher, France
54–56	Sea Island, Georgia
57–64	Contra Costa County, California

The following producers or producing groups have been responsible for the first productions of O'Neill's plays:

Play no.	Producer
3 6 8 14 17 22 23 24 25 27 28 35 38 39 41	Provincetown Players
9 10	Key Theatre
21	Washington Square Players
26 36	John D. Williams
31 32	George C. Tyler
27	Arthur Hopkins
40	Augustin Duncan
42 43 49	Kenneth Macgowan, Robert Edmond Jones and Eugene O'Neill
44 45 47	Provincetown Playhouse, Inc.
48 51 52 53 54 55 59 64	Theatre Guild
50	Pasadena Community Playhouse
60 61 62 63	Royal Dramatic Theatre

All the plays except the following had their opening night in New York City:

3 8	Provincetown, Massachusetts
32	Atlantic City, New Jersey
50	Pasadena, California
55	Boston, Massachusetts
60 61 62 63	Stockholm, Sweden
64	Columbus, Ohio

[83] *Till We Meet, Shell Shock,* and part of *The Straw* and *Chris Christopherson* may have been written at West Point Pleasant, N.J. Cf. note 4.

BIBLIOGRAPHY

I. Works by O'Neill

1. *Unpublished Sources*

CORNELL UNIVERSITY LIBRARY: The George Jean Nathan Collection of the library contains a valuable collection of letters from the correspondence between O'Neill and George Jean Nathan.

DARTMOUTH COLLEGE LIBRARY: The O'Neill Collection contains a rather extensive number of letters from O'Neill to divers addressees including John Barrymore, Benjamin De Casseres and Michael Gold.

HARVARD COLLEGE LIBRARY: The library holds typescripts of some unpublished plays, including *Now I Ask You, The Personal Equation* and *The Revelation of John the Divine*. There are also scenarios of two unwritten plays—*The Reckoning* and *S.O.S.*—and typescripts of some of the published plays. In addition the library boasts the possession of the correspondence between O'Neill and his second wife, Agnes Boulton. There are also a few other letters by O'Neill, including some to Isaac Goldberg.

LIBRARY OF CONGRESS: The library possesses typewritten versions of twenty-seven of the plays, including the following not found in manuscript form elsewhere: *A Wife for a Life, Bread and Butter, Abortion, The Movie Man, Servitude, The Sniper, Shell Shock.*

MUSEUM OF THE CITY OF NEW YORK: The museum holds longhand drafts of the following twelve plays: *Thirst, Recklessness, Warnings, Bound East for Cardiff, In the Zone, Ile, The Long Voyage Home, The Moon of the Caribbees, The Rope, The Dreamy Kid, Where the Cross Is Made,* and *Ah, Wilderness!* (The longhand drafts of the first three are revised scripts; the original longhand draft of *Thirst* is in the Yale collection.) In addition there are notes for *Ah, Wilderness!* and a typescript of *The Ancient Mariner.*

PRINCETON UNIVERSITY LIBRARY: The O'Neill Collection contains longhand drafts of the following twelve plays: *The Web, The Straw, Gold, Anna Christie, The Emperor Jones, Diff'rent, The First Man, The Hairy Ape, The Fountain, Welded, All God's Chillun Got Wings,* and *Desire Under the Elms.* There are also notes for some of these plays. In addition, the library holds the manuscript of O'Neill's only published short story, *Tomorrow,* and a number of letters from O'Neill to George Tyler.

YALE UNIVERSITY LIBRARY: The O'Neill Collection at Yale is by far the largest single depository of material. It contains longhand drafts of the following fourteen plays: *Thirst, Chris Christopherson, Marco Millions, The Great God Brown, Lazarus Laughed, Strange Interlude, Dynamo, Mourning Becomes Electra, Days Without End, The Iceman Cometh, Long Day's Journey Into*

Night, Hughie, A Touch of the Poet, and *A Moon for the Misbegotten.* There is a photostat copy of the longhand draft of *Beyond the Horizon,* the original of which I have been unable to locate. The library also holds typescripts of *Now I Ask You* and *More Stately Mansions.* For most of these plays there are extensive notes and scenarios in longhand as well as typescripts and galley proofs. A welter of notes and scenarios for plays which remained unwritten or which were destroyed, notably the Cycle plays, are included in the collection. Among the miscellaneous notes may be mentioned O'Neill's excerpts from Nietzsche's *Thus Spake Zarathustra* (transl. A. Tille). O'Neill's work diary from 1924 to 1943 also belongs to the collection as well as some unpublished poems. There is an extensive collection of letters which includes letters to O'Neill's third wife, Carlotta Monterey, to Mary Clark, Marjorie Griesser, Kenneth Macgowan, Nina Moise, Robert F. Sisk, and Harry Weinberger. The library also holds a substantial part of O'Neill's private library. (Another part of it is found at C.W. Post College, L.I.) Much of the Yale material is as yet unavailable to scholars.

For other O'Neill manuscripts, see *American Literary Manuscripts: A Checklist of Holdings in Academic, Historical and Public Libraries in the United States,* 1960, Austin.

2. *Published Sources* (in order of publication)

a) PLAYS

All God's Chillun Got Wings and *Welded,* 1924, New York: Boni and Liveright.
The Complete Works of Eugene O'Neill, 2 vols., 1925, New York: Boni and Liveright.
The Complete Plays of Eugene O'Neill, 12 vols. (Wilderness edition), 1934–35, New York: Scribner's.
The Plays of Eugene O'Neill, 3 vols., (1951) 1954–55, New York: Random House. Page references to all plays except the ones mentioned below are to this edition.
A Moon for the Misbegotten, 1952, New York: Random House.
Long Day's Journey Into Night, 1956, New Haven: Yale University Press.
A Touch of the Poet, 1957, New Haven: Yale University Press.
Hughie, 1959, New Haven: Yale University Press.
The Ancient Mariner, Oct. 1960, in *Yale University Library Gazette,* 35, pp. 63–86.
Ten "Lost" Plays, 1964, New York: Random House. This volume is a reprint of O'Neill's debut collection *Thirst and Other One-Act Plays* (1914, Boston: The Gorham Press) and the unauthorized *Lost Plays of Eugene O'Neill* (1950, New York: New Fathoms Press). The ten plays included are the following: *Thirst, The Web, Warnings, Fog, Recklessness, Abortion, The Movie Man, The Sniper, A Wife for a Life,* and *Servitude.*
More Stately Mansions, 1964, New Haven and London: Yale University Press.

b) NON-DRAMATIC SOURCES

Private letters, etc. are treated as parts of the works in which they are cited.

"Free" [poem], April 1912, *Pleiades Club Year Book.* New York. Reprinted in Sanborn-Clark, pp. 111–12.

"Eugene O'Neill's Credo and the Reasons for His Faith" [on *Diff'rent*], 2.13.1921, *New York Tribune*. Reprinted in Cargill et al., pp. 104–06.

"A Letter from O'Neill" [on *Beyond the Horizon*], 4.11.1920, *New York Times*, 6, p. 2.

"To the Dramatic Editor" [on *Anna Christie*], 12.18.1921, *New York Times*, 6, p. 1.

"Strindberg and Our Theatre," 1.3.1924, *Provincetown Playbill*. Reprinted in Deutsch-Hanau, pp. 191–93.

"Are the Actors to Blame?", 11.6.1925, *Provincetown Playbill*. Reprinted in Deutsch-Hanau, pp. 197–98.

"The Playwright Explains" [on *The Great God Brown*], 2.13.1926, *New York Evening Post*. Reprinted in Clark, pp. 104–06.

"O'Neill's Own Story of 'Electra' in the Making," 11.8.1931, *New York Herald-Tribune*. Reprinted as "Working Notes and Extracts from a Fragmentary Diary" in Frenz, pp. 3–15.

"O'Neill Says Soviet Stage Has Realized His Dreams" [letter to the Kamerny Theatre], 6.19.1932, *New York Herald-Tribune*. Reprinted in Cargill et al., pp. 123–24.

"Memoranda on Masks," Nov. 1932, *American Spectator*, 1. Reprinted in Cargill et al., pp. 116–18.

"Second Thoughts," Dec. 1932, *American Spectator*, 2. Reprinted in Cargill et al., pp. 118–20.

"A Dramatist's Notebook," Jan. 1933, *American Spectator*, 2. Reprinted in Cargill et al., pp. 120–22.

"Prof. George Pierce Baker," 1.13.1935, *New York Times*. Reprinted in Gelb, pp. 793–94.

"Eugene O'Neill's Teacher" [O'Neill's Nobel Prize address], 12.12.1936, *New York Times*. Reprinted in Frenz, pp. 41–42.

"Ibsens Innsats hyldes av Shaw og O'Neill i Uttalelse til N.T.," 6.2.1938, [letter to] *Nordisk Tidende*.

Inscriptions: Eugene O'Neill to Carlotta Monterey O'Neill, 1960, New Haven: Privately Printed.

[Dedication to Lawrence Langner], 1963, *Yale University Library Gazette*, 38, p. 37.

II. Other Works Cited

Adams, William, 1957, "The Dramatic Structure of the Plays of Eugene O'Neill," (unpubl. diss.), Stanford University.

Adler, Jacob, Dec. 1960, "The Worth of *Ah, Wilderness!*," *Modern Drama*, 3.

Alexander, Doris, May 1953, "*Strange Interlude* and Schopenhauer," *American Literature*, 25.

—— Dec. 1953, "Psychological Fate in *Mourning Becomes Electra*," *PMLA*, 68.

—— Dec. 1959, "Eugene O'Neill, 'The Hound of Heaven,' and the 'Hell Hole,'" *Modern Language Quarterly*, 20.

—— 1962, *The Tempering of Eugene O'Neill*, New York.

Anderson, Sherwood, 1925, *Dark Laughter,* New York.

Angus, S., 1925, *The Mystery-Religions and Christianity: A Study in the Religious Background of Early Christianity,* London.

[Anon.], 11.16.1924, "Eugene O'Neill Talks of His Own Plays," *New York Herald-Tribune.* Reprinted in Cargill et al.

Arbenz, Mary, 1961, "The Plays of Eugene O'Neill as Presented by the Theatre Guild," (unpubl. diss.), Univ. of Illinois.

Asselineau, Roger, Dec. 1958, *"Mourning Becomes Electra* as a Tragedy," *Modern Drama,* I.

Atkinson, Brooks, 1.17.1952, "At the Theatre," *New York Times.* Reprinted in Miller, 1965.

Bentley, Eric, 1946, *The Playwright as Thinker,* New York.

—— Summer 1952, "Trying to Like O'Neill," *Kenyon Review,* 14. Reprinted in *In Search of Theater,* (1953) 1955.

Berkelman, Robert, Fall 1959, "O'Neill's Everyman," *South Atlantic Quarterly,* 59.

Biese, Y. M., 1963, *Aspects of Expression I: Eugene O'Neill's Strange Interlude and the Linguistic Presentation of the Interior Monologue,* Helsinki.

Bird, Carol, June 1924, "Eugene O'Neill—the Inner Man," *Theatre Magazine,* 39.

Blackburn, Clara, May 1941, "Continental Influences on Eugene O'Neill's Expressionistic Dramas," *American Literature,* 13.

Block, Anita, 1939, *The Changing World in Plays and Theatre,* Boston.

Bogard, Travis, 1964, *"Anna Christie:* Her Fall and Rise," in *O'Neill: A Collection of Critical Essays* ed. by J. Gassner, Englewood Cliffs, N.J.

Boulton, Agnes, 1958, *Part of a Long Story,* Garden City, N.Y.

Bowen, Crosswell, 11.3.1946, "The Black Irishman," *PM.* Reprinted in Cargill et al.

—— 1959, *The Curse of the Misbegotten: A Tale of the House of O'Neill,* New York.

Brandell, Gunnar, 1950, *Strindbergs Infernokris,* Stockholm.

—— 1967, *Freud enfant de son siècle,* Paris.

Brooks, Cleanth, and Heilman, Robert, (1945) 1961, *Understanding Drama,* New York.

Broussard, Louis, 1962, *American Drama: Contemporary Allegory from Eugene O'Neill to Tennessee Williams,* Norman, Okla.

Brugger, Ilse, 1957, "Verwendung und Bedeutung der Maske bei O'Neill," *Die Neueren Sprachen N.F.,* 6.

Caputi, Anthony (ed.), 1966, *Modern Drama,* New York.

Cargill, Oscar, 1941, *Intellectual America,* New York.

Cargill, Oscar, Fagin, Bryllion, and Fisher, William, 1961, *O'Neill and His Plays: Four Decades of Criticism,* New York.

Carpenter, Frederic, 1964, *Eugene O'Neill,* New Haven.

Clark, Barrett, (1926) 1947, *Eugene O'Neill: The Man and His Plays,* New York.

Clemen, Wolfgang, (1951) 1966, *The Development of Shakespeare's Imagery,* London.

Clurman, Harold, 11.24.1956, "Theatre," *Nation,* 189. Reprinted in Cargill et al.

Cowley, Malcolm, July–Aug. 1926, "Eugene O'Neill, Writer of Synthetic Drama," *Brentano's Book Chat*, 5.

—— 9.5.1957, "A Weekend with Eugene O'Neill," *Reporter*, 17. Reprinted in Cargill et al.

Dahlström, Carl, (1930) 1965, *Strindberg's Dramatic Expressionism*, New York.

Day, Cyrus, May 1958, "The Iceman and the Bridegroom," *Modern Drama*, 1.

—— Dec. 1960, *"Amor Fati:* O'Neill's Lazarus as Superman and Savior," *Modern Drama*, 3.

Deutsch, Helen, and Hanau, Stella, 1931, *The Provincetown: A Story of the Theatre*, New York.

Dickinson, Thomas, 1925, *Playwrights of the New American Theatre*, New York.

Dietrich, Margret, 1961, *Das moderne Drama: Strömungen, Gestalten, Motive*, Stuttgart.

Downer, Alan, Feb. 1951, "Eugene O'Neill as Poet of the Theatre," *Theatre Arts*, 35. Reprinted in Cargill et al.

Downes, Olin, 8.29.1920, "Playwright Finds His Inspiration on Lonely Sand Dunes by the Sea," *Boston Sunday Post*.

[Dowson, Ernest], 1919, *The Poems and Prose of Ernest Dowson*, New York.

Driver, Tom, Dec. 1958, "On the Late Plays of Eugene O'Neill," *Tulane Drama Review*, 3. Reprinted in Gassner, 1964.

Ellis-Fermor, Una, (1945) 1964, *The Frontiers of Drama*, London.

Engel, Edwin, 1953, *The Haunted Heroes of Eugene O'Neill*, Cambridge, Mass.

—— 1964, "Ideas in the Plays of Eugene O'Neill," in *Ideas in the Drama* ed. by J. Gassner, New York.

Falk, Doris, (1958) 1965, *Eugene O'Neill and the Tragic Tension: An Interpretive Study of the Plays*, New Brunswick, N.J.

First Editions, Autographs & Manuscripts: Co-operative Catalog of the Middle Atlantic States Chapter of the Antiquarian Booksellers Association of America, Inc., n.d.

Flexner, Eleanor, 1938, *American Playwrights, 1918–1938: The Theatre Retreats from Reality*, New York.

Fraser, G. S., 1953, *The Modern Writer and His World*, London.

Frazer, James George, 1923, *The Golden Bough: A Study in Magic and Religion*, abridged edition, London.

Frenz, Horst (ed.), 1965, *American Playwrights on Drama*, New York.

Freud, Sigmund, 1913, *The Interpretation of Dreams* (tr. A. A. Brill), New York.

—— 1916, *Wit and Its Relation to the Unconscious* (tr. A. A. Brill), New York.

—— 1918, *Totem and Taboo* (tr. A. A. Brill), New York.

—— 1920, *A General Introduction to Psychoanalysis* (tr. G. Stanley Hall), New York.

—— (1922) 1924, *Beyond the Pleasure Principle* (tr. C. J. M. Hubback), New York.

—— (1922) 1925, *Group Psychology and the Analysis of the Ego* (tr. J. Strachey), New York.

—— 1936, *The Problem of Anxiety* (tr. H. A. Bunker), New York.

—— (1941) 1947, *Zur Psychopathologie des Alltagslebens, Gesammelte Werke*, 4, London.

——— 1948, "Selbstdarstellung," *Gesammelte Werke*, 14, London.

Gallup, Donald, Oct. 1960, "Eugene O'Neill's 'The Ancient Mariner,'" *Yale University Library Gazette*, 35.

——— 1964, "Prefatory Note" to *More Stately Mansions* by Eugene O'Neill, New Haven and London.

Gassner, John, (1940) 1954, *Masters of the Drama*, New York.

——— Summer 1951, "Homage to O'Neill," *Theatre Time*, 3. Reprinted in Cargill et al.

——— (ed.), 1964, *O'Neill: A Collection of Critical Essays*, Englewood Cliffs, N.J.

——— 1965, *Directions in Modern Theatre and Drama*, New York.

Gelb, Arthur and Barbara, 1962, *O'Neill*, New York.

Glaspell, Susan, 1927, *The Road to the Temple*, New York.

Goldberg, Isaac, 1922, *The Drama of Transition*, Cincinnati.

——— 1926, *The Theatre of George Jean Nathan*, New York.

Gorelik, Mordecai, (1940) 1962, *New Theatres for Old*, New York.

Greene, William Chase, 1944, *Moira: Fate, Good, and Evil in Greek Thought*, Cambridge, Mass.

Gump, Margaret, 1957, "From Ape to Man and from Man to Ape," *Kentucky Foreign Language Quarterly*, 4.

Hamilton, Gilbert, and Macgowan, Kenneth, 1929, *What Is Wrong with Marriage*, New York.

Hart, James, (1941) 1965, *The Oxford Companion to American Literature*, New York.

Hartman, Murray, 1960, "Strindberg and O'Neill: A Study in Influence," (unpubl. diss.), New York University.

——— Nov. 1961, "*Desire Under the Elms* in the Light of Strindberg's Influence," *American Literature*, 33.

Heilman, Robert, (1948) 1963, *This Great Stage: Image and Structure in King Lear*, Seattle.

Hewitt, Barnard, 1959, *Theatre USA: 1688 to 1957*, New York.

Hoffman, Frederick, 1945, *Freudianism and the Literary Mind*, Baton Rouge, La.

Hughes, Glenn, 1951, *A History of the American Theatre 1700–1950*, New York.

Jelliffe, Smith Ely and Brink, Louise, 1922, *Psychoanalysis and the Drama*, Washington.

Jones, Carless, Feb. 1935, "A Sailor's O'Neill," *Revue Anglo-Américaine*, 12.

Jones, Robert Edmond, (1941) [1956], *The Dramatic Imagination*, New York.

Josephson, Lennart, 1953, "En måne för olycksfödda," *Ord och Bild*, 62.

——— 1962, "Den stora dramacykeln," *Ord och Bild*, 71.

Joyce, James, 1922, *Ulysses*, Paris.

Jung, Carl Gustav, 1916, *The Psychology of the Unconscious* (tr. B. Hinkle), New York.

——— 1923, *Psychological Types—or The Psychology of Individuation* (tr. H. G. Baynes), London.

Kaucher, Dorothy, Oct. 1928, *Modern Dramatic Structure, University of Missouri Studies*, 3.

Kemelman, H. G., Sept. 1932, "Eugene O'Neill and the Highbrow Melodrama," *The Bookman,* 75. Reprinted in Miller, 1965.

Kinne, Wisner Payne, 1954, *George Pierce Baker and the American Theatre,* Cambridge, Mass.

Koischwitz, Otto, 1938, *O'Neill,* Berlin.

Krafft-Ebing, Richard von, (1906) 1922, *Psychopathia Sexualis: With Especial Reference to the Antipathic Sexual Instinct. A Medico-Forensic Study* (tr. F. J. Rebman), New York.

Krutch, Joseph Wood, 1932, "Introduction" to *Nine Plays by Eugene O'Neill,* New York.

—— April 1952, "Eugene O'Neill, the Lonely Revolutionary," *Theatre Arts,* 36. Reprinted in Miller, 1965.

—— (1939) 1957, *American Drama Since 1918,* London.

Krämer, Edgar, 1953, "Freiheit und Notwendigkeit als tragisches Problem bei O'Neill," (unpubl. diss.), Christian-Albrechts-Universität, Kiel.

Lamm, Martin, 1952, *Modern Drama* (tr. K. Elliott), Oxford.

Langner, Lawrence, (1951) 1952, *The Magic Curtain,* London.

Lawson, John Howard, (1936) 1964, *Theory and Technique of Playwriting,* New York.

Leech, Clifford, 1963, *O'Neill,* New York.

[Lewis, Gladys Adelina], 4.22.1931, *Georges Lewys, Complainant, v. Eugene O'Neill, Boni & Liveright, Inc., Horace Liveright, Inc., and Theatre Guild, Inc., Defendants, United States District Court: Southern District of New York.*

Linscott, Eloise, 1939, *Folk Songs of Old New England,* New York.

Lorimer, Katharine, 1947, "Eugene O'Neill and Modern Dramatic Technique," (unpubl. diss.), London University.

McAleer, John, Feb. 1962, "Christ Symbolism in *Anna Christie,*" *Modern Drama,* 4.

McAneny, Marguerite, Feb.–April 1943, "Eleven Manuscripts of Eugene O'Neill," *Princeton University Library Chronicle,* 4.

Macgowan, Kenneth, (1921) 1923, *The Theatre of Tomorrow,* London.

—— Feb. 1929, "The O'Neill Soliloquy: Notes on the Evolution of a Modern Technique," *Theatre Guild Magazine,* 6. Reprinted in Cargill et al.

Macgowan, Kenneth, and Rosse, Herman, 1923, *Masks and Demons,* New York.

Middleton, Richard, 1912, *Poems & Songs,* London.

Miller, Jordan, 1962, *Eugene O'Neill and the American Critic: A Summary and a Bibliographical Checklist,* Hamden and London.

—— (ed.), 1965, *Playwright's Progress: O'Neill and the Critics,* Chicago.

Mollan, Malcolm, 1.22.1922, "Making Plays with a Tragic End: An Intimate Interview with Eugene O'Neill Who Tells Why He Does It," Philadelphia *Public Ledger.*

Morgan, George Allen, 1943, *What Nietzsche Means,* Cambridge, Mass.

Muchnic, Helen, Spring 1951, "Circe's Swine: Plays by Gorky and O'Neill," *Comparative Literature,* 3. Reprinted in Cargill et al.

Mullett, Mary, Nov. 1922, "The Extraordinary Story of Eugene O'Neill," *American Magazine,* 94.

Myers, Henry, (1956) 1965, *Tragedy: A View of Life,* Ithaca, N.Y.

Mårtensson, Sigvard, 1957, *Eugene O'Neills dramatik,* Stockholm.

Nathan, George Jean, Jan. 1925, "The Theatre," *American Mercury,* 4.

―― Jan. 1929, "The Theatre," *American Mercury,* 16.

―― 1932, *The Intimate Notebooks of George Jean Nathan,* New York. Sections dealing with O'Neill reprinted in Cargill et al.

Nethercot, Arthur, Dec. 1960, Feb. 1961, "The Psychoanalyzing of Eugene O'Neill," *Modern Drama,* 3.

Nicoll, Allardyce, 1949, *World Drama,* London.

Nietzsche, Friedrich, 1896, *Thus Spake Zarathustra* (tr. A. Tille), New York.

―― 1909, *The Birth of Tragedy* (tr. Wm. A. Haussmann), Edinburgh and London.

Northam, John, 1953, *Ibsen's Dramatic Method,* London.

Olson, Esther, 1956, "An Analysis of the Nietzschean Elements in the Plays of Eugene O'Neill," (unpubl. diss.), Univ. of Minnesota.

Packard, Frederick, 1952, "Eugene O'Neill, Dramatic Innovator," *Chrysalis,* 5.

Peck, Seymour, 11.4.1956, "A Talk with Mrs. O'Neill," *New York Times.* Reprinted in Cargill et al.

Pellizzi, Camillo, 1935, *English Drama: The Last Great Phase* (tr. R. Williams), New York. A section dealing with O'Neill reprinted in Cargill et al.

Quinn, Arthur Hobson, (1927) 1937, *A History of the American Drama from the Civil War to the Present Day,* 2, New York.

Quintero, José, April 1957, "Postscript to a Journey," *Theatre Arts,* 41.

Racey, Edgar, May 1962, "Myth as Tragic Structure in *Desire Under the Elms,*" *Modern Drama,* 5.

Raleigh, John, 1965, *The Plays of Eugene O'Neill,* Carbondale and Edwardsville.

Sanborn, Ralph, and Clark, Barrett, 1931, *A Bibliography of the Works of Eugene O'Neill,* New York.

Sayler, Oliver, April 1922, "The Artist and the Theatre," *Shadowland,* 6. Reprinted in *Theatre Arts,* 41, June 1957.

Schroeter, James, Summer 1961, "The Four Fathers: Symbolism in *Oedipus Rex,*" *Criticism,* 3. Reprinted in A. Cook (ed.), 1965, *Oedipus Rex: A Mirror for Greek Drama,* Belmont, Calif.

Sergeant, Elizabeth, 1927, *Fire Under the Andes,* New York.

Shand, John, 9.19.1925, "The Emperor Jones," *New Statesman,* 25. Reprinted in Miller, 1965.

Shipley, Joseph, 1928, *The Art of Eugene O'Neill,* Seattle.

―― 1956, *Guide to Great Plays,* Washington.

Sievers, David, 1955, *Freud on Broadway,* New York.

Simonson, Lee, (1932) 1963, *The Stage Is Set,* New York.

Skinner, Richard Dana, (1935) 1963, *Eugene O'Neill: A Poet's Quest,* New York.

Sokel, Walter, 1959, *The Writer in Extremis: Expressionism in Twentieth Century German Literature,* Stanford.

Sprinchorn, Evert, 1966, 20th Century Plays in Synopsis, New York.

Stamm, Rudolf, Oct. 1949, "The Orestes Theme in Three Plays by Eugene O'Neill, T. S. Eliot and Jean-Paul Sartre," *English Studies,* 30.

Stekel, Wilhelm, 1922, *Disguises of Love: Psycho-analytical Sketches* (tr. R. Gabler), London.

Stuart, Donald Clive, (1928) 1960, *The Development of Dramatic Art,* New York.

Trilling, Lionel, 9.23.1936, "Eugene O'Neill," *New Republic,* 88. Reprinted in Cargill et al.

—— 1937, "Introduction" to *The Emperor Jones, Anna Christie, The Hairy Ape* by Eugene O'Neill, New York.

Törnqvist, Egil, Aug. 1965, "Ibsen and O'Neill: A Study in Influence," *Scandinavian Studies,* 37.

—— Feb. 1966, "Personal Nomenclature in the Plays of O'Neill," *Modern Drama,* 8.

—— 1968, "O'Neills arbetssätt," in *Drama och teater* ed. by E. Törnqvist, Stockholm.

—— Aug. 1968, "Nietzsche and O'Neill: A Study in Affinity," *Orbis Litterarum,* 23.

Waith, Eugene, Oct. 1961, "Eugene O'Neill: An Exercise in Unmasking," *Educational Theatre Journal,* 13. Reprinted in Gassner, 1964.

Valgemae, Mardi, Sept. 1967, "O'Neill and German Expressionism," *Modern Drama,* 10.

Weissman, Philip, 1965, *Creativity in the Theater: A Psychoanalytic Study,* New York and London.

Whitman, Robert, April 1960, "O'Neill's Search for a 'Language of the Theatre,'" *Quarterly Journal of Speech,* 16. Reprinted in Gassner, 1964.

Whitman, Walt, [1900], *Leaves of Grass,* Philadelphia.

Wilson, Edmund, Nov. 1922, "Eugene O'Neill as Prose Writer," *Vanity Fair.* Reprinted in Cargill et al.

Winther, Sophus Keith, (1934) 1961, *Eugene O'Neill: A Critical Study,* New York.

Woolcott, Alexander, 2.8.1920, "The Coming of Eugene O'Neill," *New York Times.* Reprinted in Cargill et al.

Woolf, S. J., 9.15.1946, "Eugene O'Neill Returns After 12 Years," *New York Times.*

Young, Stark, 1948, *Immortal Shadows: A Book of Dramatic Criticism,* New York and London.

Zeller, Marlis, 1961, "Das Symbol und seine Funktion in O'Neills 'The Emperor Jones,'" *Kleine Beiträge zur amerikanische Literaturgeschichte,* Heidelberg.

KEY TO ABBREVIATED PLAY TITLES

Ape = *The Hairy Ape*
Brown = *The Great God Brown*
Cardiff = *Bound East for Cardiff*
Caribbees = *The Moon of the Caribbees*
Chillun = *All God's Chillun Got Wings*
Chris = *Chris Christopherson*
Christie = *Anna Christie*
Cross = *Where the Cross Is Made*
Days = *Days Without End*
Desire = *Desire Under the Elms*
Electra = *Mourning Becomes Electra*
Fountain = *The Fountain*
Horizon = *Beyond the Horizon*
Iceman = *The Iceman Cometh*
Interlude = *Strange Interlude*
Jones = *The Emperor Jones*
Journey = *Long Day's Journey Into Night*
Kid = *The Dreamy Kid*
Lazarus = *Lazarus Laughed*
Man = *The First Man*
Mansions = *More Stately Mansions*
Marco = *Marco Millions*
Mariner = *The Ancient Mariner*
Misbegotten = *A Moon for the Misbegotten*
Poet = *A Touch of the Poet*
Rope = *The Rope*
Straw = *The Straw*
Voyage = *The Long Voyage Home*
Web = *The Web*
Wife = *A Wife for a Life*
Wilderness = *Ah, Wilderness!*
Zone = *In the Zone*

The index includes titles of projected plays. The abbreviations used in the text are listed within parenthesis. Information about places of composition and first production is given on p. 265; no references to this page are made in the index.

INDEX OF NAMES